Family
ETHNICITY

To the memory of my parents,
Anna Howard Russell Pipes and William Harrison Pipes, Ph.D.,
whose writings and teachings have continued to guide me

Family ETHNICITY

Strength in Diversity

Harriette Pipes McAdoo
Editor

SAGE Publications
International Educational and Professional Publisher
Newbury Park   London   New Delhi

For information address:

SAGE Publications, Inc.
2455 Teller Road
Newbury Park, California 91320

SAGE Publications Ltd.
6 Bonhill Street
London EC2A 4PU
United Kingdom

SAGE Publications India Pvt. Ltd.
M-32 Market
Greater Kailash I
New Delhi 110 048 India

Printed in the United States of America

Library of Congress Cataloging-in-Publication Data

Family ethnicity : Strength in Diversity / edited by Harriette Pipes McAdoo.
        p. cm.
    Includes bibliographical references and index.
    ISBN 0-8039-3736-9 (cloth).—ISBN 0-8039-3737-7 (pbk.)
    1. Minorities—United States. 2. Family—United States.
    3. United States—Social conditions—1980-   I. McAdoo, Harriette
    Pipes.
    E184.A1F33   1993
    305.8'00973-dc20   92-40086

93   94   95   96   10   9   8   7   6   5   4   3   2   1

Sage Production Editor: Judith L. Hunter

Contents

Introduction

HARRIETTE PIPES McADOO

Family cultural ethnicity is an increasingly important concept in our world today. As we move into the twenty-first century, families who represent diverse ethnicities make up an increasingly large percentage of the population of the United States. Our country is approaching the time when a majority of its citizens will be members of ethnically diverse families.

This diversity goes beyond social classes, racial groupings, regional differences, and even countries of origin. Ethnic identification has evolved so that it now transcends individual differences and has become *family ethnicity,* or the identification of entire families or clusters of individuals, who may or may not be aligned in racial grouping or land of origin, with certain ethnicities. Immigrants have come to the United States and have found commonalities that transcend individual countries. They have formed into clusters that are closely aligned with their continents of origin.

Family ethnicity is the sum total of our ancestry and cultural dimensions, as families collectively identify the core of their beings. Our ethnicity is fundamental to our identity. Families differentiate themselves from other groups and form linkages with families who assume similar identifications and provide reference groups for their members. Ethnicity involves unique family customs, proverbs, and stories that are passed on for generations. It includes the celebrations, the foods that are eaten, the religious ceremonies that are shared, and the stories of how the first family members came to this land. A family's involvement in its ethnicity may be ongoing and intensive or may arise only occasionally. Almost all of us are from families with ties to ethnicities. Our ethnicity is one of the most basic elements of our being.

Ethnicity is receiving increasing attention among those who study, relate with, develop policies for, and provide services to families. Such practitioners, researchers, and policymakers need to have a sound understanding of the diverse ethnicities of the families they serve and study. This book is an attempt to contribute to such understanding and to prepare us for the growing need for sensitivity to ethnic diversity.

This volume provides extensive information about the various cultural elements that different family groups have drawn upon in order to exist in the United States today. The chapter authors are intimately familiar with the groups they write about, most through membership in those groups. In a few cases, the chapter authors have gained their knowledge through intensive study of the groups they discuss.

Diverse groups are presented here in the order of the size of their populations on the North American continent. The family ethnicities of five distinct cultures—Native American, African American, Mexican American and Spanish origin, Muslim American, and Asian American—are covered in detail. Particular emphasis is placed on groups of color, because these individuals have distinct experiences of isolation and discrimination. With the numerous shifts in many facets of this nation's life, it is essential that family practitioners and researchers gain specialized information concerning the characteristics and needs of particular family groups.

The United States is now at a point in history where we can no longer be blind to the many ethnic groups, particularly those of color, that are steadily growing in our midst. Now, more than one U.S. resident in four is nonwhite or of Hispanic ancestry (Rix, 1990). If present trends in immigration and birthrates continue until the end of the twentieth century, it is predicted that the Asian American presence will increase by 22%, the Hispanic American presence by 21%, the African American presence by 12%, and Americans of European descent by only 2% (Henry, 1990). These drastic changes make it crucial for all of us to prepare for this new reality. We need to learn more about each other and to begin to reach out to and appreciate the diversity that we will all bring to the future.

Why This Volume Was Produced

The concept of producing a volume such as this one grew out of experiences I have had during my many years as a member of family organizations and as a professor. Foremost, I wanted a volume with a strong family focus on ethnicity. It is within our families that we first celebrate our ethnicity. The family focus here differs from some other texts that look at individuals or the group as a frame of reference. This book attempts to look within each group and to identify family-related issues having to do with ethnicity.

Second, I wanted to focus on families of color, for they have a particularly difficult time having their diversity acknowledged as legitimate and being accepted by the larger society. This difficulty is based on racial and religious differences from those persons who are of European descent, in spite of the ongoing emphasis on cultural diversity. There are persistent concerns, stereotypes, and misconceptions that abound about families of these groups. This volume is an attempt to provide information on research findings, ethnic practices, and policies that concern ethnic families.

I have worked to provide information on family ethnicity within professional organizations. By addressing the ethnic issues that are hidden within organizational structures, we may become knowledgeable enough to address the same issues within the professional situations that arise in these organizations. I feel strongly that professionals who work with ethnic families will be far more effective if they have accurate information about their clients. If knowledge about family ethnicity is incorporated within case histories and policies, practitioners will have richer resources with which to help families.

Appreciation of the contributions of diverse ethnic groups has grown. In my work in the two most influential professional family groups, as program vice president and president-elect of the National Council on Family Relations and as program chair of the Groves Conference on Marriage and the Family, I had the responsibility of setting the direction for national conferences, and I chose to focus on the examination of ethnicity. Several of the chapters in this book were first presented by the authors at these conferences. In fact, the title of this book comes from the conference theme I selected for the Groves Conference meeting in the Bahamas.

Each chapter provides information about such topics as the process of socialization, family values and histories, and family practices of these groups. The authors have drawn upon individual histories of family ethnicity to illustrate specific areas such as socialization, couples' relationships, treatment of elderly family members, and providing supportive help to ethnic families.

The need for this volume grew out of my work with adults in courses that viewed the diversity of family groups. I have taught courses in ethnicity, families, and family policy at several sites: Howard University, Smith College, University of Washington, University of Minnesota, and now Michigan State University. In each course, I attempted to expose students to family ethnicity in ways that would make them understand the importance of incorporating this knowledge in their practice with ethnically diverse families. As I taught these classes, using a collection of newspaper articles, reprints, selections from books, and the personal experiences of students in my classes, it became obvious that a family ethnicity book was needed.

There were some books available that represented families of various ethnic groups. Mindel, Habenstein, and Wright's (1988) *Ethnic Families in America* is an excellent text, and I have used it on several occasions. This very appropriate text gives recognition to many different ethnic groups. However, by the time the third edition was published, so many groups needed coverage that the editors were able to devote only one chapter to each group, and many were left out altogether. What was needed was a volume that would look at a few groups intensely.

The books that are related to practice present many more options. McGoldrick, Pearce, and Giordano's (1982) *Ethnicity and Family Therapy* evaluates the influence of ethnicity on family problems and therapy. Boyd-Franklin's (1988) *Black Families in Therapy* presents a fine discussion of African American families and useful procedures for promoting family functioning. Devore and Schlesinger's (1987) *Ethnic-Sensitive Social Work Practice* offers a thorough discussion of the perspectives of ethnic groups. Kumabe, Nishida, and Hepworth's (1985) *Bridging Ethnocultural Diversity in Social Work and Health* provides an intensive discussion on culture, diversity, and values. The authors present case materials on three selected ethnic groups to illustrate how practitioners can use cultural knowledge in their work with families.

Overview of This Book

The overall orientation of this volume is that we all belong to one group or another. We do not stand alone, apart from our ethnicity. It is what makes our country so strong. The cultural ties to our homelands are embedded within the society. Some ethnic groupings are more powerful than others and have been in a majority position for so long that they have come to believe that only one way of doing things, their way, is legitimate.

Even in a book concentrating on people of color, there are many groups that could not be covered. I decided, therefore, to concentrate on those families about which little is known and, for the groups about which much has already been written, to bring the best of the works of writers in the field. Even among ethnic groups of color there is much overlap and diversity. I have selected Native American or American Indian, African American, Mexican- and Spanish-origin American, Muslim American, and Asian American families for emphasis in this volume. Chapter authors were asked to focus on certain family-related aspects of the groups about which they wrote. These authors were chosen for their ability to look within their own groups and to present information that is accurate and sensitive to the particular dimensions of each ethnic group. Many of the best known and most sensitive writers on family dynamics for each group have contributed to this process.

The ethnically diverse families discussed in this volume have very little in common, but they do have some attributes that are similar. One similarity is that all of these groups want to emphasize their uniqueness and value their difference. They want to achieve a place within this country that will allow them to have a degree of comfort, to have their children succeed in school, to feel good about themselves, and to live within the United States with a degree of security. For a variety of reasons, these groups have been only partially successful in achieving these desires.

Part I presents an overall picture of the selected ethnic groups. In Chapter 1, I address the concepts of diversity that are found within and between ethnic groups, and many of the controversies that abound in society's views of cultural diversity, in such areas as social class, minority status, and acculturation versus assimilation. Doris Wilkinson then presents extensive demographic data on diverse ethnic groups in Chapter 2. In Chapter 3, Edward Kain presents birth and mortality statistics on various ethnic groups in the United States.

Part II is devoted to families whose origins are in the many cultural groups of Africa. The original immigrants came as explorers, adventurers, and indentured servants, much like those from other groups. Families developed who were not unlike the others in their areas. Then the importation of millions of enslaved Africans began. This resulted in three centuries of subjugation similar to the treatment of Native Americans, with policies designed to control work and family life. The majority of African Americans were enslaved, but small groups remained free, and others were sometimes able to purchase their freedom. The result of the history of slavery has been a mix of African cultural continuities, European values, and infusions of cultural elements from the Caribbean.

In Chapter 4, Niara Sudarkasa addresses female-headed African American families, a subject that has been the source of widespread misconceptions. Shirley Hatchett and James Jackson discuss African American extended kin systems in Chapter 5, using data from a national survey. In Chapter 6, John McAdoo's contribution concerns self-esteem and decision making in African American families, and in Chapter 7, Phillip Bowman discusses the growing marginality among African American men and how this affects fatherhood.

Mexican American and Spanish-origin families, coming from many countries and cultures, are examined in Part III. Many of the families in this group immigrated to this country in search of a better life or because they were fleeing oppression. Some families came in the eighteenth and nineteenth centuries, but the greatest influx has been in the past two generations. Of particular interest are families from Mexico, Puerto Rico, Cuba, and Central and South America. In Chapter 8, Catherine Street Chilman's presentation covers a wide range of these ethnic groups. Zulema Suárez, in Chapter 9, then discusses the unique position of Cuban families in this country, families that are seldom found in the literature. In Chapter 10, Juan Paz provides insight concerning the elderly in Hispanic families. Finally, in Chapter 11, Estella Martinez discusses the issue of parenting in Chicano families.

American Indians or Native Americans, collective terms used to describe members of several hundred different nations, existed in this land long before it became the United States. In the first chapter of Part IV, Suzan Shown Harjo presents an overview of Indian experiences in the United States, reviewing the history of the Indian nations, their subjugation and genocide, and the current efforts to bring about tribal control of the socialization of Indian children. In Chapter 13, Duane Champagne discusses kinship and political change in four Indian nations, the Cherokee, Choctaw, Creek, and Chickasaw. The general population knows so little about Native Americans that a historical analysis is important here. This is provided in Chapter 14 by Charlotte Tsoi Goodluck, who discusses in particular the special needs of those children who are cared for under the Indian Child Welfare Act. Few of us know about this group of children who have been victims of massive relocation, unemployment, and other hardships that Native Americans continue to endure.

Part V focuses on Muslim American families. The increasing attention now being given to Muslim families is matched only by the wider society's ignorance of this group. Muslims who reside in North America have come from many countries. In Chapter 15, Azim Nanji presents an overview of the concept of Muslim American family heritage, which is based on kinship and unity. He also addresses the cultural conflicts that are faced by Muslim American youth.

In Part VI, Asian Americans are discussed in terms of their countries of origin and reasons for immigration. Three different ethnic groups found among Asian Americans have been selected to illustrate both cultural differences and differences in the experience of assimilation into American society while keeping the uniqueness of their origins. The socialization of children born to Chinese immigrant families in the United States is covered in Chapter 16 by Young-Shi Ou and myself. Chinese immigration from Taiwan is explained in Chapter 17 by Chien Lin and William Liu in terms of the cultural value of *hsiao,* a complex system of obligation of child to parents. Pyong Gap Min discusses Korean immigrants' marital patterns and adjustments to marriage in Chapter 18. Vietnamese families are examined in Chapter 19 by Steven Gold, who highlights differences between the two waves of recent Vietnamese immigrants.

Part VII is devoted to discussion of ethnic sensitivity among professional practitioners in the human services. In Chapter 20, Wynetta Devore and Harlan London address the role that therapists play in the provision of family therapy. They present specific principles for ethnicity-sensitive practice, as well as a detailed practice model, for therapists of all ethnicities. The chapter also includes an annotated bibliography listing materials that can assist practitioners in their work with many different ethnic families. My final chapter closes the book with a synthesis of the issues surrounding family ethnicity and family policy orientation in the future.

As we look at ourselves, we see that our differences, our diversity, constitute the main element we have in common. We need to understand the places we have come from, the places our families have been, and the directions in which we are moving as we enter the next century. As more attention is paid to ethnicity, from both positive and, unfortunately, negative viewpoints, this book will become a resource that will add much to the discussion.

Creating this book has been a long but worthwhile process. Working with all of the different contributors has been tremendously interesting and fulfilling. I would like to thank them all for their fine efforts. In addition, I want to thank my Sage editor, Mitch Allen, for his continued support of a lengthy project. I also want to thank Jane Myers for her editorial work and LaRene Smith for helping get the final version completed. This volume is one of which we can all be proud.

PART I

Family Ethnic Diversity

1

Ethnic Families

Strengths That Are Found in Diversity

HARRIETTE PIPES McADOO

What Is Family Ethnicity?

Our sense of uniqueness, of being rooted in one space to one group, comes from our membership in families. It is through the experiences of growing up within the confines of the family that we first begin to get a sense of who we are, what we are, and what direction our lives will take. When we examine ourselves, we find that who we are and who we can become depend in great part upon who we started out to be. This is found within our families. Our ethnicity cannot be separated from our families. Within the security and insecurity of our families, as they face all of the developmental changes that families must, by definition, go through, we become firmly established in our time and place.

Many questions arise from the use of the terms *ethnicity* and *family ethnicity*. Just what do we mean by *family ethnicity*? How does it differ from ethnicity as described in earlier volumes? How do we differentiate between ethnicity and race? These questions will be explored in this examination of family ethnicity. An individual's family ethnicity clearly establishes the core of his or her being. Many of the attributes of ethnic culture are mediated through the family (Mindel & Habenstein, 1981). *Family ethnicity* has come to mean the interaction of all elements that occur within ethnic family constellations.

It is believed that we all come from one "mother" in the Nile Valley, eons ago. Our families moved out from that center to all parts of the globe. We have migrated over the centuries and have responded over the course of time to the geographical conditions of our diverse environments. Our families developed different cultures, different races, different ways of viewing the world, and different rituals as they faced the mysteries and uncertainties of life. We have diversified; each group in its own place has developed a culture appropriate to its time and its environment.

As we have come together over time in this land of the United States, we have not come equally in power and resources. Families and individuals from diverse groups came to this country to escape tyranny or poverty, they came to seek a better way of life for their families, or they were brought against their wills to work. Of the families who came to this land from European countries, some were poverty stricken and oppressed, and some were wealthy (Zinn & Eitzen, 1990). Many came with the assurance of their culture, their God, and their "manifest destiny," which has continued into the present. Native Americans, who were already here, were subjugated and decimated. Enslaved Africans were brought to shore up the economy and were denied the right to be human. Asians were brought in to labor in the western part of the country and were never looked upon as equals, but many Asians are now becoming powerful economic forces in this country. Families from Spanish-speaking lands have been in North America for centuries; some were indigenous, some were immigrants, and new ones arrive every day. Muslims were ignored by many for a while, but now have gained in importance. As we look at the various families in our country today we may well be amazed at the varieties we find. Each group brought with it its members' uniqueness; each brought parts of another culture as well as other elements of ethnicity that continue to flourish today.

Ethnicity and Culture

Cultures differ in their worldviews, in their perspectives on the rhythms and patterns of life, and in their concept of the essential nature of the human condition (Devore & Schlesinger, 1987). The impact of culture is apparent in personality and behavior, in patterns of social interaction, and in social institutions (Kumabe, Nishida, & Hepworth, 1985). Ethnicity reveals itself in the customs, rituals, values, attitudes, and personality types of individuals (Kumabe et al., 1985), but it is on an even subtler level that ethnicity becomes more salient. It can provide "feelings of well-being, and mastery over the futures of one's children," the ability to be able to have a say in what becomes of the members of one's family as they seek to move ahead in the society (Mindel & Habenstein, 1981).

Family ethnic groups, as defined by Kumabe et al. (1985), are "a collectivity of people who conceive of themselves as being alike by virtue of their presumed common ancestry and cultural heritage (race, religion, or national origin) and who are regarded by others to be a part of such a group." It is therefore not possible to think of whites as being ethnics and people of color as being racial or cultural groups. Almost all families may be considered to be from one or many ethnic groups. Glazer and Moynihan (1975) define ethnic groups to include all groups in society that are characterized by a distinct sense of difference owing to cultural tradition and land of origin. Self-perceptions and the perceptions held by those outside the group are important components of the definitions of ethnicity, including family ethnicity. We define ourselves as ethnics and this definition is reinforced by our society.

Without awareness and acceptance of their own cultural values, individuals may suffer from "cultural myopia," so that they fail to perceive the cultural differences between themselves and those in other groups (Kumabe et al., 1985). Large cultural gaps exist between many groups in the United States. In a benign and truly pluralistic society, individuals are able to function in more than one language, and persons are accepted regardless of their cultural and religious backgrounds. No special preference is given to one or another ethnic group. Clearly, the present-day United States is far from being such a society.

Minority Status and Ethnicity

The word *ethnicity* has often been used almost interchangeably with *minority status, race,* and *socioeconomic class.* The term *minority status* is not used in this book to indicate ethnic status for several reasons. First, while different ethnic groups may be technically in the minority in terms of number in the present U.S. population, we define *family ethnicity* as a status that begins in cultural locations outside the North American continent, with the exception of Native Americans. Within that context, ethnic groups of color are not minorities, but are collectively the majority of persons in the world. Recent U.S. demographic profiles show that in the near future the growing number of ethnics will alter the picture of ethnicity.

The second reason *minority status* is avoided as a descriptive phrase in this volume is that it connotes more than numerical differences—it has an insidious implication of inferiority. This concern is especially important in the socialization of children. Minority status is the view of family ethnicity from the position of the dominant group, the majority. The term has come to mean those groups who are most affected by racism and poverty (Devore & Schlesinger, 1987). A sense of superiority is assumed by those of the implied superior status. This is the gist of ethnocentrism, for no one wants to give up real or implied power. To remain technically in control, the groups in power have attempted to circumvent those who have in the past been in less fortunate positions. Yet change will come, and as populations shift, modifications will be made in the relationships among ethnic groups.

Hopps (1982) states that because so many groups have referred to themselves as minorities (women, gays, the disabled, and so on), the impact of the term in general has been diminished and another designation should be used. Hopps suggests that *people of color* is more accurate in designating persons who belong to ethnic groups. Hopps selected this term because many forms of exclusion and discrimination exist in this country, but "none so deeply rooted, persistent, and intractable as that based on color." Family members experience persistent and subtle levels of discrimination, even those persons of color whose educational and economic levels are greater than those of the majority population.

People of color who are designated to be of inferior status must pay psychologically. Negative attributions made about those of color are too often internalized by members of the group. This can be seen in some ethnic group members' attempts to become as much like members of the majority group as possible. Subjugation is the direct outgrowth of power imbalances between groups. Psychological subjugation is more insidious and manipulative than physical subjugation. When the ability to maintain control is aligned with the desire to maintain resources and services, the dominant group can maintain control. Power in turn becomes financial resources. This is seen in the treatment of newly arrived immigrant groups and of displaced Native Americans.

One means of subjugation and control is the use of stereotypes—the inability to perceive that individuals within groups do differ from each other and that all levels of classes, family types, and abilities are found within each ethnic group. The insidiousness of mental control makes it difficult for persons of color to begin the process of reeducation and political action necessary to move power to more than one group in order to have a pluralistic society. As part of a pluralistic society, we need to have social science paradigms that are built upon strengths of groups, to force reality into the theories of relationships between groups, and to point to more adequate social policies (Jackson, 1991). We need to have more realistic views formed about the status of people of color. This process is long and tedious and too often filled with violence, mistrust, and confusion, yet it must be begun.

Socializing Children in Ethnically Diverse Families

An area of continuing concern is that of explaining ethnic diversity to children. Parents of children of color face the same tasks that all other parents must complete to help their children develop into functioning, self-sufficient adults. It is more difficult to raise children to have pride in their ethnic group's concepts when the group is perceived in a negative manner by the wider society (H. P. McAdoo, 1978b). Clinical and empirical evidence has shown that there is a normal distribution of feelings of self-worth in ethnically diverse children. Some feel very good about themselves and move successfully through their developmental tasks. Others are overwhelmed by limited opportunities and poor prospects for future advancement.

The important point that needs to be made in the discussion of socialization is that differences may exist between a child's self-concept and his or her ethnic or racial identity. These are two distinct variables, and they are often at odds with each other. For example, Hispanic children may feel good or bad about themselves, with a normal distribution of self-esteem, but they may have ambivalent attitudes about being perceived as being in a low-status group. A newly arrived Vietnamese immigrant child may feel good about being part of a warm extended family, but may have mixed feelings about his acceptance in school or the perceived limits that may be placed on his mobility. African American children have been found to have normal distributions of self-esteem, but they tend to be more out-group oriented in racial matters. They tend to prefer the attributes of being white—hair, skin color, and life-style—during preschool and early childhood years.

However, they become more own-group oriented when they reach middle childhood (Cross, 1987, 1990; H. P. McAdoo, 1985). Teachers and other professionals who work with ethnically diverse children need to be aware of the differences in children's self-concepts. They need to be sensitive to the many cultural nuances that are present in North American society.

There are some dimensions of class and color that have led to limited acceptance in the wider American culture. As Cole (1990) states, bigotry is learned, and since it is learned, it can be unlearned. It is possible to eliminate racism, sexism, anti-Semitism, and ageism. Ethnic groups pitted against each other mean ill for all of North America. There is an African proverb that says, When two elephants fight, it is the grass that suffers.

Family Ethnicity:
Dimensions of Class, Color, and Gender

The concept of family ethnicity is seen as larger than just membership in a group that shares one's place of origin, or race, or social class, or religion. Within the American context, family ethnicity has grown to be more than just one's group membership. In this volume, unlike earlier books in which ethnicity was handled as the domain of European origination groups with a few minority racial groups added for flavor, the differentiation of race, religion, and land of origin is combined into one concept of ethnicity.

Ethnic group membership is probably a more important element for an individual than social class, but class has strange effects on how one moves in and out of one's group, and on how one interacts with others of different or more dominant groups. McGoldrick, Pearce, and Giordano (1982) discuss this thoroughly. Middle-class people generally find more options than those who are of lower-class status. Families in poverty tend to find themselves trapped and enmeshed within the confines of their own ethnic and social class group. Ethnic group members who are wealthy may be able to insulate themselves and move into mainstream groups, but they too must confront racism, sexism, and ethnocentrism at some point.

In spite of the growing respect for diversity, sexism is still a real barrier to individuals in different groups. Girls and women of color are often treated differently from males of color and are socialized in a number of different ways. Females may not be perceived as a threat and may be allowed to move in and out of the larger culture with greater ease. However, men and boys of Hispanic, Native American, and African American descent are often perceived by those in the larger group as threatening and volatile and are thus treated more harshly.

Although all women experience gender inequality to some extent, being a victim of exclusion on one hand does not make one immune from victimizing another person on a different basis, such as ethnicity or color (Cole, 1992). Our stereotypes of gender and ethnicity become confused in the distribution of resources. As we attempt to promote ethnic diversity, we must also be aware of the insidious impact that sexism has on families.

Social Class and Ethnicity

Persons from ethnic groups, especially those of color, have a greater probability of being from a lower-status social class. Gordon (1983) describes this association between ethnicity and social class level as "ethclass." Devore and Schlesinger (1987) note that the intersection of ethnicity and social class generates identifiable dispositions and behaviors. A unique situation exists when ethnic reality and social class intersect, for within each ethnic group there are members of all social classes.

More than one-third of African Americans and Hispanics are earning middle-class or higher incomes, yet another half continue to live "at the margin" or in poverty. All of these persons have not been treated equally by public policy, businesses, and institutions of higher education. As Wharton notes, "Monolithic generalizations just won't work anymore—if they ever did—either to describe the problems or solutions" (quoted in Magner, 1990). More attention must be paid to individual family groups, in terms of their socioeconomic levels and their ethnicity. Those who are middle class need to be bolstered, while other measures should be used to aid unskilled workers and those who are in poverty. Different ethnic groups have accomplishments and difficulties, but these cross racial and socioeconomic lines.

The majority of those who are in temporary poverty will escape it in the ways that most people end poverty—they will obtain jobs with decent wages or they will form extended family units to gain a combined income that will allow them to escape the most devastating effects of poverty. The consistent poor, a group heavily populated by women and children and by those of ethnic status, have a more difficult time ending their poverty.

The family and its extended formations are important in all classes of ethnic families. Close kinship interactions are common in many groups. The term *extended family* does not imply that all live under one roof, but that nonnuclear family members are in close interaction with one another, exchange goods and services, and keep in close or periodic contact with one another. Mobility into middle or higher statuses has not been able to extinguish the importance of family systems to persons of ethnic groups (H. P. McAdoo, 1988).

That group of individuals who form what has come to be known as the "underclass" are defined as having attitudes, values, and behaviors that are different from with those of mainstream society in North America. In several studies, neighborhoods have been defined as census tracts that have a high proportion of individuals who are out of step with the rest of society. Most of the tracts are in urban areas; more than half of the residents are African American, one-third are White, and about 10% are Hispanic.

Steinberg (1989) has made an important analysis of the concept of the underclass. He found that the concept is filled with value assumptions and that it has confused the historical and structural sources of the underclass. He additionally states that discussion of an underclass "fudges over the significance of racism" in the creation and the maintenance of this underclass.

Steinberg makes several points that are important to understand as we evaluate the impact of class and ethnicity. First, he notes a clear retrogression to the "culture of poverty" view of the 1960s and to the cultural deprivation of the 1950s by those who espouse the underclass concept. The role that racism plays in the perpetuation of class is often overlooked in the discussion of family poverty. Further, in looking at the success of some family groups and the lack of success of others, we must realize one important thing. Inherited genes or family culture do not determine economic and educational success or failure (Steinberg, 1989). Rather, inherited class advantages and disadvantages often account for the differences we see. Families pass on the advantages and disadvantages from their own experiences from one generation to the next. In this way certain ethnic groups have become entrenched in poverty.

Acculturation Versus Assimilation

Acculturation and *assimilation* are important terms that need to be differentiated. Both represent the processes that take place when ethnic and nonethnic groups, carrying different backgrounds and cultures, meet. Acculturation occurs when the various cultural threads of the ethnic and mainstream cultures become intermeshed (Kumabe et al., 1985). Assimilation, on the other hand, is a gradual process, occurring over time, in which one set of cultural traits is relinquished and a new set is acquired through participation in the mainstream culture (Kumabe et al., 1985). There is a prevailing American ethos that members of ethnic groups should assimilate into the mainstream culture. Members of diverse ethnic groups who operate in the mainstream are expected to become bicultural, while few whites feel that need (Gillian, 1990). This ethnocentric requirement saps the strength and energy of all of us.

Kumabe et al. (1985) use the phrase "acculturation continuum" to conceptualize the scale of values that confronts a person or group from an ethnic background. The continuum ranges from the traditional values of an individual's homeland, religious practices, and cultural artifacts on one end to the mainstream values of the dominant group at the other end. In reality, the other end may include more than the values of the dominant group—it may involve the ethnic person's perceptions of dominant values.

The Melting Pot Fallacy

The waves of persons who come to these shores are a portion of American history that is too often hidden away, for it embarrasses Americans. It is a continuing process that does not appear to be diminishing. Previously, the process was often hidden behind the concept of the "melting pot," an ideal under which all persons would assimilate into an American potpourri of mainstream society and would march happily into the future together. We were at one time told that the great melting pot would make our ethnicity no longer so important. What was not spoken out loud was that the pot melted only certain ethnicities. It did not pick up elements from each group and fuse a more natural entity. The pot was expected to melt away all of our differences, and we would all become North Americans, without respect to our ethnicity. While optimistic in view, this vision of reality had not occurred for oppressed people of color, but it has occurred for White ethnic groups.

Some groups were more amenable or acceptable and were allowed to "melt" faster than others. This homogenized version of the great American society appeared to occur only for one group, those of European origin. Others realized that no such event was occurring in their lives. Ethnic groups, particularly those considered to be of minority status, were not allowed to melt. They became more aware that they had to give up some valuable elements of their being in order to assimilate. Some attempted to become Americans and forget their roots, but they found themselves rudderless, without direction. Many individuals attempted to deny their own cultures through intermarriage with Europeans. Others denied their identities as they attempted to move up the occupational ladder into American acceptance. But they lacked the elements we all appreciate today as important aspects of our lives that we need to keep.

Some groups held on to their former cultures. They were seen as marginal persons who, once they received the proper education, would join the mainstream. Many groups, such as Negroes and Native Americans, felt that to deny their own heritage was simply the price one paid to become part of the American culture. They envisioned a society where people moved in or out, up or down, based solely on their abilities and perseverance. However, those who tried it found one fatal flaw— regardless of how hard they tried, mobility was limited for those of color. Diversity should be a strength, but too often it is seen as a problem, and thus a source of misunderstanding (Gillian, 1990).

The melting pot allusion has been replaced by metaphors of "unmeltable ethnics." The "salad bowl" metaphor has been used in Canada (Mindel, Habenstein, & Wright, 1988), but even this reference does not go far enough to show the effects of cultural contact and exchange. The metaphors now often used are those of a "stew" (Kelly, 1990) and a "stir fry." These may be more appropriate. Where ethnic groups come into contact with each other, they blend a little and they make an entity that is even better than all the original ingredients were alone. Each group becomes richer and more resourceful, and yet each maintains the integrity of the original ethnic group.

Current Controversies in Cultural Diversity

Like other areas of study, the study of ethnicity has gone through changes, from intense interest to periods of decline and now more recently to a resurgence of attention. While there once was a push toward assimilation into the mainstream, we are now going through a period in which individual cultures are more readily recognized and valued. Some people are developing pride in their own groups and are emphasizing family ethnicity. However, there is a growing controversy between those who oppose and those who strongly support this trend.

Caution in the emphasis on diversity is advised by Steinberg (1989), as well as by others. Steinberg describes the current celebration of ethnicity as ignoring the essential negative basis on which pluralism has been developed—that is, as a defense against discrimination. He believes that this celebration fails to recognize the precariousness of ethnic institutions, and misconstrues the significance of the recent ethnic upsurge. Giving greater attention to ethnic groups becomes part of the problem, Steinberg states, when such groups function as "false havens" during the crises that beset the larger community. The process of turning inward by a group results in the group's feeling of isolation from external events. Our society has not created alternatives for diverse cultures and for those who are part of communities based on extended family, religious beliefs, or country of origin. Ethnic families often pay homage to the past because it gives them a sense of belonging.

Zinn and Eitzen (1990), in discussing the negative outcomes of the rising ethnicity push, state that universities should not allow their student bodies to get carried away with cultural patterns. These authors believe that principles such as individual merit and accomplishment, color-blindness, and due process are lost when cultural diversity is emphasized. According to Zinn and Eitzen, when groups "celebrate their victimization," it undermines the sense of community on campus. We should "gaze upon the world through color-blind and gender-blind eyes, to regard each other as individuals rather than as group representatives." They extend their argument to an almost radical position when they state that growing diversity will lead our society to separation and eventual destruction.

This contrary position is evidence of the growing conservatism that is sweeping the country. It shows a fear of sharing power and a resistance to taking what is good from each culture while continuing to enjoy the richness of one's own group. This position calls for the subjugation of diverse cultures in favor of a culture-free world that never existed. This approach would have its merits if all groups globally would take a culture-blind view. However, experience has shown that this has not been possible in the past, and it does not seem likely in the future. One of the benefits of celebrating our differences is that through doing so we acknowledge that the differences do exist and can have value for each group member. To a large extent, people who have developed a strong sense of cultural identify, self-esteem, and positive self-aware-ness are especially apt to be nondefensive and open to learning about and accepting other cultures.

In summary, each ethnic family group of color has a different story to tell. Their lives have all been different, but there are elements of similarity as these families have come to the United States. They have been excluded not only for their ethnicity, but also for their color, their physical differences, their accents, and their economic positions in life. Their religious differences have been less accepted. To a great extent, they have been powerless. But there is a growing sense today that history must be rewritten to portray more accurately the diversities that have always existed.

2

Family Ethnicity in America

DORIS WILKINSON

Despite the universal and inevitable social, political, and technological changes that affect family structure and functioning, families in some form survive. Yet they differ significantly on a number of important variables: cultural histories, ethnic identities, bonds of kinship, patterns of residence, forms of lineage, intergenerational relationships, socioeconomic characteristics, and an array of institutionalized attitudes and beliefs. Because of variations in their social biographies and the centrality of these nurturing units in all societies, each system should be examined with sensitivity and caution (Allen, 1978a, 1978b; McLanahan, Wedemeyer, & Adelberg, 1981; Palisi, 1966; Staples, 1971a, 1971c; Staples & Mirandé, 1980).

It has been aptly expressed that families are the primary agents for perpetuating social class status, life-styles, values, nationality and racial distinctions, and concomitant cultural histories. With respect to ethnic traditions, they function to transmit "the native tongue"—a language system— and hence the fundamental beliefs and folkways of an ethnic heritage. In highly heterogeneous societies such as ours, where race has been established as paramount in status ascription, families respond differently to the legacies and social interpretations of race in their unique modes of coping with the consequences of group definitions (Thompson & Van

AUTHOR'S NOTE: An earlier version of this chapter appeared as "Ethnicity," in M. Sussman & S. Steinmetz (Eds.), *Handbook of Marriage and the Family.* Copyright 1987 by Plenum Publishing Corp. Reprinted by permission.

Houten, 1970, p. 43). Differential responses reflect the immense heterogeneity in all facets of life among ethnic populations.

This chapter has several objectives. The primary one is to review and discuss selected works that provide a general picture of the diversity in family constellations among four prominent ethnic groups. Another aim is to present selected quantitative data and research results on significant demographic processes that impinge on family systems. To date, most of the information on minority families[1] has tended to mirror biases intrinsic in the nation's dominant culture. To counteract these biases an attempt has been made to incorporate the array of conceptual frameworks, vocabularies, theoretical arguments, and models offered by contemporary minority scholars. Many who are members of the ancestral groups presented have focused not only on social science assumptions about the family but also on family strengths from their perspectives (R. Lewis, 1981; Montiel, 1973).

The family characteristics of four racially distinct ethnic populations will be examined: Afro-American,[2] Asian American,[3] American Indian,[4] and Americans of Hispanic ancestry or Spanish origin.[5] The criteria used in selecting and designating these as minorities were ancestry and social history, placement in the stratification hierarchy in the country of settlement, race, and nationality and cultural heritage as these differ from those of the dominant sector. Restricted access to sources of economic and political power constitutes the essence of the subjugated minority classification. This discussion thus relies on a systematically derived and realistic conceptualization of the term *minority* as having as basic components *ancestry* and *locus in the stratification system*.

The labels used indicate self-identification by the respondents who participate in population surveys. It is of interest to note here that the ethnic designations emerge both from formal criteria, such as national heritage or country of birth, and from self-classification, although they may not denote clear-cut scientific definitions of biological stock. Defining *ethnic populations* in terms of descent, ethnicity, or ancestry means that the reference is to the origin, the lineage, the nationality group, or the country in which the person or the person's ancestors or parents were born. With respect to this definition, in a 1979 special U.S. Census report on ethnicity and language, "persons reported their ancestry group regardless of the number of generations removed from their country of birth. Responses to the ancestry question reflected ethnic group(s) with which persons identified but did not necessarily indicate the degree of attachment or association the person had with the particular ethnic groups(s)" (U.S. Bureau of the Census, 1982, p. 19).

The rationale for concentrating on the families of the four populations selected is based on several historically salient and socially relevant facts:

(1) They are separated from the dominant group by racial heritage and access to the sources of economic and political power.

(2) They constitute the largest ancestral minorities in the United States, and their numbers are growing, individually and collectively.

(3) The histories of American Indians and Afro-Americans predate those of many of the other ethnic immigrants.

(4) Although quantitative studies are few, these groups' cultures, life-styles, and forms of social organization have been described extensively in the social and behavioral science literature.

(5) As groups, they represent politically active and potent voting blocks.

(6) A large proportion of their families have an association with federal, state, and local governments, particularly in the area of public assistance.

(7) Some of these racial and ethnic populations have had a major impact on changes in American society and culture. (Wilkinson, 1969)

Delineating boundaries for racial and ethnic minority populations is not an easy task. Designations vary, depending on research objectives and the responses of the groups surveyed. As a result, the lack of consistency in definitions often means that data about ethnic minorities, in particular, are not comparable. For example, in the 1980 U.S. Census, the mother's heritage was used to classify persons who could not provide a simple response to the race item on the questionnaire. In contrast, earlier census procedures relied on the respondent's father's race. This procedural modification altered the comparability of 1970 and 1980 data.

Data comparability is also affected by inconsistencies in self-classification. Disparities in such reporting have modified the counts and the comparability of the "white" and "other" categories (U.S. Bureau of the Census, 1981b). In 1980, persons of Spanish ancestry reported their racial status differently than in the 1970 census. A much larger proportion specified their race as "other." Further, most of those who marked this category and wrote in a Spanish affiliation such as Mexican, Venezuelan, or Latino were reclassified as "white" a decade later (U.S. Bureau of the Census, 1981a, p. 3). These fluctuations in self-racial designation thus resulted in a much larger proportion of the Spanish-origin population being classified as "other" in 1980 than in the previous decade.

In the 1970 census, 93% of the population of Spanish heritage was classified as "white," whereas in 1980, only 56% reported "white" as their race. It is important to mention such shifts in identification, as they are pertinent to our understanding of the beliefs, the changing consciousness, and the collective self-perceptions of ethnic minority families. Not only does the practice of fluctuating ethnic/racial classifications indicate modifications in census methodology, it also symbolizes transitions in the social structure and reveals the political significance assigned to ethnic status and race in American society. What is sociologically relevant is that changes in ethnic identity are correlated with the historical and political epoch as well as with age, age at arrival in the country for immigrants, educational status, place of residence (Rogler & Cooney, 1980), and family identities and interactional patterns.

Definitions

Some of the basic concepts used in this discussion require clarification. In sociology, the concept of *minority* represents a generic, all-inclusive label refers to persons who are not simply a numerical minority but who also constitute a socially, politically, and economically subordinated population. The term has referred to specific racial and ethnic groups that share a common race, national heritage, and language and who are not in the dominant sector.

Despite multiple interpretations of the concept, in this discussion of ethnic diversity in family life, *minority* will be used in the conventional sociological sense. Most of the criteria for the designation are applicable to the aforementioned racial and ethnic populations. Each has a common ancestry and is smaller in size than the dominant group. Each has fewer opportunities, less political power, lower economic status, and hence lower family income than the majority population. Further, all of the minority sectors have experienced social discrimination, exclusion, and political subordination in some form. These varied experiences have resulted in specific behavioral modes of adaptation, ranging from mass revolts and passive resistance to acquiescence.

Predictably, family life has been affected by the experiences of and the responses to minority status.

By *racial* is meant an anatomical designation based on biological criteria. More precisely, a *race* is a category of persons who are related by a common heredity or ancestry and who are perceived and responded to in terms of external features or traits. Although the members of a racial subdivision are characterized by a relatively distinct combination of physical attributes, those in an *ethnic group* share not only a national heritage but also a distinct set of customs, a language system, beliefs and values, indigenous family traditions, rituals, and ceremonials. Ethnicity thus includes a common cultural history and familial and other institutions. Basically, an *ethnic population* is a "group"[6] of people who are of the same nationality or ancestry and who enact a shared culture and life-styles. Individuals and hence families may, however, be in the same racial category but in different ethnic groups.

From the mid-1970s to the present, growing numbers of scholars have emphasized internal bonds and cohesion as well as the need to understand the nature and causes of family problems (Canino, Earley, & Rogler, 1980; Hill, 1972; Jiménez-Vásquez, 1980; Lacy, 1975; Martin & Martin, 1978; Maunez, 1973; Mirandé, 1979; Montiel, 1970; Nievera, 1980; Nobles, 1974; Padilla & Ruiz, 1973; Peters, 1974; Sue & Wagner, 1973; Wilkinson, 1978a, 1980a).

It is important to point out that this discussion and review does not involve making extensive contrasts in differential family functioning or unwarranted comparisons among racial and ethnic minority families that have vastly distinct and cumulative social histories. Rather, the aim is to present variations *within* given populations and to accent similarities in salient demographic and family institutional properties where these exist.

Demographic Patterns

Population Distributions

During the 1960s and 1970s, growth was evident in racial and ethnic minority populations in the United States. The largest sector continues to be the Afro-Americans; Hispanics rank second. Although persons of Spanish descent now number between 12 million and 15 million and constitute the second largest minority in this country (Alvirez, 1981,

p. 11), the classification denotes an extremely dissimilar ethnic category. Its heterogeneity is demonstrated by the inclusion of the following Hispanics: Latinos, Mexican Americans or Chicanos, Puerto Ricans, Dominicans, Cubans, and other persons from Central and South America and of Spanish heritage. The diversity represented is anchored in biological heritage as well as in unique cultural histories and experiences that interlace the institutional character of the family (Mann & Salvo, 1985).

Table 2.1 provides a summary of recent estimates for the racial and ethnic clusters being discussed. The size of each of the groups is quite variable. A number of ecological processes and demographic trends, such as fertility and the numbers immigrating, along with the reporting of multiple ancestry (U.S. Bureau of the Census, 1982), have contributed to the population differentials between and within the categories for the years shown. For example, as mentioned above, "persons of Spanish origin reported their race differently in the 1980 census than in the 1970 census," and this discrepancy in identification has altered the counts and the comparability of the available population data on Hispanics (U.S. Bureau of the Census, 1980c, 1981a, 1981b, p. 3). Further, as previously indicated, the 1980 census relied on the mother's ancestry to classify persons who did not give a single response on the racial status item. A decade earlier, the procedure involved using the race of an individual's father for respondents participating in the census.

Hispanics. Hispanics, or persons of Spanish origin, constitute a highly diverse population (U.S. Bureau of the Census, 1980c, 1981a; U.S. Department of Labor, 1971; Ventura, 1982). This ancestral and cultural diversity pervades family life-styles. As the data in Table 2.1 show, at the beginning of the 1970s there were about 5 million persons of Mexican heritage in this country. An estimated 1 million persons of Spanish origin were of Puerto Rican descent. Of the total estimate of 15 million Hispanics in 1980, the majority were of Mexican ancestry. The others were distributed approximately as follows: 15% were Puerto Rican, 6%-7% were Cuban, 7% were of Central or South American origin, and 11% were classified by the Census Bureau as "other" Spanish (Gurak, 1981, p. 6; Nieves & Martinez, 1980; U.S. Bureau of the Census, 1980c, 1980d). In 1980, the Cuban population of this country was estimated at 803,226 people, representing a substantial increase from its 1970 population status. The majority of Cuban families remained concentrated in Florida.

Afro-Americans. Afro-Americans, or Blacks, are the largest racial minority in the United States, with a history in this country dating back to the sixteenth century. One notable characteristic of this group is that

Table 2.1   U.S. Population by Race and Ethnicity for Selected Racial and Ethnic Groups, 1970 and 1980

Racial/Ethnic Category	1970	1980	Percentage Change
American Indian	792,730	1,361,869	+71.8
African American/Black	22,580,289	26,488,218	+17.3
Chinese	435,062	806,027	+85.3
Filipinos	343,060	774,640	+125.8
Japanese	591,290	700,747	+18.5
Mexican American	4,532,435	8,740,439	+92.8
Puerto Rican	1,429,396	2,013,945	+40.9

SOURCE: U.S. Bureau of the Census (1981b, Table 1).
NOTE: The 1970 figures for Mexican Americans and Puerto Ricans are rough estimates and are derived from U.S. Census reports of the population. The 1980 total Spanish-origin population was about 15 million. Differences between 1980 and 1970 U.S. Census counts by Spanish origin affect the comparability of data. The 1980 data on Mexican ancestry relfect misreporting in the Spanish origin category. (U. S. Bureau of the Census, 1982b).

it is young; approximately 37% of its members are under age 18. As the data in Table 2.1 show, Afro-Americans totaled about 26 million in 1980, representing a 17% increase over the 1970 figure. In contrast to most of the other racial and ethnic minority populations, the 1980 figure constituted only a slight increase (U.S. Bureau of the Census, 1981b). Current estimates put the population at around 30 million.

Asian Americans. Like Hispanics, Asian Americans are an exceptionally dissimilar ethnic minority (Endo, 1980; Endo, Sue, & Wagner, 1980; Fujii, 1980b; Lyman, 1970, 1971, 1974; Pian, 1980). There is no complete consensus on who is an Asian. With respect to the classifications used in population surveys and in the U.S. Census, the groups most often included in this category are Burmese, Cambodians, Chinese, Filipinos, Japanese, Koreans, Malaysians, Guamanians, Pakistanis, Indonesians, Vietnamese, and Samoans. In the U.S. Census, some of these have been designated as "others," meaning unclassified ethnic or racial populations. Yet, classifying these diverse ethnics as Asians obscures the extent of variation in their national heritages, languages, beliefs, customs, and systems of family organization (C. L. Johnson, 1977; Kalish & Moriwaki, 1973; Liu, 1966; Liu & Yu, 1975; Muramatsu, 1960; Sue & Kirk, 1973).

In 1970, Asians constituted about 1% of the U.S. population (U.S. Bureau of the Census, 1973). With the dramatic entry of Indochinese refugees in 1975, the counts rapidly increased (Cordova, 1980, p. 139). Of those admitted since the spring of 1975, an estimated 89% were Vietnamese. The remaining percentages were divided among Laotians, Hmongs (mountain-dwelling peoples from China, Laos, Vietnam, and Thailand), and Cambodians (Aylesworth, Ossorio, & Osaki, 1980, p. 64). Contrary to newspaper accounts, the Vietnamese and the other Asians were quite different from each other with respect to skills, occupational status, educational attainment, and family life-styles and values.

Asian Americans have always been a culturally diversified population, the dominant subdivisions in the United States being the Chinese, the Filipinos, and the Japanese (Endo et al., 1980; Pian, 1980). The Japanese are the largest group, currently approaching 1 million. With sustained immigration and a reduction in mortality for the nation as a whole, their numbers continue to rise. Chinese and Filipinos rank second and third, respectively. Existing data reveal that these sectors also increased in the 1970s. Although most of the growth in these two ethnic populations has been the result of immigration, in contrast, it is estimated that about two-thirds of the Japanese increment can be attributed to births (Kaplan & Van Valey, 1980, p. 216). It is of interest that, at the beginning of this decade, Koreans constituted the fourth-largest and fastest-growing Asian group (U.S. Bureau of the Census, 1981b, p. 7).

American Indians. The American Indian population is increasing, but the patterns of growth are difficult to measure precisely because of shifts in racial identification and delays in the dissemination of current statistics. The growth shown in Tables 2.1 and 2.2 is due both to a rise in the birthrate and to changes in classification procedures. A number of other factors have also contributed to growth in the American Indian population: increased life expectancy at birth, improved census procedures, the value placed on children, residential mobility, and tribal folkways and mores.

Around 1500, an estimated 840,000 Indians were residing in the United States. More than four centuries later, the numbers claiming Indian and Alaskan Native ancestry have not altered appreciably. Recent data reveal, however, that the Indian population is growing at a rate that is four times the national average (Kaplan & Van Valey, 1980, p. 214). Several demographic processes have influenced this growth rate: (a) a sustained rise in the birthrate, (b) a reduction in infant mortality, and (c) increasing numbers of persons identifying themselves as having Indian ancestry. Further, the growth reflects modifications in the methods for classifying persons of Indian heritage and improved data-gathering procedures. Table 2.2 presents the estimated population counts and percentage changes for American Indians from 1900 to 1980.

Table 2.2 American Indian Population in the United States: 1900 to 1980

Year	Estimated Population	Change From Preceding Year (percentage increase or decrease)
1980	1,361,869[a]	+71.8
1970	792,730	+51.4
1960	523,591	+46.5
1950	357,499	+3.5
1940	345,252	+0.6
1930	343,352	+40.5
1920	244,437	−11.7
1910	276,927	+16.8
1900	237,196	—

SOURCE: U.S. Bureau of the Census (1981b).
NOTE: Years are census years; *change* refers to change from the preceding census.
a. This figure has been projected to 1.5 million.

Regional Variations

Residential patterns vary by ethnic classification; these patterns are associated with differing immigration histories, community values and mores and hence with variations in the institutional nature of the family. Whereas Puerto Rican families are disproportionately clustered in New York (Gurak & Rogler, 1980), those of Mexican Americans constitute only a small portion of the Hispanic population in New York City. Their families and communities are located primarily in the southwestern part of the country.

Like Puerto Ricans, the majority of Afro-Americans reside in metropolitan areas. At the end of the 1970s, an estimated 56% were central-city residents, and only 20% lived in the suburbs of metropolitan areas. At the beginning of the 1980s, "twelve states had a Black population of 1 million or more," with New York ranking first, followed by California and Texas (U.S. Bureau of the Census, 1981b, p. 1). Most, however, continued to live in the southern part of the country. In seven southern states and in the District of Columbia, they constituted 20% or more of the total population. Among the southern cities with Black majority populations were Atlanta, Birmingham, New Orleans, Richmond, and Wilmington. This spatial clustering in a specific region of the country "reflects a change in the long-term pattern of a large net outmigration of Blacks from the South" (U.S. Bureau of the Census, 1981b, p. 1).

Further, the current ecological distribution of Black families is based on economic and social variables (Edwards, 1970).

Moreover, among American Indians, place of residence and residential mobility are intricately interwoven with family behavior (Ablon, 1964; DeGeyndt, 1973). For the American Indian, life on the reservation merges with the family life cycle. The Bureau of Indian Affairs estimated that more than three-fourths of Indians were living on or near reservations at the end of the 1970s. Excluding Alaska, the areas designated as reservations at the time totaled about 267. Slightly more than half of these were tribally owned lands (Blumenthal, 1976). Some were individually owned allotted lands, the majority of this type being dual-allotted tribal lands. The relationship of Indian customs, beliefs, rituals, and daily family life to the land has been captured vividly in the historical and contemporary literature (Blanchard & Warren, 1975; Blumenthal, 1976; Deloria, 1970; Hostbjor, 1961; Red Horse, 1981).

In recent years, several major land-related issues have emerged. For example, in New Mexico, Navaho Indian ranchers, Pueblo leaders, and social workers informed a U.S. Civil Rights Commission panel that traditional customs were being disrupted by energy development. Because family and tribal beliefs incorporate the sacredness of ancestral burial sites, abuse of such areas is perceived as desecration of valued observances. In Connecticut, Indian tribes requested laws to protect the burial grounds of their ancestors. As recently as 1982, Kumeyaay Indians filed suit in Los Angeles for permission to exhume the remains of ancestors so that they could rebury them on the reservation. The year before, a group of Navahos and an allied group of Hopis requested that a federal judge stop a proposed ski resort in Arizona. Manifesting the deeply entrenched values of their culture, they felt that construction would desecrate the sacred mountain range and anger their gods. Such events illustrate the traditional links among Indian customs, family practices, and tribal lands. Many tribes today are involved in land disputes.

Although American Indians live in all parts of the country, nearly half of the population is concentrated in the West. Slightly more than one fourth reside in the South, and this region of the country is experiencing an increase in its Indian population. Such changes in community of residence eventually become cultural transitions, because regions differ not only in geography, but also in modes of production, social customs, folkways, religious beliefs, and dietary practices. Thus the place where families reside forms a cultural settlement.

In the 1970s, nearly half of American Indian families lived on or near reservations located in Arizona, Alaska, California, Minnesota, New Mexico, North Carolina, Oklahoma, South Carolina, South Dakota, Washington, and Wisconsin. Ten years later, California had the largest population, with Oklahoma, Arizona, New Mexico, and North Carolina ranking second, third, fourth, and fifth. As a proportion of the total population, the American Indian sector was highest in two states: New Mexico and South Dakota.

In addition to regional variability, there are numerous tribal affiliations, with distinct languages and customs. In 1970, the largest tribes were the Apache, Cherokee, Chippewa, Choctaw and Houma, Creek, Alabama and Coushatta, Iroquois, Lumbec, Navaho, Pueblo, and Sioux tribes. The Navaho ranked first in size and the Cherokee ranked second. Other well-known tribes included the Cahuilla, Cheyenne, Comanche, Delaware, Menominee, Mandan-Hidatsa, Mohawk, and Osage (Kaplan & Van Valey, 1980, p. 214). Recognizing and understanding the nature of distinct tribal identities are essential, because these identities are associated with diversity in language, family forms, traditions, life-cycle rituals and ceremonies, patterns of lineage, and kinship relationships (Association of American Indian Affairs, 1974; J. Brown, 1970; Deloria, 1978; Farris, 1976; Harmsworth, 1965; Medicine, 1969, 1975; Virgil, 1980; Wissler, 1966).

The social consequences of urban versus rural residence must also be considered in analyses of Indian family organization. Often, there is continuous movement between reservations and urban communities for some individuals and families. Further, growing numbers are leaving rural areas and reservations for city life. Many also return to their families on the reservation. In 1960, about one-third resided in urban centers. Yet, 10 years later, nearly half lived in such communities. Thus the American Indian population, like other earlier rural and traditional peoples, is increasingly becoming an urbanized one. Life-styles originating from prior tribal affiliations and customs interacting with urban migration have an effect on the character of the family. Future studies of these relationships must take into account the fact that the existing data are general and do not lend themselves to detailed descriptions of the specific ways of life of any one tribe. It is, however, important to understand that tribal identities vary and that these are integrated with family organization.

Unlike the regional patterns for Afro-Americans and Puerto Ricans, most Asian American families are concentrated in California. In 1970, an estimated 40% of Filipinos, 39% of Chinese, and 35% of Japanese lived in that state alone. A decade later, large numbers of Pacific Islanders and Asian families resided in California, Hawaii, New York, Illinois, Texas, New Jersey, and Washington (U.S. Bureau of the Census, 1983). Although recent immigrants have not been settling exclusively in the western part of the country, that section continues to have a larger proportion of Asians than any other region. California ranked first for each group except Hawaiians and Asian Indians; other states varied in distributions of the different populations. At the beginning of the 1980s, New York ranked second, with the highest concentrations of Chinese and Koreans. Also, Hawaii had the largest proportion of Filipinos and Japanese, and Texas had the largest number of Vietnamese. Asians and Pacific Islanders constituted 60% of the total Hawaiian population (U.S. Bureau of the Census, 1981b, p. 2). What may be ecologically pertinent, because of the impact of regional location on family life-styles and behavioral codes, is that Asians and Pacific Islanders are becoming more dispersed (U.S. Bureau of the Census, 1973, 1983).

Data in Table 2.3 show the 1970 and 1980 populations and the percentage change for Chinese, Filipinos, and Japanese by regions. The Chinese live in larger numbers outside the western part of the country, in contrast to the other Asian ethnics. At the beginning of the 1970s, slightly more than 25% lived in the Northwest, and nearly 20% lived in New York State (Kaplan & Van Valey, 1980, p. 216). Although the country of origin and its accompanying norms and values contribute to family diversity among Asians, regional location and patterns of residential mobility have an impact on family income status and behavior. Place of residence can affect family member occupational opportunities and thus the economic security of the household.

In contrast to Asian American families, Puerto Ricans are disproportionately clustered in New York (Gurak & Rogler, 1980; Mann & Salvo, 1985). Mexican Americans, on the other hand, form a relatively minor sector of the Hispanics in the city and state (Samora & Lamanna, 1967; Thurston, 1974). Their families had settled centuries earlier in New Mexico, Arizona, California, and Texas. It has been observed that this phenomenon of residential selection has "created numerous distinct Hispanic communities" (Gurak & Rogler, 1980, p. 2) and consequently distinct family milieux (Alvarez, 1973; Baca Zinn, 1980, 1982; Samora & Lamanna, 1967). For example, large numbers of Hispanics are "concentrated in ethnically specific pockets or enclaves" (Zavaleta, 1981, p. 1; see also Samora & Lamanna, 1967). These resi-

Table 2.3 Population of Chinese, Filipinos, and Japanese for 1970 and 1980 by Regions

Ethnic Group and Region	1970 Population	1980 Population	Percentage Change
Chinese			
Northeast	115,777	217,730	+88.1
North Central	39,343	72,905	+85.3
South	34,284	90,616	+164.3
West	245,658	424,776	+72.9
Filipinos			
Northeast	31,424	75,104	+139.0
North Central	27,824	79,945	+187.3
South	31,979	82,596	+158.3
West	251,833	536,995	+113.2
Japanese			
Northeast	38,978	46,930	+20.4
North Central	42,354	44,426	+4.9
South	30,917	44,636	+44.4
West	479,041	564,755	+17.9

SOURCE: U.S. Bureau of the Census (1981b).

dential boundaries, interacting with unique histories, predictably contribute to community and family diversity. This relevant social fact explains the variability in intergenerational relationships, family customs, and marital patterns, particularly rates of out-group marriage. With respect to the latter, it has been found that where ethnic groups such as Puerto Ricans are closely grouped, rates of ethnic intermarriage decrease (Collado, 1980, p. 5).

Moreover, a number of sociological investigations have focused on a subculture that evolves in ethnically specific areas (Penalosa, 1967). What social scientists have discovered about children of Hispanic ancestry is that those who grow up in Hispanic communities maintain close ties with their cultural heritage. Growing up, they play with other children whose backgrounds are similar to their own. Unlike American Indians and Asians, they share not only values and beliefs that are rooted in indigenous family traditions, but also a language. Basically, their regional distributions are as follows: Mexican American children and their parents reside primarily in southwestern states and selected parts of the

Midwest; Puerto Rican families are concentrated in three Middle Atlantic states—New York, New Jersey, and Pennsylvania; and large numbers of Cuban and Central and South American families are found in Florida, New York, and Texas (Zavaleta, 1981, pp. 1-2).

Size and Composition

Ethnic diversity in family structure is revealed in the variations in size and composition. For example, compared with all families in the United States, those of Afro-American and Hispanic descent tend to be large. In 1979, nearly 33% of Hispanic families consisted of five or more persons, compared with 18% of all families in the United States (U.S. Bureau of the Census, 1980d, p. 50). Although the proportions of Hispanic and non-Hispanic ever-married women who had at least five children decreased between 1970 and 1978, Hispanic women continued to have large families. Yet, as in other ethnic groups, Hispanic families vary in size and composition.

By the end of the 1970s, 3 of every 10 families of Hispanic origin and 1 of every 4 Afro-American families had five or more members. About 41% of Afro-American families had female householders,[7] "compared with 15 percent for families of all races combined" (U.S. Bureau of the Census, 1980d). The average size of Afro-American households in the mid-1970s was 3.3 persons. If this reduction in household size indicates a pattern, it would coincide with national trends of declining fertility and simultaneously increases in the numbers of young people living alone (U.S. Bureau of the Census, 1978, p. 100).

According to the data available from the U.S. Department of the Interior (1977), American Indian families are reported as large, primarily because of more accurate statistical reporting, greater interest in Indian history and family life, a measurable reduction in infant mortality, and a sustained high birthrate. In the mid-1970s, the "rate of 30.5 live births for each 1,000 Indians and Alaska Natives was 2.1 times as high as the U.S. 'All races' rate of 14.8" (U.S. Department of the Interior, 1977, p. 2).

Birth and fertility rates vary among Hispanics, and Hispanic mothers tend to be younger than most non-Hispanic mothers, with the exception of Afro-Americans. In 1979, the Hispanic birthrate was 25.5 births per 1,000 population. The fertility rate was 100.5 births per 1,000 women 15-44 years old. The fertility rate for Mexican American women (119.3) was greater than the rate for Puerto Rican women (80.7) (Ventura, 1982,

p. 2). No special meaning, however, can be attributed to these differences other than the uniqueness of family values (Fernández-Marina,
Maldonado, & Trent, 1958; Steward & Steward, 1973).

One-Parent Structures

Unlike the modal family forms among Asians and American Indians,
those of Puerto Ricans and Afro-Americans are characterized by a high
proportion of one-parent households. These are typically headed by
females. Yet, for the nation as a whole, there was a dramatic growth in
single-parent households in the 1970s. Whereas two-parent families
decreased by 4%, those with one parent increased by 79%: "In 1970,
about 11 percent of all families with children living at home were
maintained by one parent, but by 1979, this proportion had increased to
19 percent" (U.S. Bureau of the Census, 1980a, p. 3). At present, the
majority of these single-parent families are maintained by mothers,
despite a rise in the number supported by fathers. One distinguishing
feature of single-parent families is a large number of children.

It has been observed that for Afro-Americans, "as income increases,
the proportion of female-headed families decreases and conversely,
male-headed family structures increase" (Blackwell, 1975, p. 41). This
premise appears to apply to other minorities when family structure is
associated with socioeconomic status. Current estimates reveal that
"one in three Puerto Rican families is headed by a woman" (Nieves &
Martinez, 1980, p. 94). These households tend to be poor and disproportionately concentrated below the poverty level. There are some
predictions that such family forms, which have a historical basis, will
continue to increase among Puerto Ricans and other ethnic populations
(Cooney, Rogler, & Schroeder, 1980).

At present, the rate of growth in single-parent households among
Puerto Ricans appears to be increasing. In 1970, about 13% of Mexican
American families were maintained by women, but 24% of Puerto
Rican families had a female householder with no husband present. By
the end of the 1970s, the Puerto Rican rate had escalated to 40%, whereas
the rate for Mexican Americans had increased only slightly (Gurak, 1981,
p. 7). This structural dissimilarity emanates from variations in male and
female responses to displacement and exposure to Anglo life-styles, as well
as from differences in their cultural origins. Thus at the end of the 1970s
Mexican American families had fewer one-parent households and fewer
children than Puerto Rican families. Along with fertility differentials,

ethnicity, and familial values, socioeconomic factors have also contributed to the variability among Hispanics in single-parent units.

The available data on the single-parent form are consistent in presenting a direct correlation between the sex of the householder and family economic status. Recently, it was suggested that Afro-American women who work and maintain their families might serve as models for "all women of the proletarianized class" (Dobbins & Mulligan, 1980, p. 209). But the position of the female head of a household operates against this possibility, for, as noted, one of the striking changes in the poverty population in the past two decades has been the rise in the number of *poor* families with a female householder. This occurrence has been referred to as the *feminization of poverty*. Further, the poverty rate for persons in Afro-American families supported by a woman remains much higher than the rate for persons in comparable white families. These minority women are not members of a proletarian class. Even if they were, their social history and sustained ascriptive status are unparalleled.

Family History and Culture

Because the family ancestral and cultural histories of Asian Americans are highly diverse and their life experiences in the United States have been quite varied (Liu, 1966; Lyman, 1974; Sue & Kirk, 1973), only African Americans, American Indians, Puerto Ricans, and Mexican Americans are discussed in this section (*Pacific/Asian American Mental Health Research Center Research Review,* 1983). Each family institution for these groups has also had a distinct historical biography (Berry, 1958). In addition, each has encountered, in unique ways, external events such as value and behavioral transformations resulting from immigration and movement to and from central cities. Unlike all other ancestral groups, American Indian or Native American families and those of African heritage have occupied an unprecedented status in this country's economic, political, and social structure (Billingsley & Greene, 1974; Blassingame, 1972; Frazier, 1968; Gutman, 1965; Haley, 1976; Hare, 1976; Lammermeier, 1973; Pinkney, 1975; Wilkinson, 1969, 1974, 1978b, 1980b).

Afro-Americans

For Americans of African ancestry, the system of slavery, with its concordant attitudes, "may have militated against black family stability" (Pinkney, 1975, p. 98). The family's mode of adaptation to this dehumanizing form of social organization gave rise to prototypical and enduring kinship systems, which, in turn, may have contributed to the emergence of distinct cultural traditions (Gutman, 1965; Mack, 1971; Staples, 1971a). What we do know is that, in its evolution, the African American family persisted because of its affectional ties, the maintenance and strength of bonding, and multigenerational networks (Martin & Martin, 1978; Nobles, 1978; Wilkinson, 1978a, 1979).

The unique nature of the contemporary Afro-American family as a system interrelated with other institutions in the larger social milieu has required articulation for some time. In the analysis of any family constellation, a number of theoretical perspectives is possible. Unfortunately, in the majority of instances where families of African ancestry have been studied, these families have been evaluated primarily using the frame of reference of social problems.

In this chapter, minority families are not considered from a social problems perspective. Rather, the Afro-American family is described within the context of the social ecology and culture of both Black and white America, the family's historical character in a plantation system, the prevailing disparities in opportunities for members' upward mobility, and the differing sources of achievement. These social facts, in turn, have contributed to class and cultural variations in family organization and functioning. Despite economic and value distinctions, the family remains an essential part of the fabric of Afro-American communities.

Further, within each community there are a variety of strata, each with class-specific life-style behaviors. Socioeconomic factors impinge on the modes of family interaction, child-rearing practices, and customs, as well as member life chances. The ability of contemporary Afro-American families to meet their basic needs is directly linked to their placement in the stratification hierarchy.

Under slavery, class distinctions were obliterated; as a sanctioned form of social organization, enslavement constituted a massive disintegration of the former cultural life of Africans. One of the most disastrous results of slavery for the African family was that the slave husband was not the head of the household. This point is relevant here because the powerlessness of the male to support and protect his family for two and a half centuries has had a deleterious, pervasive, and enduring impact on family relationships (Blackwell, 1985; Cade, 1970; Wilkinson & Taylor, 1977).

American Indians

Before the seventeenth century, most of the inhabitants of this country were American Indians (U.S. Bureau of the Census, 1982, p. 2). Sharing a similar history of subordination with Americans of African heritage, American Indians were forced to adapt to pervasive disruptions in tribal society and later to what has been described as government indecisiveness on policies of assimilation versus pluralism (Berry, 1958). American Indians' family lives have been intertwined with government policies and with social changes and acculturation. Unlike the families of the other ancestral groups in the United States, American Indian parents and their children have had a long-term association with the federal government. This relationship has been defined by a territorial arrangement that influences tribal and family life extensively. For example, the United States has held in trust millions of acres of land for Indian tribes. The administrative responsibility for this territory, which continues to serve as the land base for most Indian families, rests with the Bureau of Indian Affairs.

Although their families have not been subjected to enslavement as have those of Americans of African descent, as a group Indians have experienced conquest, dislocation, cultural disintegration, spatial segregation, and, consequently, predictable ethnic identity and family problems (D. Brown, 1970). Recent case studies have shown that their personal estrangement and continued isolation are correlated with family problems and high rates of alcoholism, suicide, runaways, and crime on the reservations (Westermeyer, 1977). Yet, in order for individuals or families to be eligible for social services, they must be members of tribes recognized by the federal government. For some services, it is necessary to claim one-fourth or more Indian heritage (U.S. Department of the Interior, 1977, 1980).

According to some social scientists, the unparalleled historical conditions of Afro-Americans and American Indians are associated in the present with unique types of family patterns, particularly in the areas of composition, life-styles, husband-wife and parent-child interaction, the form and content of socialization, and mode of family adaptation. Because of intense emotional and economic needs, nuclear families in isolation from relatives and even from older members have not been found frequently in the past. Although variable, kinship bonding and obligations to relatives remain essential in familial interaction. Even today, relations with kin involve much more than long-distance "help patterns." They include residential propinquity, obligatory mutual aid, active participation in life-cycle events, and central figures around whom family ceremonies revolve. These patterns are similar in some respects to the role sets found in many Hispanic families (Baca Zinn, 1975). Relatives live near each other and become involved in the daily lives of the members of the kinship unit. Women play fundamental roles in these extended systems (Red Horse, Lewis, Feit, & Decker, 1978; Rubel, 1966; Spindler, 1962; A. Williams, 1980; Witt, 1974). In many American Indian tribes, the descent of children and the ownership of property are traced through the mother's line. The observation has been made that, "as matrilineal people, American Indian women are carriers of tribal credentials" (Keshena, 1980, p. 250). It is important to point out here also that the centrality of women is a major aspect of the family configurations of all the ethnic groups described.

Puerto Ricans

Frequent social mobility and residential dispersion have affected relations between Puerto Rican parents and their children. Traditional norms of obedience and respect for adults, rules pertaining to endogamy, and those governing male-female behavior have been modified. Many coping behaviors have emerged. One indicator of "adjustment to life on the mainland has been the increase of marriage of Puerto Ricans with non-Puerto Ricans" (Fitzpatrick, 1971, p. 94), although their rate of intermarriage is lower than that for more recent immigrant groups (Gurak & Rogler, 1980, p. 5).

Most Puerto Rican families live in inner cities and in "ethnically specific enclaves" (Zavaleta, 1981, p. 1) and thus have an opportunity to interact with other Puerto Ricans. Life in central cities, however, has its own peculiar problems: unemployment, frequent residential mobility, high crime and drug abuse rates, and marital dissolution. Puerto Rican females, for example, appear to have higher divorce rates than other Hispanic women (Alvirez, 1981, p. 12). Further, in urban centers, Puerto Ricans appear to remain single in greater proportions than most of the other Hispanics. This may simply be a consequence of the age distribution, which includes large numbers of young among the population. It is essential to understand these demographic and ecological patterns and trends among Puerto Ricans and other ethnic minorities that affect family organization.

Moreover, Puerto Rican women on the island have been exposed to social situations in which their roles reflect mainland values. They are accustomed to working, to occupying positions of prestige, and consequently to being out of the home. On the island, historically, they have been represented in the political and literary spheres: "Throughout Puerto Rico, one will find female mayors; and in the legislature, there are senators and assembly women" (Correa, 1980, p. 5). Women have thus played active, integrated roles as wives, mothers, and workers. Like Mexican American women, they have also been socialized to a set of cultural norms anchored in a belief in male authority, but this sex-typed ethic is not the negative feature that it has been claimed to be in much of the family literature.

The explicit codes of conduct for the sex-specific behaviors of Hispanic males and females are integral parts of their cultural ideology and their learned system of status differentiation. Historically, male dominance has been a prominent aspect of Hispanic social organization, and in Puerto Rican and Mexican American families, expressive and conventional duties for mothers and wives prevail (Gonzales, 1980; Sánchez, 1973). But, as previously indicated, this fact discloses the premium placed not only on effective family organization but on a rational division of labor. The prevailing distorted notions about extreme paternal rigidity and a negative *machismo* ethic do not reveal the affectional roles of husbands and fathers (Goodman & Beman, 1971; Rubel, 1966).

Mexican Americans

Many of the external influences on Puerto Rican families also affect those of Mexican heritage. It has been asserted that the fundamental beliefs of Mexican culture do not coincide with those of Anglo society (Fernández-Marina et al., 1958; Hamilton, 1973; Mirandé, 1977). Although there are predictable generational and class differences within Mexican American communities and among families, understandably those reared in a Mexican environment do not share assumed ideal middle-class Anglo-American norms, such as deferred gratification (Burma, 1963, p. 22). In Mexican culture there is a greater emphasis on the present and on meeting the needs of the collective: *la familia* (Mirandé, 1979; Rubel, 1966).

Furthermore, there are several distinguishing aspects of Mexican American expectations and family interaction that should be discussed. Although these are similar to the behavioral precepts of other Hispanics, they vary by virtue of differences in history and culture, family customs, immigrant status, regional location, and occupational and economic positions. Like other families of Spanish descent in the United States, those of Mexican ancestry tend to ascribe significance to solidifying beliefs, such as (a) the integral nature of the family in daily living; (b) the functional dominance of males, complemented by a positive and traditional role for women; (c) the reinforcement of sex role distinctions through child-rearing practices; (d) strong kinship bonds; (e) the "centrality of children"; (f) the repression of feminine attributes in males; and (g) a precedent for the male as head of the household (Mirandé, 1979, 1980; Mirandé & Enriquez, 1979; Penalosa, 1968). As previously indicated, these differ in scope and intensity from the beliefs of other Hispanics because of separate histories, behavioral prescriptions, and the configuration of familistic values to which the members are socialized.

Family interaction is of paramount importance among Mexican Americans (Kenkel, 1985). The intimate involvement of personalities is a prominent feature, and children are at the center of family life. However, a number of dramatic social events and conditions, such as migration, unemployment, illegal-alien status, and discrimination, have resulted in modifications in some of these fundamental traits. Increasingly, families are becoming similar to Anglo-American middle-class structures (Penalosa, 1968, pp. 407, 409). This trend perhaps indicates a class metamorphosis from a lower socioeconomic status to an ethnic group similar to European immigrants of a few generations ago, such as the Italian Americans (Penalosa, 1967).

Exposure to a changing political environment has had a direct effect on women's roles in the family system. There has been, for example, a lessening of the woman's customary adherence to the values and conventions of her family of origin. New levels of aspiration to independence and professional status, as well as less dependence on male authority, also characterize contemporary role shifts for women. Despite modifications in the traditional habits and behaviors that have shaped Mexican American culture and have affected husband-wife interaction, particularly role expectations for women, the family remains the strongest source of emotional strength and support (Díaz-Guerrero, 1955; Mirandé & Enriquez, 1979). Although the family constitutes the nucleus of Hispanic life, it is undergoing transformation (Kenkel, 1985).

As indicated earlier, there is considerable heterogeneity within the Hispanic population, resulting in significant differences in family styles and customs. For example, Puerto Rican women, like Mexican American women, tend to have large numbers of children: "First and second generation Mexican women have a greater tendency to continue having children after the age of 35" (Gurak, 1981, p. 9). In addition to fertility differentials, there are basic marital and residential distinctions. These result not only from established practices but also from variations in immigrant status, employment opportunities, and encounters with discrimination. There are also considerable differences in these experiences from those of the other racial and ethnic groups. For example, "direct discrimination does not hit the Mexican American as severely" as it does the Afro-American (Bullock, 1978, p. 159).

For Mexican Americans and Puerto Ricans, migration and adjustment to a new status and cultural environment—specifically American middle-class folkways—are among the processes contributing to change in family organization. Some of the internal transitions are reflected in the family lives of Asian Americans and American Indians, such as (a) an increase in the participation of mothers in occupational activities outside the home; (b) a rise in nontraditional male and female role expectations, which are modifying conventional family observances; (c) decreasing authoritarian structure with respect to the father role and a greater emphasis on egalitarianism (Cromwell & Cromwell, 1978); (d) the acquisition of knowledge of the English language on the part of children, with accompanying redefinitions of the father-offspring relationship in particular; and (e) status attainment increasingly based on individual achievement rather than on family productivity (Jiménez-Vásquez, 1980). The content and form of these changes vary considerably with the cultural histories and experiences of Hispanic families (Baca Zinn, 1980; Durrett, O'Bryant, & Pennebaker, 1975; Fitzpatrick, 1971; Mirandé, 1980; Montalvo, 1974; Murillo-Rohde, 1976; Perez, 1979; Project on the Status and Education of Women, 1975).

Kinship Relationships

Despite the sharp demarcation in sex role behaviors, male and female relatives provide basic intergenerational links in ethnic families. Arrangements based on cohesiveness and kinship bonding were illuminated in the social science literature at the end of the 1950s, when prevailing theories of isolated nuclear structures were questioned (Sussman, 1959). Decades later, social scientists unveiled help patterns that continue to filter throughout American Indian, Afro-American, Asian American, Mexican American, and Puerto Rican family life cycles.

Hispanics

Although the basic unit for Mexican Americans tends to be nuclear, with strong emotional ties (Thornburg & Grinder, 1975, p. 352), as Chicano culture is exposed to constant and rapid environmental changes and modernization, extended kin associations become more and more important (Mirandé, 1979). Generally, in Hispanic families, close relationships with maternal and paternal grandparents are fundamental. Of special importance are the emotional ties with the mother's relatives. Maternal aunts often serve as brokers, providing a link between parents and other adults in the family. Actually, the aunt functions as a "second mother" or a mother substitute. She is the one who responds to the problems of all family members, which range from requests for financial assistance to consultations (Jiménez-Vásquez, 1980, pp. 224-255). She thus enacts a set of roles that are quite similar to those found in Afro-American families, especially among the lower and working classes.

Kinship forms vary among the different ethnic populations. For example, *la familia* among Hispanics is quite distinct in structure and composition from the extended bonds found among Asian Americans and Afro-Americans. In the Spanish language, *la familia* is a broad concept that may include single households, combinations, and/or all extended relatives. Thus its form and function depend on the emotional and financial capabilities of the central families. Although the most frequent household type among Chicanos is nuclear centered, the norm is geographic propinquity and strong kinship ties among family units, especially in times of need (Sena-Rivera, 1979).

Like those for others of Spanish ancestry, extended kin units function as connecting links to basic institutions such as the church and the school in Puerto Rican communities. Although families are becoming spatially nuclear, emotional closeness and mutual aid networks among relatives have been preserved. Puerto Rican parents and their adult offspring tend to reside close to each other. This practice is manifested in Puerto Ricans' regional distribution in central cities. As noted earlier, minicommunities of families often live in the same block of a neighborhood. A similar ecological pattern of neighborhood concentration is found among Japanese, Chinese, Filipino, and other Asian Americans. Apparently, the legacy of the extended system, with strong emotional ties clustered in nearby residential areas, remains an important aspect of Hispanic American, Asian American, American Indian, and Afro-American family bonding (Billingsley, 1970; Conner, 1974; C. L. Johnson,

1977; Martin & Martin, 1978; H. P. McAdoo, 1978a; Palisi, 1966; Wilkinson, 1979).

Afro-Americans

Although kinship relations are salient, the majority of Afro-American families reflect a nuclear model. Extended relatives may reside in the immediate household. One trend that is transforming composition and stucture or form has been the decline in the proportion of families with a husband and wife present. In the mid-1970s, those with a husband and wife accounted for slightly more than 60% of all American families of African heritage. In contrast, three decades earlier, that figure was estimated at nearly 80% (U.S. Bureau of the Census, 1978, p. 100). A significant consequence of this change in structure has been a substantial rise in the proportion of Afro-American households maintained by a woman (U.S. Bureau of the Census, 1980a, p. 3). Such families often encounter emotional and financial difficulties, but frequently these are offset by social support and financial assistance provided by relatives.

Kinship systems among Afro-Americans tend to be interdependent and multigenerational. In many respects, they resemble those of other ethnic minority families (H. P. McAdoo, 1978b). They are characterized by intimate involvement and a set of unwritten obligations to consanguineal and conjugal relatives regardless of age. Among the most important properties are affectional bonds connecting several generations; a central family member who occupies a leadership position, establishes behavioral codes, and participates in the socialization of the children; an expectation of responsibility for the children on the part of the fathers; an intense communal orientation toward family members; the interdependency of relatives on each other for emotional, social, and material support; an absorption mechanism for taking in those unable to care for themselves; and a mutual aid system (Martin & Martin, 1978; Wilkinson, 1979, p. 397). Despite class distinctions and social changes that influence family solidarity as well as upward mobility, relations with kin are fundamental in the Afro-American family system (Billingsley, 1970; H. P. McAdoo, 1978a, 1978b).

Asian Americans

Variations in cultural backgrounds, class differences, and recency of immigration contribute to diversity in the kinship forms among Asian

American families (Lyman, 1971). However, the retaining of functional liaisons with relatives through established customs and a chain-migration pattern are typical (Boyd, 1971, 1974; Pian, 1980). Such occurrences mirror and amplify the unique placement of their families in the economic and social structure of the United States.

Furthermore, the different Asian American populations have entrenched norms and role expectations pertaining to caring for the aged, who are usually older relatives. Most often, an elderly parent lives in the same household as the adult children (Fujii, 1980a; Kalish & Moriwaki, 1973; Osako, 1980, p. 227). Responsibilities to aged parents and to close relatives are fundamental to the family institution among Japanese, Chinese, and Filipinos, although changes are taking place in the modes of assisting kin, the degree of internalization of contemporary American family values, and economic and cultural backgrounds and life-styles (Cheung, Cho, Lum, Tang, & Yau, 1980; Conner, 1974, 1977; Ishizuka, 1978; C. L. Johnson, 1977; Kalish & Yuen, 1971; Kim & Mejia, 1976; Li, 1975; Liu, 1966; Liu & Yu, 1975; Lyman, 1974; Montero, 1980; Muramatsu, 1960; Osako, 1976; Yanagisako, 1975).

American Indians

Although American Indians, like Asians, are a people experiencing continuous transitions, there are qualities of strength within their families, and affinal and consanguineal bonds are sustained through profoundly embedded customs (R. Lewis, 1981). Despite tribal as well as urban versus rural residential distinctions, kinship ties are of supreme importance. In fact, "extended family networks remain as a constant regardless of family life style patterns" (Red Horse et al., 1978, p. 71). These networks include several households of significant relatives that tend to assume a "village-type" character. Transactions within and among them occur within a community context (Red Horse et al., 1978, p. 68). Variations in household composition and intergenerational relationships are indicators of unique tribal histories, customs, and values; life on particular reservations and in urban communities; the changing roles of women (Gilfillan, 1901; Granzberg, 1973; Harmsworth, 1965; Jimson, 1977; Medicine, 1969); techniques of adaptation to urban dislocation; past "deculturation" (Ablon, 1964; Boggs, 1953; Hallowell, 1963; Unger, 1977; Westermeyer, 1977; A. Williams, 1980); and individual and family problems and needs (Ackerman, 1971; Kuttner & Lorinez, 1967; Streit & Nicolich, 1977; Tyler & Thompson, 1965). Yet, the community-family configuration is a mark of an integrated social organization that serves to offset the ravages of perpetual displacement (Attenave, 1977).

Marital Patterns

Urbanization, industrialization, "deculturation," war, evolving roles, and social changes have affected marriage and divorce trends. Because of their relevance to diversity in family interaction and the attention given them in the past four decades, two events are of particular concern here: (a) trends in the marital status of women and (b) the phenomenon of interethnic and interracial exogamy. Residential mobility (specifically, movement to urban centers), new contacts in the workplace, and changing mate selection and marital practices have resulted in an increase in interracial and interethnic marriages and a dramatic rise in divorce rates.

Asian Americans

In the traditional Asian family, marriage and unity are the foundation of social organization. Divorce and intermarriage are simply not characteristic. For example, "the ancient Chinese family was patriarchal, family centered, male dominated" (Mirandé, 1979, p. 97), and stable. These traits remain, and marriage continues to be essential to family solidarity and cultural transmission (Fillmore & Cheong, 1980; Osako, 1980).

Recent studies have shown that Asian American families share strong kinship associations, fewer children than the national average, declining authoritarianism, a high proportion of marriages outside the specific ethnic group (Kitano & Kikumura, 1980), and a smaller percentage of divorced women than in other ethnic populations. Moreover, in contrast to U.S. families as a whole, those of Chinese, Japanese, and Filipino heritage tend to be more stable, to have lower divorce rates, and to have fewer families with female heads.

Nearly "half of Asian American women are primarily housewives" (Hirata, 1980, p. 173), a position that differs from the marital status of significant proportions of Puerto Rican, Mexican American, and Afro-American women. In 1970, more than 60% of women from the three dominant Asian American ethnic populations were married. Among Japanese American women alone, age 16 and older, two-thirds were married. This proportion contrasts sharply with the marital status of Puerto Rican and Afro-American women today, a large number of whom reside in households with no husband present (U.S. Bureau of the Census, 1980a, 1980c).

The frequent occurrence of interracial marriage among Asians is worth noting because of its relevance to the family environment. As early as the 1930s, researchers discovered that the Japanese in Hawaii had high rates of out-group marriage (R. Adams, 1937). Since then, studies of exogamous unions have dealt specifically with the numbers of women marrying outside their ethnic groups. Although a larger proportion of Japanese women who practice exogamy marry white males than either Chinese or Filipino women, a significantly higher percentage of Filipino women who practice exogamy marry males of Spanish descent (U.S. Bureau of the Census, 1973). There are several sociological explanations for this phenomenon. Place of residence and occupation are important explanatory variables. Further, many Asian American women who marry outside their ethnic groups live in urban centers. They tend to have high-status jobs and to emphasize upward mobility for themselves and their families (Cheng & Yamamura, 1957; Kikumura & Kitano, 1973). The desire to enhance status and the tendency toward assimilation are prominent.

The assumption of marital mobility for Asian women who practice exogamy has been scrutinized. In fact, one study of Asian intermarriage in Los Angeles County for 1960-1961 found that, on the average, Japanese, Chinese, and Filipino women married men with lower occupational statuses than they themselves held (Mittlebach & Moore, 1968). Despite the limited data in this important area of marital relations, correlations have been found between socioeconomic status and intermarriage. It has been suggested that, if Asian women do marry downward, there may still be a compensatory element in that they marry into the majority group (Hirata, 1980, p. 330). What is known from most of the available literature is that social class factors, interacting with a multiplicity of personality needs, play a prominent role in exogamous unions (DeVos, 1973).

Moreover, the increasing numbers of Chinese, Japanese, and Filipino interethnic marriages portend new social changes. Macrosocietal developments and their consequences not only affect family interaction and traditional institutions but may eventually alter the conventional system of ethnic classification (Kikumura & Kitano, 1973, p. 34). Further, the social psychological and familial consequences of those marriages that experience difficulties include some of the same ones encountered by other ethnic minorities; planning where to live, selecting a school for the children, deciding how to rear the children to have a positive identity, and being concerned about peer-group pressures and community attitudes toward the family. Asians, however, experience fewer of these problems than do members of other racial minority families (Endo et al., 1980).

Afro-Americans

Although marriage provides the foundation for the Afro-American family, single households and divorce have become common. An important indicator of changes in traditional family structure is the proportion of families that include both a husband and a wife (U.S. Bureau of the Census, 1978, p. 100). In the 20-year period between 1940 and 1960, the marital status distribution for the Afro-American population showed a larger proportion of men and women who were married than had been true in earlier years. It has been asserted that, "in this century, the percent of married was at its peak for Blacks" during that 20-year period (Glick, 1981; U.S. Bureau of the Census, 1978, p. 101).

The trends in marital status patterns for Blacks have been basically similar to those for the white population. In the mid-1970s, 81% of Afro-American males who were 35-44 years old were married. For females in this same age range, slightly less than three-fourths were married (U.S. Bureau of the Census, 1978, p. 110), and an estimated one-tenth were divorced.

In most of the census years since 1890, larger proportions of men than of women in their middle years have consistently been reported as married (U.S. Bureau of the Census, 1978, p. 101). The factors that account for the disparities in marital status between the sexes include age at first marriage, rate of remarriage, variations in the age structure, and differential rates of intermarriage, as well as the possibility of misreporting and census errors in calculations. What is important here is that, like other racial and ethnic minority families, those of African ancestry are experiencing considerable reorganization and structural change. The rise in divorce rate, the escalating economic insecurity of husbands and fathers, the growing number of single households headed by females, and an increase in interracial marriages since the 1960s have all eroded the traditional Afro-American family institution.

As a consequence of the historical position of Americans of African descent in the stratification system, the subject of interracial marriage has elicited a multiplicity of behavioral science interpretations and emotional responses. Because racial status and associated symbolic meanings are entrenched in the dominant political structure and ideological system, these variables assume distinct connotations in the context of Black-white dating, mating, and marriage. Although social controls both within the family and outside it have operated against such liaisons, racial exogamy has become a frequent occurrence. On the other hand, endogamy does prevail as the norm for the selection of marital partners in the majority of racial and ethnic minority families.

With the advent of social changes in the 1960s, interracial marriages, primarily between Afro-American males and white females, rose. Of the estimated 65,000 interracial married couples in 1970, more than 63% involved Black husbands and white wives. By 1977, the number of such couples constituted an estimated 95,000, a 131.7% change in that seven-year period! However, there have been few studies of the life-styles, child-rearing practices, and marital behaviors in these families. It has been suggested that the "small amount of scientific investigation of racial intermarriage in this country is testimony to what could be termed a degree of myopia in contemporary American sociology" (Barnett, 1975, p. 23).

Several social consequences for family organization and interaction emanate from interracial unions. These involve collective status incongruence and ambiguities in the content of socialization, particularly with respect to the self-concept development of the children. Recently, the serious ramifications of these issues have been revealed in divorce cases where some fathers have requested custody of children on the grounds that their offspring are genetically Black and that, therefore, *their* offspring would be denied an Afro-American identity and heritage. The potential psychological pressures on children have been observed as critical. Among the most frequent tensions for interracial families as a whole arise from problems concerning difficulty in deciding where to live in relative comfort, not being able to maintain close affectional ties with kin, being constantly exposed to public responses to the emotional symbolism of the Black male-white female union (Golden, 1975, p. 9), occupational adjustment difficulties, and awareness on the part of the children of the subordinated position and inferiorized status of the father throughout history (Beigel, 1975; Wilkinson, 1975a, 1980b; Wilkinson & Taylor, 1977).

American Indians

Interracial marriage is also increasing among American Indians. It is estimated that more than one-third of all Indians marry outside their ethnic group (Scheirbeck, 1980). These alliances are the result of a number of social conditions: residence in metropolitan areas, new occupational opportunities, frequency of contact with other ethnic groups, higher educational status, and the desire for and perceptions of the possibility of assimilation. Although tribal marital customs remain, the practice of interethnic marriage has affected Indian cultural identity, traditional tribal values, and the institutional context of the family (Boggs, 1953; Boyer, 1964; A. Williams, 1980).

Hispanics

Converging with the marital patterns among Asian Americans, there has been considerable exogamy among Hispanic ethnics (Bean & Bradshaw, 1970; Fitzpatrick & Gurak, 1979). Although Puerto Ricans have relatively low rates of exogamy, Hispanics from Central America and Cuba tend to have high rates of interethnic marriage. Duration of stay in the country of residence, the degree of racial similarity and perceptions of assimilation, regional location, social class variables such as education and occupation, and frequency of contact contribute to variations in intermarriage rates (Murguia & Frisbie, 1977; Wilkinson, 1975a). Within each occupational stratum, exogamy tends to increase with distance from immigrant status for Asians and Hispanics. In addition, within each generation, marriage outside one's ancestral group "increases steadily with the socioeconomic status of the groom" (Mittlebach & Moore, 1968). Interestingly, "the second generation exogamy rates for the non-Puerto Rican Hispanics are high even when compared to European ethnic groups, while those of Puerto Ricans are relatively low" (Gurak, 1981, p. 8). More recent data suggest that the intermarriage rates for Mexican Americans may be on the decline (Murguia & Frisbie, 1977). Women of Hispanic origin have higher rates of intermarriage than do Hispanic males, especially in the second and third generations. Interestingly, marriages between Puerto Ricans and other Hispanics are relatively frequent (Gurak, 1981, p. 8). The variable forms of exogamy are indicative of differences in values, social class position, frequency of contact, the extent of assimilation, and the degree of internalization of the dominant sector's social distance attitudes.

More than a decade ago, the majority of Puerto Rican and Mexican American women were married (U.S. Bureau of the Census, 1980c). However, as noted earlier, there has been a substantial increase in female-headed families among Puerto Ricans. For example, in the 1960 and 1970 U.S. Census data, an increase in such households with own children under 18 was found in the states of New York, New Jersey, and Pennsylvania (Cooney et al., 1980). Despite the structural transitions, family and kinship ties are highly valued.

Socioeconomic Characteristics

It is axiomatic that diversity among minority families is manifested in life-style characteristics based on income and the educational and employment status of the head of the household. Most of the available data on income, however, are confounded for Hispanics and Asians by the combining of ethnic populations. However, it can be safely stated that, with the exception of Asians and Pacific Islanders, the economic position of racial and ethnic minority families is generally low.

Hispanic and Afro-American families are underrepresented at the higher income and educational levels. The proportion of Hispanic families with annual incomes less than $5,000 is about twice the proportion for families not of Hispanic heritage. For Afro-Americans, the proportion is about three times that for white American families (National Center for Health Statistics, 1979, p. 4). Thus the stratification pyramids are quite distinct for the different populations and consequently for the families within them.

A number of values, behavioral customs, and life-cycle events in ethnic families are directly correlated with disparities in social and economic status. Understandably, the ability of families to meet the fundamental needs of their members is intricately interwoven with their placement on the economic ladder (Billingsley, 1968, p. 145).

Among Afro-Americans, upper-class persons are more likely than working- and lower-class persons to have grown up in nuclear families with norms of obedience to adults and with strong fathers (Billingsley, 1968). These values are characteristic of upper- and upper-middle-class families, regardless of race or ethnicity. Although the poor occupy an economically powerless location in the stratification system, it has not yet been empirically substantiated that their families share a "culture of poverty."

Occupational Status

Asian Americans. The position of women in the professions and as members of families varies with ethnicity and with customary definitions of the woman's roles. For example, in comparison to other ethnic minorities, Filipino and Chinese American women have a "higher percentage employed in the professions" (Osako, 1980, p. 163). For both males and females, the "majority of Filipino immigrants settling in the East are younger highly educated professionals (e.g., medical doctors, registered nurses, accountants, engineers, etc.)" (Cordova, 1980, p. 142). These achievements elevate the socioeconomic status of the family and enrich its values (Kim & Mejia, 1976; Loo, 1980).

Puerto Ricans. More than one-third of Puerto Ricans in the United States live at or below the poverty level. The majority of single-parent Puerto Rican families live in poverty. In two-parent households, women are less likely to work outside the home, and fewer of them are in the labor force. Generally, unemployment rates are high, and the median family income is slightly more than half the nation's average (Nieves & Martinez, 1980, p. 93). Overall, median family income tends to be lower for Puerto Rican than for other Hispanic families. Puerto Rican men tend to have longer periods of unemployment than do other Hispanic males (Alvirez, 1981, p. 13). Even in families with the husband present, Puerto Rican males often encounter difficulty securing jobs (Mizio, 1974, p. 81). In contrast to Mexican American males, they also have longer periods of being without work. What accounts for these disparities in socioeconomic levels and the concomitant experiences? There are several explanations for the low socioeconomic attainment of Puerto Rican males: stresses of migration, concentration in lower-paying jobs, difficulties related to life in central cities, the preponderance of families with unskilled female heads, and language and structural barriers.

American Indians. Rural and urban American Indian families also have organizational and interactional characteristics that are associated with social and economic factors as well as with distinct tribal histories. They have large families (Scheirbeck, 1980, p. 64), and their occupational and income status are low. Husbands and fathers tend to be unskilled or to lack the training for jobs in urban communities, and they hold low-paying jobs. If families reside in rural communities, the women who work outside the home are likely to be found in semiskilled service occupations. Where families live in urban centers, the women can be found holding white-collar positions. Low educational achievement, combined with a large proportion of men and women relegated to service and semiskilled jobs, results in Indians' having one of the lowest median incomes of any sector in the U.S. population. Recently, many American Indians have expressed dismay about the recession and federal budget cuts. Tribal and family living are being affected by widespread unemployment among Indians across the country.

Themes in the Literature: Changing Historical Perspectives

Although the civil rights revolution ushered in widespread concern about the varied depictions of ethnic family life, thorough analyses of Hispanic and American Indian families, in particular, are relatively recent. In the 1950s, writings about ethnic minorities were primarily anecdotal presentations, limited case studies, subjective essays, and time- and space-restricted ethnographies by social workers and others (Díaz-Guerrero, 1955; Dohen, 1959). With the advent of the politically conscious 1960s, studies were designed to explore a wide range of topics pertaining to majority-minority relations and ethnic families and communities. Some of the results, based on an array of data-collection techniques, expanded foci on realistic issues such as employment needs and mental health problems (J. Brown, 1970; Cabezas, 1977; Correa, 1980; Díaz-Guerrero, 1955; Fong & Cabezas, 1980; Ikeda, Ball, & Yamamura, 1962; Jaco & Wilber, 1975; Nagel, 1975; Nava, 1973).

Hispanics

Descriptions of Hispanic families in the previous decade provided insights into demographic, social, and cultural distinctions within this multiethnic population (Gurak & Rogler, 1980). In fact, ethnically specific frames of reference for examining Chicano parents and their children were not crystallized until the 1970s (Mirandé, 1977; Sena-Rivera, 1979). One of the more insightful contributions about those of Mexican heritage was presented in the late 1960s by Penalosa (1968), who offered a new perspective for analyzing Mexican American culture and traditions. It was based on the premise that earlier studies tended to display positive tones about Mexican American families, but that those centering on families *in the country of origin* carried negative tones. Other Chicano social and behavioral scientists criticized the myths, the pathological models, and the pejorative depictions of Chicano family organization. "Insider" views were based on the assumption that a general model of life among Mexicans was necessary for a full understanding of husband-wife and parent-child interaction and to reduce cultural biases on the part of researchers.

In the 1970s, a growing body of the data collected on Hispanics began to be produced by Hispanic scholars. Emphasis was placed on the history of Mexicans in America (Cabeza de Baca, 1972; Carrillo-Beron, 1974; Grebler, Moore, & Guzman, 1970; Rendón, 1971), their general family characteristics (Alvirez & Bean, 1976; Mirandé, 1979; Murillo, 1971; Padilla & Ruiz, 1973; Temple-Trujillo, 1974), and the evolution of their adaptations to American culture (Alvarez, 1973). Simultaneously, many young writers initiated systematic inquiries into the subjective and conflicting images of Chicano people and their culture, as well as into the myths in the literature about Mexican American men, women, and family environments (Mirandé, 1977; Montiel, 1970; Riccatille, 1974; Rincón, 1984; Nieto, 1974; Suárez, 1973). It was observed that, as no hard data existed on Mexican Americans, myths and generalizations abounded (Mirandé, 1977, p. 747). These portrayed Mexican American men and women and their families and customs in negative ways (Montiel, 1978; Shepro, 1980, p. 120) and thus perpetuated stereotypical images and distorted interpretations under the "banner of science" (Montiel, 1973).

The economic development of Chicano communities (Alvirez & Bean, 1976) and earnings differentials for male workers (Poston, Alvirez, & Tienda, 1976) were the subject of research in the mid- to late 1970s, along with the tensions associated with marital decision-making power and methods of family conflict resolution (Cromwell, Corrales, & Torsiella, 1973). One study of particular interest, using a sample of 274 spouses (88 Anglos, 88 Afro-Americans, and 98 Chicanos), found that ethnicity did not constitute a sufficient explanation for variance in perceptions by spouses of decision making. The emphasis was on who makes the determination about purchasing a car or contacting a doctor, whether or not the wife will work, how much the family will spend on food per week, and what will be the interaction among the children and with whom they will play (Cromwell & Cromwell, 1978, p. 754). In one hypothesis, it was assumed that "the relative degree of patriarchy perceived by husbands and wives will be greatest for Chicanos, intermediary for Anglos, and least for Blacks" (Cromwell & Cromwell, 1978, p. 752). The informative result was that, for the three ethnic groups, egalitarianism in conjugal decision making was the norm as defined by the wives and their husbands. Whereas Chicano couples tended to agree on who dominated, Afro-American husbands and wives disagreed on the outcomes (Cromwell & Cromwell, 1978, p. 755).

It should be noted here that the components of decision making typically examined are not problems fundamental for husbands and wives in ethnic minority families. Rather, their collective concerns revolve around meeting basic economic needs, providing quality life experiences for their children, maintaining employment, developing coping strategies in response to mobility, and controlling perpetual external pressures.

As indicated above, ethnic endogamy has been another important topic studied in the social science literature. A considerable portion of the data on Hispanic intermarriage indicates that there are generational differences in the practice of marrying outside one's ancestral group. Younger Mexican Americans are more antitraditionalist and thus tend to practice exogamy more frequently than those from older generations (Mittlebach & Moore, 1968). Among Mexican Americans, as well as other minority groups, there is also an association between the socioeconomic status of the man and the rate of interethnic marriage. In Mittlebach and Moore's (1968) study of marriage licenses in Los Angeles County in the 1960s, 40% of the marriages involving Mexican Americans were exogamous. Interestingly, women were found to practice exogamy more frequently than men. Perceptions of opportunities for assimilation and expectations for upward social mobility are among the explanations for this occurrence.

Coinciding with the feminist movement, Puerto Rican and Chicano women and their families began to be studied in the social and behavioral science literature in more positive or appreciative tones (S. Delgado, 1971; García, 1980; Longeaux y Vásquez, 1972; Lopez, 1973; Montiel, 1973; Suárez, 1973; Viera, 1980). A few of the findings revealed that, despite exposure to the women's movements, Mexican American women's feelings about their traditional roles and family responsibilities were only slightly altered (Gonzales, 1980; Nieto, 1974). Basically, the deeply rooted sex role behaviors, sexual mores, and familistic conventions associated with being wives and mothers, as well as feelings of estrangement from the Anglo women's movement (Hamilton, 1973; Mirandé, 1979; Nieto, 1974; Vidal, 1971)—sentiments shared with Asian, Afro-American, and American Indian women—have remained intact. Explanations for this adherence to ingrained role definitions are based on the "centrality of children" and internalized husband-wife and mother-father role relationships that oppose the goals of the women's movement. In fact, extreme feminists have been viewed by many in ethnic minority groups as antifamily.

Between 1960 and 1970, two divergent foci monopolized the sparse writings on Puerto Rican families and their communities in the United States and on the island (de Rodriguez, 1973). As indicated earlier, these were the "culture of poverty" thesis (O. Lewis, 1965; Sexton, 1965) and migration trends. Because migration transformed family structure and functioning in myriad ways, patterns of social mobility and subsequent changes in Puerto Rican culture were studied (Fitzpatrick, 1971; Taeuber, 1966). Of special concern has been the impact of migration to the mainland on parent-child interaction, effective parental role functioning, and consequently the significance of the helping professions in meeting the needs of family members (Mizio, 1974). In the 1970s, critiques of earlier behavioral science and historical portrayals of families of Hispanic origin escalated (Mirandé, 1977; Montiel, 1970; Riccatille, 1974; Vásquez, 1970; Vidal, 1971; Ybarra, 1977).

Some of the literature of the 1970s provided a new perspective on prevailing disputes over "momism" versus "machismo," (Sánchez, 1973), as well as on the nature of Puerto Rican community social habits that affect family members' interaction and adjustment. Investigations in the late 1960s and early 1970s by Hispanic and non-Hispanic scholars explored Puerto Rican families' experiences with child rearing and emphasized socialization and the emotional development of children (Maunez, 1973; Moran, 1973; Muñoz, 1973; Santiago, 1973). Home-school conflicts were found to be encountered frequently in Puerto Rican families (Canino & Canino, 1980; Montalvo, 1974).

American Indians

Before the 1960s, there were ethnographic portraits and social work reports on Indian family life and the experiences of children in tribes such as the Chippewa (Hilger, 1951) and the Arapaho (Hilger, 1952). These writings tended to be descriptive personal accounts of daily activities, tribal rituals, and ceremonials. There were no analyses of the needs of different tribal families.

In later years, there were case studies on the hazards of boarding schools (Beiser, 1974; Brightman, 1971), the mental health risks of such schools (Krush & Bjork, 1965), the dilemmas associated with adoption practices (Byler, Deloria, & Gurwitt, 1974; Davis, 1961; Farris, 1976; Lacy, 1975), and the emotional difficulties encountered in attempts to adapt to dislocation (Fitzpatrick, 1971). There were calls for assistance in finding solutions, yet many of these problems remain and warrant not merely descriptive accounting but practical resolutions. Increasingly, Indians are becoming more vocal about their family and community needs.

Many of the difficulties that American Indians continue to confront, which affect their life chances and family functioning, were disclosed in the 1970s. Juxtaposed with poverty and its correlates—substandard housing, high infant mortality rates, tuberculosis, and other health problems—persistent bureaucratic neglect of children was divulged. Among the prevailing issues are those centering on the quality of education for Indian children, the disadvantages of boarding schools (Dlugokinski & Kramer, 1974), and the psychological stresses related to adoption (Byler et al., 1974). Simply keeping children in school is a continual family and community problem for many tribes on the reservations, as well as for families living in urban areas. Although the majority of Indian children of school age are enrolled in school, the dropout rate for those in both public and private high schools tends to be high.

With the advent of the 1970s, descriptions of the physical and mental health of Indian children as well as their educational achievements were offered along with accounts of American Indian history (Bird, 1972; D. Brown, 1970; Deloria, 1970; McLuhan, 1974), the status of Indian women (J. Brown, 1970; Spindler, 1962; A. Williams, 1980; Witt, 1974), and the totality of family experiences, which differ by tribal affiliations. As a result of the ideological and value orientations underlying the women's movement, more recently specific attention has been devoted to the educational needs of Indian girls (Scheirbeck, 1980).

In the mid-1970s, the various images and multiple intersecting roles of Indian women as mothers, wives, and workers began to constitute a subject of interest (R. Green, 1975). It was recognized that, although modern Anglo roles are not compatible with Indian tribal customs, many fundamental needs of Indian women have been neglected in the literature *and* in their own societies. In 1976, the Conference on the Educational and Occupational Needs of American Indian Women, sponsored by the National Institute of Education, explored a number of Indian women's problems and their unfulfilled expectations (Blanchard, 1980; Keshena, 1980; A. Williams, 1980). Today, there is a North American Indian Women's Association, which has as its mission the improvement of the home, family life, and the community (Blanchard, 1980).

Asian Americans

Understandably, Asian American families differ not only from American Indian families but also among themselves. Asian American children do not have a history of being sent to boarding schools, of high dropout rates, or of severe emotional traumas resulting from continual displacement (Aylesworth et al., 1980). Further, their families have manifested a high degree of stability, less internal modification, and fewer conflicts revolving around women's roles. These differences are understandable, as the cultures and social experiences of Chinese, Japanese, and Filipino Americans are substantially distinct from those of the American Indians. In fact, as pointed out earlier, in contrast to the marriages of Puerto Rican and Afro-American women, the marriages of Chinese, Japanese, and Filipinos display a greater degree of permanence, and there is a high level of family solidarity. The majority of Asian American women are housewives with husband present (Hirata, 1980, p. 173), although not all of them are married to Asian American men.

Aside from the studies in the 1960s of internal family dynamics and, more specifically, of child-rearing practices of Asian parents (Guthrie & Jacobs, 1966; Kitano, 1961, 1964; Kurokawa, 1968; Scoffield & Sun, 1960), a frequent focus of social science research has been on changing marital customs, particularly on mate selection among women. As early as the 1950s, the subject of interracial marriages began to dominate inquiry into Asian American marital patterns. Following the Korean War, interest centered specifically on the cultural changes that affected Filipino American marriages (Hunt & Coller, 1956) and the adjustment problems of Japanese war brides (Kim, 1972, 1980; Kimura, 1957; Schnepp & Yui, 1955; Strauss, 1954). Soon attention was directed not only to interethnic marital trends among Japanese, Chinese, and Filipinos in the aftermath of the war (Barnett, 1963; Burma, 1963), but also to the psychological motives and the relational problems underlying these marriages (Beigel, 1975; Gordon, 1964; Strauss, 1954; Teicher, 1968).

Twenty years after World War II and during the height of the Vietnam era, the sociological subjects of interest were war brides, identity conflicts of children, and the general adjustment difficulties faced by Chinese and Japanese women married to white servicemen (DeVos, 1973). Deviance and social problems were often the key analytic concepts. The relevance of ethnic boundaries for Japanese who practiced exogamy became a topic of consideration (Kikumura & Kitano, 1973; Kim & Mejia, 1976; Tinker, 1973). Specifically emphasized were the tensions in transethnic families as evidenced by the clinical casework examinations of Japanese wives of Americans (Kim, 1972).

Patterns of acculturation in Chinese-Caucasian dating (Weiss, 1970) were also explored. Interracial marriages were viewed within the context of assimilation and social class factors. It was found that the higher the socioeconomic status, and the more frequent the contact with persons of another ethnic or racial group, the greater the likelihood of out-group dating and marriage. This substantiated proposition provided one explanation for the intermarriage trends among the members of other ethnic minorities. There were also studies of the economic status and employment patterns in Asian families in which special attention was given to the marital and parental roles of women and to the mental health consequences of urbanization and migration (Berk & Hirata, 1972; Ikeda, Ball, & Yamamura, 1962; Homma-True, 1980; Sue & McKinney, 1975; Sue & Sue, 1971; Sue & Wagner, 1973).

Afro-Americans

Historical and social science inquiries were simultaneously designed in the 1970s to focus on the significance of the family institution in the Afro-American population. One highly perceptive analysis of kinship functioning enriched current thinking about the structural, emotional, and economic continuity among many generations (Martin & Martin, 1978). Black social scientists investigating social class and value differences among Afro-American families were the first to capture their strength and resiliency rather than the presumed deviant and negative features (Blackwell, 1985; Hill, 1972; Staples, 1971a, 1971c; Willie, 1977). They provided extensive descriptions of the supportive and instrumental functions of kinship linkages. Among the most salient were the provision of mutual aid and emotional support to the nuclear household.

Research findings indicate that, like Mexican Americans, those of African heritage were and still are familistic, with paternal and maternal relatives perpetuating vital ties in multigenerational and nuclear units. The bilateral kinship bonds actually represent economic arrangements penetrated by intense emotional loyalty. These bonds complement the nuclear structures that evolved after World War II with the migration of Afro-Americans to northern industrial communities. During that era, individualism emerged as an orientation dominating family values.

As a result of critiques of the matriarchy thesis (Staples, 1977), new concepts and interpretations were introduced in research on Afro-

American families. Many social scientists observed that, although there have been innumerable macrostructural barriers to manhood in families of African ancestry, the female-headed household is not an obstacle; rather, it is the consequence of "the marginal economic position of the black male" (Staples, 1977, p. 136). In recent years, the matriarchal concept has been reexamined and is now considered neither a "reality" nor a deviant form when it is simply a matrifocal or matricentric arrangement. Sociologists have recognized that the instrumental roles of wives who work continue to be essential in helping to maintain middle-class status for large numbers of households (Hill, 1972). In most Afro-American two-parent families, men, not women, are the householders or heads (Blackwell, 1985). Thus in husband-wife units "dominance is shared between the mother and the father *or* is vested in the father" (Pinkney, 1975, p. 107). In fact, family stability is correlated with maternal employment, with dual-career patterns, with kinship associations (H. P. McAdoo, 1978a), and with the male as head of the household.

As the 1970s came to an end, the findings from research on Afro-Americans tended to accentuate familial continuity and stability, the survival of kinship linkages, social class variations in husband-wife and parent-child interaction and in family size and composition, the survival strategies of women (Cazenave, 1980; Kane & Wilkinson, 1974; Nobles, 1978), heterogeneity in life-styles, the affectional bonds with aged parents, patterns of friendship among the elderly (Jackson, 1972), and the socialization and value orientations of youth (Wilkinson, 1975b). Allen (1978b) summarized themes from earlier investigations in an insightful critique of three prevalent conceptual models of Afro-American families: structural-functional, interactional-situational, and developmental or life cycle. Allen also presented three competing perspectives dominant in the research literature: the cultural equivalent, the cultural deviant, and the cultural variant. Since World War II, the cultural deviant scheme has generated numerous deficit-oriented studies (Wilkinson, 1978b, 1980a). Yet, the appropriate model for analyses of American families of African ancestry is perhaps the cultural variant one. Concomitantly, the developmental frame of reference is viewed as the most useful *conceptually* (Allen, 1978a).

On the other hand, it has been suggested that a unitary theoretical paradigm should not be used to generate research for the study of Black family organization. Considerable diversity exists and emanates from significant differences in demographic origins, social class backgrounds, economic status, residential location, and patterns of mobility (Blackwell,

1985). This diversity and the varying conceptual perspectives for examining it negate the likelihood of constructing a single empirically testable and useful model for probing the differing types of Afro-American family organization (Allen, 1978a, p. 126). This principle is applicable to attempts to develop monolithic schemes for examining the structure and functions of other racial and ethnic minority families as well.

Research Priorities

Although each ethnic and racial minority family complex presented has been described primarily within its own demographic and cultural structure, three important similarities have been found to be characteristic: *kinship bonding*, *multigenerational links*, and the "*centrality of children*" (Cazenave, 1980). Of special interest has been the maintenance of *generational continuity* in a decade of nucleated and single-parent households. Although cohesiveness for American families in general, via kinship associations, was made prominent at the end of the 1950s (Sussman, 1959) and in the early 1960s (Litwak, 1960a, 1960b), thorough analyses of the functioning of extended support systems among racial and ethnic minorities did not occur until the mid-1960s (Bernard, 1966; Billingsley, 1968; Boyd, 1974; Hays & Mindel, 1973; Heiss, 1975; Hill, 1977; Martin & Martin, 1978; Martineau, 1977; H. P. McAdoo, 1978a, 1978b). There is a need for research on the network of relations in minority families and on those psychological forces that sustain them in an era of continuous social change and economic stress.

Status of Women

Awareness of the changing roles of ethnic minority women, another important area for future analysis, is a recent subject that is less a consequence of the women's movement than of the civil rights revolution (Cade, 1970; Hamamsy, 1957; Lott, 1980; Nieto, 1974; Wilkinson, 1970). Most policy-directed emphases in government and special funding programs pertain to women in the dominant population. One specific direction for social science inquiry might be the major status transitions experienced by minority women and the accompanying changes in their role expectations and achievement aspirations as wives, mothers, and workers. Among the questions for which we might seek answers are the following:

(1) What are the consequences of modifications in women's roles for family stability among racial and ethnic minorities?

(2) What are the fundamental concerns of these women as mothers and wives and as blue- and white-collar workers?

(3) What can local, state, and federal governments, as well as the private sector, do to meet the needs of minority women who are single parents and those who are in dual-career marriages?

(4) What processes occur in ethnic family integration and functioning when *emergent* role definitions are internalized and enacted?

(5) How can opportunities for the advancement of minority women in the managerial, technical, and professional work force be enhanced so that these women will be able to meet their families' economic, health, and educational needs?

The employment problems and accompanying stresses confronting women in ethnic minority families require adequate documentation in the behavioral and social science literature (R. Green, 1975; Medicine, 1975; Metcalf, 1976; Spindler, 1962; A. Williams, 1980; Witt, 1974). It has been observed that, "while the women's movement has sought to liberate all women, it has focused more on the needs of middle-class Anglo women" (Mirandé & Enriquez, 1979, p. 1) than on the unique experiences of minority women. What this statement reveals is the need for useful data on demographic, occupational, and marital trends among those who are politically powerless and for practical and realistic studies of the impact of changes in their roles on the family. Hispanic social and behavioral scientists, recognizing this need, have called for research that examines the cultural and ecological factors correlated with the acquisition of new roles, with family tensions, and especially with the emotional difficulties experienced by children and youth (Canino & Canino, 1980; Canino et al., 1980; Moran, 1973; Santiago, 1973; Zambrana, 1980), the occupational positions of Puerto Rican women (Correa, 1980), and the consequences of these. Further inquiry is needed into intrafamilial dynamics among ethnic populations and particularly into the changing status of women as this affects family functioning (Baca Zinn, 1975, 1980; S. Delgado, 1971; García, 1980; Longeaux y Vásquez, 1972; Lopez, 1973; Mirandé & Enriquez, 1979; Suárez, 1973; Viera, 1980; Ybarra, 1977).

Among the priorities for minority parents and kin are the following: obtaining stable employment, elevating family economic position, strengthening resources, securing adequate health care and other necessary services, locating affordable housing, finding constructive ways to rear children in impoverished communities, controlling husband-wife and parent-child conflict, establishing educational priorities for offspring, and maintaining responsibilities for elderly parents (Cheung et al., 1980; Montero, 1980). Understanding the traditions of families in the same racial category but in different social strata will permit the discernment of adaptive and life-style distinctions among them and an interpretation of the uniqueness of their needs. Actually, *needs* should constitute the focus of attention, rather than family *forms*.

Summary

This chapter has incorporated, for the most part, writings reflecting indigenous, though varied, and relatively positive orientations to four minority family configurations. Although the contributions are sparse and are different in emphases, techniques of analysis, and conceptual models, many of the social science biases about minority husband-wife relationships and parent-child interaction can be offset by the perspectives offered (Montiel, 1973; Wilkinson, 1978b, 1979). Blending the frames of reference used by scholars writing in the 1950s and 1960s with those of a new generation of scientists will enable us to make better predictions about minority family life.

Specifically, kinship network paradigms (Litwak, 1960a, 1960b; Litwak & Szelenyi, 1969; Sussman, 1959, 1970) should be incorporated in studies of ethnic minority families. Given the economic constraints and the depletion of resources, it is important to comprehend how mutual aid among relatives can be sustained. Where to house elderly parents and grandparents will become an increasing problem. Two decades ago, it was recognized that, because the aged population is growing, "studies of housing for older people cannot ignore the aid variable" (Sussman & Burchinal, 1962, p. 329).

The research topics formulated and even the interpretations of the results in the future should be culturally specific. Assumptions regarding ethnic family organization must not emanate from models of pathology or deviance or structural determinism. Rather, theories ought to be based on the fact that, despite disparities in form and in functioning, families remain the primary types of social arrangements for American Indians, Afro-Americans, Mexican Americans, Asian Americans, and Puerto Ricans. Differences among them are merely the consequence of

unique demographic and ancestral backgrounds, cultural histories, ecological processes, and economic origins and statuses. These have been
considered here to enable us to understand the diverse contextual and
institutional nature of minority families.

Notes

1. Minority families differ from those in the majority population on the basis of race,
ancestry, and other characteristics. They are part of a socially, politically, and economically subordinated population. Differential treatment is a significant consequence of
minority status. The dominant minority groups (or populations) in the United States are
Blacks or Afro-Americans, Chicanos or Mexican Americans, Puerto Ricans, and Japanese, Chinese, and Filipino Americans.

2. In the 1980 U.S. Census of population, *Black* was used to designate persons who
identified themselves as Black or Negro as well as others who indicated their ancestry or
national origin as Jamaican, Black Puerto Rican, West Indian, Haitian, or Nigerian (see
U.S. Bureau of the Census, 1981a). In this discussion, *Afro-American* will be used
interchangeably with *Black*. This classification refers to any American of African descent.

3. In many population reports, Asians and Pacific Islanders are often combined. The
category *Asian* includes persons who indicate their race as Asian Indian, Chinese,
Filipino, Hawaiian, Guamanian, Korean, Japanese, Samoan, or Vietnamese (U.S. Bureau
of the Census, 1981a, p. 7). Only three Asian groups are examined in this presentation:
Chinese, Japanese, and Filipinos.

4. Frequently, American Indians are referred to as *Native Americans*. In recent years,
they have requested to be identified as American Indians. They are combined with
Eskimos and Aleuts in the 1980 census. Also included as American Indians are persons
who classified themselves as members of an Indian tribe but who did not specify their
race or ethnicity as American Indian.

5. Persons designated as Hispanic or of Spanish origin are those who report themselves
as Chicanos, Mexican Americans, Mexicans, Mexicanos, Puerto Ricans, Cubans, Central
or South Americans, or others of Spanish ancestry. Self-identification or perceived ethnic
identity and national heritage constitute the basis for classifying participants in the U.S.
Census as persons of Spanish descent. Such persons may be of any race (see U.S. Bureau
of the Census, 1981a).

6. Although *population* has a specific demographic and statistical meaning, it will be
used here synonymously with *group*. In this sense, *population* will refer not only to the
total number of individuals occupying a given area but also to a group of persons or
individuals having qualities or characteristics in common, such as ancestry, cultural
background, and racial and ethnic identity. Although the standard definitions of *population* differ from the sociological conception of *group, population* does provide a useful
general translation of the latter concept.

7. The terms *householder* and *head of family* are used interchangeably, although the former replaced the latter in the 1980 U.S. Census. This shift in labeling is the consequence of social changes and had resulted in the Bureau of the Census (1980b) "reconsidering its longtime practice of always classifying the husband as the head when he and his wife are living together. . . . In the 1980 census, the householder is the first adult household member listed on the census questionnaire" (p. 149). All persons who occupy a house, an apartment, or a single room occupy a *household*. Thus a household includes persons living alone, related family members, and unrelated persons, if any, such as lodgers (U.S. Bureau of the Census, 1980b, p. 150).

3

Race, Mortality, and Families

EDWARD L. KAIN

One of the most important changes affecting family life over the past century has been the dramatic decline in mortality. At the turn of the century, orphanhood was a common event, and death touched nuclear families much more often than today. In 1900, infant mortality was 10 times its current rate, and maternal mortality was more than 80 times the current level. The expectation of life at birth has increased from less than 50 to nearly 75 years. While these changes have had a tremendous impact upon both individual development and family life, very little research has focused on the importance of mortality shifts in understanding social change and families in the United States (Uhlenberg, 1980).

During this period of rapid change, variations in death rates between racial and ethnic groups have remained an important part of the differential distribution of mortality in this country. In their classic study of mortality differentials, Kitagawa and Hauser (1973) found that Blacks in this country have the highest mortality rates, while Japanese have the lowest. Native Americans had the second highest mortality rates, followed by Chinese and whites. Unfortunately, high-quality mortality data on all racial and ethnic groups in this country are not available for all historical periods. Because of these limitations, this chapter will

AUTHOR'S NOTE: An earlier version of this chapter was presented in a poster session at the annual meetings of the National Council on Family Relations, Dallas, Texas, November 1985. A slightly abbreviated version of the chapter appears as the concluding section of Chapter 4 in my book *The Myth of Family Decline: Understanding Families in a World of Rapid Social Change* (Lexington Books, 1990).

contrast the mortality experiences only of Blacks and whites and will examine the implications of these mortality differences for family life.

This chapter examines historical changes in race differences in mortality in three different ways. First, several measures of mortality in three cohorts[1] separated by 40 years (1900, 1940, and 1980) are compared to illustrate social change in mortality. Race and sex differences highlight the importance of diversity within cohorts as well as between cohorts. Second, variation by race, gender, and ordinal position of children is explored to illustrate how the early life experiences of Americans have been differentially affected by death. Third, several aspects of later periods in life are examined to point to the continued impact of race and gender as variables that modify the implications of mortality change upon the lives of individuals within families.

Summary demographic measures of mortality, such as the expectation of life at birth and age- or group-specific mortality rates, are useful for illustrating trends in the overall patterns of mortality. These population statistics do not, however, illuminate the implications of changing mortality for family life. Using a life-course framework, Uhlenberg (1980) has helped to illustrate the profound changes that have occurred in families because of these shifts. His data were calculated comparing three cohorts in the white population: 1900, 1940, and 1976. His analyses suggest the impact of changing mortality upon several stages of life: childhood, young adulthood, middle age, and old age. This chapter starts with the foundation laid by Uhlenberg and examines how race and sex differences in mortality rates have had an impact upon the early life experiences of Black and white families since the turn of the century. In particular, the focus is on the lives of children. While Uhlenberg's emphasis was on intercohort variation, this chapter focuses on intracohort variation and points to the importance of race, gender, and ordinal position in modifying the impact of change in mortality upon the early life-course experience of individuals within the family. Several illustrations are also provided that demonstrate the effect of mortality differences within a cohort on later stages of life.

The chapter is divided into three sections. The first asks the question, Why should we be interested in intracohort differences in mortality? Several measures of mortality are compared in three cohorts to illustrate the large variations within cohorts by both race and gender. The second section uses a life-course framework to illustrate the effects of some of these mortality changes on the lives of children, and how the variables of race, sex, and ordinal position predict very different experiences of mortality for children in families. The final section provides some brief suggestions about intracohort variation in the experience of mortality in other stages of life and summarizes some of the intracohort variations in mortality and its impact upon family life.

Why Should We Be Interested in Intracohort Differences in Mortality?

Ryder (1965) suggests that intercohort comparisons can help us to understand social change and intracohort comparisons can help illuminate diversity within a cohort. Since the turn of the century, mortality rates have drastically declined in the United States. This is true in every measure of mortality—from infant and maternal mortality rates to expectation of life at birth. In each cohort, however, race and sex differences are evident. The race differences at the turn of the century painted strikingly different pictures for the life chances of Blacks and whites (see Table 3.1). In 1900, for example, the expectation of life at birth was 48.2 years for white men and 51.1 years for white women. The corresponding figures for the Black population were 32.5 years and 35.0 years. By 1980, whites continued to have longer life expectancies, but the race difference had declined to approximately 6 years, compared with 16 years at the turn of the century (see Table 3.2).

The data in Tables 3.1 and 3.2 clearly illustrate that both race and gender are important variables in predicting mortality rates throughout this century. In all three cohorts, the expectation of life at birth is higher for whites than for nonwhites and, within racial groups, it is higher for women than for men. (National data on mortality vary in their quality from year to year. Many years do not provide data in racial categories. When such data are available, the most common tabulation is in two categories—"white" and "Black and other." The 1940 data used in this chapter, for example, do not differentiate Blacks from other groups. In every year, however, Blacks constitute at least 95% of the "Black and other" category. Although there are appropriate political reasons to avoid the term *nonwhite,* that unfortunate word will be employed at times in this chapter to ease readability.) Table 3.2 illustrates, however, that the historical trends in race and sex differences are moving in opposite directions. This difference merits further explanation.

Table 3.1 Expectation of Life at Birth by Race and Sex, United States, 1900, 1940, 1980

Year	White		Black and Other	
	Male	Female	Male	Female
1900	48.2	51.1	32.5	35.0
1940	62.8	67.3	52.3	55.5
1980	70.7	78.1	63.7	72.3

SOURCE: Data for the first two cohorts are from *Historical Statistics of the United States*; 1980 data are from the *Statistical Abstract of the United States* and compare only Blacks and whites.

Historical Changes in Sex Differences in Mortality

Within racial groups, the sex difference in expectation of life at birth has been increasing.[2] One explanation of this trend is the dramatic decline in maternal mortality rates since the turn of the century. From the point of conception, the male of the human species has a higher age-specific mortality rate than the female. Whereas the sex ratio (the number of men per 100 women) is approximately 124 at conception, it drops to about 104 for full-term births (Rossi, 1985). At birth, most societies report a slight excess of males over females (Schryock, Siegel, et al., 1975), but by adulthood, women outnumber men, and current cross-national data indicate that the life expectation at birth is higher for women than for men in virtually every society worldwide, in spite of extremely high maternal mortality rates in some cultures (United Nations, 1980). As a result, when maternal mortality begins to decline, the sex difference in life expectation at birth increases. The decline in maternal mortality rates in the United States is illustrated in Table 3.3, which compares three different cohorts. (The cohorts compared in the other tables in this chapter do not correspond directly to Table 3.3, as data for 1900 are unavailable on these variables. The goal is to compare cohorts that are approximately 40 years apart.) This table illustrates that while the maternal mortality rate has declined in both racial groups, the relative magnitude of race differences has actually increased over time. In 1915, nonwhite groups had a rate that was 1.76 times that of whites. By 1980, this ratio had increased to 2.86. The most plausible explanation for this increase is that medical technology and services, which have been

Table 3.2   Race and Sex Differentials in the Expectation of Life at Birth, United States, 1900, 1940, 1980

Year	Sex Difference (female-male)		Race Difference (White-Black and Other)	
	White	Black and Other	Male	Female
1900	2.9	2.5	15.7	16.1
1940	4.5	3.2	10.5	11.8
1980	7.4	8.6	7.0	5.8

SOURCE: Data for the first two cohorts are from the *Historical Statistics of the United States*; 1980 data are from the *Statistical Abstract of the United States* and compare only Blacks and whites.

responsible for the precipitous decline in maternal mortality, are more available to white women because of social class (particularly income) disparities between whites and other racial groups in our society. A considerable number of developed countries have maternal and infant mortality rates lower than those of the United States, and this is often attributed to the lack of national programs that support children and families. Programs and policies that provide for things as varied as child-care services, maternity and paternity leaves, sick leave for parents when a child is ill, and medical benefits for mothers and children regardless of income are sadly lacking in the United States relative to many other industrialized countries (Bronfenbrenner, 1982; Kamerman & Kahn, 1978, 1981).

Historical Changes in Race Differences in Mortality

Social class differences (in access to medical services, nutrition, adequate housing, and so on) are most likely the major reason for the persistence in race differences in expectation of life at birth that is evident in Table 3.2. The three cohorts compared at 40-year intervals illustrate that the race difference has declined over time for both males and females. In 1900, white women and men outlived Black women and men by about 16 years. By 1980, the advantage of whites over Blacks had declined to 7 years for men and 5.8 years for women. This change is a result of a combination of declines in various age-specific measures of mortality. As Table 3.3 illustrates, however, the changes have not always occurred at the same rates for Blacks and whites. While the maternal mortality rate has declined faster for whites than for Blacks,

Table 3.3   Race Differences in Maternal and Infant Mortality Rates, United States, 1915, 1940, 1980

| Year | Maternal Mortality Rate | | | Infant Mortality Rate | | |
	White	Black and Other	NW/W	White	Black and Other	NW/W
1915	60.1	105.6	1.76	98.6	181.2	1.84
1940	32.0	77.4	2.42	43.2	73.8	1.71
1980	.7	2	2.86	11.1	19.1	1.72

NOTE: The maternal mortality rate = deaths per 10,000 live births; the infant mortality rate = deaths per 1,000 live births.

this is not true of the infant mortality rate. The ratio of nonwhite to white infant mortality has remained relatively constant throughout the century. Thus, although infant mortality rates are one-tenth the magnitude they were in 1915, the white infant mortality rate is still about half that of other racial groups.

Summary measures of mortality clearly illustrate the importance of race and gender as predictors of variation within a cohort. They do not, however, provide a very clear picture of how the change in mortality rates has affected the lives of individuals. The next section of the chapter takes a closer look at the implications of intracohort and intercohort variation in mortality upon one stage of life—childhood.

Implications of Intracohort Differences in Mortality for Childhood

Uhlenberg (1980) used life table values to calculate the probabilities of different mortality-related events (such as orphanhood or loss of spouse) occurring in various cohorts. The methods from his paper are used here to examine three types of intracohort differences in the life-course experience of children. Uhlenberg clearly illustrates the impact of mortality change upon family life during this century. This impact has varied considerably between racial groups within each cohort, however. This section will use the variables of race, sex, and ordinal position to illustrate some of this variation.

Life Chances During Childhood

In preindustrial societies, the periods of highest age-specific mortality are infancy and childhood. As nutrition, sanitation, and medical technology improve, their combined effects limit the number of infant deaths during childbirth and due to early childhood diseases, thus dramatically increasing the chances of survival to adulthood. Many of these changes began throughout the eighteenth and nineteenth centuries in the United States, yet the rapid rate of decline in infant and childhood mortality continued well into the twentieth century. Table 3.4 illustrates that the probability of survival for the 1900 cohort was considerably less than that of cohorts later in the century.

Just as striking are the race and sex differences in the probability of a child surviving to adolescence. To take the extreme example, in 1900 the probabilities of a Black male surviving to adolescence were slightly better than three in five. In contrast, a white female's chances of survival were better than four in five. When intercohort and intracohort differences are compared, the difference between Blacks and whites in 1900 is as large as the 40-year difference between white cohorts in 1900 and 1940.

Loss of a Sibling

Another way to think about how the variation in mortality affects the lives of children is to examine the probability that a child will have one or more siblings die. Table 3.5 uses differential mortality rates to contrast the probabilities of loss of a sibling if we assume that the child has two siblings, one sister and one brother. This association results in an underestimate of both social change and social diversity, because of the patterning of fertility over time and by race. Since the turn of the century, the total completed fertility of women in this country has dropped from more than four to fewer than two. Throughout the period, Blacks have had a higher fertility rate than whites. Thus a child in 1900 would be likely to have more than two siblings (resulting in an underestimate of his or her probability of losing a sibling to death), and a child in 1978 would be likely to have fewer than two siblings (resulting in an overestimate of his or her probability of losing a sibling to death). Similarly, within each cohort, a Black child would, on the average, have more siblings than a white child, thus underestimating the race difference in the probabilities of losing a sibling to death. Throughout this chapter, the estimates that are derived are conservative estimates of both intercohort and intracohort differences. They are meant to illustrate the diversity of experiences when only one variable—mortality—is exam-

Table 3.4 Race and Sex Differences in the Probability of Death to
Children, 1900, 1940, 1980

| | Probability of Surviving From Age 0-15 | | | |
| | White | | Black and Other | |
Year	Male	Female	Male	Female
1900	.78	.83	.64	.68
1940	.93	.95	.90	.92
1980	.98	.99	.97	.98

SOURCE: Probabilities calculated from life table values in U.S. Department of Health and Human
Services (1982, Table 5-4; 1985, Table 6-2).
NOTE: Data for 1900 are for death registration states and include only Blacks in the "Black and other"
category. Data for 1940 and 1980 are for the full United States. Blacks always constitute at least 95%
of the "Black and other" group. Data for 1980 include only Blacks in the "Black and other" category.

ined. Other variables, such as fertility, rather than moderating the
effects of mortality, tend to accentuate the differences. This will be
discussed in the final section of the chapter.

Race is clearly a powerful factor in predicting whether or not a child
is likely to have one of his or her siblings die. In all three cohorts, Black
children are about one and a half times as likely as white children to
have this experience. In 1900, the chances were about 1 in 3 that a white
child would lose a sibling before reaching age 15. For Black children,
the probability of this event was more than 1 in 2. By 1980, the
experience was much less likely for both racial groups, with the chances
being only 3 in 100 and 5 in 100 for whites and Blacks, respectively.

Incidence of Orphanhood

While the loss of a sibling may have implications for children in
terms of household responsibilities; the number of people within the
household with whom affection, food, and other resources must be
shared; and the emotional trauma of death, it is clear that the death of
a parent is far more significant. Social insurance was unknown in 1900,
and the death of either parent, particularly the father, could mean an
overnight move from relative financial security to destitution. If the
child was older when the event occurred, an unplanned transition into
adulthood and the status of head of household, or at least that of major
breadwinner, could be one result of orphanhood. Table 3.6 presents the
probabilities of a child who is born when both parents are 25 years old

Table 3.5   Race Differences in the Probability of Death of a Sibling Before a Child Reaches Age 15, 1900, 1940, 1980

Year	*Probability of One or Both of Two Siblings Dying*		
	White	*Black and Other*	*Black and Other/White*
1900	.35	.56	1.6
1940	.12	.17	1.4
1980	.03	.05	1.7

SOURCE: Probabilities calculated from life table values in U.S. Department of Health and Human Services (1982, Table 5-4; 1985, Table 6-2).
NOTE: This table assumes that the child has two siblings—one sister and one brother. As a result, it underestimates the rates for nonwhites relative to whites and the rates of earlier cohorts versus later cohorts, given differential fertility between races and between cohorts.

losing one or both parents. The first column indicates the probability of a child's father dying before the child reaches age 15. The next three columns illustrate the probabilities of losing a mother, the probabilities of losing either parent, and, finally, the chances of losing both parents before the child reaches age 15. Again, we see that within each cohort, Black children are much more likely to have a parent die than are white children. In the 1900 cohort, for example, the chances were about 1 in 5 that during childhood a Black child would have his or her father die. The probability of this happening for a white child was closer to 1 in 10. The chances were 1 in 3 that a Black child who was born when both parents were age 25 would lose one or the other of his or her parents. Black children in this cohort were three times likelier than their white counterparts to lose both parents. In the 1940 and 1980 cohorts, the race difference in this final column is accentuated. Black children are about 10 times as likely to be doubly orphaned before they reach the age of 15.

A comparison of the variation between cohorts is again instructive in considering the importance of race as a factor in how children experience mortality. The probabilities in all four columns have a striking pattern in which the chances of Black children being orphaned are 40 years behind those of white children. While mortality is declining for both race groups, because of the continuing mortality differential, the rates for Blacks in the 1940 cohort roughly match those of whites in the 1900 cohort, and the rates for Blacks in 1980 roughly match those of whites in 1940.

Table 3.6 Race Differences in the Probability of an Earlier-Born Child Being Orphaned by the Age of 15, 1900, 1940, 1980

Year	Probability of Father Dying		Probability of Mother Dying		Probability of Either Parent Dying		Probability of Both Parents Dying	
	White	Black and Other	White	Black and Other	White	Black and Other	White	Black and Other
1900	.12	.19	.11	.17	.22	.33	.01	.03
1940	.05	.13	.04	.12	.09	.23	.002	.02
1980	.03	.07	.01	.03	.04	.10	.0003	.002

SOURCE: Probabilities calculated from life table values in U.S. Department of Health and Human Services (1982, Table 5-4; 1985, Table 6-2).
NOTE: This table assumes that the child was born when both parents were age 25 and is thus an "earlier-born" child.

Importance of Ordinal Position

Table 3.6 illustrates the probabilities of orphanhood when it is assumed that the child is born early in the reproductive careers of the parents (at age 25 for both parents). The ordinal position of the child clearly plays a role, however, in a society where adult life expectation is shorter and the end of life overlaps with the years of childbearing and child rearing. Later-born children are much more likely to experience orphanhood. This is illustrated in Table 3.7, which mirrors the previous table but assumes that the child is born when both parents are age 35. The contrast between Tables 3.6 and 3.7 gives a conservative estimate of the importance of ordinal position, since the reproductive careers of parents (particularly in cohorts around the turn of the century) usually begin before 25 and usually end after 35. Nonetheless, the contrast between the tables is quite striking. Here we find that Black children who are "later born" have a 1 in 4 chance of losing their fathers and a 1 in 4 chance of losing their mothers while they are still in childhood. The probability of losing one or the other parent is better than 2 in 5, and the chances are greater than 1 in 20 that a Black child will have both parents die before he or she reaches age 15. As with earlier tables, the probabilities of orphanhood are much lower for white children in all three cohorts, and again there is a striking similarity in the probabilities by race if we compare the Black rates to those we find for whites 40 years earlier.

Loss of a Member of the Immediate Nuclear Family

It is clear from these data that successive cohorts of children have had radically different experiences of mortality in terms of the loss of siblings or parents. Further, these experiences vary considerably by race, with white children being much less likely to have a sibling or a parent die. Table 3.8 combines the information from previous tables and asks the question, What are the chances of having either a sibling or a parent die while you are a child? Again, we are assuming a family that has two siblings—one sister and one brother. The first two columns assume that the child is born when both parents are 25 (and is thus an "early-born" child) and the second two columns assume that the child is "later born," when both parents are age 35. In the latter case, we find that the probabilities of a Black child experiencing the death of a nuclear family member were three in four for the 1900 cohort. Remember that this underestimates the probability of that occurrence because completed fertility rates for both Blacks and whites were higher than

Table 3.7 Race Differences in the Probability of a Later-Born Child Being Orphaned by the Age of 15, 1900, 1940, 1980

Year	Probability of Father Dying		Probability of Mother Dying		Probability of Either Parent Dying		Probability of Both Parents Dying	
	White	Black and Other	White	Black and Other	White	Black and Other	White	Black and Other
1900	.16	.25	.14	.24	.28	.43	.02	.06
1940	.09	.21	.07	.19	.15	.36	.006	.04
1980	.05	.12	.03	.06	.08	.18	.002	.007

SOURCE: Probabilities calculated from life table values in U.S. Department of Health and Human Services (1982, Table 5-4; 1985, Table 6-2).
NOTE: This table assumes that the child was born when both parents were age 35 and is thus a "later-born" child.

three in 1900. (The 1980 estimate of nearly one in four Black children losing a nuclear family member to death also is a biased estimate because of the assumption of a completed fertility rate of three.) By 1980, Black children were more than twice as likely as white children to have a member of their nuclear family die while they are still in childhood, regardless of whether they are born early or late in their parents' reproductive lives.

All of the measures discussed above point to the importance of examining not only differences between cohorts when we look at the impact of mortality upon family life, but also the differences within cohorts, using such variables as race, gender, and ordinal position. These three variables by no means exhaust the variables of importance. Clearly, the experiences of Black and white children vary by social class as well as by such factors as region and residence. The relationship between variables has changed over time as well. In early cohorts, mortality rates were higher in urban areas because of crowding and poor sanitation. In more recent cohorts, rates for many types of mortality are higher in rural areas, where access to sophisticated medical technology is limited. The importance of some of these other variables is discussed briefly in the concluding section of this chapter. First, however, it is instructive to move beyond childhood and give a few examples of intracohort variation in the impact of mortality upon other stages of the life course.

Implications of Intracohort Differences in Mortality for Other Stages of Life and for Family Life in General

Uhlenberg (1980) moves beyond childhood and clearly illustrates the impact of mortality decline upon other stages in life. I have kept the major focus of this chapter upon childhood in an attempt to look at the importance of variations within cohorts (diversity between Blacks and whites) as well as between cohorts (social change). I would now like to note briefly some of the implications of intracohort variation in mortality for these later stages of the life course; the chapter then concludes with a review of some of the major issues raised by an analysis that includes examination of race differences in the experience of mortality.

Early Adulthood and Marriage

Variation in mortality within a cohort has a variety of impacts upon decisions about life-course transitions in early adulthood. As noted

Table 3.8 Race Differences in the Probability of Death to a Nuclear
Family Member Before a Child Reaches Age 15, 1900, 1940,
1980

Year	Probability of Death to a Family Member of an Earlier-Born Child		Probability of Death to a Family Member of a Later-Born Child	
	White	Black and Other	White	Black and Other
1900	.49	.70	.53	.75
1940	.20	.36	.25	.47
1980	.07	.15	.11	.23

SOURCE: Probabilities calculated from life table values in U.S. Department of Health and Human Services (1982, Table 5-4; 1985, Table 6-2).
NOTE: This table assumes that the child has one brother and one sister.

above, if a child is orphaned, the transition to adulthood may happen at an earlier age as entry into the labor force becomes a necessity. Elder (1974) has illustrated that historical events such as the Great Depression also may operate to speed up the assumption of adult responsibilities, and may have implications for educational attainment and other activities that take place in early adulthood. The number of people available for marriage is also affected by mortality shifts and historical events. For instance, a war reduces the number of men available to women as spouses. Sex differences in mortality from any cause may have an impact upon the marital chances of a cohort completely separate from the needs and desires of the individuals in that cohort. (It is currently the case, for example, that during the marriageable years there is an extreme imbalance in the sex ratio among Blacks in this country, with many fewer men than women.) One must note that mortality is not the only factor that affects the sex ratio. In particular, differential migration either within or between countries may significantly alter the sex ratio of the marriage market in any particular geographical region.

After marriage, differential mortality by gender has an impact upon the length of both marriage and widowhood. Table 3.9 illustrates that the probability of a couple living long enough to celebrate their fortieth anniversary has increased dramatically throughout this century. (The probabilities assume that both people are married at age 25.) In 1900, the chances were slightly less than one in three that a white couple would both live long enough to celebrate their fortieth anniversary and were less than half that for Black couples. By 1980, the chances were approximately two in three that a white couple would live long enough to celebrate this occasion, while the probability for a Black couple was less than one in two. These calculations do not, of course, include the probability that a marriage will end in divorce. Uhlenberg's work, however, indicates that couples today are more likely to stay together in their first marriage up to the fortieth anniversary than their counterparts were at the turn of the century. While the divorce rate has risen dramatically, especially since the late 1950s, the mortality rate has declined at an even faster rate. Long marriages are more common now than they were in the past (Uhlenberg, 1980).

The part of our population that is growing most quickly is the "older old"—those who are 75 years of age and above. The increase in the probabilities of surviving to this last stage of the life course can be found in Table 3.10. As in all the tables in this chapter, sex and race differentials are pronounced within each cohort. Women are more likely to reach both the ages of 75 and 85, and the sex difference has increased over time. By 1980, women in both race groups were twice as likely as men to reach the age of 85. Race differences persist as well, but there has been a slight decline in those differences over time. The final columns of Table 3.10 illustrate a radical transformation of the latest stages of the life course. In 1900, it was an extreme rarity for both spouses to survive to the age of 85 in either racial group. The chances were only 6 in 1,000 for a white couple and 2 in 1,000 for a Black couple that they would both reach age 85. (These probabilities all use expectation of life at age 25 as a base for calculation.) By 1980, while still unusual, such couples were more than 10 times as likely to exist. The probabilities in 1980 were 7 in 100 for whites and 4 in 100 for blacks.

The Importance of Other Variables

The probabilities presented in this chapter must be considered illustrative, at best. The reader should keep several important caveats in mind while examining the data. First, probabilities assume an independence of events that is highly unlikely in the case of mortality in families. Members in a family share the same environment—the same ecological setting, as it were. The shared nutritional status, physical and social environment, access to medical services, safety or dangerousness of neighborhood, and social class of family members (not to mention shared genetics) would all suggest that a family member who is at risk for higher mortality shares that higher risk with other family members.

Table 3.9 Race and Sex Differences in the Probability of Surviving to a Fortieth Wedding Anniversary, 1900, 1940, 1980

Year	Probability of the Wife Surviving		Probability of the Husband Surviving		Probability of Both Surviving	
	White	Black and Other	White	Black and Other	White	Black and Other
1900	.57	.39	.53	.36	.30	.14
1940	.74	.47	.64	.43	.47	.20
1980	.86	.75	.75	.58	.65	.44

SOURCE: Probabilities calculated from life table values in U.S. Department of Health and Human Services (1982, Table 5-4; 1985, Table 6-2).
NOTE: This table assumes that both spouses married at age 25.

Table 3.10 Race and Sex Differences in the Probability of Reaching Old Age (the "Older Old") Alone and With Spouse, 1900, 1940, 1980

| | Probability of Survival to Age 75 | | | | | | Probability of Survival to Age 85 | | | | | |
| | Male | | Female | | Both | | Male | | Female | | Both | |
Year	White	Black and Other	White	Black and Other	White	Black and Other	White	Black and Other	White	Black and Other	White	Black and Other
1900	.29	.17	.33	.20	.10	.03	.07	.04	.09	.06	.006	.002
1940	.37	.24	.48	.29	.18	.07	.10	.08	.16	.12	.02	.01
1980	.49	.34	.70	.55	.34	.19	.19	.13	.39	.28	.07	.04

SOURCE: Probabilities calculated from life table values in U.S. Department of Health and Human Services (1982, Table 5-4; 1985, Table 6-2).
NOTE: This table assumes that both spouses married at age 25. Probabilities of survival are calculated from age 25, not from birth.

This points to the importance of examining the role of other variables in predicting variation in the experience of mortality within cohorts. The national data used in this chapter do not allow such analyses historically, but several variables stand out as being of particular importance. As noted above, region of residence as well as residence in a rural versus an urban area are important factors. It is possible, for example, that race differences may have been greater in the South earlier in this century than they are for current cohorts. The rural versus urban dimension may also have had important implications for specific cohorts. Some cities experienced extremely high mortality during specific epidemics (such as the flu epidemic of 1917), and the impact of these events upon families was immediate and long lasting.

Variables such as region and residence may also be of importance in predicting additional variables that are linked to the experience of mortality in significant ways. Rural families, for example, are more likely both to be poorer than urban families (a predictor of higher mortality) and to have many more children (which increases the probability that one of the children will die during childhood and that the mother may die during childbirth). While this chapter clearly illustrates the importance of looking at intracohort variation in terms of variables such as race, sex, and ordinal position of children, a model that includes the true complexity of the social world would illustrate even more extreme differences in how mortality has affected the lives of children in families of all racial and ethnic groups throughout this century in the United States.

Some Specific Implications of Race Differences in Mortality

It is also likely that some of the factors that continue to differentiate Black and white families in the United States can be related, at least in part, to differences in the experience of mortality. Black women have been much more likely to work outside of the home than have their white counterparts throughout this century (Hunter, 1984; Kain, 1982). This difference has been decreasing in recent decades, as more and more white women (of all marital statuses) are working outside of the home. In the early part of the century, married Black women were much more likely to work than were their white counterparts, largely because of the low wages and poor labor market available for Black men (Hunter, 1984). An additional cause of the larger labor pool of Black women is the higher Black mortality rate, which increased the probability of widowhood in the Black population.

The labor of both women and children is one strategy for the family economy to survive in times of stress (see Moen, Kain, & Elder, 1983).

Another possibility is the pooling of resources of several families or subfamilies, including sharing a residence. Just as Stack (1974) finds that the maintenance of an extended network of kin is functional for modern urban poor Black families, such an extended kin group makes sense in a world of high mortality, where death is a common occurrence and the immediate nuclear family cannot be viewed as a stable unit that will provide security in a harsh world.

We must take care not to overemphasize the importance of mortality differentials in predicting other variations in family patterns, but it is clear that the simple fact that death rates have declined, and that these declines have varied by race, has major implications for how individuals experience family life. In the decade of the 1980s, a new cause of death has emerged in the epidemic of HIV infection. Recent data indicate that HIV infection and AIDS disproportionately affect Blacks and Hispanics in this country. From 1981 through 1987, Black and Hispanic men were nearly three times as likely to contract AIDS as were white men. Black women's relative risk during the same period was 13 times that of white women, while Hispanic women's risk was nearly 9 times that of white women. The differentials are even larger when pediatric cases are examined (Curran et al., 1988). Because mortality from AIDS is concentrated among people who are in the 25- to 44-year-old age group, it will lead to substantial decreases in life expectancy. As a result, variation in mortality by race will continue to be an important part of the lives of families as we enter the next century.

Variation in mortality has too long been neglected as an important determinant of how families operate in their day-to-day existence. Death is a central factor in the organization and the patterning of the life course. Only when we begin to provide it with a place in the matrix of variables affecting individuals as they move through life can we understand family change and family diversity in the United States.

Notes

1. For the reader unfamiliar with demographic terms, *cohort* refers to any group that experiences something at the same time. In demographic research it is usually used more specifically to refer to a *birth cohort*—all of the people born in a particular year.

2. For an expanded discussion of race and sex differences in mortality, as well as other factors related to variation in death rates, see Kain (1987), in which I place the race differences described in this chapter into a broader time frame.

PART II

African American Families

4

Female-Headed
African American Households

Some Neglected Dimensions

NIARA SUDARKASA

There has been considerable speculation and misinformation in the scholarly literature as well as in the popular media about the causes and consequences of female-headed households among African Americans. Amid
the confusion and controversy, over the years, policymakers have proposed
and developed various "solutions" to the "problems" supposedly embodied
in and engendered by Black families headed by women. Such "solutions"
have been well intentioned but often misguided because they attempted to
address problems and issues that were only half understood. A sound
analysis is not only relevant to the formulation of policy, it is indispensable
to it. If we are to develop a program of action to assist female-headed
households, we must have a clear conception and complete analysis of the
circumstances of their development as well as their form and function.

In this chapter, I will comment on the following six points, which I
feel are important to keep in mind as we seek to clarify, amplify, and
demystify the data on households headed by African American women:

AUTHOR'S NOTE: Earlier versions of this chapter were presented at the conference
"Woman to Woman: Single Parenting From a Global Perspective," sponsored by Delta
Sigma Theta Sorority, Inc., Nassau, Bahamas, 1987, and at the symposium "Women of
Color" at Virginia Commonwealth University, 1989.

(1) A key to understanding contemporary African American family structure, whether headed by women, by men, or by couples, is a knowledge of the earlier structure of African extended families out of which they evolved. It is particularly important to understand that as these African-derived extended families evolved in America, they embraced households headed by single parents, most of whom were women, as well as households headed by married couples.

(2) Female-headed households are not all the same. They differ in terms of the dynamics of their formation and their functioning.

(3) Marital stability and family stability are not one and the same. Female-headed households have been and can be stable over time.

(4) There are demographic and socioeconomic reasons why many African American female-headed households are now and have always been a predictable and accepted form of household organization.

(5) There is a need to appreciate that women may be primary providers and heads of households in families with both parents present as well as in situations where they are the only parent in the home.

(6) It is necessary to refute the notion that female-headed households are the main cause of the deplorable conditions of poverty, crime, and hopelessness found among Blacks in many inner cities.

First, in order to understand families and households among African Americans, one must realize that these groupings evolved from African family structure, in which coresidential extended families were the norm (Sudarkasa, 1980, 1981, 1988a). To varying degrees in different parts of the United States, the organization of many African American households and families still reflects that extended family background. It is important to mention this because many researchers and policymakers studying Black families look only at *individual households* and therefore miss the "web of kinship" (Fortes, 1949) and patterns of cooperation that tie these households together.

Historically, in parts of America where conditions permitted it, different constituent families within large Black extended families built their houses near each other on commonly owned land, thereby creating living areas resembling African compounds. Two of my former students, Dr. Mary Faith Mitchell and Mr. Bamidele Agbasegbe Demerson, found such patterns in the Sea Islands off the coast of South Carolina in the early 1970s (Demerson, 1991). In fact, such clusters of individual households, headed by couples or by single women, could be found in various parts of the South before African-Americans began to lose control over much of the land they had acquired after slavery.

In many places, even where households were or are spatially separated from one another, cross-residential or transresidential cooperation was and continues to be an important factor in rearing children, providing financial support in times of need, caring for aged family members, and providing shelter for various kinfolk who need it from time to time. These patterns of cross-residential cooperation are not static. They have changed over time, but the work of contemporary scholars such as Carol Stack (1974) and Joyce Aschenbrenner (1975) shows that these patterns of cooperation have been a very important factor in the survival of Black families in cities as well as in rural areas throughout America. Thus many female-headed households have had *bases of support* in other households.

Unfortunately, however, in the United States today, the poverty that engulfs the majority of African Americans is threatening the very survival of these traditional self-help extended family networks. This sea of poverty has a particularly negative impact on households headed by women. Yet, we must not forget that most female-headed households among the poor would be in an even worse condition without the extended family networks and patterns of cross-residential cooperation that do still exist.

The second point to be stressed in this chapter is the need to understand that different dynamics underlie the formation and functioning of different types of female-headed households. These households may represent entirely different phases in the developmental cycle of a family group. For example, households headed by young, never-married women are different from households headed by widows. The latter are appropriately understood as a phase in the life cycle of what was a two-parent household. The former may be an incipient two-parent household or it may remain a female-headed household throughout the life of the mother. Households headed by widows and older mature women who are divorced or separated from their husbands or mates predictably function differently from those headed by younger mothers. Thus age as well as maturity and previous marital status of the household head need to be taken into consideration in any discussion of households and families headed by women.

In this connection, it is very important to note that the pattern of young mothers living alone with their children, a pattern discussed a great deal today, is a relatively recent phenomenon among African Americans. In the 1950s, when I was a teenager, young Black women who had children outside of wedlock usually lived in households headed by their mothers, grandmothers, parents, grandparents, or other senior relatives. They did not live alone. The younger the mother, the longer she would probably live with other adults.

It is my hypothesis that the phenomenal rise in the number of single-parent households among African Americans is as much a consequence of a change in residential patterns as it is the result of a higher incidence of teenage pregnancies. The large number of isolated households headed by young single mothers today is directly related to public welfare policies and public housing policies that, over the years, discouraged and/or disallowed the multigenerational households that were characteristic of Black families, whether they were headed by women or by married couples (Sudarkasa, 1980; Jewell, 1988).

The breakup of multigenerational female-headed households and multigenerational two-parent-headed households automatically results in a higher incidence of households headed by young women. Where, for example, in the past a woman, her adult son, two adult daughters, and the daughters' children might have been found living in one household, we now might find the mother and the son in one household and each of the daughters and their children living in separate households. Thus we have three female-headed households to be counted by the census takers, where 30 or 40 years ago we probably would have had only one.

My third point relates to the need to expunge the misconception that marital stability and family stability are one and the same, and that family stability can be found only in two-parent households. In several of my earlier papers, I stressed that traditional Black female-headed households were built around several adult consanguineal or "blood" relatives rather than around a single adult woman (Sudarkasa, 1980, 1981, 1988a). Such consanguineally based households typically included a woman, some of her adult children, perhaps a sister, and the dependent children of one or more of the women. The core of adult relatives was often a stable unit that remained together over time and provided an environment for bringing up children that could be just as supportive as an environment provided by a two-parent family.

Many writers have tended to focus on the absent father in such households, while neglecting the critical support provided by adult males in the roles of sons, brothers, and uncles. Some of these men lived with their mothers or sisters in female-headed households. Others headed households that were a part of the extended family network on which their mothers or sisters depended. In both circumstances, these men provided important role models for the children as well as financial and emotional support for their kinswomen. Although today many Black males do not have jobs that would enable them to continue this pattern of support for their female relatives, some still provide financial assistance to their mothers and sisters as well as to their wives or girlfriends.

The main point here is that discussions of family stability that focus only on the roles of husband and wife or father and mother overlook the stability and support that traditionally have been provided by a nucleus of consanguineal relatives in African American households headed by women. The instability of the marital bond cannot be taken as an infallible barometer of family instability among African Americans because they have maintained the African commitment to "blood" kin and have used those bonds of kinship as building blocks for a significant proportion of their households and families.

A fourth point that needs to be addressed concerns the legitimacy of female-headed households as an alternative form of domestic organization among Blacks. Andrew Billingsley (1968) pointed out more than two decades ago that, historically, about 25% of Black families had been headed by women—a minority to be sure, but a significant number. Nowadays, the proportion of Black families headed by women approaches 50%.

As African American scholars and professionals, we must acknowledge, unequivocally, that female-headed households have been, and are, one accepted form of domestic organization in our communities. Such households have always been a "legitimate" (though not necessarily the most preferred) family form among African Americans. Blacks have historically understood and accepted that some women had to conceive and/or rear children without husbands if they were going to have children at all.

Underlying this acceptance was and is the fundamental fact that African Americans, like their African ancestors, still place a high value on having children. As I said in a paper published more than 15 years ago, the maiden aunt is a rarity, almost an anomaly, among Africans and peoples of African descent (Sudarkasa, 1975). The high value we place on children has always meant that African American women could have children out of wedlock without the stigma that fell to many white women in the same situation. Charles S. Johnson (1934, pp. 66-69), the eminent sociologist of the first half of the twentieth century, long ago pointed out that Blacks did not stigmatize children as "illegitimate" simply because their parents were not married when they were born. Parenthetically, I might note that white women are now demanding the right to be single mothers and to rear their children without stigma.

African Americans understood that a number of factors made it impossible for all women to have or to rear children within the framework of marriage. Unlike Africa, where polygamy (or, more technically, polygyny) was sanctioned, in the United States a man could have only one wife at a time. Yet, factors such as the higher birthrate for females over males, earlier deaths of males, the migration of males in search of work, and the incarceration and execution of large numbers of Black males during their prime reproductive years converged to cause a relative scarcity of males in relation to females in many Black communities.

Some men responded to the realities of this unequal sex ratio by having serial marriages and/or common-law living arrangements with various women. Other men remained legally monogamous while maintaining liaisons with other women. But we cannot "blame" men, as many are wont to do, for these domestic patterns, any more than we can "blame" women for their behavioral responses to the shortage of men. Many women have sought the companionship of married men because they saw themselves as having no options. Moreover, many African American wives have accepted the pattern of what contemporary Africans now call "outside wives," because they know they have to share their husbands or risk losing them altogether. Among African Americans as among ostensibly monogamous Africans, as long as the husbands give public respect and recognition to their legal wives, many of these women tolerate their husbands' infidelities as a preferable option to divorce.

These realities must be taken into account when we analyze the phenomenon of single motherhood. Of course, we are rightly concerned about curbing the rising number of teenage pregnancies and the consequent number of households headed by young single women. But we must be realistic about the *totality* of the phenomenon we are addressing. Female-headed households are not just the consequence or the result of teenage pregnancies. Many are alternative forms of family organization that mature Black women have adopted in the face of the demographic, economic, political, and social realities of Black life in America.

The fifth point that needs to be clarified concerns the role of women as coproviders or sole providers in households where both husbands and wives are present. Because most of the discussion of family and household dynamics assumes male headship whenever a male is present, the female-headed household with a male spouse present is virtually unexplored in the literature.[1] Yet we know that the unemployment of Black males has led to the existence of a number of households where wives or girlfriends are the sole providers and the de facto heads of "two-parent" households.

This raises the more general point of a need to understand all types of domestic arrangements in which women assume all or most of the responsibility for providing for themselves and their children. The anthropological and historical data show that, regardless of household structure, in most parts of the world in most social classes, women have been coproviders or primary providers for themselves and their children. We have not sufficiently focused our attention on this fact under conditions where women live *with their husbands* to be able to understand what is different when they live alone with their children or with their children and other family members.

As female scholars, we should be the last to be seduced by the myth of the male provider, if by that is meant "sole provider." Historically, women have worked in the fields, in the marketplace, in factories, and in the home to shoulder much of the responsibility for the support of their children and themselves. It is equally true, historically, that much of the wealth generated by men has gone to support and validate their political, social, economic, and military positions in society, rather than solely or even mainly toward the ongoing material needs of their families.

It is only within a relatively brief period of Western history that women and children in the privileged classes have been supported more or less entirely by men. And even there, researchers in women's studies have shown that the value of the in-kind contribution of these women to their domestic units has been greatly underrated. Moreover, for women in the very elite classes, it is not so much their husbands who have supported them as it is the masses of people in the lower classes whose work has supported them both.

The more typical pattern that we find in the world is not one of male providers but of male and female coproviders in support of their families. Women have usually been and will continue to be a major source of material and financial support as well as the major source of emotional support for their children. In the case of African American women, if we want to explore fully their contributions as heads of households, we need to include an examination of their economic roles in families where they live with their husbands or mates as well as those in which they live as single parents.

My last point in this chapter focuses on the need to expose the myth that female-headed households are the root cause of the deplorable conditions in which many Blacks find themselves in urban ghettos. As I wrote in an article in *Sisters* magazine, this myth is hardest to overcome because many Blacks themselves have accepted it as truth (Sudarkasa, 1988b). They have been led to believe that Black family structure is the main cause of the high rates of crime, unemployment, school dropouts, teenage pregnancies, drug abuse, and disaffection among young people in many of our inner cities. Their views are shaped by scholars and journalists who refuse to acknowledge that those African Americans whom William Julius Wilson (1987) calls the "truly disadvantaged" are caught in a black hole of poverty that is not of their own making and that creates vicious cycles of deprivation that most cannot escape.

Of course, some of the African American family patterns developed in response to abject poverty have themselves become factors in perpetuating the distressing conditions in many inner cities. But the structure of the Black family (which in this context usually refers to female-headed households) cannot be labeled the root cause of the wretched conditions of poverty; the reverse is more probably the case. In fact, it is virtually impossible to envision a change in family structure so long as the systemic unemployment of males and other conditions of poverty and deprivation persist. Moreover, the evidence is unequivocal that most two-parent families in the ghettos are often powerless to combat the drugs, crime, and degradation that grow out of the conditions of poverty in which they live.

Ironically and sadly, one reason it is difficult to wipe out drug-related crime in Black communities is that some families, particularly those headed by women, have come to depend on the income they receive from the young men who are the ones mainly involved in illicit drug traffic. In the face of the chronic and systemic unemployment of young Black males, drug money becomes the alternative to no money at all. Too often, the relatives of young drug dealers look the other way when members of their community seek to mobilize to stamp out narcotics. This dependence on the underground economy, which of course is not unique to African Americans, is one of the patterns that must be broken if we are to rescue Black families who are long-term victims, even if they think of themselves as short-term beneficiaries, of the illegal drug traffic and the violence it breeds.

All the evidence we have shows that the social pathologies that are allegedly caused by Black family structure rapidly improve when people in poverty are provided with skills and jobs to earn a decent living. William Julius Wilson's book *The Truly Disadvantaged* (1987) demonstrates that the extraordinarily high rates of unemployment and despair among young Black males, along with the violent drug subculture that offers them easy money and continuous highs, are the root causes of crime and degradation in the inner cities. Eliminating these conditions will require a relentless and total war on drugs and unemployment, not war on Black families.

Conclusion

As we formulate plans and seek models for improving African American families, we must not be seduced by the myth that only the nuclear family can provide the stability and support necessary to ensure the survival and success of our communities in the twenty-first century. Rather, we should explore ways in which the values of cooperation and reciprocity that allowed female-headed households to thrive within the context of the extended family can be revived and rekindled in the context of the realities of family organization of the present day.

In the arena of public housing, we need to call for policies that do not disallow or discriminate against extended family households. These multigenerational domestic units can be an answer to the problems facing young single mothers living alone, struggling to find the support that would enable them to go out to work to sustain themselves and their children. Elderly mothers and grandmothers now living alone with time on their hands could look after the children of these young working mothers, as elderly Black women did in the past.

We also need to use African American institutions such as churches, sororities, fraternities, and other community groups to begin private initiatives to bring together adults from different generations and both genders to discuss and plan for the African American family of the future. These organizations can mobilize financial resources to design and build new types of housing units that would accommodate families of varying sizes and configurations. Rather than assume that a family unit must be the proverbial nuclear family of husband, wife, and two children, we must recognize that the key to the survival of African Americans has always been the *flexibility* and *adaptability* of our family organization. We must remember that our first effective economic and social networks were extended family networks. We can now use ties of kinship and friendship to create new domestic networks for the new age, networks that will embrace and affirm families that are headed by women, by men, or by both.

Note

1. Since this chapter was written, a very important paper on the concept of *provider* has come to my attention (Hood, 1986). It explores a number of points raised here.

5

African American
Extended Kin Systems

An Assessment

SHIRLEY J. HATCHETT
JAMES S. JACKSON

Much has been written about the importance of the extended family for the survival of African Americans (e.g., Billingsley, 1968; Hill, 1972; H. P. McAdoo, 1981). A great deal of this discussion came in the mid-1960s, in the aftermath of the controversial Moynihan (1965) report. This report generated a decade-long debate on the viability of African American families and the appropriateness of various research perspectives. Critical reviews by Black scholars, among them Staples (1971c) and Allen (1978a), countered the indictment of the Black family as dysfunctional with arguments that much prior research on Black families had, as a consequence of research perspectives and limited samples, presented views of these families as deviant and/or fraught with pathology. Other scholars also came to the defense of Black families by expanding their empirical investigations in terms of both sampling and statistical methodologies (e.g., Heiss, 1975; Scanzoni, 1971).

At issue has been the structure of the African American family and its supposed consequences for family members, particularly children. The great diversity of structures among Black families, particularly the large proportion of female-headed households, raised questions of functionality in a society where the nuclear family was seen as the most viable and functional form. Staples (1980) and others have criticized a reliance on a household-based definition of family and family functioning in Black family research. Indeed, two decades ago, pioneering research on kin networks and extended kin behavior in the general population seriously questioned the image of the isolated nuclear family advanced by early social theorists. Litwak (1960b), Reiss (1962), and Sussman and Burchinal (1962) found not only that modified extended family behavior was a part of modern urban life but that it was not dysfunctional for either mobility or modernization (also see G. R. Lee, 1980). Also, recent interest in social support has expanded investigations of extended kin networks, which are now being viewed as an important resource for both individual and family coping.

Scholars stressing the strengths of Black families have emphasized these families' great intra- and extrahousehold extendedness and the historical assumption by the extended kin system of functions generally fulfilled within the nuclear family household (Aschenbrenner, 1973; Hays & Mindel, 1973; Hill, 1972; Martin & Martin, 1978; Shimkin, Shimkin, & Frate, 1978). These features of the Black family belie the assessment of its viability without consideration of family behavior across household boundaries.

African American extended kin behavior has been viewed both as an adaptive response to situational constraints in America (Aschenbrenner, 1973; Billingsley, 1968; Hill, 1972; Stack, 1974) and as a vestige of West African culture (Herskovits, 1941; Nobles, 1974; Sudarkasa, 1980). This debate ensues from the larger one over the Black family in general, where the particular forms and functions of Black families have been discussed and presented in the literature as being deviant, adaptive, or culturally variant (Allen, 1978a). Sudarkasa's (1980) assessment of the influence of African heritage upon Black family structure bridges the adaptation versus cultural survival argument. Sudarkasa suggests that the type and quality of adaptations to slavery and life in America were perhaps facilitated by the West African heritage of Blacks. From her studies of West African culture, she contends that African extended family traditions may have proved useful for preserving family ties and for the socialization of children in spite of the disruptive aspects of social oppression.

Martin and Martin (1978) define the Black extended family as follows:

> a multigenerational, interdependent kinship system which is welded together by a sense of obligation to relatives, is organized around a dominant figure; extends across geographic boundaries to connect family units to an extended

family network; and has a built in mutual aid system for the welfare of its members and the maintenance of the family as a whole. (p. 1)

In their view of the extended family, individual households are sub-families connected to a base household or households of the family of origin. Characteristics of Black extended kin systems noted most frequently in the literature can be summarized as follows: (a) a high degree of geographical propinquity; (b) a strong sense of family and familial obligation; (c) fluidity of household boundaries, with great willingness to absorb relatives, both real and fictive, adult and minor, if need arises; (d) frequent interaction with relatives; (e) frequent extended family get-togethers for special occasions and holidays; and (f) a system of mutual aid (Aschenbrenner, 1973; Feagin, 1968; Hays & Mindel, 1973; Hill, 1972; Martin & Martin, 1978; Martineau, 1977; H. P. McAdoo, 1978a; Shimkin et al., 1978; Stack, 1974). This last aspect of Black kin systems has received considerable attention in the last decade in research on the role of social support in the functioning and survival of special Black subpopulations, particularly single mothers and the elderly (H. P. McAdoo, 1977, 1983; Taylor, 1983).

Much of the research on Black extended kin networks has been qualitative in nature. Notable exceptions are found in the works of Harriette Pipes McAdoo, as well as in the works of Taylor, Jackson, and Quick (1982) and Taylor (1983), which are based on the same data used in this chapter. These studies, although substantively rich, have the same shortcoming as the qualitative studies—lack of representativeness.

Most of our knowledge of Black extended kin behavior comes from small, often nonrepresentative, local samples. In an effort to expand our knowledge of Black extended kin systems, we present an empirical assessment of four aspects of Black extended kin systems: geographical propinquity of kin, subjective closeness of kin, frequency of interaction with kin, and frequency of aid received from kin. These analyses are based on data from a large national sample of Black American adults. This survey allowed assessment of extended kin networks among various subgroups as well as an examination of the relationship between various aspects of Black extended kin systems.

Methodology

Our data come from the National Survey of Black Americans (NSBA), a national cross-sectional study of Black adults 18 years old and older, conducted by the Program for Research on Black Americans at the Survey Research Center at the University of Michigan during 1979 and 1980. A total of 2,107 respondents were interviewed in a multistage probability sample of Black households in 76 different communities in the continental United States. This was an equal probability sample, wherein every Black household had the same chance of selection; the intent was to get a nationally representative sample of Black Americans in all walks of life.[1] The analyses presented here are based only upon selected respondents who were either heads of household or spouses of heads at the time of interview (nearly 82% of all respondents).[2]

The measures of characteristics of extended kin systems were included in a large general questionnaire that covered many aspects of African American life: neighborhood, family, friends, work and unemployment, mental and physical health, coping and help seeking, and racial identity.

Geographical propinquity of kin was measured for both immediate family members and other relatives. The primary residence of the majority of immediate family members was determined as falling within one of seven response categories: "in this household," "in this neighborhood," "in this city," "in this county," "in this state," "in another state," and "outside the country." For analysis, these categories were coded from 1 to 6 according to proximity to the respondent's household (the "household" category was deleted). The geographical proximity and density of other kin were derived from a series of seven questions: "How many of your relatives, not in your immediate family, live in the following areas . . . in this household, in this neighborhood, in this city, in this county, in this state, in another state, and in another country?" An additive index of these items, with the exception of "household," was constructed, with each item weighted according to proximity to the respondent's household.

The subjective closeness of kin was measured by a single item that asked, "Would you say your family members are very close in their feelings to each other, fairly close, not too close, or not close at all?" (categories were scored 4-1, respectively). The frequency of interaction or contact with kin and the frequency of aid received from kin were measured by the following questions:

Frequency of interaction with kin: "How often do you see, write or talk on the telephone with family or relatives who do not live with you?"

Frequency of aid received from kin: "How often do people in your family— including children, grandparents, aunts, uncles, in-laws and so on—help you out? Would you say very often, fairly often, not too often, or never?"

The frequency of interaction with kin was coded 1-6, with the highest value indicating frequent interaction. The frequency of aid was similarly scored on a scale of 1-4.

Results

In assessing extended kin systems of Blacks on the whole and for various subgroups, we treated each of the variables described above as dependent variables in multiple classification analyses (Andrews, Morgan, Sonquist, & Klem, 1973).[3] Included as predictors in these analyses were several sociodemographic variables—sex, age, family life cycle,[4] household income, region, and urbanicity. In addition, both indicators of geographical propinquity of kin were included as predictors of subjective closeness of kin. Subjective closeness, both measures of geographical propinquity for the analysis of interaction with kin, and all of the preceding variables were used as predictors of aid received from kin. The causal relationships implied in these models may not be sufficient, however. Reciprocal influences among some of the variables are possible. For the most part, the decision to include these predictors in the various analyses derived from the literature, which suggests the importance of various sociodemographic variables, kinship ideology, and geographical propinquity, as well as kinship propinquity, in determining interaction with kin and exchanges of aid (Leigh, 1982; Reiss, 1981; Reiss & Oliveri, 1983).

Geographical Propinquity of Kin

A large proportion of the respondents reported a high level of geographical propinquity of both immediate family members and other relatives. More than half of the respondents reported that most of their immediate family members were located in their cities of residence—household, neighborhood, or city; 7% said most of their immediate family lived in their own household, 7% said most of their family lived in the same neighborhood, 39% said the same city, 6% the same county, 15% the same state, and 26% said most family members lived in another state. Less than 1% of the respondents indicated that most of their immediate family members lived outside the United States.

With respect to other relatives, respondents tended to have more relatives living in their cities, counties, states, and other states (respec-

Table 5.1 Relative Importance of Predictors of Two Indicators of Geographical Propinquity of Kin

Predictors	Eta	Beta
Proximity of immediate family members		
age	.14***	.11
family life cycle	.14***	.11
degree of urban development	.10***	.10
region	.10***	.07
household income	.02	.06
respondent's sex	.03	.02
$R^2 = .04$; R^2adj = .03		
Proximity and density of relatives		
age	.17***	.15
family life cycle	.16***	.09
degree of urban development	.08***	.09
region	.10***	.08
household income	.03	.07
respondent's sex	.04	.00
$R^2 = .06$; R^2adj = .04+		

NOTE: R^2 is the measure of variance explained in the model. R^2adj is the estimate of explained variance if predictors used in the model are applied to a different sample for same population. The adjustment is made to degrees of freedom in the model.
***$p < .001$.

tively, for the category of "many," 27%, 20%, 27%, and 34%) than in their neighborhoods (for "none," 60%) and another country (for "none," 85%). For the collapsed proximity and density of relatives index, 42% of the respondents had a low score, 32% a medium score, and 26% a high score.[5]

Table 5.1 shows bivariate and multivariate measures for each predictor included in multiple classification analyses for both indicators of the geographical propinquity of kin.[6] For both indicators, significant bivariate associations were found for all of the variables except sex and household income. Age, family life cycle, degree of urban development, and region emerged in the multivariate model as the most significant predictors of both indicators of geographical propinquity. Tables 5.2 and 5.3 present the unadjusted and adjusted (for the effect of other predictors) means for all categories of each predictor. Their relationships with both indicators can be summarized as follows.

Table 5.2 Proximity of Immediate Family Members by Age, Family Life
Cycle, Degree of Urban Development, and Region

Predictors	Class Mean	Adjusted Mean	SD	N
Age				
18-34	4.0	4.0	1.4	524
35-54	3.7	3.7	1.4	520
55-64	3.8	3.9	1.4	175
65-101	3.5	3.5	1.4	235
Family life cycle				
young never marrieds	3.6	3.4	1.4	56
older never marrieds	3.5	3.5	1.5	36
ever marrieds	3.7	3.7	1.5	294
young marrieds	3.9	3.8	1.3	55
marrieds with children	3.8	3.8	1.4	496
single parents	4.0	4.0	1.4	326
older marrieds, post-child launching	3.4	3.6	1.4	148
older childless marrieds	3.4	3.5	1.4	43
Degree of urban development				
large urban areas	3.9	3.9	1.4	687
smaller urban areas	3.8	3.7	1.4	461
less urban and more rural areas	3.5	3.6	1.4	306
Region				
Northeast	3.7	3.7	1.4	271
North Central	4.0	4.0	1.4	318
South	3.7	3.8	1.4	778
West	3.6	3.6	1.4	87

Age. Persons 18-34 and 55-64 years of age are more likely to have immediate family members at a closer distance than those 35-54 and those over 65, with the latter the least likely to have immediate family members close by. The relationship of age to proximity and density of relatives follows a negative linear pattern, with the proximity and density of relatives decreasing with age.

Family life cycle. Generally, never-married persons of all ages, married persons whose children have left home, and older childless married persons report less propinquity of immediate family members than those in other family life-cycle stages. The highest geographical pro-

Table 5.3 Proximity and Density of Relatives by Age, Family Life Cycle, Degree of Urban Development, and Region

Predictors	Class Mean	Adjusted Mean	SD	N
Age				
18-34	26.4	25.9	13.0	546
35-54	23.4	23.5	12.6	556
55-64	22.8	23.3	13.4	195
65-101	19.9	20.1	12.2	252
Family life cycle				
young never marrieds	25.2	23.7	13.4	59
older never marrieds	18.7	19.7	10.8	36
ever marrieds	21.3	22.3	13.3	321
young childless marrieds	25.1	24.0	11.3	56
marrieds with children	24.8	24.5	12.5	529
single parents	25.9	24.9	12.9	350
older marrieds, post-child launching	22.2	23.4	13.0	152
older childless marrieds	19.3	21.3	13.0	46
Degree of urban development				
large urban areas	23.0	23.2	12.5	748
smaller urban areas	23.5	23.2	13.0	482
less urban, more rural areas	25.8	26.1	13.7	319
Region				
Northeast	21.9	22.7	12.1	289
North Central	25.2	25.6	13.8	349
South	24.1	23.6	12.9	817
West	21.2	21.9	11.4	94

pinquity of immediate family members is found for single parents living with children. The pattern is different for the reported density and proximity of other relatives. For this variable, older married persons and older childless married persons report the lowest density and proximity of relatives and single parents the highest.

Urbanicity. The relationships differ for each indicator. The mean geographical proximity of immediate family members decreases as the degree of urban development decreases. Just the opposite happens for the proximity and density of relatives; this increases as the degree of urban development increases.

Region. The mean proximity of immediate family members is greater in the North Central region for Black Americans than in other regions. The lowest mean proximity of immediate family members is found for respondents in the West. This relationship holds for the other indicator of geographical propinquity.

All of these predictors explain only a very small, although statistically significant, proportion of the variance in each of the indicators.

Subjective Closeness

As the literature has suggested, there is an overwhelming perception of family solidarity among Black Americans. More than 90% of all respondents in our sample reported that their family members were "very close" or "fairly close" in their feelings toward each other.

Bivariate and multivariate measures of association for each predictor of perceived subjective closeness of kin are found in Table 5.4. Significant bivariate relationships were not found for sex, age, degree of urban development, or the proximity of immediate family members. The family life cycle evidences the most impact in the multivariate model, followed closely by the proximity and density of relatives and region. The unadjusted and adjusted means for categories of these predictors are shown in Table 5.5. Their relationships with subjective closeness are summarized below.

Family life cycle. Older never-married persons perceive the lowest mean subjective closeness of kin. They are followed by older childless couples. The highest perceived closeness was found for young childless couples and older couples whose children have left home.

Proximity and density of relatives (collapsed). Perceived subjective closeness increased as the geographical density and proximity of relatives increased.

Region. Respondents in the Northeast and the West perceived less family solidarity than those in the South and the North Central region.

These predictors together explained only 3% of the variance in subjective closeness of kin ($R^2 = .06$, R^2 adjusted = .03).

Interaction With Kin

Black Americans appear to maintain fairly frequent contact with their kin. More than two-thirds of all respondents reported contacting their relatives by phone call, letter, or visit at least once a week. A total of 17% said they contacted relatives a few times a month, 7% said at least

Table 5.4 Relative Importance of Predictors of Subjective Closeness of Kin

Predictors	Eta	Beta
Family life cycle	.15***	.13
Density and proximity of relatives	.12***	.12
Region	.10**	.10
Household income	.06	.09
Age	.04	.07
Proximity of immediate family	.06	.05
Respondent's sex	.01	.04
Degree of urban development	.06	.03
$R^2 = .03$; R^2adj = .02		

$**p < .01$; $***p < .001$.

Table 5.5 Subjective Closeness of Kin by Family Life Cycle, Indicators of Geographical Propinquity of Kin, Region, and Income

Predictors	Class Mean	Adjusted Mean	SD	N
Family life cycle				
young never marrieds	3.4	3.5	0.8	43
older never marrieds	3.0	3.0	1.1	26
ever marrieds	3.4	3.4	0.8	227
young marrieds	3.7	3.7	0.5	35
marrieds with children	3.5	3.5	0.7	362
single parents	3.4	3.4	0.8	241
older marrieds, post-child launching	3.7	3.6	0.6	114
older childless marrieds	3.4	3.4	0.8	35
Proximity and density of relatives (collapsed)				
few relatives, far away	3.4	3.4	0.8	625
	3.6	3.6	0.6	120
many relatives, close	3.6	3.6	0.6	338
Region				
Northeast	3.3	3.3	0.9	202
North Central	3.5	3.5	0.7	245
South	3.5	3.5	0.7	570
West	3.4	3.4	0.8	66
Annual household income				
less than $5,000	3.4	3.4	0.8	263
$5,000-$9,999	3.4	3.4	0.8	284
$10,000-$19,999	3.5	3.5	0.7	305
$20,000 and above	3.5	3.5	0.6	231

Table 5.6 Relative Importance of Predictors of Interaction With Kin Among Black Americans

Predictors	Eta	Beta
Subjective closeness	.31***	.30
Proximity of immediate family	.28***	.24
Respondent's sex	.18***	.18
Household income	.09**	.15
Family life cycle	.13**	.13
Degree of urban development	.12***	.09
Proximity of relatives	.17***	.08
Age	.09*	.05
Region	.08	.02
$R^2 = .24$; R^2adj $= .22$		

*$p < .05$; **$p < .01$; ***$p < .001$.

once a month, 6% said a few times a year, 5% said once a year, and less than 2% said they never contacted their relatives.

Table 5.6 presents bivariate and multivariate measures for each predictor of the frequency of interaction with kin. All of the predictors except region showed significant bivariate relationships with the frequency of interaction with kin. Table 5.7 presents the unadjusted and adjusted means for the five most important predictors in the multivariate model. These relationships can be summarized as follows.

Subjective closeness. There is a fairly strong relationship between the perception of family solidarity and the frequency of interaction with kin. The greater the feeling of family solidarity, the more frequent the interaction.

Proximity of immediate members. The closer one lives to family members, the more frequent the interaction.

Sex. Women had a higher mean frequency of interaction with relatives than men.

Household income. Interaction increased as income increased.

Family life cycle. The highest mean frequency of interaction with kin was found for older never-married persons, followed by older persons whose children have left home, single parents, ever-married persons, and young childless married persons. Married persons with children at home and older married persons without children had lowest mean frequencies of interaction with kin.

Table 5.7 Frequency of Interaction With Relatives by Subjective Closeness of Kin, Proximity of Immediate Family, Sex, Income, and Family Life Cycle

Predictors	Class Mean	Adjusted Mean	SD	N
Subjective closeness				
not close at all	2.9	3.0	1.8	36
not very close	3.8	3.8	1.7	65
fairly close	4.5	4.5	1.4	340
very close	4.9	4.9	1.3	640
Proximity of immediate family				
other country	3.7	3.7	1.4	9
other state	4.2	4.2	1.5	342
same state	4.5	4.6	1.5	181
same county	5.1	5.2	1.3	58
same city	5.1	5.0	1.2	427
same neighborhood	4.8	4.7	1.6	64
Sex				
men	4.3	4.3	1.5	417
women	4.9	4.9	1.4	664
Annual household income				
under $5,000	4.5	4.4	1.7	262
$5,000-$9,999	4.6	4.6	1.4	284
$10,000-$19,999	4.8	4.8	1.3	305
$20,000 and above	4.8	5.0	1.2	230
Family life cycle				
young never marrieds	4.4	4.6	1.6	43
older never marrieds	4.5	5.0	1.8	26
ever marrieds	4.6	4.8	1.5	227
young marrieds	5.0	4.7	1.1	35
marrieds with children	4.5	4.4	1.4	361
single parents	4.9	4.8	1.4	240
older marrieds, post-child launching	4.7	4.8	1.4	114
older childless married persons	4.4	4.5	1.5	35

Subjective closeness of kin and geographical closeness of immediate family members are the most important predictors of the frequency of interaction with kin. Sex, family income, and family life cycle follow in predictive importance. Although urbanicity, region, and age were related to the frequency of interaction with kin at the bivariate level, controlling for the other predictors greatly decreased their predictive power in the multivariate model. Together, all predictors explain 22% of the variance in this variable, indicating the overall utility of this model for predicting interaction with kin.

Differences also emerge across regions and levels of urban development. However, these two variables are significant predictors only of subjective closeness of kin and geographical propinquity of kin. Persons living in the western region of the country tend to perceive less family solidarity, tend to live further from immediate family members, and have less dense and geographically close kin networks. The West is the most recent site of Black migration (other than reverse migration to the South). This subjective isolation from kin may be partially due to the West's distance from the South, where the bulk of Black Americans resided before migration and where half still live. The significant associations among geographical closeness, density of kin, and subjective closeness may help to explain the lower perceptions of family solidarity among Black westerners.

Urbanicity is important only in predicting the proximity of immediate family members. Persons in more rural areas report being more isolated from their family members than those in other areas. Socioeconomic status (SES), as measured here by family income, is important in predicting subjective closeness and interaction with kin. Perceptions of family solidarity and interaction with kin both increase as income increases. This has important implications for social support as measured by frequency of aid received. Both of these variables are important predictors of the frequency of aid.

Aid Received From Kin

Mutual aid, perhaps the most important function of the extended family because of its implications for social support, was assessed indirectly in our study. Respondents were asked only about aid or help received and not about help given. However, the literature suggests that norms of reciprocity may exist that obligate people to repay family members in kind or with related goods, services, or support when they are in need (Martin & Martin, 1978; Stack, 1974). In this light, the item used here can be seen as an indicator of mutual aid, although admittedly one-sided.

Slightly less than half of our respondents reported that family and relatives helped them either "very often" or "fairly often": 21% said they received help "very often," 21% "fairly often," 28% "not too often," and 29% reported never receiving help. All in all, more than two-thirds of our sample reported receiving some help from family members.

Table 5.8 shows bivariate and multivariate measures for each predictor of aid from kin. All of the sociodemographic variables were significantly related to aid from kin at the bivariate level, with the exceptions of region and urbanicity. Table 5.9 shows the unadjusted and adjusted means for the variables having the most impact in the multivariate model: subjective closeness, family life cycle, and frequency of interaction with kin. Their relationships with aid from kin can be summarized as follows.

Subjective closeness. The higher the perceived family solidarity, the more frequent was reported aid from kin.

Family life cycle. Aid was received most frequently by never-married persons (mostly the young). Next in frequency of aid received were couples with children, single parents, and couples whose children had left home. Those with the lowest mean frequency of aid were older childless couples.

Frequency of interaction with kin. The more frequent the interaction or contact with kin, the more frequent the reported aid. Subjective closeness of kin is the most important predictor of aid from kin. Next in importance are family life cycle and frequency of interaction with kin.

Together, the predictors in this model explained 14% of the variance in the reported frequency of aid from kin. These results suggest that high family solidarity, particular family life stage, and frequent interaction with kin are important requisites for the frequent exchange of goods, services, and socioemotional support across family households.

Summary and Discussion

This study assessed four aspects of Black extended kin systems using data from a large nationally representative sample of Black Americans. Our data came from a questionnaire covering many aspects of Black American life, thus limiting the scope of our investigation in this area. Our indicators are, therefore, very general. We attempted to tap overall

Table 5.8 Relative Importance of Predictors of Aid Received From Kin

Predictors	Eta	Beta
Subjective closeness	.28***	.22
Family life cycle	.20***	.18
Frequency of interaction with kin	.25***	.18
Respondent's sex	.08**	.07
Region	.10*	.07
Proximity of immediate family	.10	.05
Degree of urban development	.06	.05
Household income	.10*	.05
Age	.13***	.03
Density and proximity of relatives	.10***	.02
$R^2 = .17$; R^2adj = .14		

$*p < .05$; $**p < .01$; $***p < .001$.

perceptions of family solidarity, the general geographical propinquity of unspecified immediate family members and relatives, and the general frequency of all kinds of interaction with and aid from kin. We hoped to substantiate a number of claims in the literature about the Black extended kin system, particularly with respect to the prevalence of sentiments and behaviors for the total population and for various subgroups. We also hoped to gain some insight into correlates of several aspects of Black extended kin systems.

In answer to our first query, we found an overwhelming perception of family solidarity among Black Americans. Nearly 9 of every 10 respondents said their families were "very" or "fairly" close. Also, the degree of geographical propinquity to immediate family members and the proximity and density of other kin were fairly high. The proportions reporting fairly frequent interaction or contact with relatives and frequent aid from kin were likewise substantial, indicating a fair amount of extended kin behavior among Black Americans. More than two-thirds of our respondents reported contacting relatives at least once a week, and more than two-thirds reported receiving help from relatives.

Much research on the Black family has presented a rather monolithic, undifferentiated view of Blacks. This is the result, for the most part, of the use of small, limited samples. Our findings indicate that there are differences in extended kin behavior across various subgroups of Blacks. The differences for subgroups defined by six sociodemographic variables

Table 5.9 Frequency of Aid From Kin by Subjective Closeness, Family Life Cycle, and Frequency of Interaction With Kin

Predictors	Class Mean	Adjusted Mean	SD	N
Subjective closeness				
not close at all	1.6	1.9	1.1	34
not very close	1.9	2.1	0.9	60
fairly close	2.4	2.4	0.9	298
very close	2.8	2.7	1.1	568
Family life cycle				
young never marrieds	2.8	3.0	1.0	40
older never marrieds	2.3	2.6	1.2	22
ever marrieds	2.3	2.3	1.1	197
young marrieds	2.6	2.4	1.1	31
marrieds with children	2.7	2.7	1.0	331
single parents	2.6	2.5	1.0	225
older marrieds, post-child launching	2.6	2.5	1.1	87
older childless marrieds	1.8	1.9	0.9	27
Frequency of interaction with kin				
hardly ever, never	2.0	2.2	1.2	55
a few times a year	2.2	2.2	1.0	54
at least once a month	2.2	2.2	1.0	76
a few times a month	2.4	2.4	1.1	155
at least once a week	2.6	2.6	1.0	271
nearly every day	2.8	2.7	1.0	349

can be summarized as follows. Significant differences by sex were found only for the frequency of interaction with kin and frequency of aid received from kin. Women were more likely to report frequent interaction with kin, as well as frequent aid. A number of studies have reported similar differences between men and women.[7] Women have been seen as the primary movers in extended kin systems. Some of the literature, notably work by Stack (1974), has presented images of high and intense levels of extended kin behavior among lower-SES Blacks. These findings, coupled with classical hypotheses about social mobility and extended kin behavior, have given the impression that perhaps this behavior is less prevalent at higher SES levels. Harriette McAdoo (1978a), in her study of Black middle-class families, has offered evidence to refute this argument. These data, based on a larger and more representative sample of Blacks, bring some focus to the overall picture of SES and extended kin behavior. There are, indeed, differences across income groups within the Black population, and higher-SES, not lower-SES, persons appear to have greater activity within kin networks. This suggests that higher-SES persons may also benefit more from these behaviors.

We included measures of both general life cycle (age) and family life cycle or stage within our analyses. For the most part, the impact of life span or age is captured by our family life cycle variable. Although significant bivariate relationships were found for age and all four aspects of extended kin behavior examined here, age remained an important predictor for only one behavioral aspect after the effect of family life cycle was discounted. For the most part, older Black Americans are more geographically isolated from kin, both immediate and other relatives. This may be the result of such factors as the deaths of same-age and older immediate family members and the greater geographic mobility of successive generations of Blacks.

Family life cycle, on the other hand, is an important predictor of all four aspects of Black extended kin behavior. Understanding the patterns found across family life cycle for each variable perhaps requires an assessment of the salience of relational propinquity, particularly in regard to parents and children, in extended kin systems. For example, never-married persons of all ages, married persons whose children have left home, and older childless couples reported being more geographically distant from their parents, siblings, and children. These patterns seem to reflect changes in living arrangements caused by children leaving the nest and establishing independent households. A similar pattern emerged for the other general indicator of geographical proximity of kin. Married persons whose children have left home and older married persons who are childless reported lower density and proximity of relatives.

The results for frequency of interaction and aid, as well as family solidarity, also fit this general pattern. Overall, the lowest mean frequency of interaction with kin was found for married persons with children still at home and older childless married persons, indicating that much of the interaction with relatives may be with children outside of the home. The lowest mean reported frequency of aid from relatives was found among older childless adults. Other research has found that frequency of aid reported decreases as age increases (Taylor, 1983). When family life cycle was introduced into our analyses, this age relationship disappeared. Those reporting less frequent aid are, for the most part, older married persons who do not have children. The cycle of aid this suggests is that parents help children up to some point, and then the direction of aid reverses. The importance of children also appears in the patterns found for perception of family solidarity. Older childless couples and older never-married persons were more likely to feel that their families were not close.

Our final objective in this chapter is to contribute to some insight into the correlates or determinants of the various aspects of Black extended kin systems. To this end, we note that we found that the variables included in the models for subjective closeness of kin and both measures of geographical propinquity did not fare well, explaining only a small fraction of the total variance in these variables. The models for the frequency of interaction with kin and aid received from kin did much better. From these models, we found that subjective closeness of family solidarity is the most influential predictor of both behaviors. The next two most important variables for interaction with kin were geographical proximity of immediate family and sex of the respondent. The prominence of the measure for immediate family in this model over that for other relatives is consistent with the literature, which suggests an influence of kinship propinquity on interaction with kin (Leigh, 1982). The important variables for predicting aid from family members, aside from subjective closeness, are frequency of interaction with kin and family life cycle.

In sum, we have to some degree substantiated claims in both lore and literature about the general nature of Black extended kin systems. Black Americans, on the whole, are very much involved in extended kin systems.

We hope that we have also contributed to the debunking of the myth of the monolithic Black family. Just as there are differences across various subgroups of African Americans in other aspects of family structure and function, there are differences in extended kin systems and behaviors.

Notes

1. Whereas previous large samples of Blacks have tended to overrepresent Blacks in large urban areas and in areas of high Black density, the NSBA utilized sampling and screening procedures designed to give appropriate representation to all Blacks, particularly those in low-density areas.

2. For this study, head was determined as follows: If a household contained a couple (man and wife or man and partner), the man was designated the head; if there was no couple, the most economically dominant person was designated as head; if no one was economically dominant, the person closest to age 45 was designated as head.

3. Multiple classification analysis is a technique analogous to dummy variable regression. It examines the interrelationships between several predictor variables (of any measurement level) and an interval-dependent variable within an additive model.

4. The family life cycle variable was created by the recoding and combining of information from several variables—household composition, parental status, marital status, and age. The resulting categories are as follows: (1) young never-married persons (30 years old and under), (2) older never-married persons (more than 30 years old), (3) ever-married persons (all divorced, separated, or widowed persons not living with own children), (4) young married persons with no children (less than 46 years old), (5) married persons with children in the household, (6) single parents with children in the household, and (7) older married persons whose children are no longer at home and older married persons who have never had children (46 and older).

5. The full index ranges from 1 to 63. The categories 1-3 of the collapsed version are derived by combining categories 1-20, 21-23, and 34-63, respectively.

6. Eta is a bivariate measure indicating the ability of the predictor to explain variation in the dependent variable. Eta^2 is the correlation ratio. Beta is analogous to eta but based on the adjusted means in the multivariate model. It is also analogous to the standardized regression coefficient.

7. Reiss and Oliveri (1983) discussed a number of these studies in their examination of the role of women in facilitating and structuring kinship ties.

6

Decision Making and Marital Satisfaction in African American Families

JOHN LEWIS MCADOO

Many African American scholars are beginning to provide us with a more balanced picture of African American family relationships and adjustments to life in the United States. This chapter focuses on decision-making patterns and self-esteem within all social classes of African American families. Studies on power relationships within African American families are evaluated, and an attempt is made to determine whether one person is seen as dominant in the family and to determine the degree to which dominance or equality in decision-making influences how the partners feel about themselves in that relationship. The degree to which decision-making patterns differ by social class is also explored.

Traditional researchers who use an exchange theory approach to studying families have left seriously underdeveloped several important concepts in their theory that would help explain power relationships in African American families. These concepts include inheritance from their ancestors of an expectation of cooperation and reciprocity as opposed to competition within the family unit and the effects of institutional racism and economic inequality on the family's ability to thrive and prosper. African families were expected to cooperate in the social, economic, child-rearing, and other tasks within their families and communities. Among African Americans, cooperation in decision making has often been essential, because for most families both spouses have had to work to overcome the lower wages earned by the husband. Shared responsibility has been seen as a way to mitigate the effects of society's negative evaluation of African Americans as an ethnic group.

The African American Experience

African families were expected to cooperate in the economic, child-rearing, and other tasks within their communities. Sometimes communities competed with one another for economic and social advantages, and the family's survival depended upon how well each member carried out designated tasks. While in some African communities women were selected to lead the family and men to lead in others areas, cooperation played a more important role in family decision making than ability to bring resources to the family unit or to control resources.

During the enslavement period, African American children called their parents' slave shipmates aunts and uncles. While they were not really related, these fictive kin were socially obligated to provide nurturance and support to the children (Gutman, 1965, pp. 185-230). The thread that kept the African American family together was a social exchange network embedded in a value and belief system based upon the norm of reciprocity—a commitment to collective cooperation that permeated all of the institutional structures within African American communities (Jewell, 1988, pp. 11-33).

African American values dictate that competition between individuals begins and ends with the mate selection process. When spouses are won or are married, they are expected to work cooperatively for the good of the marital unit. A family's survival depends on spousal cooperation in the gathering of scarce resources in order to be able to exchange them with others in their society. The perceived power of the family unit may be seen as depending on the unit's ability to survive and defend itself.

Institutional racism has influenced both the study and the life outcomes of African Americans in several ways. Family scholars have continued to evaluate African American family structure as being different in spite of the evidence that it is similar to that of white families. The term *matriarchal* is applied negatively to African American families when they are no different in their structure from White families. The assumption that women who lead families are somehow bad or create problems for the family relationship and socialization of children is both erroneous and sexist.

The society itself has created economic differences between African Americans and whites. From 1954 to the present, African Americans with the same education, occupational status, and employment history as their white male counterparts have earned about 57% of what whites make. The difference persists across socioeconomic levels (J. L. McAdoo, 1990; Wilson, 1987). Thus we have created a glass ceiling on the economic resources that the African American father can bring to his family.

The overall effect of the earning of fewer resources for the same type of work has caused resentment and economic and social stress among African American families. The lack of adequate housing and educational opportunities, higher crime and incarceration rates, inadequate health care, and higher infant mortality and deaths related to cancer and other disease within African American communities may be tied both directly and indirectly to the inadequate resources within the African American family. The overrepresentation of African American males in unemployment and underemployment statistics is also a result of racial barriers to employment.

This report focuses on only those studies in which both husbands and wives were present. As Staples (1971b) has correctly asked, "Who does the female in single-parent households dominate if no man is around?" African American married couples, according to the Bureau of the Census (cited in Rix, 1990, pp. 350-398), make up 51% of the African American population. Female-headed families make up an additional 43%, and male-headed families make up 6% of the families. Married-couple African American families had a median income in 1985 that was nearly triple the median income of families headed by a woman alone—$27,182 versus $9,710 in 1986. The exclusion of female-headed households here is an attempt to control for extremes in economic influences as well as family structural differences (H. P. McAdoo, 1990).

Literature Review

Resource theory posits that family decision making is highly dependent on who has the greater economic resources within the family. Historically, in American culture, the husband was seen as the provider and was assumed to dominate decision making in all aspects of family life because of his position. Proponents of this economically based theory have noted three indices of success in the community that influence power differentials within the family: (a) The higher the husband's occupational prestige, the greater his voice in marital decisions; (b) the higher the husband's income, the greater his power; and (c) the higher the husband's status based on occupation, income, education, and ethnic background, the more power he has to make decisions (Gillespie, 1971).

Modern proponents of the theory have modified it to include the notion of exchanges. This theory suggests that marriages are maintained by a balance of resources controlled by each partner and needed by the other (Sexton & Perlman, 1989). Thus the greater the equity in the performance of family roles, the greater the equity in marital power. In addition, perception of shared power is as important in determining marital power as are actual resources exchanged. It is interesting to note that this change in theoretical orientation came about as a result of increased participation of white women in the labor market.

An extension of the theory to add the concept of cooperation could lead to a better understanding of the way power or social relationships are organized within African American families. At present, this point of view suggests that families who are denied resources, who find themselves denied equal access to occupational and educational opportunities and forced to concentrate continuously on survival, are in no condition to compete internally for power.

While there is considerable criticism of the way family power is measured, most studies continue to ask both the wife and husband who makes the final decisions in eight areas of family life: what job the husband would take, what car to buy, whether or not to buy life insurance, where to go on vacation, what house or apartment to take, what job the wife should take, what doctor to use when someone in the family is sick, and how much money the family should spend on food (Blood & Wolfe, 1960). These questions have been used along with others to determine the degree of power that each member of an African American family has in the relationship.

Hyman and Reed (1969) reexamined the results from three national surveys for evidence of the dominance of wives in the lives of African American families. They examined data from the cross-national inquiry on civic culture done by the National Opinion Research Center in 1960 regarding who made decisions in the family of origin and in the respondent's own families if married; the 1951 Gallup Poll, which included a question on which parent had been influential in childhood; and the Survey Research Center's 1965 study on political socialization of high school seniors to determine the relative influence of two parents on decision making. All of the surveys contained both African American and white respondents. In all three surveys, the actual white pattern of responses was almost identical to that of African American families. The pattern of wives' influences in the decision-making process had increased in both groups.

Hyman and Reed attribute ethnic spousal differences found in these studies to a pseudocomparative design or fictitious comparison, in which the comparative data for paternal dominance in decision making for whites were imputed on the basis of the analysts' beliefs rather than measurement. One questions why, in light of a study completed more than 30 years ago, non-African American researchers, in the absence of data, continue to express the belief that patterns of decision making in African American and white families are different and to imply that these differences are the reasons for the problems experienced by African American families.

Blood and Wolfe (1960) interviewed a small number of African American wives and found that African American families were different because the responses of the wives, who were alleged to claim being the dominant power, indicated that the family power patterns deviated from the cultural norm of father domination or equality in decision making. However, a reanalysis of Blood and Wolfe's data indicated no significant differences in African American and white responses to the questions related to who made the final decisions in the family.

Mainstream researchers in the past have focused on the most economically depressed, most problematic of African American family structures and suggested that the outcomes found were representative of all African American families, regardless of socioeconomic status and income (J. L. McAdoo, 1988). This apparent racial bias in sample selection and inability to control for social class or economic resources by these researchers lend some credibility to the belief in some African American communities that social science is used to justify and maintain the status quo.

What have African American researchers to say about the decision-making process in African American families? Several researchers have used Blood and Wolfe's (1960) questions in conducting studies related to decision making in families. All asked each spouse separately to respond to the questions. A few had spouses either play a game where decisions were reached or asked questions about the reasons for joint decision making or both, allowing either of the spouses to make the final decision. Some had the families discuss the reasons for differences in their separate choices in terms of decision making.

Middleton and Putney (1960), in a comparative study of 40 middle- and working-class African Americans and whites, found that the normative decision-making response was egalitarian for both groups. The researchers had spouses fill out questionnaires separately and then asked them to compare their responses; if either spouse changed responses on two-thirds of the items, the family was labeled patriarchal or matriarchal, depending on which spouse made the changes. If either spouse made at least one-third but less than two-thirds of the decisions, the family was labeled egalitarian. Working- and middle-class African American husbands were found to win as often as their wives in a majority of the families. African American families were found to be slightly, although not significantly, more egalitarian than white families.

Mack (1978a), in a partial replication of the Putney and Middleton study, evaluated 80 couples using the Blood and Wolfe questionnaire. She also controlled for ethnic group and social class. She found that, regardless of race, working-class husbands reported significantly more decision-making power than did middle-class husbands. In an evaluation of time each spouse spent in discussing an issue, no gender, race, or class differences were noted. Both middle- and working-class African American and white husbands tended to perceive themselves as the slightly more dominant partner in the marriage. Middle-class African American and middle- and working-class white mothers also saw their spouses as slightly more dominant in the relationship. However, African American lower-class mothers perceived themselves as the most dominant.

In a study of power relationships in 52 economically secure working-class African American families, Hammond and Enoch (1976) noted that both the spouses indicated an overall egalitarian decision-making pattern. Husbands seemed to have more say in what job the husband was to take and what car to buy.

Hammond and Enoch (1976) also did a comparative analysis of their Memphis study, Blood and Wolfe's (1960) Detroit study, and Centers, Raven, and Rodrigues's (1971) study of families in Los Angeles. While all of the Memphis subjects were African American, only 10% of the Centers et al. study were African American. However, about 62% of the Detroit and Los Angeles samples were working-class. Hammond and Enoch's findings suggest a similarity of decision-making responses across all three groups. African American and white families, regardless of social class, reported themselves to be egalitarian in family decision style. Evaluations of occupational level, spousal employment, and relative status difference revealed no differences in spousal evaluations of family power.

Hammond and Enoch's (1976) findings provide some additional support for Willie and Greenblatt's (1978) case studies, which found the overall pattern of middle- and working-class spouses to be egalitarian. Willie and Greenblatt noted that middle-class spouses acted as partners out of necessity and developed an egalitarian pattern of interaction in which neither spouse has ultimate authority. Working-class families felt that cooperation was basic to their survival as a family unit, and their egalitarian way of making decisions was based upon this. However, each spouse had assigned roles that could change during stress or in times of family crisis.

Non-African American researchers have also reported no differences among African American and ethnic groups. Cromwell and Cromwell (1978) found both husbands and wives reporting equality in decision making in 450 African American, Chicano, and white families. They found that African American families tended to disagree on who had the power: 25% of the wives reported matriarchal decision structures, but only 9% of their spouses agreed with them. Husbands perceived themselves as more dominant than their wives perceived them to be, and wives perceived themselves as more dominant than their husbands perceived them to be across ethnic groups. Finally, although there were spousal differences in reporting, the subjects did not support the notion of masculine dominance in decision making across ethnic groups.

Grey-Little (1982), in a study of marital quality and power processes among African American couples, found no significant gender differences in the impact of power patterns and global marital quality. A significantly greater proportion ($p < .001$) described their marriage as husband-led. In comparing husband-led, wife-led, and egalitarian families, husband-led families were found to be higher in marital satisfaction and positive regard, and reciprocity subscale scores for families, followed by egalitarian-led families. The wives in wife-led families were found to be least satisfied with their marriages.

Very few studies have evaluated the relationship between family power and marital satisfaction. Zollar and Williams (1987) found, in evaluating data collected in 1972 and 1984 for the National Opinion Survey, that African Americans who were married were more satisfied with their lives than those who were not. Married women were generally more satisfied than men. Thomas (1990) explored the determinants of global life happiness and marital happiness in dual-career African American couples. Almost 98% of respondents, both men and women, were found to be either somewhat or very happy with their marriages.

A large majority of the couples were happy with their friendships, their relationships with their children and each other, their marital condition, and their health. Many of the spouses expressed satisfaction with finances, work and career, leisure activities, and the communities they lived in.

In summary, the data from both small and large samples across socioeconomic status and geographic location indicate that decision-making patterns, power relationships, and marital satisfaction for African American families resemble those of white families. The patterns may be similar within socioeconomic status and/or gender. Very few matriarchal families were seen in the studies reviewed here, and the few that identified such a family decision pattern had conflicting spousal reports.

The questions I want to answer in this report are as follows: To what extent do African American husbands and wives in this sample perceive their family power structure differently? What is the relationship between perceived family power, marital satisfaction, and self-esteem in these families?

Sample

A total of 40 middle-income African American families living in the Baltimore-Washington, D.C., metropolitan area were invited to participate in the study. Married couples were selected if both spouses were African American, both were employed, and they had at least one child under the age of 18 in the home. The subjects were interviewed in their own homes. Gender bias in the interviewing process was controlled by using same-gender interviewers.

Each spouse was interviewed separately on questions related to life satisfaction and self-esteem using the Blood and Wolfe questions. The scoring for each question was as follows: 1 = father always and father more than mother decides in most cases, 3 = both spouses share equally in the decision, and 5 = mother always and mother more than father decides in most cases. In addition, subjects were asked how satisfied they were with their spouses and their marriages. The responses ranged from very satisfied to very unsatisfied.

Interviewers also used the Rosenberg (1965) self-esteem scale, which asks respondents whether they strongly agree, agree, disagree, or strongly disagree with 10 statements such as "On the whole, I am satisfied with myself." A high score on the scale indicates that subjects have high regard for themselves, or high self-esteem, which, according to Rosenberg, simply means that the individuals respect themselves and consider themselves worthy. It does not mean that they consider themselves to be any better or worse than others; rather, individuals with high self-esteem recognize their own limitations and have some expectation that they will grow and improve.

Findings

In response to questions related to global satisfaction with the marriage, husbands' and wives' responses were similar—97% of the subjects reported being satisfied with their spouses, and 85% were either very satisfied or satisfied with their marital and family lives. A total of 80% of the spouses reported that they had good relationships with their spouses.

When spouses were asked to list the positive aspects of their marital relationships, they mentioned having a companion (34%), friendship (34%), mutual support (34%), communication (31%), similarity in goals and interest (13%), religion (13%), and trust and mutual respect (9%).

When wives and husbands in this sample were asked to explain their feelings about their family life, 34% felt that the relationship was loving, supportive, and comfortable; 31% were very satisfied with their marriage because their children were rewarding; and 21% had similar goals in the marriage. Only 6% of the spouses reported being unhappy with the marital relationship because of marital disagreements and perceived lack of respect. One spouse reported that work-related problems interfered with his marital happiness, and another reported that lack of a positive social life made marital life unsatisfactory for her.

The spouses were asked separately about family decision making to determine any differences in their perceptions as to who made the decisions. As to decisions about what car to buy, the husbands' mean response of 2.5 and the wives' mean response of 2.7 indicated that both felt the decision was made jointly. In contrast, both the husbands (mean = 1.8) and the wives (mean = 1.9) agreed that the husbands made the final decisions about what jobs they would take. Both the husbands (mean = 3.4) and the wives (mean = 3.8) agreed that they would jointly decide whether the wives would work. No significant gender differences were found in the responses.

The husbands' and wives' responses to decision questions related to what insurance to buy (mean = 2.8), what house to buy (mean = 3.0), which doctor to see (mean = 3.8), what to do when illness occurs (mean

= 3.67), how to spend food money (mean = 3.2), what television programs to watch (mean = 3.2), children's jobs (mean = 3.5), and children's curfew (mean = 3.1) were all in the egalitarian range. No significant gender differences were found in any of the questions. Wives (mean = 4.0) saw themselves as slightly more likely than their husbands (mean = 3.8) to make decisions related to birth control. However, the difference was nonsignificant.

In summary, the African American spouses in this study shared equally in the major decisions in the family. Their responses were similar to the findings of TenHouten (1970), Mack (1978a), Hammond and Enoch (1976) and Willie and Greenblatt (1978). No significant gender differences were found in the total decision-making score of the sample. More than 90% of the sample were very satisfied on the global measure of marital satisfaction. This finding was similar to the findings of Zollar and Williams (1987).

In response to questions about the spouses' self-esteem, no gender differences were found. Both the husbands' (mean = 14) and the wives' (mean = 13) scores were in the moderately high positive range. The overwhelming majority of African American husbands and wives indicated that elements of cooperation, mutual support, communication, trust, and mutual respect were the most positive aspects of their marital relationships.

Conclusion

African American families have been found across several studies to exhibit the same kinds of family decision-making patterns as families of other ethnic groups. There appear to be no significant social class and few gender differences in African Americans' egalitarian family pattern. African American families were found to be satisfied with their marital lives regardless of family decision-making styles. The families in this study also valued themselves highly within their marital relationships. While all of the studies discussed here were small, the sampling across the nation can lead us to have some confidence that the conclusions reached would not be significantly different from the family decision patterns of other ethnic groups.

Mainstream social scientists, on the other hand, have interpreted the similar ethnic group findings differently, sometimes negatively. It has been suggested that the conceptual framework of either choice and exchange or resource theory has led some social scientists to biased interpretations based on the assumption that one group has to be on the bottom, or has to lose, in any exchange of resources. Further, social scientists have assumed that the decision-making responses in families would be different between white ethnics at the top and African Americans at the bottom of the economic ladder. However, no empirical studies have been found that provide support for these assumptions related to African American families.

The study presented here has demonstrated that African Americans, perhaps because of limited resources, tend to be more cooperative than other groups in their relationships and decision-making patterns. The families in this study felt good about themselves individually and their marital relationships, regardless of the pattern of decision making that took place in the family. There appeared to be a high emphasis on shared decision making and responsibility.

The findings in this and other studies of decision making and marital satisfaction suggest a need for a theoretical framework that encompasses an understanding of the context in which ethnic families function, their decision making, and a broader range of relational patterns. However, it would appear that a theoretical framework may be only as useful as the ability of the observer to control his or her own bias in doing research on or providing therapy to families that may be ethnically different from the observer.

What the findings in this and other studies on African American families suggest to family theorists, family researchers, family sociologists, and others who study the family is that we need to take some care in studying African Americans and any other ethnic group to eliminate political and social bias in interpretation of behaviors, attitudes, and beliefs. The exploration of values and history of the transformation of the culture of any ethnic group may help to provide a more positive context for understanding that culture and the people who are most influenced by it.

Finally, we need to identify and understand universal trends across ethnic groups and study those areas that are peculiar to particular ethnic groups. For African Americans, the cultural value of cooperation in decision making, while a strong cultural imperative, may turn out to be a universal pattern that they have operationalized to help them survive and thrive within the American community.

7

The Impact of Economic Marginality Among African American Husbands and Fathers

PHILLIP J. BOWMAN

Throughout African American history, the quality of family life among Black fathers has largely depended on their ability to cope with discouraging family role barriers—especially as economic providers (Frazier, 1939; Gutman, 1977; Staples, 1982; Wilkinson & Taylor, 1977). These researchers show that many Black fathers, even during chattel slavery, managed to respond in adaptive ways despite structural barriers to responsible family roles.

In recent years there has been an impressive upsurge of research attempting to remove a serious blind spot in existing literature by investigating the family roles of Black husband-fathers who remain with their families. Focusing primarily on middle-income families, researchers have begun to document systematically the high level of involvement among Black husband-fathers in child rearing (Allen, 1981), nurturant interactions with children (J. L. McAdoo, 1988), family decision making (Mack, 1978b; Staples, 1976; Willie & Greenblatt, 1978), and the economic provider role (Cazenave, 1979). These studies indeed provide valuable descriptive findings on Black husband-fathers. More theory-oriented empirical research on representative samples is needed to clarify factors that threaten and promote the quality of their family life.

Past studies suggest that persistent economic marginality among Black fathers may not only erode perceptions of family life quality, but may also be a pivotal risk factor for the growing numbers who become dislocated from their children and families (Farley & Allen, 1987; Liebow, 1967; Marsiglio, 1987; Wilson, 1987). An ongoing program of research seeks to provide additional insight into economic marginality, adaptive cultural resources, and family life quality among Black husband-fathers in a national sample (Bowman, 1988, 1989, 1990c).

Until recently, father absence was not the statistical norm in African American communities. The majority of Black households with children under 18 years old were two-parent families until the 1980s (Glick, 1988; Gutman, 1977), but this is now changing. Black families with children are now more likely than other families to have no husband-father present.

Most existing studies on Black fathers, unfortunately, have emphasized the pervasiveness of maladaptive responses to familial role difficulties (e.g., Bowman, 1989; Evans & Whitfield, 1988; Gary, 1981). This literature has tended to depict Black fathers as absent from their children's households (Burton & Whiting, 1961; Earl & Lohman, 1978; Hetherington, 1966), marginally involved in familial roles (Liebow, 1967; Rainwater, 1966; Scanzoni, 1975), or otherwise pathological (Anderson, 1989; Moynihan, 1965; Rubin, 1974; Shin, 1978).

The Research Model

The general conceptual orientation to the present study is presented schematically in Figure 7.1. This social psychological model focuses on structured economic marginality experienced by Black fathers as the major precursor of provider role strain (arrow A). In turn, both objective and subjective aspects of provider role strain threaten the quality of their family lives (arrows A and B). Hence emphasis is placed on the harmful psychosocial effects of specific dimensions of chronic provider role strain that are rooted in macroeconomic inequalities. A second notion is that intergenerational ethnic patterns often reaffirm adaptive cultural resources among African Americans, which, in turn, can enhance their family life quality and psychological well-being (arrows C and D). Therefore, among economically marginal Black fathers faced with chronic provider role difficulty, the retention of cultural resources may help them to maintain more satisfying family lives.

Next, background literature that supports this research model is briefly highlighted, followed by the presentation of methods and descriptive results for the present study. In addition to the descriptive

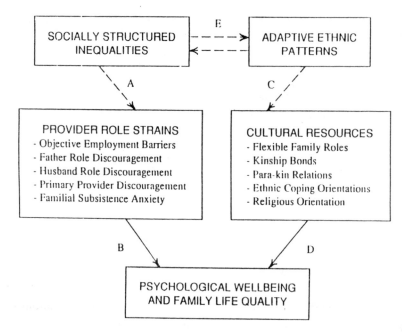

Figure 7.1. Interrelationships Among Major Classes of Variables in Provider Role Strain-Cultural Resource Model

findings, a related discussion also considers ongoing theory-oriented research and practical implications.

Economic Marginality

Since the transition from slave to free labor, economically marginal Black fathers have experienced particular difficulty in the family provider role (Frazier, 1939; Gary, 1981; Wilkinson & Taylor, 1977). However, the specific structural sources of their economic marginality have shifted systematically over the years. During earlier historical periods, the provider role difficulty of Black fathers stemmed primarily from enslavement, followed by underemployment in low-paying sectors of dual agricultural and industrial labor markets (Du Bois, 1903; Frazier, 1939; Gutman, 1977). Increasingly, however, the problem of Black male underemployment is compounded by chronic joblessness as unskilled manufacturing and operative jobs are rapidly eliminated by postindustrial technological change (Bowman, 1988). Thus, despite gains from the civil rights movement, chronic joblessness continues to exacerbate the economic marginality of Black fathers in the final decades of the twentieth century (Wilson, 1978, 1987). Growing joblessness has also dampened optimism that early twentieth-century industrialization would provide the necessary opportunity for Black fathers to assume greater economic responsibility within their families.

As we approach the twenty-first century, national employment trends make Frazier's (1939) early vision increasingly unlikely. The rapid displacement of unskilled industrial jobs is directly linked to alarming increases in chronic unemployment, job search discouragement, and labor market dropout rates among Black males (Bowman, 1988; Wilson, 1978). Black men are hit hardest because they have disproportionately depended on the most vulnerable manufacturing jobs for their economic livelihood for a half century. As Black male joblessness has increased, there has been a systematic decline in both the number of husband-wife families and the number of teenaged mothers who marry within Black America (Farley & Allen, 1987; Wilson, 1987). These correlations do not warrant a conclusive causal interpretation, but more definitive tests of a causal hypothesis have important theoretical as well as social policy implications. It appears quite plausible that growing joblessness among Black fathers may not only promote intrafamilial strains, but also increase the dissolution of existing husband-wife families and discourage new marriages for the next generation.

Family Provider Role Values

Strong personal values for the family provider role among fathers of all races may intensify the level of strain and distress produced when performance difficulty occurs (Hood, 1986). Studies have shown that the family provider role has a very high valence within the masculine identities of both middle-income (Cazenave, 1979) and low-income (Liebow, 1967) Black fathers. Cazenave (1979) found that, for his sample of middle-income letter carriers, being a man meant first and foremost taking care of one's family as a responsible husband and father. This salient aspect of masculine identity was associated with the virtues of hard work, ambition, firm guiding principles, and warm emotional investment in other areas of family life.

Liebow's (1967) widely cited study of economically marginal Black men found that high aspirations in the family provider role were not limited to working-class fathers. Most of the Black males in his restricted sample of "street corner men" married early, "with high hopes of becoming good family providers, husbands, and fathers; but they failed, at first financially and then emotionally." Liebow also notes that when "the father lives with his own children, his occasional touch or other tender gesture is dwarfed by his current obligations. No matter how much he does, it is not enough" (p. 87). A more recent study revealed that unmarried Black fathers of children born to teenaged mothers expressed strong commitments to responsible fatherhood, but economic barriers often frustrated their provider role performance (Marsiglio, 1987).

Although based on small, unrepresentative samples, the foregoing studies clearly support the salience of the family provider role for Black fathers regardless of social class standing. The most pressing issue for future research has been raised by Cazenave (1981) in a critical review of existing literature: "What happens to Black men who accept society's notion of what it takes to be a man but are denied the resources to 'earn' their masculinity through traditional channels?" (p. 77). Cazenave refers to this as a "double bind," and the related concept of provider role strain provides the basis for a coherent theoretical model to guide future research and intervention.

Provider Role Strain

For greater conceptual clarity and specificity, provider role research on Black fathers can build on a diverse role strain-adaptation literature (Bowman, 1988, 1989; Cohn, 1978; Merton, 1968; Pearlin, 1983). In this context, provider role strain involves performance difficulty, which may have multiple causes, but is sometimes structurally built into the family provider role. Provider role strain includes both objective difficulty and subjective reactions to such difficulty, which impede the achievement of valued goals. The basic premise is that Black fathers and husbands want to be responsible providers but this may not always be easy and has sometimes even been impossible. However, their perceptions of and reactions to discouraging provider role barriers may distinguish maladaptive from more adaptive modes of coping. Historically, despite a salient value for the primary family provider role in their masculine identities, economic marginality has more often made it difficult for Black fathers to fulfill such expectations.

In contrast to psychological approaches, early sociological formulations emphasized the structural determinants and consequences of role strain. For example, Merton's (1968) theory of anomie emphasized maladaptive social structural consequences of chronic strain in major life roles. In Goode's (1960) model, institutional processes shape interpersonal mechanisms through which perceived role strain is produced; he also proposed that interpersonal role bargains can be negotiated to reduce perceived strain and societal discord. More recently, psychologists have begun to examine negative emotional consequences of chronic role strain, as well as how various personal resources and strategies facilitate individual coping (Baruch & Barnett, 1986; Kahn, Wolfe, Quinn, Snoek, & Rosenthal, 1964; Pearlin, 1983). Building on existing studies, an ongoing program of research seeks to provide new insight into the social psychology of role strain and adaptation of African American males (Bowman, 1984, 1988, 1990b, 1990c). The central goals are to investigate systematically (a) how objective and subjective aspects of role strain exacerbate maladaptive psychosocial consequences of structured inequalities, and (b) how cultural resources, related cognitive strategies, and developmental variables facilitate more adaptive modes of coping.

Adaptive Ethnic Resources

The conceptual model in Figure 7.1 emphasizes the adaptive influence of ethnic or cultural resources among economically marginal Black fathers faced with growing provider role strain. As depicted by arrow E, intergenerational ethnic patterns are viewed as both outcomes (strategic adaptations) and causal factors (reciprocal agents of changes) in shifting racial inequalities. Researchers generally agree that the distinct form of familial, religious, and other ethnic or cultural resources within Black communities is, to some degree, a response to economic inequality (Billingsley, 1968; Frazier, 1939; Hill, 1972). However, several scholars suggest that cultural resources such as extended kinship structures, flexibility of family roles, strong kinship bonds, spiritual beliefs, and ethnic coping orientations also reflect authentic African traditions (Du Bois, 1908/1969; Herskovits, 1941; Nobles, 1974, 1988; Sudarkasa, 1988). According to these Africentrists, such cultural resources represent distinct African forms that have merely been adapted to meet the shifting exigencies of American life. Regardless of debates about their origin, African American cultural resources appear to be transmitted systematically from one generation to the next (e.g., Bowman & Howard, 1985; Martin & Martin, 1978). Moreover, studies document the adaptive utility of such cultural resources in promoting both social structural changes (Morris, 1984) and familial and individual coping (Hill, 1972; R. Jones, 1980; H. P. McAdoo, 1988; Stack, 1974).

The Present Study

Guided by the foregoing research model, descriptive findings are presented in this chapter from a national sample of Black husband-fathers who remain with their families. The use of national probability data permits analyses that go beyond studies based on small, unrepresentative samples. These national data provide more accurate estimates of economic, cultural, and family life variables among Black husband-fathers throughout the entire United States. A social psychological approach looks beyond objective economic marginality to also explore provider role perceptions and subjective cultural strengths as well as family life satisfaction. Are Black husband-fathers more likely to be employed than unmarried fathers or husbands without children? Do husband-fathers perceive their efforts to be responsible family providers as successful, or have large numbers become discouraged? To what extent have they retained adaptive cultural resources that may help them cope with discouraging provider role difficulty? Compared with other Black men or women, how satisfied are Black husband-fathers with their family lives?

Methods

The data analyzed to investigate the above questions were collected in a cross-sectional survey of the Black adult population living in the continental United States (Bowman, 1983; Jackson & Gurin, 1987; Jackson, Tucker, & Bowman, 1990). This national survey was conducted by researchers at the University of Michigan's Institute for Social Research based on a rigorous multistage, area probability sampling design (Kish, 1965). The procedure was carefully implemented to ensure that every Black household in the nation had the same chance of being selected for the interview. Specialized screening techniques helped produce a sample that more accurately represents all noninstitutionalized Black adults than in past studies. During 1979-1980, highly trained interviewers matched on race and other characteristics completed 2,107 face-to-face interviews, with an overall response rate of 67.1%. In line with the African American population, the majority of the sample resided in the South (53%), followed by the North Central region (22%), the Northeast (19%), and the West (6%). A full 80% of the sample was made up of urban residents; 20% lived in rural areas. Respondents ranged in age from 18 to 101 years, and included 1,310 females and 797 males. An extensive 2-hour interview schedule was used to collect data in several major areas: social background, employment experience, support networks, life stress, psychological well-being, and health. Despite the use of many single-item indicators, several specialized techniques enhanced the meaningfulness of these measures. Focus group and back translation procedures helped in the development of more culturally sensitive indicators; moreover, a series of pretest and random probe procedures further improved the quality of each measure. Data from the subsample of 372 Black men who were both fathers and husbands are the major focus of this study.

Results

Provider Role Strain: Objective and Subjective Indicators

Does employment-unemployment status differentiate Black husband-fathers from unmarried fathers or those without children? As shown in Table 7.1, married men in the national sample were clearly the most likely to have jobs; this was true for both husband-fathers (75%) and husbands with no children (77%). By contrast, unmarried fathers (58%) and women, regardless of marital and parental status (between 59% and 48%), were most often jobless. Hence, among Black fathers, joblessness appears to be a major factor distinguishing the growing numbers of unmarried fathers from traditional husband-fathers. Unmarried fathers, as well as unmarried mothers, were the most likely to be unemployed, which indicates that they were jobless but actively seeking or interested in work. Women with no children, regardless of marital status, were least active in the labor force, with more than one in four reporting no interest in a job (because of being a homemaker, a student, retired, or the like).

What are the role perceptions of Black husband-fathers as they strive to fulfill expectations as responsible family providers? Despite the relatively low level of joblessness, pervasive underemployment in low-paying jobs may still restrict successful provider role functioning among Black husband-fathers. How much do these husband-fathers worry about their families' ability to meet expenses and bills? Do they perceive

Table 7.1 Comparisons of Black Husband-Fathers and Other Population Subgroups on Employment Status (in percentages)

| | Men | | | | Women | | | |
| | Fathers | | No Children | | Mothers | | No Children | |
Employment Status	Married (N = 372)	Single (N = 202)	Married (N = 47)	Single (N = 162)	Married (N = 390)	Single (N = 607)	Married (N = 62)	Single (N = 227)
Employed	75	58	77	65	59	50	56	48
Unemployed	12	31	2	27	26	34	18	25
Not interested in job	13	11	21	9	14	16	26	27
Total	100	100	100	100	100	100	100	100

128

themselves as successful primary family providers or as adequate providers for their wives or children? About 60% of husband-fathers in this national sample worried at least "a little" about their families' economic hardships, with 16% reporting that they worried "a great deal" (Table 7.2). Many husband-fathers felt that they had done no better than "fairly well" as primary family providers (40%), as responsible husbands (29%), and as successful fathers (23%). However, it is also important to note that 60%, 71%, and 77%, respectively, felt that they had done "very well" as primary providers, husbands, and fathers.

Adaptive Ethnic Resources: Objective and Subjective Indicators

To what extent do Black husband-fathers retain adaptive cultural resources as a source of empowerment in the face of discouraging provider role difficulties? Table 7.3 presents data on five cultural patterns that may be important resources for Black husband-fathers as they strive to cope with underemployment, growing joblessness, and provider role difficulties. Husband-fathers were asked questions about the flexibility of their family roles as indicated by the objective presence of multiple economic providers. In addition, questions also focused on subjective cultural resources such as the perceived closeness of family bonds, para-kin friendship bonds, racial consciousness or system-blame ideology, and religious beliefs. About two in every three Black husband-fathers lived in households with at least two earners (64%). Moreover, a similar proportion perceived their families as being very close (63%), retained strong para-kin friendships (67%), and expressed a consciousness of racial barriers (68%). Most striking, a full 84% reported being at least "fairly" religious, with 37% confessing a "very high" level of religious commitment.

Family Life Satisfaction

Are Black husband-fathers more satisfied with their family lives than other Black men or women? As revealed in Table 7.4, more than half of the husband-fathers were "very satisfied" with their family lives (57%). Husband-father family life satisfaction is similar to that among unmarried fathers (52%) and all other comparison groups except married Black men with no children (77%). Apparently, having a job and a wife, but no stress related to providing for and raising children, may elevate family life satisfaction. However, among most Black men who do father children, we need a better understanding of (a) how objective and subjective aspects of provider role strain operate to erode the quality of

Table 7.2 Distribution of Black Husband-Fathers on Provider Role Indicators

	N	%
Family subsistence anxiety: How much do you worry that your total family income will not meet your family's expenses and bills?		
not at all	139	40
a little	121	34
a lot	35	10
a great deal	57	16
total	352	100
Primary family provider role: Given the chances you have had, how well have you done in taking care of your family's wants and needs?		
very well	210	60
fairly well	130	37
not too well	12	3
total	352	100
Husband role: Given the chances you have had, how well have you done at being a good husband to your wife?		
very well	250	71
fairly well	102	29
not too well	0	0
total	352	100
Father role: Given the chances you have had, how well have you done at being a good father to your children?		
very well	271	77
fairly well	81	23
not too well	0	0
total	352	100

family life and (b) the manner in which the retention of objective and subjective cultural strengths may facilitate adaptive coping with discouraging provider role barriers.

Summary and Implications

As increasing numbers of jobless Black fathers face difficulty as family providers, research on husband-fathers who somehow manage

Table 7.3 Distribution of Black Husband-Fathers on Sociocultural Indicators

	N	%
Multiple family providers: How many people in your household, including yourself, give money to support your household?		
one	128	36
two	209	59
three or more	19	5
total	356	100
Cohesive familial bonds: Would you say your family members are very close in their feelings to each other, fairly close, not too close, or not close at all?		
not too close	19	5
fairly close	112	32
very close	226	63
total	356	100
Para-kin friendship bond: Not counting your wife, do you have a best friend? Do you have any friends that you feel very close to?		
no close friend	63	18
close friend	53	15
best friend	240	67
total	356	100
Racial consciousness: In this country if black people do not get a good education or job, it is because (1) they have no one to blame but themselves, or (2) they haven't had the same chances as whites in this country?		
blame Blacks themselves	115	32
blame racial barriers	240	68
total	355	100
Religious orientation: How religious would you say you are—very religious, fairly religious, not too religious, or not religious at all?		
not too religious	56	16
fairly religious	169	47
very religious	131	37
total	356	100

to succeed in the provider role becomes more crucial. The rapid growth in unskilled industrial jobs during the first half of the twentieth century provided unprecedented opportunities for Black fathers to become responsible economic providers for their families. However, as automation

Table 7.4 Comparisons of Black Husband-Fathers and Other Population Subgroups on Family Life Satisfaction (percentage)

| | Men | | | | Women | | | |
| | Fathers | | No Children | | Mothers | | No Children | |
	Married (N = 372)	Single (N = 202)	Married (N = 47)	Single (N = 162)	Married (N = 390)	Single (N = 607)	Married (N = 62)	Single (N = 227)
Very satisfied with family life	57	52	77	43	50	51	52	60

continues to displace unskilled industrial jobs, growing numbers of Black fathers must cope with chronic joblessness and related provider role strain (Bowman, 1988). Traditional literature on Black fathers has primarily focused on the family deserters, the irresponsible or pathological fathers. Because of this negative literature, we currently know very little about Black husband-fathers who somehow manage to remain responsible family providers despite adversity.

This national study of Black husband-fathers provides a descriptive profile as a basis for ongoing hypothesis-testing research, theory building, and intervention. Results represent accurate estimates of the economic status, provider role perceptions, cultural strengths, and family life satisfaction among husband-fathers throughout the nation. More than half of the fathers in the national sample were also husbands, but their numbers continue to decrease as they are replaced by unmarried fathers who face more severe economic marginality (Bowman, 1988; Cross, 1985).

Research Directions

Research on Black husband-fathers can provide valuable insight into the nature, antecedents, and consequences of success as well as failure in the family provider role (Bowman, 1990b, 1990c; Cazenave, 1979; Taylor, Leashore, & Tolliver, 1988). Compared with Black husband-fathers, unmarried fathers and single men without children were clearly more economically marginal. Therefore, the general tendency for Black husband-fathers to perceive themselves as effective primary providers may indeed reflect their relative employment success compared with unmarried Black fathers. Moreover, provider role efficacy among employed Black fathers may encourage more active involvement in other areas of family life and further reinforce their sense of family life satisfaction (Allen, 1981; J. L. McAdoo, 1988; Willie & Greenblatt, 1978).

Future inquiry needs to unravel the links joining provider role perceptions, masculine identity, family satisfaction, and psychological well-being among both married and unmarried fathers (Cazenave, 1979, 1981). Because of the growing economic displacement of Black men, studies also need to clarify further the various psychosocial consequences of chronic joblessness and related provider role perceptions (Bowman, 1989). For example, the majority of husband-fathers in the national sample expressed some level of anxiety concerning family economic hardships. Moreover, a significant proportion (between 40%

and 23%) also perceived some level of difficulty as primary providers, husbands, and fathers. Does such provider role discouragement exacerbate the harmful effects of objective employment difficulty on psychological well-being or family life quality among husband-fathers? Do flexible family roles and the tendency for Black husband-fathers to retain cohesive family bonds, para-kin friendships, system-blame ideology, and strong religious beliefs facilitate adaptive coping? Are these adaptive cultural strengths equally helpful to husband-fathers who remain with their families and the even more economically marginal unmarried fathers? Are there systematic shifts in provider role strain-cultural adaptation dynamics as Black fathers progress through the life cycle from young adulthood to old age?

Ongoing studies, based on the national sample of Black fathers utilized in this study, have begun to address these critical questions (Bowman, 1989). Three recent studies have investigated the multivariate effects of both provider role strain and cultural resource predictors on the psychosocial functioning of Black fathers (Bowman, 1990b, 1990c; Bowman & Sanders, 1989). As expected, husband-fathers who perceived success on the provider role indicators were especially happy with their lives, while those who perceived difficulty expressed a greater sense of personal unhappiness with life as a whole (Bowman, 1990c). Husband role discouragement, or perceived difficulty in the husband role, was associated with greater life unhappiness than was objective unemployment or other subjective aspects of provider role strain. With respect to cultural resources, strong religious beliefs and perceived family closeness were more powerful predictors of personal happiness than multiple family earners, having a best friend, or system-blame ideology. However, despite their protective effects, these two cultural retentions failed to offset the more powerful deleterious effects of provider role adversity.

Similar to findings on personal happiness, a second multivariate study of Black husband-fathers also found that provider role discouragement exacerbated harmful effects of objective employment difficulty on global family life satisfaction (Bowman, 1990b). However, while low personal happiness was most strongly linked to husband role discouragement, low family satisfaction was about equally associated with three other dimensions of provider role strain—objective unemployment, father role discouragement, and family subsistence anxiety. Family closeness and religious belief were the most powerful cultural resource predictors of both personal happiness and family satisfaction. However, the relative effects of these two pivotal cultural strengths were reversed for the two distinct psychosocial outcomes. Religious belief was the most powerful predictor of personal happiness, but family closeness was more important to family life satisfaction. Hence these findings suggest a resource-outcome specificity principle. Strong kinship bonds may be especially crucial for adaptive familial outcomes, while religious beliefs may be more directly linked to religion-related behaviors and psychological well-being. A related study of unmarried fathers suggests that specific provider role strain and cultural resource effects on psychosocial well-being may shift systematically as Black fathers proceed across the life cycle from early adulthood to mid-life to old age (Bowman & Sanders, 1989).

Theoretical Issues

Guided by the role strain-adaptation paradigm, theory-driven studies should build on the foregoing research to specify further any pivotal social psychological mechanisms that mediate both maladaptive and adaptive responses to provider role difficulty (Bowman, 1989, 1990b, 1990c; Bowman & Sanders, 1989; Pearlin, 1983; Sarbin & Allen, 1969).

Subjective cultural strengths, which are transmitted across generations, appear to reduce harmful effects of provider role barriers and to facilitate adaptive coping (Bowman, 1990b, 1990c). The relatively powerful effects of family closeness and religious beliefs corroborate a growing literature on indigenous cultural strengths among African Americans (e.g., Herskovits, 1941; Nobles, 1988). Future inquiry must also further clarify effects of flexible family roles, para-kin bonds, ethnic coping orientations, and other cultural strengths that have proven to have adaptive value for African Americans (Bowman, 1989; Bowman & Howard, 1985; Hill, 1972; Stack, 1974). In the absence of such cultural resources, chronic provider role difficulties may more often produce a sense of helplessness, which increases risk for maladaptive emotional, behavioral, and health problems (e.g., Miller & Norman, 1979). Studies on Black fathers that clarify how indigenous African American ethnic patterns reduce a sense of helplessness and facilitate adaptive cognitions can inform cross-cultural psychology (Triandis et al., 1980-1981). Black husband-fathers who retain cultural strengths may perceive, interpret, and process information about provider role adversity in more adaptive rather than maladaptive ways (Bowman, 1984, in press; Bowman, Jackson, Hatchett, & Gurin, 1982; Neighbors, Jackson, Bowman, & Gurin, 1983).

Studies also need to investigate how cultural resources facilitate the role adaptation process during different stages of the life cycle. Research on life-cycle antecedents and consequences of provider role difficulties among husband-fathers is especially crucial to future theory development (Bowman, 1989, 1990a; Bowman & Sanders, 1989). For example, pivotal educational role difficulties during childhood and adolescence may elevate risks for both chronic joblessness and related provider role discouragement among husband-fathers in the adult years. Persistent student role difficulties in the preadult years may impede the school-to-work transition during early adulthood, which, in turn, may lead to more serious provider role strain in middle age. Moreover, provider role failure during the middle adult years may carry over into chronic despair and related psychosocial problems as older adults reflect on their life accomplishments. Research on successive role strain and adaptation processes across the adult life cycle may provide new insight into pivotal developmental antecedents and consequences of chronic provider role strain.

Preventive Intervention

Provider role studies among Black husband-fathers can also facilitate efforts to design effective interventions and social policy. Community-based organizations have already begun to develop innovative male responsibility programs targeted at high-risk populations. In line with the maxim that "an ounce of prevention is worth a pound of cure," primary prevention efforts targeted at young Black males must continue to go beyond the mere treatment of symptoms. Culturally sensitive intervention strategies should seek to promote more constructive modes of coping with economic marginality through the mobilization of indigenous ethnic resources within African American communities. Moreover, early intervention efforts to promote achievement among preadult Black males in educational settings may be an especially cost-effective way to prevent chronic provider role problems among jobless husband-fathers.

In addition to early educational intervention, social policies that help reduce structural barriers at the macrosocial level are also necessary for comprehensive primary prevention (e.g., Bowman, 1988; Wilson, 1987). In addition to affirmative action, responsive employment/training and industrial policies can directly address the differential impact of rapid reindustrialization on chronic joblessness among displaced Black males. Policy initiatives must be comprehensive enough to address the interrelated sequels of chronic joblessness, welfare dependency, and related family provider role problems that result from rapid displacement of Black fathers within a postindustrial labor market. For example, viable work-sharing policies could encourage more cooperative family support from employed Black fathers as well as from mothers (H. P. McAdoo, 1984; Smeeding & Zill, 1990). In contrast to current welfare policies, work sharing would not weaken cooperative father-mother family bonds and would reduce the so-called feminization of family poverty. Increased financial contributions from fathers may also help reduce the unemployment crisis among their teenaged children, who too often enter the labor market prematurely because of inadequate household income within Black families. Without more informed preventive measures, the provider role difficulties that currently threaten stable Black husband-wife families may become even more devastating as we move into the twenty-first century.

PART III

Mexican and Spanish-Origin American Families

8

Hispanic Families
in the United States

Research Perspectives

CATHERINE STREET CHILMAN

The impact of the Hispanic population on American society is enormous and diverse, having many implications for family research, professional practice, and public policies. Scholars and professionals need a deeper understanding of the variety of Hispanic individuals and families in this country.

Although it is common to view all Hispanic families in this country as being similar in values, beliefs, behaviors, resources, and concerns, such sweeping assumptions are seriously erroneous (Andrade, 1982; Cortes, 1980; de Silva, 1981; Frisbie, 1986; Mirandé, 1977; Staples & Mirandé, 1980). These families are far from homogeneous; they represent a number of different national and ethnic origins, vary by social class, speak a variety of dialects, have differing histories, differ in immigration and citizenship status, and live in various regions of this country. Details about the various groups appear in later sections of this chapter.

The first part of this chapter provides general immigration and demo-graphic facts about each of the major Hispanic groups in the United States. The second section discusses some of the chief social and psychological research findings regarding these families, and the last section sketches some implications for research, clinical practice, and public policy.

Some Current Issues in Immigration

Until 1945, legal immigration to the United States was mainly governed by an act of Congress of 1924, which was amended in 1952. This used the national origin system, which favored Western Europeans over Asians and Pacific peoples. In general, there was a ratio for each nation in the world that limited immigrants to numbers proportional to the population makeup of the United States in 1920 (for example, about one-fourth of immigrants granted entry were from Great Britain). However, the independent countries of the Western Hemisphere were afforded unlimited entry under this act.

In 1965, new legislation abolished restrictions against Asian and Pacific peoples. However, it imposed limits on immigration from the Western Hemisphere, with a quota of 120,000 persons a year being established. Preference was given to those with occupational skills judged to be needed in this country (LaPorte, 1977).

Because of severe economic and political problems in their own countries, larger numbers of Hispanics have sought to enter the United States than provided for under immigration laws. Thus many illegal aliens have recently entered this country, particularly from Mexico and Central and South America. Portes (1979) holds that the current large waves of illegal immigrants, most of whom are Mexicans, could be prevented from entering the United States, but that business and industry do not want this to occur. These workers are a cheap source of labor, and the fact that they are illegal creates an advantage for their employers, because they are highly vulnerable employees.

The Immigration Reform and Control Act of 1986 offered legal status in the United States or amnesty to illegal aliens who could prove they had resided continuously in this country since before January 1, 1982. More liberal amnesty provisions were developed for agricultural workers. The amnesty program includes sanctions against employers who hire illegal aliens and provisions for stepped-up border patrol and immigration service enforcement agents. The goal is to deter further illegal immigration while offering the protection of legal status to aliens who have lived here since before January 1, 1982 (Applebome, 1988).

Aliens applying for jobs had to apply for amnesty by the end of August 1987 to be hired for work that year, but applications were low and only about half of the estimated 2 million illegal aliens in this country had applied for amnesty by January 1, 1988, even though the deadline for such application was May 1, 1988. Most observers agree that the major impediment to this application was fear that families would be broken up, because some members of a number of families lacked documentary proof that they had lived continuously in the United States since before January 1, 1982. In fact, it is probable that many family members did not live in this country before 1982 and that, of those who were here at that early date, a number probably had moved back and forth across the border. Attempts were made in Congress in 1987 to amend the legislation to protect family unity and grant amnesty to all family members if some members had gained amnesty or were eligible for it, but these amendments failed to pass.

The family issue is but one difficult aspect of the immigration problem. There are powerful economic and political pressures in countries of origin inducing immigrants to cross the border, whether these immigrants can gain legal entry or not. At the same time, many Hispanics south of the United States yearn to enter this country because of the relative economic gains and personal freedoms it appears to offer. Moreover, the long border between the countries is very difficult to police adequately, and a number of U.S. employers desire the cheap labor provided by illegal immigrants who fear discovery and deportation.

It is essential for family researchers, policy and program personnel, and practitioners to recognize the severe problems families face when they have immigrated to this country illegally. As suggested earlier, they are extremely vulnerable to employer exploitation. They also live in constant fear of discovery and are therefore difficult to reach if they need assistance. Further, they are ineligible for public aid and must rely on private sources for help. Immigration, in and of itself, poses a number of problems for families; illegal immigration severely escalates these problems.

Population Characteristics

There are difficulties in defining the term *Spanish origin*. Recognizing that census reports do contain some errors, it is helpful, nonetheless, to consider the data they present. According to these reports, there were more than 12 million persons of Spanish origin in the United States in 1979: 7.3 million Chicanos, 1.7 million Puerto Ricans, 800,000 Cubans, 800,000 Central or South Americans, and more than 1 million persons of other Spanish backgrounds. The total number of Hispanic-origin people in the United States increased by 33% between 1970 and 1979, with the fastest-growing group being Mexican—which grew by 62%. The majority of Hispanic families live in Arizona, California, Colorado,

New Mexico, Texas, Florida, and New York. These families are largely concentrated in 10 of the nation's 305 metropolitan areas, with especially large numbers in New York and Los Angeles.

Age

The median age of the Hispanic population is fairly young when compared with the remainder of the population. This difference in age level is both a result and a cause of the higher fertility rate of Hispanic families. This comparatively youthful age has a number of other implications for public policy, including the likelihood that programs for children and adolescents will have a disproportionate number of Hispanics in them.

Educational Levels

On the average, members of Hispanic families, particularly the elderly, have lower educational levels than any other population group in the United States (U.S. Bureau of the Census, 1980c). These lower levels of education for most Hispanics are partly a result of the recent migration of many of them, as well as the poverty and low levels of public education in their former countries. Continuing problems of low educational achievement for many Hispanic Americans, including children and youth, is a matter of intense concern, especially because it adversely affects their future employment opportunities.

Employment and Income

Racial discrimination is apt to be another important factor in the high rates of unemployment of those Puerto Ricans who have dark skins and are classed as nonwhites—an effect of the African, Indian, and Spanish mix of their native land. Racial discrimination, still present in the United States, often comes as a shock to immigrants who have experienced much less of this in Puerto Rico (M. Delgado, 1987).

Spanish American men and women are more apt than the rest of the population to be in blue-collar and service occupations. This is especially true for people of Mexican and Puerto Rican origin. Women are more apt than men to be in white-collar occupations. The great majority of Hispanic families live in urban areas today. There has been a massive shift away from farm employment, mostly because of the industrialization of agriculture. However, on average, there has been little advancement in occupational level.

Hispanic women are generally paid at a lower wage level than either white or African American women. This is also true for those Hispanic men who are in clerical occupations or who are factory operatives. On the other hand, Hispanic men who are in professional or managerial fields earn more, on average, than Black men in these occupations but considerably less than white males.

As of the 1980 census, more than 50% of all female-headed Hispanic families were below the poverty line, including 72% of Puerto Rican families, 49% of Chicanos, and 38% of other Hispanic families. For all groups, two-parent families with the wife in the labor force had the highest income, and one-parent families had the lowest annual income: about $25,000 for white one-parent families, $15,000 for African Americans, and $18,000 for Hispanics (U.S. Bureau of the Census, 1983a). In general, families with young children had the lowest average annual income in the nation. Overall, a large percentage of the children lived in impoverished families—a shocking and tragic fact. Minority children were in particularly adverse situations: 46% of Black families with children had incomes below the poverty line. This was the case for 39% of Hispanic families and 16% of white families. (See also the section below on implications for public policy.)

Marital Stability

The 1980 census data for five southwestern states show that rates of marital stability are about the same for Mexican Americans, Cuban Americans, and Anglo-Americans, with divorce and separation rates of about 25% for these groups (U.S. Bureau of the Census, 1980c). However, both Blacks and Puerto Ricans experienced rates of about 40%. Mexican Americans and Cuban Americans had a far lower remarriage rate than did Anglos, but the reasons for this are unknown. Interestingly, Mexican American divorce rates rise with higher levels of education for women, though the reverse tends to be true for Anglos (except for those women with graduate educations). Frisbie (1986) speculates that Mexican American women with higher levels of education tend to become more acculturated to American patterns and are, therefore, more accepting of separation and divorce; however, this may be an overly simple explanation.

Precise data regarding unmarried parenthood among Hispanic Americans tend to be missing. However, studies of unmarried adolescent mothers reveal that Hispanic girls are fairly similar to other adolescent women (*Family Planning Perspectives*, 1983). Although premarital chastity has been emphasized within the culture, this norm has been drastically eroded in recent years. Thus nonmarital intercourse and pregnancy have become increasingly common. Although the parents of pregnant teenage girls usually consider illegitimate childbearing a serious problem, they tend to welcome the baby into the family if the young woman decides to keep her child and not get married—a decision she frequently makes.

Fertility

According to the 1980 census, Hispanic women had higher birthrates than did either Blacks or Anglos; however, those rates have been declining somewhat in more recent years. For example, only a little more than one-third of the women aged 15 to 44 had three or more children in 1980, compared with almost half of this group in 1970. Estrada (1987) notes that these high rates are caused by a number of factors: the youthful age structure of the Hispanic American population, large families and high fertility rates of incoming immigrants, and traditional, though fading, negative attitudes toward birth control. These attitudes are partly associated with the fact that the huge majority of Hispanic Americans are Catholic.

Large families are most likely to be characterized by low levels of employment, education, and income. This is found for such families in most parts of the world. Therefore, although these data can be interpreted as the consequence of high fertility, analyses also show that high fertility is a result of little education, unemployment, and poverty and the hopelessness, alienation, and lack of medical care they often engender (Chilman, 1968, 1983). High fertility also tends to go with low levels of modernization and a predominantly agricultural society (Chilman, 1968). There is evidence that the birthrate for Hispanic American families is currently declining in association with rising levels of education, urbanization, and employment of Hispanic women. Increased availability of low-cost, high-quality family planning services also has been helpful, although addition of Spanish-speaking personnel to the professional staffs of such service agencies is frequently needed (J. Jones, 1985).

Language

The vast majority of Hispanics in this country are bilingual. Two-thirds of those who speak Spanish report that they also speak English well or very well (Estrada, 1987). A recent Institute of Social Research survey of Mexican American households in the Southwest and Midwest revealed that the majority of adults interviewed spoke both English and Spanish. There was general consensus among the respondents that the speaking of Spanish was very important. Most thought there ought to be bilingual education in the schools. There was a generally strong feeling of ethnic identity, with many of the younger members of the population showing a particularly enthusiastic movement in this direction (Arce, 1982).

Many of the elderly and recent immigrants speak only Spanish, and many Hispanics, in general, chiefly speak Spanish within the family. As with other immigrant groups, it is common for the children to learn English before the parents do and for family members who are mainly confined to the home (often the elderly and mothers of young children) to speak English far less well than those who are in school or employed. This can create a number of disruptive family problems and is another indication that professionals who seek to work with Hispanic families should be bilingual, so that they can converse directly with all family members (Bernal, 1982; Falicov, 1982; Garcia-Preto, 1982).

Variations by National Origin

In the discussion that follows, emphasis is placed on the family-related cultural patterns of various Hispanic American groups. There are two reasons for this emphasis: (a) most of the associated research and clinical observations reported in the literature emphasize cultural patterns and (b) these patterns are important in affecting individual and family behaviors, although not as important as much of the literature, including the following discussion, would suggest.

It is essential to recognize that cultural patterns by themselves do not determine an individual's behavior, although they may strongly affect his or her values, attitudes, and norms. Each person's behavior is also strongly affected by her or his temperament, special abilities and limitations, physical condition, age, life situation, and total developmental experience within the family and elsewhere. Moreover, the behavior of families is an outcome of the interaction of the individuals within them, plus the family's size, structure, history, developmental stage, and total situation—as well as cultural patterns.

Thus these patterns constitute one of a number of complex factors that affect familial behaviors and those of family members. For instance, Baca Zinn (1980) perceptively wrote that cultural values are important in family life, but should be studied in social context. They become fully meaningful only when they are related to historical, economic, residential, and other structural factors. Although they are important dimensions of families, they do not by themselves determine, or fully explain, family organization. Rather, one needs to study actual behaviors of families as well as their expressed beliefs (Baca Zinn, 1980, pp. 68-69). One also needs to take into account the economic resources of a family. For instance, members of an extended family may live together out of economic need rather than preference. Younger relatives may provide support for aging kin—again, more because of necessity than because of cultural norms.

The historical background of a people also influences the behavior of its members in a number of subtle and not-so-subtle ways. Among other things, history, including legends, affects the self-image of group members as well as their perceptions of people of other national origins. Thus brief historical sketches of various Hispanic groups are provided below.

Puerto Ricans

Puerto Rico was a Spanish colony from the time of its discovery by Columbus in 1493 until the United States invaded and annexed it in 1898 during the Spanish-American War (Fitzpatrick, 1981; Garcia-Preto, 1982). Although Puerto Rico gained increasing control over its own affairs during the next half century, becoming a commonwealth in 1952, real political control over the island remains in the United States today. This fact has spawned understandable resentment among Puerto Ricans, with some groups agitating for complete independence, some for statehood, and others for continued collaboration with the United States and the resulting benefits of this partnership, perceived by some as outweighing the costs. These varying positions naturally affect the attitudes of Puerto Ricans who come to the United States; it can be expected that a number would continue to harbor antipathy toward this country, with resulting barriers to acculturation.

As a people, Puerto Ricans are of many colors, from completely Negroid to completely Caucasian, and they must face the difficult problem of racial prejudice in the United States (Fitzpatrick, 1981). Poverty has been widespread in Puerto Rico, a central reason for the large migration to the continental United States. Cultural patterns are highly variable, affected by the kind of occupation pursued, the region of the island (such as isolated rural areas, farm villages, or urban areas), and social class status. Fitzpatrick (1981) cites a number of studies of family life and socialization in Puerto Rico, but most of them were carried out during the 1950s and

1960s and are therefore now rather out of date. There seems to be almost no research regarding Puerto Rican family life in this country. Thus in their discussions of the topic, both Garcia-Preto (1982) and Fitzpatrick (1981) tend to rely chiefly on clinical observations.

According to Garcia-Preto (1982), the dignity of the individual and respect for each person, regardless of her or his status, is of basic importance to most Puerto Ricans. This also pertains to respect for authority within the family as well as elsewhere. "The rules for respect are complex. For instance, Puerto Ricans think that a child who calls an adult by his or her first name is disrespectful. To make direct eye contact with strangers, especially women and children, is also unacceptable" (Garcia-Preto, 1982, p. 172). Garcia-Preto writes further that Puerto Ricans strongly favor self-control and an appearance of calm; they tend to attribute stressful situations to external factors and to express stress indirectly through somatic complaints.

Traditionally, Puerto Ricans place a high value on the family's unity, welfare, and honor. Emphasis is on commitment to the group, rather than the individual, and on familial responsibilities, including obligations to and from the extended family.

The double standard of sexual morality has been instilled as a basic value, with emphasis on modesty and virginity in women, sexual freedom among men, and, simultaneously, the obligation of men to protect the honor of the women in the family. This double standard has been considerably eroded in recent years, owing to the impact of changing cultural patterns in the United States and in Puerto Rico itself. Clearly defined sex roles have been common, but this pattern is changing, especially as more and more women find employment outside the home.

Parent-youth conflicts are observed by clinicians to be common among Puerto Rican families in the United States, especially among recent immigrants. As often happens with immigrants, traditional family values and roles are frequently challenged by children and adolescents as they seek to become completely "Americanized" in our highly individualistic, competitive society. As parents feel they are losing control, they often become more authoritarian, emphasizing responsibility, obedience, and respect toward the family. This tends to escalate the conflict, which may become particularly intense and harmful because the support of a homogeneous neighborhood and extensive family network is generally lacking—aids that had been of important assistance in their former island home (for further details, see Fitzpatrick, 1981; Garcia-Preto, 1982).

The above observations concerning Puerto Rican cultural patterns should be viewed with a certain amount of skepticism, especially with regard to Puerto Rican families in this country. As noted earlier, cultural patterns vary from group to group within Puerto Rico and also within the United States. The latter variation is strongly affected by the reasons, timing, and conditions of immigration and the region of the United States to which the immigrants came. For instance, the existence of large Puerto Rican communities within New York City and the constant movement back and forth, to and from the island, tend to reduce ready acculturation and shifts from more traditional family roles. This movement has a deep impact on the family, as it reinforces many links to the island and fosters continuous dismantling and reconstruction of family life (Rodriguez, Sanchez, & Alers, 1980). Puerto Ricans who have moved to other regions, such as in the Midwest, less readily find compatriots and may, therefore, take on American ways, including egalitarian family patterns and individualism, more quickly. However, they may also suffer more from a sense of loneliness and isolation.

As indicated earlier, Puerto Ricans, on the average, tend to have more economic, occupational, familial, and educational problems than other Hispanic groups in this country. The reasons are unclear, but such problems are probably a result of such factors as the poverty in Puerto Rico, from which they have fled; poor economic and social conditions in New York City, where most of them live; racism; lack of facility in the English language; perhaps, in some cases, a search for the more generous public assistance grants in New York as against Puerto Rico; and slow acculturation to this country because of frequent travel back and forth to the homeland.

A large percentage of Puerto Ricans in this country receive public assistance. This is partly a result of their ready eligibility for this aid because they are citizens of the United States, an outcome of Puerto Rico's status as a commonwealth of this country. This status also makes it possible for them to move readily to the U.S. mainland without immigration restrictions. Their citizenship status, in sum, confers certain privileges on them and makes them different from other Hispanic groups seeking entry to, and citizenship in, this country.

Mexican Americans

Most Mexicans are of mixed Spanish and Indian descent. Their national heritage goes back many centuries to Indian civilizations that existed before the arrival of the Spanish explorers in the early 1500s. During the seventeenth, eighteenth, and nineteenth centuries, Spain extended its rule over the region that is now Mexico, California, and the southwestern United States. Mexico finally obtained its independence from Spain in 1821, but it was a weak country with little control over its vast territory (Kraus, 1959).

The rule by the United States over what is now the American Southwest and was previously part of Mexico dates only from the Mexican War of 1848—a war that ended in victory for the United States and the acquisition of lands that now include Arizona, California, Nevada, Utah, and Wyoming. Texas, which had recently (1835) won its independence from Mexico, was annexed by the United States in 1844. Thus, for a number of Mexicans in this country, their roots in what is now American soil far predate the arrival of the Anglos (Falicov, 1982). It is natural that Indian-Spanish heritage remains strong and that many continue to have feelings of resentment toward the United States. Although some Mexican Americans have been in this country for many generations, the majority are either first- or second-generation immigrants.

Resentment toward this country has been perpetuated and, at times, strengthened by discriminatory and often exploitative behaviors by some Anglo-Americans toward many Mexicans in the United States and toward Mexico itself (Alvirez, Bean, & Williams, 1981). However, this resentment is mixed with admiration and envy of this country, which, potentially at least, offers many more opportunities than Mexico does for economic advancement.

At different time periods there have been large waves of Mexican immigration to the United States for political reasons (for example, flight from the violence of the Mexican Revolution of 1910) and for economic reasons (for example, the flight from crushing poverty and unemployment in Mexico in recent years). Most Mexican Americans in the United States continue to suffer discrimination today, with limited access to good housing, education, and jobs. They are often exploited by employers, especially if they are illegal immigrants. They also have high rates of both unemployment and early school leaving.

Although most Mexican Americans live in the Southwest, some have migrated to other parts of the country. For instance, some have lived in midwestern cities for three generations or more. As in the case of other immigrant groups, those who live near the borders of their "mother" country are less likely to acculturate readily than those who live far from their native land. For example, Mexicans who live in Chicago are more apt to become Americanized quickly than are those who live in southern Texas.

Much more has been studied and written about the family patterns of Chicanos (the appellation that many of today's Mexican Americans prefer) than any other Hispanic group in the United States. Earlier research tended to assume that Mexican and Mexican American life family patterns were essentially the same. It was generally believed that Hispanics were all highly familistic, with authoritarian, patriarchal patterns, including machismo for males and submissiveness for females. It was also held that premarital virginity and high fertility norms were characteristic of these families.

Andrade (1982) has summarized numerous studies and reports that an exaggerated supermother figure emerges from a summary of impressions of Mexican American women: the unceasingly self-sacrificing, ever-fertile woman without aspirations for herself other than to reproduce. Andrade comments that several of the investigations from which this interpretation emerged were carried out in rural settings by Anglos, many of whom were males, unfamiliar with the culture or the situation they were investigating. Notably, almost all of these studies investigated lower-class samples, thus confounding ethnicity with socioeconomic status. Moreover, samples tended to be small and nonrandom (Andrade, 1982, p. 229).

Both Andrade (1982) and Mirandé (1977, 1979) emphasize that early writings about Hispanic family patterns (especially those about the Chicanos) were quite erroneous in stressing lack of egalitarian behaviors between husbands and wives. Mirandé (1979, p. 474) proposes that the concept of the all-dominant and controlling Chicano male is largely mythical. He criticizes unfounded psychoanalytic interpretations that interpret the machismo concept as a pathological defense against the Mexican American male's feelings of inadequacy engendered by the adverse effects of discrimination and poverty. Mirandé also stresses that there are many kinds of Mexican American families, with differing culture patterns. These patterns vary in accordance with recency of immigration, place of residence, socioeconomic status, degree of intermarriage with other ethnic groups, age, urbanization, and employment of women outside the home.

According to Mirandé (1979), more recent studies have shown an egalitarian family pattern in the behaviors of urban as well as rural Chicano families. One Mexican American study project found, in both Los Angeles and San Antonio, that the families were not patriarchal, as had been frequently assumed (Grebler, Moore, & Guzman, 1973). Rigid differentiation of sex role tasks was lacking, and both men and women shared in homemaking and child rearing as needed. However, fathers tended to have a stronger role outside the family, and mothers were usually the dominant persons in the day-to-day matters of child rearing and homemaking—a point also made by Baca Zinn (1980). See also Cromwell and Cromwell (1978), Hawkes and Taylor (1975), and Staton (1972) for generally similar findings.

Mirandé (1977) describes the Chicano woman as the center of the family and the mainstay of the culture. As with many other ethnic groups, the mother tends to perpetuate the language and values of the "old country" and is usually a source of warmth and nurturance within the home.

The father is seen as the authority figure in many Chicano families. He is usually warm in his relationships with younger children, but more controlling as they get older. He often appears to be aloof and uninvolved in the details of family matters. Although he is seen by himself and others as the family leader who has power, the culture also includes a strong sense of related paternal responsibility.

Children are taught to carry family responsibilities, to prize family unity, and to respect their elders. However, the peer group becomes very important to adolescent boys as they grow older. Traditionally, girls stay at home with their mothers until marriage, but Chicanas (Mexican American females) today are struggling for greater equality with both men and Anglos. They wish to keep their ethnic identity, but they also desire more flexibility in family and other roles.

The culture also emphasizes the family as a basic source of emotional support, especially for children. Support is provided not only by the parents, but also by grandparents, uncles, aunts, cousins, and friends. For example, although there has been a great deal of rural-urban migration among Hispanic populations, it appears that many Chicanos continue to live in comparatively large, intact kinship units where there are extensive networks of relatives who are helpful and supportive (Arce, 1982). No sharp distinction is made between relatives and friends, with the latter being considered as virtually kin if a close relationship has been formed. The term *compadrazo* is often used for this relationship. However, the pattern of close extended family relationships tends to fade among third- and fourth-generation families and among those who are upwardly mobile (Alvirez et al., 1981).

Bean, Curtis, and Marcum (1977) carried out an analysis of 1969 data from 325 Mexican American couples who were members of a stratified sample in the Southwest. They found, among other things, that couples with egalitarian relationships were highest in their marital satisfaction—hardly a surprise. In general, the authors found little to support the concept that Mexican American families have cultural patterns that are different from those of Anglo families and unique, culturally related sources of marital satisfaction. This point is also made by Zapata and Jaramillo (1981), who compared a small sample of Anglo families to Mexican American ones in two southwestern cities. They found that differences in perceived family roles and alliances pertained far more to differences in socioeconomic status than to ethnicity.

Vega, Patterson, et al. (1986) provided helpful information regarding selected family patterns of a group of southwestern urban Mexican American and Anglo parents with fifth- and sixth-grade children ($N = 147$ in each group). Using the Family Adaptability and Cohesion Scale II (Olsen, Russell, & Sprenkel, 1982), observers rated these families for the above characteristics. They also used an acculturation scale developed by Cuellar, Harris, and Jasso (1980). As might be expected, Vega, Patterson, et al. (1986) found that levels of acculturation varied for the Mexican Americans according to their length of residence in the United States and their socioeconomic status.

The majority of both groups had family scores that corresponded to national norms of high-satisfaction, low-stress families in similar stages of family development and of similar family size. Low socioeconomic status families were somewhat more likely to have scores associated with high stress and low satisfaction.

Ybarra (1982) studied 100 married couples in Fresno, California, and found that there was a broad range of conjugal role relations, including shared family and marital roles, especially when the wife was employed. A similar finding was obtained by Baca Zinn (1980), who carried out intensive research with a small sample of Mexican American families. In some cases the mother was employed outside the home and in others she was not. Maternal employment caused a shift in family roles, and the fathers helped more at home in nontraditional ways. This finding was also obtained by Cooney, Rogler, Hurrer, and Ortiz (1982) in a New York study of Puerto Rican couples and by Vasquez and Gonzalez (1981) in a study of Chicanos.

It appears, therefore, that the same general principle applies to both Puerto Rican and Mexican American families and, indeed, to families of many other population groups: A woman's power in relationships within and outside the family tends to increase when she is employed outside the home and when she has acquired a high level of education and independent income. The researchers cited above report that when these role shifts occur in Hispanic families, there is often considerable associated stress—a finding surely not unique to Hispanic families.

Vega, Kolody, and Valle (1986), in another study of Mexican Americans in San Diego, interviewed almost 2,000 immigrant Mexican women. More than 20% of them had experienced marital disruption through separation or divorce. Responses of the group to a widely used depression rating scale revealed that these divorced or separated women were significantly more depressed than the married ones, especially if they had a low occupational-economic status—a finding often also obtained for other groups of divorced or separated women (Hetherington, Cox, & Cox, 1978; Wallerstein, 1985). Vega, Kolody, and Valle (1986) also found that the widows and never-married mothers in their sample were not particularly apt to be depressed, but the reasons for this finding are not clear.

Lack of a confidant for those in marriages disrupted by separation or divorce was strongly associated with depression. It seems likely that marital disruption and the resulting lack of a supportive confidant would be especially difficult for immigrants (both men and women) because they often lack the extended family relationships and community membership left behind in their native lands, factors especially poignant for persons, such as Mexicans and other Hispanic people, who have been embedded in strong family and neighborhood networks (Falicov, 1982) and for those who do not speak English.

It should be recalled that, as shown in the first section of this chapter, Mexican Americans have higher rates of poverty and unemployment and lower educational-occupational status than is the case for Anglos. Although their situation, on average, is more favorable than that of Puerto Ricans and Blacks, it is still not good. Low educational achievement, including early school leaving, is one important cause of the problems of this group, as discussed in somewhat more detail in a later section of this chapter.

Cuban Americans

Cuban Americans have a rather different background and immigration history than either Puerto Ricans or Mexican Americans (see Suárez, Chapter 9, this volume). Cuba had been a colony of Spain for hundreds of years before the intervention of the United States in 1898, following an insurrection of some Cuban groups against oppressive Spanish domination. American motivations for intervention were mixed: Some liberal groups supported the Cuban cause of independence from

Spain, but more powerful groups were swayed by their economic and political interests in this strategic island (Dulles, 1959).

After victory in the Spanish-American War, the United States established a strong political hold on Cuba, inducing rebellions, especially on the part of those people who were victims of the one-crop sugar economy and land ownership by the very few. The Cuban revolution of 1959 brought Castro and a predominantly socialist government into power and created fear and resistance in the United States, especially among those who, correctly or incorrectly, equated the Castro government with Soviet intrusion into the Western Hemisphere. At the present time, barely contained conflict between the United States and Cuba continues. One result of this conflict has been differing waves of immigration from Cuba to this country (Bernal, 1982; Dulles, 1959).

Many of the first wave of Cuban immigrants made a poor adjustment to the United States, partly because of their own troubled and disadvantaged backgrounds (Bernal, 1982). A serious public policy issue has arisen concerning government plans to deport some of those Cubans who have criminal records and the resistance of many to being deported. Cuban immigrants have settled chiefly in metropolitan areas such as Miami, New York, and Chicago. Although the different immigrant groups vary enormously in a number of ways, they also share a general cultural heritage.

Although formal research regarding Cuban American families seems to be lacking, Bernal (1982) presents a summary of largely clinical observations. The traditional Cuban emphasis on familism, including the extended family, appears to be much like that found in other Hispanic countries. According to Bernal, the double standard of sexual morality, along with the concept of male dominance, has prevailed in Cuban culture as well. However, as shown above concerning Mexican and Puerto Rican families in the United States, when women work outside the home, egalitarian values and behaviors tend to emerge.

Bernal cites several small studies from the 1970s to the effect that younger and second-generation Cubans become acculturated to the United States more quickly than older or first-generation immigrants. As in reports regarding Puerto Rican families and immigrant families from many countries, the cultural differences between children and their parents often lead to youthful rebellions, authoritarian parental reactions, and considerable family stress. Bernal observes further that Cubans tend to regard themselves as a special people, perhaps because of their homeland's strategic political and economic importance to other nations over the centuries. This sense of being special may lend a feeling of superiority to some Cubans, with allied attitudes of chauvinism, racism, and classism, which may be viewed by some observers as arrogance and grandiosity. However, as in the case of Puerto Rican Americans, more research about Cuban American families is needed before much can be said about the ways in which they are like or different from other families in this country.

Immigrants from Central and South America

Very little has been written about the family patterns of other Hispanic immigrants. According to L. Cohen (1977), two-thirds of the immigrants from Central and South America during the 1970s were women. Most had children whom they left behind with their maternal grandmothers. These women often came on student or tourist visas or crossed the border illegally. They frequently had kin and friends who helped them come into this country and find work. They were afraid to bring their young children with them, and often dreaded returns home to visit for fear they could not reenter the United States.

These women were usually never married, separated, divorced, or widowed. They had a harder time than men in getting employment because of both sex and ethnic discrimination (L. Cohen, 1977). Despite low wages, most sent money home to help their families. They found it hard to bring their children to this country because it is difficult to gain permission for immigration of whole families to the United States. Much more needs to be learned about immigrant families in the United States from many parts of Central and South America, but there appears to be limited research about them.

Some Implications for Practice

The foregoing reports of recent research tend to emphasize that Hispanic families in the United States today appear to be changing their traditional cultural patterns and are generally similar in their behaviors to "mainstream America." However, it is important to recognize that most of this research has investigated only Mexican American families. Also, as is true of much research, it has analyzed overall differences between groups who more or less represent the general population. On the other hand, clinicians deal with troubled families who are seeking help and do not, therefore, usually represent the average family. The Hispanic families known to these practitioners are apt to be unusually problem laden. Although the observations of clinicians tend to provide rather biased and negative views of individual and family traits, these views can have important value in a number of ways. They can provide useful insights to other clinicians, they can provide clues to human characteristics that are difficult to identify through more formal research, and they can suggest hypotheses for further study of subsets of group data—for example, of census data that show particularly high rates of early school leaving among Puerto Rican and Mexican youth.

Both Andrade (1982) and Baca Zinn (1980) provide insights that are especially valuable for clinicians. They note that traditional cultural values are still important to many Hispanic families, in that they represent deeply rooted aspirations, if not actual behaviors. Aspirations are significant, especially in the public sense; that is, most people, including Hispanics, wish to appear to be living according to their professed values, even though they cannot consistently maintain these ideals. For example, a Chicano father may wish to appear as the dominant authority in his family, even though, in actuality, he may be forced to behave within the home in an egalitarian fashion.

Falicov and Karrer (1980) have written perceptively of therapeutic work with disturbed Hispanic-origin families. They urge therapists to strive for a deep understanding of the cultural values as well as actual behaviors of each family with whom they work. For instance, it can be important to give recognition to the woman as the "perfect submissive, ever-protective, all-giving" mother who subscribes to traditional family values but, simultaneously, help that woman to behave in ways that are more adaptive to contemporary conditions, which may call, for instance, for her to grant greater independence to her growing children. This can be interpreted, of course, as appropriate and caring maternal behavior.

Falicov and Karrer point out, further, that intergenerational conflict is common, especially when the older generations were born and reared in another country. Traditionally, there is a close alliance among daughters, mothers, and grandmothers. Especially in today's rapidly changing, more androgynous society, this alliance, with its rigid insistence on highly differentiated sex roles, tends to be dysfunctional and a threat to the unity of the dyadic relationship of husband and wife as well as to the adaptive behaviors of other members of the family.

Cardes (1983) cites Szapocznik, a psychologist who directs a mental health treatment and research center in Miami, who found that intergenerational differences in speech and acculturation to U.S. culture greatly exacerbate family conflict. Mothers who are isolated within their homes because of childbearing responsibilities, language difficulties, and traditional concepts of women's all-encompassing maternal functions often find it particularly difficult to adapt to the larger, predominantly Anglo society. In their role as "culture bearers" for the family, their relative lag in acculturation to the world outside the home can lead to severe marital and parent-child conflicts. Falicov and Karrer (1980) suggest that situations of these kinds may be assuaged through helping the whole family to see that the mother's participation in community life may be salutary for all concerned. For instance, support groups of women in fairly similar situations have been found to be beneficial.

The adverse effects of ethnic and racial discrimination on Hispanics and other oppressed minority groups in this country cannot be overlooked. This tends to operate in many settings. Its intensity varies by region of the country, state of the economy, availability of jobs, density of population groups, skin color, facial characteristics of individuals, degree of acculturation, language facility, and immigration status. The general corrosive effects of discrimination on individual and family behaviors, well-being, aspirations, and self-image have been well documented elsewhere (for example, see Peters & McAdoo, 1983). This calls for particular sensitivity and awareness on the part of therapists as well as family advocacy and social change activists to promote needed programs and policies, as suggested in the next section.

When one considers the heavy impact of the multiple stresses of cultural and language differences, discrimination, recent migration for many, illegal immigrant status (for some), and separation from family members (in numerous cases), it becomes apparent that members of the helping professions need extensive knowledge and skills to assist Hispanic families who become troubled. In this process, it is important for professionals who work with Hispanic families to be aware of natural support systems within the ethnic community.

It is also important for professionals who work with Hispanic families to be proficient in Spanish and to be sensitive to the nuances of courtesy in interpersonal, including familial, relationships. Further helpful suggestions for therapeutic work with Hispanic families can be found in excellent relevant chapters appearing in McGoldrick, Pearce, and Giordano's (1982) *Ethnicity and Family Therapy*.

According to Delgado and Delgado (1982), there are a number of different kinds of support systems in Hispanic communities, including the extended family, folk healers, religious organizations, merchants, and social clubs. *Botanicas* are shops that sell herbs as well as records and novels in Spanish. *Bodegas* are grocery stores, but they also serve as information centers for the Hispanic community, providing such information as where folk healers can be found. *Clubs sociales* provide recreation as well as links to community resources, including employment and housing.

The family consists not only of blood relatives, but also of special friends who furnish reciprocal support called *como familial*. There is also the ritual kinship of *compadrazo*: Persons of this status participate in baptisms, first communions, confirmations, and marriages, and often serve as parent substitutes.

Folk healers exist in Mexican, Cuban, Puerto Rican, and other Hispanic cultures in the United States. There are different healers for emotional, physical, and spiritual problems. Persons working with Hispanic families need to learn as much as possible about these healers and about the other kinds of natural support systems mentioned above within the particular communities with which they are involved.

Some Implications for Public Policy

Immigration

Clearly, immigration problems have not been solved by recent legislation. Although this issue does not apply to Puerto Ricans, it does apply to other Hispanics. Although a persuasive case can be made for permitting all family members to gain legal immigrant status in this country if one member has such status, difficult issues may arise: How are family members to be defined, especially in respect to the extended family? Can this country provide employment for all adult family members who wish to immigrate? Would this kind of immigration provide the labor supply the country may require? What of the possible increase of people who become dependent on welfare programs? Can this country provide all the social, health, and educational services that this population may need?

Moving beyond the immigrant family question, there are further knotty political, social, and economic problems associated with immigration policy. A consideration of these questions is far beyond the space constraints of this chapter; suffice it to say that it behooves those of us who are concerned about public policy and Hispanic families to become increasingly informed and politically active regarding immigration issues and their underlying causes.

Employment

As shown earlier in this chapter, Hispanic families in the United States have somewhat higher rates of unemployment than do Anglo families; rates are particularly high for Puerto Ricans—34% in 1979, a rate that may well have risen since. Moreover, on average, Hispanics are paid inadequate wages and work in low-level jobs. Although their situation is partly a result of inadequate educational-occupational training and ethnic or racial discrimination, a more fundamental problem exists in this nation's economic structure, with its growing tendency toward a two-tier employment situation: a shift toward extremely technical jobs for the exceptionally competent and highly trained few and low-level, poorly paid, primarily service jobs for the many who are less advantaged.

Special employment problems exist for those Hispanics who lack legal immigrant status, as we have seen. This is tied to problems of immigration policy. One approach, suggested by Portes (1979), seems to make considerable sense: the use of labor contracts with employers, as used in Western Europe, that allow nonresident nationals to enter the country and remain so long as their employment lasts. On the other hand, what happens if their employment terminates and they are loath to return to their countries of origin?

Income

The lower average income of Hispanic families in this country is obviously tied to higher rates of unemployment and low occupational levels. Part of the high poverty rate for Hispanic families, especially for Puerto Ricans, is associated with their relatively high proportion of female-headed families. There has been a marked increase in the poverty rates for all families with children since 1980. These rates are especially high for one-parent families and are chiefly a result of large cuts in welfare programs during the Reagan administration together with inflation, falling wage levels, and growing rates of unemployment among both males and females with limited education and few technical skills.

Besides efforts to improve the employment situation, as sketched above, improvements in income assistance programs are needed, including restoration of funds cut from Aid to Families with Dependent

Children programs, health services for poor people (more generous Medicaid and related provisions), increased food stamp allowances, stepped-up subsidies for and construction of low-income housing, and expansion of social and health services, including family planning, for moderate- and low-income families (Chilman, 1988). As discussed earlier, these services, and indeed all public programs in areas with Hispanic populations, should be offered in Spanish as well as in English and with appropriate sensitivity to cultural patterns and problems of immigration.

Education

Improvement of education programs for Hispanics is a crucially important issue, especially considering the high rates of early school leaving among so many young Puerto Ricans and Mexican Americans, among others. Although graduation from high school far from guarantees that a person will get a good job, failure to graduate virtually guarantees that he or she will not.

Whether or not public school programs should be bilingual is a matter of acrid controversy and a topic too specialized and complex to discuss adequately here. Much more research is needed to further our understanding of which factors appear to be most closely associated with the academic failures and successes of selected Hispanic groups and which approaches appear to be associated with improved academic performance. It is likely that educational problems are as closely tied to the income, employment, housing, health, and immigration problems of families as they are to the nature of school programs themselves; this is one of the many issues that calls for further investigation.

Some Implications for Research

As we have seen, there has been relatively little research devoted to Hispanic American families. Most studies have focused on selected marital attitudes and behaviors of Mexican American couples. The majority of these studies have looked at what significant differences, if any, are to be found between these couples and their Anglo counterparts, especially in matters pertaining to traditional male-dominant behaviors and segregated, rigidly defined sex roles. No significant differences between groups have been found, and it seems that these particular questions do not need further general exploration with respect to Mexican Americans. However, they might well be asked in studies of particularly problem-laden subgroups, as well as Puerto Rican, Cuban, and other Hispanic families in this country, with the appropriate use of demographic controls.

Research has far from answered a number of other questions that might be raised about Hispanic family relationships, including further exploration of the impact on marital and parent-child relationships of recent immigration, extended families, unmarried parenthood, divorce, remarriage, unemployment, substance abuse, and family violence.

Much more needs to be known about Hispanic child-rearing beliefs, attitudes, goals, and behaviors with respect to the various ethnic and social class groups and in association with child development outcomes in such areas as school achievement, parent and child satisfaction, crime and delinquency, and youth employment. In this regard, Estella Martinez's contribution to this book (Chapter 11) is particularly welcome.

9

Cuban Americans

From Golden Exiles
to Social Undesirables

ZULEMA E. SUÁREZ

Cuban Americans are the third largest group of Latino descent living in the United States. Numbering about one million, they constitute 6% of the country's Latino population. Knowledge about this minority is limited, in part because of the recency of Cuban migration (the bulk of Cubans migrated after 1959), and in part because interest in Latino communities has been just as recent (Bean & Tienda, 1988). In fact, the U.S. Census Bureau did not publish tabulations on people of Cuban birth or parentage until 1970 (Bean & Tienda, 1988). As a result, public knowledge of Cuban Americans has primarily been determined by the political and economic climates at the times of their arrival and by the media. This has resulted in the proliferation of numerous stereotypes that mask important dimensions of the Cuban American reality. For example, while the early Cubans were dubbed the "golden exiles," the latest wave has become known as "social undesirables."

This chapter examines some of the stereotypes and conditions of Cuban Americans and provides information to promote a more accurate

AUTHOR'S NOTE: The work reported in this chapter was supported in part by an Inter-University Program for Latino Research/Social Science Research Council postdoctoral fellowship.

understanding of the strengths and perils of this immigrant community. Because, unlike Mexican-Americans and Puerto Ricans, the bulk of Cuban Americans are considered to be political refugees, a status that has affected their adjustment, a brief history of their migration is provided.[1] The climate of opinion and the U.S. economy at the times of the Cubans' waves of arrival have determined the kinds of receptions they encountered and the kinds of adjustment policies that were enacted. Hence a brief discussion is included of how the different waves were received in the United States and the stereotypes that emerged in the public arena. The accuracy of these stereotypes is challenged through a look at the adjustment of Cuban Americans, with an emphasis on potentially at-risk segments of this ostensibly well-to-do population. Wherever possible, this group is placed within the context of other Latino American immigrants.

Brief History of Migration

Massive Cuban migration to the United States is recent. Despite small migration flows dating back to the past century, Cubans did not leave the island in great numbers until Fidel Castro came to power in 1959 (Boswell & Curtis, 1984; Moore & Pachon, 1985; Portes & Bach, 1985; Rogg & Homberg, 1983). Prior to that time, only 50,000 Cuban Americans were living in the United States (Queralt, 1984). Having reached power with the overwhelming support of many sectors of Cuban society, Castro began to lose followers as his communist tendencies became evident. His declaration in 1961 that his regime would follow Marxist-Leninist ideology precipitated an unprecedented exodus of refugees (Wenk, 1969). As much as one-tenth of the island population has been estimated to have left after 1959 (Rogg & Homberg, 1983).

Cuban migration occurred in what scholars call "waves." Former government, banking, and industrial officials had migrated in limited numbers (Wenk, 1969), but immigration became very difficult after 1961, when the United States and Cuba severed diplomatic relations. The first wave occurred between January 1961 and October 1962, the time of the Cuban missile crisis, and included more than 150,000 Cubans. The second wave, occurring between November 1962 and November 1965, brought only an estimated 75,000 because of restrictions imposed by the Cuban government. The third wave, spanning December 1965 to March 1972, brought another 275,000. Most of these arrived via the Freedom Flights, an airlift that brought 3,000 to 4,000 passengers a month. Unlike those in the earliest waves, who were primarily escaping political persecution, about 40% of the airlift group were students, women, and children who were joining their relatives (Bean & Tienda, 1988).

Small groups of refugees continued to arrive, but through a third country, such as Spain. The last and most controversial wave took place between April and September of 1980. More than 125,000 left Cuba through an unorganized boatlift via the port of Mariel under extremely hazardous and chaotic circumstances. Although many came voluntarily to join family members, a significant portion were forced to leave by the Castro government (Gil, 1983). The Mariel exiles are discussed in more detail below.

The Different Waves and Their U.S. Reception

The early immigrants were mostly, but not all, white and from the upper, middle, and professional sectors of the Cuban population (Bernal, 1982). Because of their white skin, their education, and the strong state of the U.S. economy at the time, these golden exiles were graciously and enthusiastically received. Some have argued that these Cubans were so welcomed because they embodied the anticommunist sentiment of the time and were used as symbols to the world of the hazards of communism (Casuso & Camacho, 1985; Pedraza-Bailey, 1980). The unique and massive Cuban Refugee Program was established by the U.S. government to help with their resettlement (Hernandez, 1974; Pedraza-Bailey, 1980). The program retrained selected groups of skilled and professional workers (i.e., teachers, college professors, doctors, optometrists, and lawyers). Approximately 70% of the emigrés were aided by this program.[2]

Despite the fact that each successive wave brought people of lower socioeconomic, educational, and occupational levels than the one preceding it, the newest arrivals were able to ride on the reputation of the earlier waves and were greeted with the same goodwill. Hence Cuban Americans became characterized as ambitious and extremely hardworking.

The Golden Exiles

That a segment of the Cuban American community became economically successful because of the entrepreneurial skills and the capital some brought to this country sustained the image of the golden exile. In fact, the Cuban impact on Miami has been ubiquitous and striking. Portes and Bach (1985) report that the number of Cuban-owned businesses in the Miami area increased from 919 in 1967 to 13,000 in 1985. Cubans are credited with revitalizing the sagging economies of both Miami and West New York, New Jersey, the two cities where they are most highly concentrated (Wilson & Portes, 1980).

Yet, according to Casuso and Camacho (1985), "the stereotype of the Cuban as a self-made business success neglects a large portion of the population" (p. 19). Although Cuban Americans, like other refugee populations, have a greater percentage of professionals and entrepreneurs among their ranks than nonrefugee migrants, almost one-third of the Cuban American labor force in 1980 held jobs as operators, fabricators, and laborers; 1 in 10 Cuban American families were living below the poverty level in 1979.[3] Moreover, these figures do not include the latest entrants, whose socioeconomic profile is lower than that of the earlier waves (Bach, Bach, & Triplett, 1981; Boswell & Curtis, 1984).

With a 1980 median family income of $18,650, Cuban Americans have higher earnings than Mexicans ($14,510) and Puerto Ricans ($11,168) (Bean & Tienda, 1988). However, there are several reasons for this apparent advantage over other Latino groups. First, the Cuban American population is about 16 years older than the other two major Latino groups, whose median age is 21 (Bean & Tienda, 1988). Because they are older, Cuban Americans have proportionately more persons participating in the labor force, fewer unemployed, and more workers at the peak of their earning power than Mexican Americans, Puerto Ricans, or the total U.S. population (Queralt, 1984). Second, Cubans' higher family income may also be attributed to multiple earners. In 1980, more than 50% of Cuban American families contained two or more earners (Bean & Tienda, 1988). It may also be that some of these earners have more than one job. And third, the ethnic enclave has traditionally provided Cuban Americans with job opportunities that they otherwise might have lacked.

Finally, when considering the relative economic advantage of Cuban Americans, several things should be kept in mind. First, income will differ according to nativity, geographic location, and degree of acculturation. For example, although Cuban American economic well-being can be attributed to participation in an ethnic enclave, Cubans in enclave jobs are paid as much as 16% less than Cuban men working in areas with lower Latino density (Bean & Tienda, 1988). Second, despite their education, Cuban Americans, like other refugees, experience considerable downward mobility (Hernandez, 1974; Rogg, 1974; Rogg & Cooney, 1980), with the added disadvantage that years of labor market experience in Cuba have virtually no effect on earnings in the United States (Chiswick, 1982). Labor market experience in the United States, on the other hand, has a substantial effect on earnings, but Cubans are still a fairly new immigrant group, with nearly 80% foreign-born. This suggests considerable within-group differences.

The Social Undesirables

Despite the fact that by the time of the Mariel exodus Cuban emigrés were increasingly demographically representative of the island population itself (Boswell & Curtis, 1984), this last wave was characterized as having an overrepresentation of criminals, prostitutes, and other institutionalized persons forced into exile (Bach et al., 1981). Consequently, the Mariel entrants became the objects of wide media coverage and bitter public debate (Portes & Bach, 1985). Unlike the golden exiles of the early waves, who were met with open arms, this group was met with great ambivalence and hostility. Americans were angry because they felt Castro was making a mockery of the United States (Harris, 1980). Not only was he refusing to discuss an orderly departure program from the island with the United States (U.S. Department of State, 1980), but the Cuban press was claiming that Cuba was ridding itself of social undesirables (Bach et al., 1981; Gil, 1983). Moreover, conditions in the United States had changed since the arrival of the first waves. Because of the high unemployment and inflation of the late 1970s, the Mariel entrants were seen as one more burden on an already overburdened economy (Bach et al., 1981). Eventually, even the older Cuban emigrés became resentful and fearful that association with the newer immigrants would taint their upstanding image (Fradd, 1983).

Research shows, however, that the entrants are generally undeserving of their negative stereotype. Although about 16% of this group had been incarcerated in Cuba, this migration also represented the source Cuban population more closely than ever before (Bach et al., 1981; Portes & Bach, 1985). Overall, the entrants were neither marginal to the Cuban economy nor out of the social mainstream. Most had been employed their entire adult lives and had average educational levels.

One difference between the Mariel entrants and the previous waves, which perhaps contributed to their undesirability in this country, was race. Nonwhites were more significantly represented in this wave than in previous cohorts. Whereas an estimated 30% of the Mariel entrants were nonwhite, only 5% of prior Cuban immigrants were (Portes & Bach, 1985). Some have reported the nonwhite portion of the Mariel group to be as high as 40% (Moore & Pachon, 1985). Also, unlike earlier cohorts, this last wave included a significant number of single men who did not have relatives in this country.

Adjustment

Perhaps it is because Cuban Americans have done relatively well economically that mainstream society has paid minimal attention to their vulnerability as refugees/immigrants. Another reason may be that as Latinos, Cuban Americans have been victims of the familism stereotype. The Latino family has too often been credited with enhancing the adjustment of its members and serving as a buffer against a variety of stressors (see Rogler et al., 1983). This romantic stereotype, however, has been based on the traditional family structure in the country of origin and has clouded the problems confronting the Latino, and in this case the Cuban, immigrant family.

Migration is an extremely stressful process that stimulates changes in the family (Grant, 1983b) and in the immigrants themselves. Whether voluntary or involuntary, the effects of migration have been linked to psychological stress and, ultimately, to a range of mental, physical, and social disorders (David, 1970). Despite the apparent good adjustment of Cuban Americans as a whole, one must be attentive to the side effects inherent in their refugee/immigrant status. Not surprisingly, segments of this population have been particularly vulnerable to the stressors of migration and are potentially at risk for maladjustment (e.g., depression and familial conflicts).

The Cuban Family

Immigration has resulted in considerable upheaval for Cuban families. Although Cuban Americans are more likely to live in extended families than are other Latino subgroups or the Black and white non-Latino populations (Bean & Tienda, 1988), the consensus among Cuban scholars seems to be that the Cuban American extended family is disintegrating (Hernandez, 1974; Queralt, 1984; Szapocznic, Scopetta,

Arnalde, & Kurtines, 1978). But the greatest tension has come from intergenerational conflicts between old world Cuban parents and their American or Americanized children (Gil, 1968; Szapocznic & Kurtines, 1980; Szapocznic et al., 1978). As with other immigrant groups, problems occur when second-generation and Cuban-born youth adopt American attitudes and behaviors at a faster rate than their parents who were born and raised on the island. According to Szapocznic and his colleagues (1978), the development of marked intergenerational differences in behavioral acculturation within the nuclear family is the source of widespread behavioral disorders (particularly of antisocial behaviors) and family disruption in Cuban immigrants.

Cuban American Women

Cuban American women were able to find work before their men were and were not as threatened by doing menial jobs when they first arrived, leading some scholars to conclude that women adjusted more easily than men (Boswell & Curtis, 1984). Yet, despite a dearth of empirical literature, there is evidence that the transition from wife and mother in Cuba to the new role of working woman has been difficult for many Cuban American women and their families (Lavender, 1986). Prior to the revolution, the majority of Cuban women were homemakers and mothers. Unaccustomed to working outside the home, they were forced to take full-time jobs in addition to continuing their responsibilities at home. Years after migration, Cuban American women maintain one of the highest rates of labor force participation by women in the United States. According to the U.S. Census, 64% of Cuban American females were employed in 1980. Rodriguez and Vila (1982) suggest that this dramatic role change has been very stressful and has led to marital problems because it is threatening to the traditional Cuban male. Indeed, the rate of marital instability among Cuban immigrants (21%) is equivalent to that of non-Latino whites and slightly lower than that of Mexicans (23%) (Bean & Tienda, 1988). Others argue, however, that this change in marital roles has resulted in a more egalitarian Cuban marriage (Boswell & Curtis, 1984).

Although Cuban American women are more likely to work outside the home than are other Latino and non-Latino women, they seem to be at a disadvantage in the labor market. Their earnings increase by only 2.4% for each additional year of schooling, while other Latino women receive a 5.8% return for the same amount of education (Bean & Tienda, 1988).

Also, Cuban women entering the United States after 1964 have earned significantly less than their native-born (statistical) counterparts.

Cuban American Youth

Although growing up in a bicultural environment may have its advantages, it can also be a liability (Boswell & Curtis, 1984). For some Cuban American youths, this has led to an identity crisis: They are neither completely Cuban nor completely American. While being part of both worlds, they also feel estranged from both. Because some lack sufficient proficiency in either English or Spanish, their economic and personal opportunities may be severely restricted (Boswell & Curtis, 1984). This cultural struggle may explain why a 1974 needs assessment of the Cuban American community in Dade County, Florida, found a significant number of high school dropouts and youth offenders (Hernandez, 1974). Almost 89% of Spanish-surnamed offenders in the caseloads of youth counselors in a district unit of the county were Cuban American. It is not known, however, what percentage of the Spanish-surnamed population of Miami was Cuban at that time.

In another needs assessment done at about the same time, Cejas and Toledo (cited in Hernandez, 1974) estimated that at least 40.7% of the Spanish-surnamed students in eight schools located in two predominantly Spanish-speaking target areas of Miami dropped out of high school before graduation. The dropout rate for the entire school population in Dade County at the time was estimated at 27%. A more recent study indicates that the dropout rate for Latinos in Miami (of which 80% were Cuban American) increased almost 28% during 1979 (Diaz, 1980). The rate for Black Miamians dropped 2.2%, while the rate for non-Latino whites increased 3.5%. The dropout rate in West New York, where the second greatest concentration of Cubans live, noticeably increased, from 4% in 1968 to 17.3% in 1979 (Rogg & Cooney, 1980).

The Elderly

Because Cuban Americans tend to be older than other Latino groups, they have a greater percentage of elderly members. Szapocznic (1980) has highlighted the plight of the Cuban American elderly. He argues that the mental health of this population is not only seriously threatened by the usual predicaments confronting the aged, it is also exacerbated by many other disadvantages and complications concomitant to the

Cubans' special status of forced migration and minority status. Social isolation and loneliness, loss of country, loss of status, and the effects of transplantation are cited as some predicaments of aging that would not have been experienced by these elders had they remained in their native country. Their lack of knowledge of the language and American ways prevents them from assimilating. This renders them incapable of negotiating the system they are most likely to depend upon: the social services delivery system. Szapocznic and his colleagues' work supports Hernandez's (1974) earlier findings: One-third of the elderly sample they surveyed reported feeling lonely and isolated. Other psychosocial problems noted as affecting this population were language barriers, discriminatory institutional policies, and mental illness.

Economically, the Cuban American elderly are primarily dependent on SSI (if they never worked in the United States or if their social security benefit is very low), Social Security, Medicare, Medicaid, and food stamps. In Miami, the Cuban elderly are reported to constitute a higher percentage of the SSI and Medicaid rolls than any other ethnic group in the city (Diaz, 1980). Perhaps this high participation in public programs explains why the Cuban elderly have been found to be experiencing medical access problems. According to a recent study, elderly respondents of Cuban origin are less likely to see a doctor than are younger Cuban Americans (Schur, Bernstein, & Berk, 1987).

The Mariel Entrants

The Mariel entrants were exposed to even greater stressors in this country than were their predecessors. Because they arrived a month after the Refugee Act of 1980 was signed, they were not eligible for refugee status. Instead, they were granted a special status known as "entrants—status pending" (Boswell & Curtis, 1984). This enabled them to enter the country, but the details of their stay were to be determined later. In addition to the anxiety aroused by this uncertain status, only a restricted range of social services was available to them. Some entrants did not receive needed medical and mental health care from private institutions because they did not have Medicaid cards (Gil, 1983). This was quite different from the government's treatment of the early cohorts.

At least initially, the negative media publicity received by this group and the accompanying stigma jeopardized their chances of finding honest employment. According to Estevez (1983), not only did the entrants arrive at a time of high unemployment, but the new job offers they received began to dwindle as media reports on the alleged criminal records of the entrants became widespread.[5] Moreover, the negative attitude toward the Mariel entrants was generalized to many of the "old" Cuban Americans, who to this day remain among the harshest critics of these latest entrants (Boswell & Curtis, 1984). This further decreased the new migrants' employment opportunities, because the majority of Cuban American wage earners were employed by other Cubans (Portes & Bach, 1985).

Another factor that might affect the adjustment of some entrants is the difference between the sending and receiving countries. According to the literature, stress seems greater for those whose native culture differs radically from that of the adopting community (David, 1970). In addition, Portes (1969) argues that one of the factors aiding the acculturation of earlier Cuban emigrés was that they came from a capitalistic order, and so the ethic of the upper and middle sectors was very similar to the ethic of individualism held in this culture. It can be inferred that even the healthy segment of the Mariel group would have greater difficulty adjusting to the new culture because nearly half of the entrants grew up in postrevolutionary Cuba (Bach et al., 1981).

How Stereotypes Affect Interethnic Relations

The stereotypes of Cuban Americans in the United States have affected interethnic relations. According to Queralt (1984), the stereotype of the economically successful Cuban exile caused problems in Cuban Americans' relations with other minority groups because Cubans were still often seen as golden exiles who were socially distant from other minority groups (also see Casuso & Camacho, 1985). She further argues that political differences, such as Cuban Americans' conservative outlook, in contrast to the more liberal activism of Mexican Americans and Puerto Ricans, also prevented better understanding between Cubans and these groups. Indeed, the overwhelming majority of Cuban Americans support the Republican party (Boswell & Curtis, 1984; Moore & Pachon, 1985). However, some argue that Cuban conservatism can be linked to passionate anticommunist feelings and to dissatisfaction with the foreign policies of the Democrats. Although the majority of the Cuban emigrés initially supported Democratic party candidates, they began to vote Republican after the Bay of Pigs fiasco and the Cuban missile crisis (when the United States agreed not to invade Cuba). Many Cuban Americans were also unhappy with President Jimmy Carter's handling of the Soviet stationing of weapons and troops in Cuba during 1980 (Boswell & Curtis, 1984).

Cuban American political affiliation can be expected to change with future generations. There is some evidence that preference for Republican candidates weakens with length of residence (Boswell & Curtis, 1984). As the younger generation of Cuban Americans, whose memories of Cuba have dwindled relative to those of older refugees, come to positions of power, their political concerns increasingly turn to domestic issues (Boswell & Curtis, 1984; Casuso & Camacho, 1985).

Cuban Americans in Miami have also experienced friction with the non-Latino community because they are perceived to be clannish. Many English-speaking residents resent the pervasiveness of the Spanish language; approximately 94% of Cuban Americans reported Spanish as their household language in the 1980 census (Bean & Tienda, 1988). At least in part as a result of such tension, 30,000 non-Latino whites moved out of Dade County between 1970 and 1980. Those who stayed, however, were instrumental in the 1980 repeal of a law passed in 1973 declaring Dade County a bilingual jurisdiction, which made Spanish the second official language for such things as election ballots, public signs, and local directories (Moore & Pachon, 1985).

Although Cuban Americans may hold on to their language and other cultural vestiges, the evidence does not support this clannish stereotype. As a group, Cuban Americans are more likely to out-marry than are Mexican Americans and Puerto Ricans (Boswell & Curtis, 1984). Although in 1970, 17% of Cuban-descent women had married non-Cubans, 46% of second-generation Cuban American women had married non-Cuban men by 1980. This compares with 33% and 16% for Puerto Rican and Mexican American women, respectively.

Cuban Americans have the highest rate of naturalization of any immigrant group (Bean & Tienda, 1988; Moore & Pachon, 1985). While approximately 80% of Cuban Americans become naturalized, only 12% of Mexican Americans do so during a comparable time. This can be viewed as evidence that, contrary to popular belief, Cuban Americans want to participate in and be part of mainstream society.

Summary

This chapter has documented and challenged the stereotypes of Cuban Americans in an effort to increase understanding of this relatively new minority group. Although the earlier Cuban immigrants benefited from being perceived as golden exiles, successive waves have suffered discrimination as a result of this and other stereotypes. Because of the perception of Cubans as successful professionals and entrepreneurs, the needs of the lower strata of Cuban American society have not been recognized or programmatically addressed.

Not surprisingly, given this stereotype, one repeatedly hears the argument that, because of their alleged affluence, Cuban Americans should not be allowed the privileges afforded other Latino groups. But, as Bean and Tienda (1988) point out, the economic success of the entrepreneurial segment of the Cuban American population has not been widely shared, as it has profited from the existence of low-wage, unskilled Cuban workers who have become the working class of the golden exiles. Thus Bach (1980; cited in Bean & Tienda, 1988) has concluded that with each successive wave the prerevolutionary Cuban social structure was transplanted to Miami "with all the implications of unequal wealth, power and prestige."

As seen in this chapter, despite a lack of empirical evidence, several segments of the Cuban American population are potentially at risk. Dispelling the stereotypes about this ethnic group can ensure that disadvantaged Cuban Americans do not fall through the cracks, so to speak, and can decrease the prejudice and isolation that members of this group may be experiencing. As things stand, like the bicultural Cuban American youth, Cuban Americans in general are not completely accepted by other Latino groups or by mainstream society. They do not seem to fit anywhere except with each other, yet they are condemned for being clannish. On the other hand, what has been perceived by outsiders as ethnocentricity may really be group cohesiveness, a cohesiveness that, according to Bean and Tienda (1988), has been instrumental in facilitating the initial adjustment and success of this group. Nonetheless, there are significant divisions within the Cuban American community, as shown by the tensions between the earlier and later waves.

Numerous questions about Cubans in the United States remain to be answered. Will this ethnic cohesiveness continue to ensure the survival of the Cuban American community, or will it lead to its decline? Will future generations contribute to the expansion and protection of the enclave economy? If the ethnic enclave does not survive, what will be the fate of future generations? Will they have the resources to join mainstream society or will they be relegated to the same positions that Mexican Americans and Puerto Ricans now occupy? Research and time will help to answer these questions, but the answers must be sought before it is too late.

Notes

1. Although Cubans, up to the Mariel boatlift, were characterized as refugees, there is evidence that the motivation for migrating changed over time (Portes, Clark, & Bach, 1977; cited in Boswell & Curtis, 1984). Whereas the earliest waves were clearly migrating for political reasons, later waves (starting with the 1970s) are believed to have been prompted primarily by economic motives rather than by political and religious persecution.

2. According to Moore and Pachon (1985), the U.S. government appropriated more than $1 billion to the Cuban Refugee Program between 1969 and 1979.

3. Cuban American educational attainment is higher than that of Mexican Americans and Puerto Ricans but lower than that of the non-Latino population (Boswell & Curtis, 1984). When compared with the Latino population as a whole, Cuban Americans are better educated, but they are not as well educated as the "other Spanish origin" group, which mainly includes immigrants from Central and South America, the Dominican Republic, and Spain.

4. This act significantly reduced the number of Cubans who were allowed legal entry into the United States (Boswell & Curtis, 1984). Breaking with tradition, the United States no longer granted Cubans refugee status; those seeking entrance had to apply on an individual basis, like other nonrefugees.

5. Although this group was characterized as social undesirables, only an estimated 4% (about 5,000) were hard-core criminals (Boswell & Curtis, 1984). Also, the so-called Mariel crime wave, according to some scholars, was a product of the sensationalization and overestimation of the crimes committed by this group and to the underestimation of the crime increase attributable to other (perhaps illegal) Hispanic immigrants (McCoy & Gonzalez, 1982; cited in Fradd, 1983). In fact, although a 1982 grand jury report showed that Mariel Cubans' percentage of arrests (16%) was twice that of the pre-Mariel groups (9%), both groups had lower rates of arrest than all other comparison groups (whites, Blacks, and other Latins or Caribbeans).

10

Support of Hispanic Elderly

JUAN J. PAZ

The uniqueness of the Hispanic elderly's family support derives from their natural helping system. Hispanic natural helping systems have a social structure that places the elderly at the center of the social network. The Hispanic family is an interdependent and interactive kinship network consisting of various generations. This family allows for mutual and reciprocal helping relationships among its various members, both nuclear and extended, and between the generations of the family system (Valle & Vega, 1982).

The Hispanic natural helping system is conceptualized as the elderly's main helping system. This system aids the elderly in performing vital nurturing tasks; the larger society, the sustaining system, is at the periphery. The system includes: (a) members of the immediate family—the husband, wife, and children; (b) the extended family—aunts, uncles, and cousins; (c) the *compadrazo* system, which is a system of church sponsors or godparents; (d) the *barrios,* also known as the *colonias,* consisting of friends and neighbors; and (e) the larger society, placed last in importance in the social order.

The concepts under study are set within the context of social systems theory, wherein human behavior is studied by viewing individuals in the situations in which they find themselves. The major principle tested in this study was the development of healthy self-esteem and a sense of mastery in the elderly, which often depends on positive reinforcement and information from their families. Hispanic elderly for the most part find themselves living within two cultures—the Hispanic culture and the culture of the dominant American society.

Culture is viewed as having a direct bearing on how the elderly view themselves and whether they perceive themselves as in control of their lives. Hispanic families are families in transition and are able to adapt to the demands placed on them by the larger cultural system, which itself is in a constant state of flux.

Social Systems, Self-Esteem, and Family Support

The Hispanic elderly are seen as occupying a central role within the family to which is ascribed respect (*respeto*), status (*su lugar*), and authority (*su experiencia y sabiduria*). According to Maldonado (1975), a warm and receptive attitude exists toward the elderly among Hispanic families. Older Hispanic individuals are conceptualized as having developed an awareness of their significance in society. They are seen as possessing a positive self-esteem and sense of mastery, and an inner strength. They feel they have something to offer younger generations.

Within the larger sustaining system, Hispanic older persons are recognized as being in triple jeopardy. They are old, poor, and belong to an ethnic minority group (Miranda & Ruiz, 1981). The larger sustaining system places higher value on youth, on persons who are productive members of society, and on persons who are white. The Hispanic elderly belong to groups that have been devalued and do not enjoy respect, status, and authority.

The vast majority of Hispanic elderly individuals are cared for by their immediate family members as well as by members of their extended family networks in their communities. For the most part, they depend on their families to provide the services they require. The values of the larger American society are seen by some as eroding traditional Hispanic values. As Hispanic families become more upwardly mobile, their elder members grow more socially isolated. The pressures of modernization and the advance of postindustrial society are seen as negatively affecting the role of the Hispanic elderly (Maldonado, 1975). Contrary to this position, Gibson (1985) views the Hispanic family as maintaining traditional family values. These values are carried out in the form of new behavioral expressions. One point of agreement between these perspectives is that the elderly are still seen as holding a central place in the family structure.

Method

The areas investigated were (a) the support and social reciprocity of the elderly and their families and (b) the elderly persons' perceptions of their self-esteem and mastery. The protocol included sections on family supports, the Rosenberg Self-Esteem Scale (1965), which measures self-esteem, and Pearlin's Mastery Scale, which measures an individual's control over his or her life (see Pearlin, Lieberman, Menaghan, & Mullan, 1981). The research instrument was translated into Spanish using conventional translation and interpretation methods. Particular attention was given to translating the questionnaire into the Spanish used in the Southwest United States, and three bilingual persons conducted the interviews.

Sample

Data were gathered in the barrios of two southwestern cities, Phoenix and Tucson, Arizona, selected for their high concentration of Hispanic family units. A total of 50 elderly persons were interviewed at each of the two sites. The elderly individuals in both communities have historical roots in the Southwest, in some cases dating back to before Arizona became a state. Most individuals identified themselves as being of Mexican descent, with some basic common values, including language, a preference for living in barrios in proximity to their families, and a shared sense of community.

The interviewers went to housing complexes with a large concentration of Hispanic families and every third housing unit was selected to identify elderly who could potentially participate in the study. The researchers were also assisted in recruiting participants by the economic development company that operates the housing complex, and received the endorsement of well-known aging advocates in both communities.

In Phoenix, the interviewees lived in an urban setting in a housing development containing 175 housing units built around a frequently used senior citizens' center. In Tucson, the elderly were interviewed in a housing development and a neighborhood center for the Hispanic elderly.

The population sample of 100 consisted of 68 females and 32 males. The larger proportion of women is explained by the fact that Hispanic women live longer than do Hispanic men. Of the 100 respondents, 65 lived alone and 45 were married and living with their spouses.

The majority of the elderly interviewed were born in the United States; only 39% indicated they were born in Mexico. From the total group, 80% reported that their fathers were born in Mexico and 77% that their mothers had been born in Mexico. The majority of the elderly had less than an eighth-grade education. One-third considered themselves to be bilingual, but 97 out of 100 chose to be interviewed in Spanish.

The vast majority (94%) of the elderly were unemployed or retired. The majority lived below or near the poverty level; 85% depended exclusively on Social Security for their income. Few respondents were receiving retirement income, and only 4% of the women indicated they received a widow's pension.

Results

Family Support

Most of the elderly had family support networks to help them cope with the realities of old age. Fully 90% indicated that they had someone whom they trusted and could confide in. Only 9% of the elderly indicated they had no one to trust and confide in. Most of the elderly identified their families as their caregivers. The majority (68%) stated that if they needed personal attention and care over a long period of time, usually a son or daughter would care for them. The remainder indicated that there was no one to care for them.

A significant relationship between family support and self-esteem was found ($F = 2.21$, $p = .041$). The relationship between family support and mastery was also statistically significant ($F = 2.21$, $p < .041$). Family support strongly influenced both the elderly's self-esteem and their sense of mastery.

Intergenerational Caregiving and Social Reciprocity

The elderly were asked to identify some of the functions they perform for their families on a Social Reciprocity Scale developed to measure levels of interaction between the elderly and their families. It consisted of an eight-item scale with Likert scale responses. Possible scores ranged from a low of 8 to a high of 32. For 93 valid observations, the mean Social Reciprocity Score was 18.79 ($SD = 4.81$). The elderly are performing important family functions such as *placticas* (talks), religious education, and social support.

The elderly were asked if they helped their families across the generations as caregivers. The responses were mixed: 72% sometimes helped their children with the problems of their own children, and one-third cared for their children and grandchildren when they were sick.

One of the most important activities of families is to communicate with their elderly members. The majority (55%) of the elderly had *placticas* or talks with their children or grandchildren, and 72% had been actively engaged in passing on religious beliefs to the younger members of their families. This suggests that while the elderly are actively involved and emotionally close to their families, they are able to recognize their limitations due to changes resulting from age.

Self-Esteem and Mastery

In Spanish, self-esteem is translated as *valor personal,* an expression related to an individual's sense of worth and inner strength. The Rosenberg Self-Esteem Scale (1965) was used to measure the level of the elderly's self-esteem. The scale consisted of 10 Likert items, with possible scores ranging from a low of 9 to a high of 36. For a total of 93 observations, the elderly had a mean self-esteem score of 26.19 ($SD = 2.93$). This suggests that the elderly had a high level of self-esteem and a balanced sense of self-worth.

They respondent felt that they had been successful in life and indicated that raising a family is a measure of success. Most felt that they were persons of value. However, 63% felt useless at times because they could not perform some of the same physical functions in old age that they were once able to do. The inability to work affected their sense of worth. Some felt they had lost some of their autonomy. The fact that they had to ask someone else for help to perform a task they could once do themselves served to diminish their sense of self. It appears that these elderly respondents defined success in life as the ability to be athletic and to raise a family, and diminished physical abilities and inability to work contributed to a diminished sense of self.

The Mastery Scale developed by Pearlin and Schooler (1978) was used to measure the elderly's sense of control over their own lives. The scale consists of seven items with Likert-type responses, with scores ranging from a low of 7 to a high of 28. For a total of 93 observations the elderly had a mean score of 18.51 ($SD = 3.14$). The elderly had a high sense of control over their own lives.

These findings suggest two concepts: First, having some measure of control over one's health contributes to a positive sense of control over one's life; second, mental determination to engage in and complete a task is a primary human value that contributes to a positive sense of mastery. Most of the respondents felt they had control over the things that happened to them. Many spoke about the fact that they had led healthy lives, which contributed to their sense of control. The majority felt they could do just about anything they set their minds to. They prized their ability to *cumplir,* to be able to complete the tasks they set out to do. A strong positive relationship was found between self-esteem and mastery ($r = .578$, $p < .001$).

Implications for Practice and Policy

One key principle regarding supportive practice with the Hispanic elderly is that there is a need to help families cope with the problems of their elderly family members. For the Hispanic elderly, the family can be conceptualized as a natural support network that provides needed emotional support as well as facilitating the acquisition of resources. With established strong kinship bonds, many define their own sense of self as being derived from their families. The elderly view themselves not only as individuals, but also as members of a collective self. The elderly's self-esteem and mastery are directly influenced by their family support.

Many of the respondents in this study said, in effect, Help my children, my family; if you help them, you are helping me. The family can serve as a source of support and help as well as a potential source of stress. There are times when a person is unable to cope effectively with a particular problem. In these situations, an elderly person may decide to ask for help at a social service agency. What is the role of the social worker in working with this type of client? One key strategy would be to redirect the elderly person back to his or her family and then to work with both the family and the elderly client to cope effectively with the presenting problem. The role of the practitioner would be to strengthen the family's ability to provide the needed assistance. This strategy may at times have to be carried out in the home environment, which would necessitate the social worker's making home visits as well as preparing for working with a family system. The family would be included as an integral part of the treatment or service plan and would become an active partner in helping to improve the elderly person's affect. At other times an elderly client may need help in separating the family's needs from his or her own.

The high level of self-esteem and sense of mastery found among the elderly in this sample suggests that they are empowered individuals.

They possess the inner strength and character to deal with the problems of life. In Spanish, one can say that these persons have developed *firmeza de caracter para lidiar con la vida.* On the other hand, individuals who possess a low level of self-esteem and sense of mastery are unable to draw upon any resources to cope with life's problems. These persons are often powerless and vulnerable to the stresses of old age.

Within a mental health setting, when an elderly client has a strong sense of self-esteem and mastery, the family is seen as a major contributor to the positive affect. However, when an older person is experiencing a low level of self-esteem and mastery, it would be incumbent upon the practitioner to assess whether the presence or absence of family support is contributing to this low level of affect. Therapists working in the mental health field need to consider that family members can play a vital role in helping older persons. The active involvement of a member of the elderly client's family in a treatment mode has the potential to contribute to improved affect.

When the Older Americans Act (U.S. Senate, 1985) was passed by Congress, its focus was to help elderly persons live with dignity in their old age. The act was the first far-reaching policy attempt to address the needs of all elderly persons in the United States. However, this legislation tends to isolate the elderly from other generations of the family. Family support plays a crucial role in the well-being of the elderly. Data from the Administration on Aging have revealed that participation by minority elderly persons in Older Americans Act-funded programs has declined during the past decade (U.S. House of Representatives, 1987). Reanalysis and reformulation of policies aimed toward helping the elderly are needed; steps should be taken to promote the well-being of the elderly within the family. Emphasis regarding the Hispanic elderly ideally should shift aid from individual elderly persons to more services to families with needy elderly members.

The family is a vital social structure that serves to help Hispanic elderly to cope with the problems of age. The individuals in the Hispanic elderly sample reported on here were found to be engaging in dynamic interactive relationships with their families—not only were their families helping them, they were helping their families. As a result, these elders were found to possess the necessary character strength, or *firmeza de caracter,* to cope with the vicissitudes of being old, poor, and members of a minority group.

11

Parenting Young Children in Mexican American/Chicano Families

ESTELLA A. MARTINEZ

As the most youthful and fastest-growing ethnic minority in the United States, the Mexican American population has been the subject of extensive speculation and predictions. Mexican American family life has been of particular concern because of the group's high immigration and fertility rates. The rearing of Chicano children is particularly salient because Hispanics, particularly Mexican Americans and Puerto Ricans, are the least educated major group of Americans (Blea, 1992; Education Commission of the States & State Higher Education Executive Officers, 1987; National Council of La Raza, 1986; U.S. Bureau of the Census, 1990). Low levels of educational attainment are often attributed to childhood socialization.

Research on Mexican American child rearing is limited, much of it is dated, and the findings are inconsistent. Results and descriptions have been supported by some researchers but contradicted by others. Despite a relatively recent increase in empirical research, there remains much conjecture about family socialization patterns and recitation of dated work (Vega, 1990). Empirical research, however, refutes many misconceptions, stereotypes, and myths, providing evidence that child rearing in Mexican American families is as diverse as the families themselves.

Group Identification

Fundamental to the understanding of children's socialization is identifying the group. Hispanic group identifiers such as *Chicano, Mexican*

American, and *Latino* are sometimes used interchangeably; however, the terms have different connotations for individuals who identify themselves as such. *Latino* refers to Latin American origin—that is, to Central or South America—as well as to Hispanic North Americans. *Spanish, Spanish American,* and *Hispano* refer either to persons who immigrated to the United States from Spain or to descendants of Hispanic or Indo-Hispanic ancestors who resided in today's Southwest when it was under Spanish and later Mexican rule.

The terms *Chicano, Mexican,* and *Mexican American* are used interchangeably in this chapter; however, it is acknowledged that the terms have different meanings for individuals. Chicanas (feminine) and Chicanos (masculine) who identify themselves as Chicano (the cultural group) recognize and take pride in their racial mixture, especially acknowledging Indian or Native American ancestry and, perhaps more important, are consciously aware of their social and political oppression in American society. *Chicano* is, therefore, a political identifier. Persons who identify themselves as Mexican American are making a bicultural statement about being American while simultaneously acknowledging their ethnicity. Those U.S. citizens who identify themselves as Mexican are making a statement about their ethnic loyalty or preference. *Hispanic* is the global identifier applied to this extraordinarily diverse subpopulation of North Americans by the U.S. Bureau of the Census (Martinez, 1988a). This diversity and the confusion over nomenclature contribute to misunderstandings about Hispanic families.

Studies on Child Rearing

Kearns (1970) studied 50 Anglo, 50 Mexican American, and 50 Papago Indian mothers of first-grade children in the urban area of Tucson, Arizona. Personal interviews were conducted in the homes of the subjects in their preferred language by interviewers of matched ethnicity. Interviewers recorded subjects' responses in shorthand and transcribed them later for rating. The research instrument was a self-report measure of maternal child rearing based on a structured oral interview, an adaptation of the rating scales developed by Sears, Maccoby, and Levin (1957) for their classic study, *Patterns of Child Rearing.*

Significant differences were found among the groups on the dimensions of strictness, restrictions on children, and permissiveness for aggression toward other children. Since socioeconomic status (SES) was controlled by including only lower-SES subjects, Kearns concluded that

186 Parenting in Mexican American Families

significant differences among Papago, Mexican American, and Anglo child-rearing practices are cultural. Among her subjects, Mexican American and Papago patterns of child rearing appeared to be governed to a large extent by traditional values and practices. Bonds with tradition appeared to be weakened among the Anglo mothers. Although Kearns generalized her results to patterns of child-rearing practices, the results of the study also applied to child-rearing attitudes, which her interview schedule also measured.

Kagan and Ender (1975) investigated the preferred reinforcement patterns of 16 urban Anglo-American, 16 urban Mexican American, and 16 rural Mexican mothers. American mothers were selected at random at a park in Riverside, California, and ranged from upper middle to lower economic class, as determined by family income. Rural Mexican mothers were chosen at random from the town of San Vicente, Mexico, where most families live slightly above subsistence level.

Subject participation was obtained by requesting that a mother-child pair spend time interacting in a game-like situation at a table, while the experimenter tallied mother responses. Prior to the experiment, family demographics and the amount of family income were obtained. During the experiment, measures were taken of the mother's responses to the success or failure of her child. The experiment consisted of each mother giving her child chips, taking chips away, or doing nothing when her child succeeded or failed to reach the child's predetermined goal in pressing a tally counter a specific number of times during timed intervals.

Analysis of the findings suggested a tendency for higher-income mothers to discriminate between success and failure more than lower-income mothers. Although neither group of American mothers discriminated between boys and girls in giving chips, they did give significantly more chips on success than on failure trials. Rural Mexican mothers gave almost as many chips following failures as they did following successes. Mexican American mothers, however, took more chips away from their children on failure trials.

The overall differences among mothers tended to be related to both economic and ethnic variables. The behavior of the two American groups was similar, except that Mexican American mothers were generally more punitive. Regression analysis of the results, however, indicated that the more frequent use of punishment by Mexican American mothers was a function of their lower economic level, and not of their culture. The researchers concluded that parental reinforcement patterns may function to maintain cultural and economic class differences. Thus

Kagan and Ender's findings on punishment suggest that Mexican American mothers of lower SES have a tendency toward authoritarian child-rearing practices.

Griswold (1975) studied Anglo, Black, and Mexican American mothers to gain information about child rearing as a function of ethnicity and SES. Her 114 subjects were from an Arizona metropolis: 52 were Anglo, 32 were Black, and 31 were Mexican American. SES of the Anglo mothers was 24 upper-, 18 middle-, and 10 lower class. Among Blacks, there were 11 upper-, 10 middle-, and 10 lower-class mothers. The Mexican American group comprised 11 upper-, 10 middle-, and 10 lower-class women. Mothers were identified through their second-grade children of dual-parent families, but the children were not included in the study as subjects. Two questionnaires were administered: the Maternal Information Needs and Attitudes Assessment (MINAA) and the Parent as a Teacher Inventory (PAAT).

Nonstatistical analysis of MINAA responses indicated that Mexican American and Anglo mothers expressed greater need for child-rearing information. Mexican Americans showed greater concern about their children's school experiences than did Anglos or Blacks. Mexican Americans and Blacks expressed more pride in their children's increasing independence, assumption of responsibility, and obedience. Mexican Americans were the least likely to consult agencies, services, institutions, and printed matter for help in child-rearing concerns. Mexican Americans and Blacks reported that they turned to their mothers and other family members for help in child rearing more often than did Anglos. Mexican Americans and Anglos regarded participation of both parents in child rearing, assurance and support from both parents, religious and moral faith, and a routine life-style as somewhat more important for children's proper adjustment than did Black mothers.

Conclusions were based on the statistical analysis of the PAAT, which measured creativity, frustration, control, play, and the teaching-learning process. Ethnic background had a significant effect on every variable except frustration; however, the major source of variance was between Anglo and Black mothers. There were no significant differences between Anglo and Mexican American or between Black and Mexican American mothers. In addition, SES had a significant effect on all the variables measured. The major source of variance was between upper- and lower-class mothers; however, variance on control, play, and teaching-learning was also attributed to differences between middle- and lower-class SES. Significant variance on control was attributed to differences between upper- and middle-class SES. Due to the higher proportion of Anglo upper- and middle-class mothers, Griswold was cautious about generalizing her findings. Nevertheless, the results of her study suggest that Mexican American mothers tend to have authoritarian child-rearing attitudes.

Some researchers have concluded that Mexican American parents have permissive attitudes toward child rearing. Durrett, O'Bryant, and Pennebaker (1975) interviewed 29 white, 30 Black, and 31 Mexican American pairs of mothers and fathers about their child-rearing orientations and techniques. The subjects were all low-income families with 5-year-old children enrolled in Head Start. A 91-item Q sort was individually administered to the parents in the home, in their preferred language of either Spanish or English. The Q-sort items were arranged by the subjects on a continuum of importance according to goals, methods, and perceived reactions to their children.

Measures of child-rearing orientations were achievement, authority, protectiveness, stressing of individual responsibility, control of emotions, and the positivity of the parent-child relationship. Measures of child-rearing techniques were consistency or lack of it; use of positive reinforcement, guilt, and aversive control; and physical punishment.

White and Black "parents reported being more authoritative (e.g., stressing respect for adults) than did Mexican-American parents" (Durrett et al., 1975, p. 871). The example—stressing respect for adults—suggests that authoritativeness disagrees with Baumrind's (1971) definition that the authoritarian, not the authoritative, mother "believes in inculcating such instrumental values as respect for authority" (p. 22).

Durrett and her associates also found that fathers of Black and white children were more achievement and success oriented than their Mexican American counterparts. Mexican American parents scored lowest on the category emphasizing individual responsibility and were significantly more protective. Mexican American parents stressed somewhat greater control of emotions than the other parents and were most consistent in their methods of reward and punishment. Use of reward when the child displays good behavior was a favored method of Black parents, but Black fathers also reported more use of strict arbitrary rules. Mexican American and white mothers reported using significantly more guilt in child rearing than did Black mothers. The groups did not differ significantly on the positivity of their parent-child relationships.

Durrett and her associates concluded that techniques of socializing children are similar among the groups, but that the parents' desired ends differ. This suggests that low-income Mexican American, white, and Black parents express different child-rearing "orientations" but have similar child-rearing "techniques." If the statistically significant findings are categorized according to Baumrind's (1971) definitions of permissive, authoritative, and authoritarian patterns of parental authority, the data suggest that the Mexican American parents' child-rearing practices tend to be authoritarian while their child-rearing attitudes are permissive.

Bartz and Levine (1978) compared the child-rearing attitudes of 152 Chicano mothers and fathers with those of 143 Anglo and 169 Black parents to identify unique ethnic child-rearing patterns. The research subjects, who resided in a low-SES urban community in Kansas City, Missouri, were randomly selected from public and parochial elementary school rosters. A survey questionnaire was administered in their homes in English or Spanish by interviewers of matched gender and ethnicity. When both parents participated, they were interviewed simultaneously but in different rooms. The questionnaire consisted of 25 statements selected from the Parent Attitude Research Scale (PARS) and the Cornell Parent Behavior Inventory (Cornell), both adapted for use with lower-class parents. The 17 statements selected from the PARS measured five factors labeled Acceleration of Autonomy, Casual Use of Time, Equalitarianism, Value Strictness, and Devalue Permissiveness. The eight Cornell items were labeled Lack of Support and Lack of Support Plus Lack of Control and were restated to measure parental perceptions of child rearing.

Comparisons by ethnicity on the seven factors indicated that the parents did not differ in their child rearing, but in the degree of their emphasis on particular attitudes or desired behaviors (Bartz & Levine, 1978). Levine and Bartz (1979) found that Chicano parents differed from Anglos and Blacks on six of the seven factors measured:

(1) Chicanos and Blacks, more than Anglos, pressed for early assumption of responsibility. This finding is in contrast to Durrett et al.'s (1975) findings on the same measure.

(2) Blacks, more than Chicanos and Anglos, pressed for wise time use.

(3) Chicanos were least likely of the groups to stress equalitarianism.

(4) Chicanos were more likely to value permissiveness than were Anglos.

(5) Chicanos and Anglos reported that they offer less support than Blacks.

(6) Chicanos and Anglo parents also reported that they are less controlling than Black parents.

No significant differences were found among the three groups on the strictness factor. The researchers indicated that this lack of significance suggests that all three groups value strictness in child rearing (Levine & Bartz, 1979, p. 171), but concluded that "Hispanic childrearing is quite permissive" (p. 175) in the low socioeconomic class.

Further analysis showed that education was nonsignificant as a control variable for all factors except one. "The higher the level of education, especially in Chicano families, the greater the belief in equalitarianism" (Bartz & Levine, 1978, p. 714). The levels of education for the sample were not given.

Levine and Bartz (1979) concluded that Chicanos, as a group, were more permissive and less equalitarian than Anglo and Black parents in their child-rearing attitudes. Cross-ethnic differences in attitudes, however, were more attributable to Chicano fathers than to mothers. F ratios on the seven factors suggested that Chicano fathers and mothers stressed acceleration of autonomy more than Anglo mothers. Chicano fathers, and not mothers, tended to devalue equalitarianism, support, and control. The conclusions—devalue equalitarianism and devalue control—appear contradictory. If equalitarianism is devalued, the implication is a lack of equality between parent and child, in which case control on the part of the parent would be expected.

The researchers further concluded that since Chicanos were less equalitarian than Anglos and Blacks, their findings were consistent with descriptions of the relatively authoritarian Hispanic family. These conclusions provide conflicting information, some of which may be attributed to the labels assigned to the categorical variables of the research instrument.

From his descriptive survey of the literature, Staton (1972) determined that Mexican American parents teach their children submission and obedience to the authority of their father. The mother, consequently, becomes the family affectional focus for the children. Although fathers would play with young children, attend to their needs, and demonstrate affection for them, they maintained authority and demanded respect from their children. As the children approached puberty, the fathers increased their distance in order to maintain authority.

Staton determined that Mexican American mothers and daughters tended to be close as a result of their male-dominated world and the daughters' training for their adult female role. The mother-son relationship was also described as close, with the mother serving as a permissive and affectional figure for the son. Many of these descriptions of traditional family roles have changed and may be considered stereotypical.

More recent descriptive studies characterize child rearing in Mexican American families as warm, nurturing, and affectionate, with emphasis on traditional respect for males and the elderly (Alvirez, Bean, & Williams, 1981; Delgado, 1980; Mirandé, 1977; Mirandé & Enriquez, 1979; N. Williams, 1990; Zuniga, 1992). In the families Williams (1990) studied, working-class couples either shared somewhat equally in disciplining their children with husband being stricter or the wife was the main disciplinarian. Among the professional class there were three subtypes of couples. In one group, the husband was the chief disciplinarian or disciplinarian of last resort. In the other, husbands and wives shared child discipline. In a third smaller group, wives were the chief disciplinarians in the family. Regardless of social class, the nature of discipline was found to shift considerably as children grow older.

Other researchers have also found that the child rearing of Mexican Americans is diverse, ranging from permissive to authoritarian to authoritative and consisting of varied child guidance practices. In their study of Mexican American perceptions of parent and teacher socialization roles, Para and Henderson (1982) interviewed 95 Chicano parents of lower and middle socioeconomic levels. The 70 subjects classified as middle-class were attending a community college and were employed in skilled or higher occupations. The 25 lower-class subjects were receiving welfare and/or public housing benefits.

The interview instrument consisting of 22 items calling for open-ended responses was administered in each subject's preferred language of either Spanish or English. It was developed by the researchers to elicit information on parents' child management practices, sex-role perceptions relating to children, age-related behavioral expectations, activities and qualities valued in children, learning outcomes and focus of responsibility, and aspirations and expectations for their children.

Most parents in both groups had a number of different means of controlling and guiding the behavior of their children. Explanation was used by 68% of the parents, and there was no difference by SES of subjects. The majority of parents in both groups reported the use of positive reinforcement, and about one-half of each group also used negative reinforcement. The two groups differed in reports of verbal punishment, with middle-class parents reporting significantly less use. Overall, physical punishment was used by fewer parents than any other category. When compared with practices using positive reinforcement, lower-status parents reported using both verbal and physical punishment to a significantly greater degree than did the middle-class parents. Analyzing these findings from the perspective of Baumrind's (1975, 1978) patterns of parental authority, the practices of lower- and middle-class Mexican American parents in this study ranged from authoritative to authoritarian.

Findings on the other areas of investigation by Para and Henderson (1982) revealed no statistically significant differences between lower- and middle-class subjects with the exception of learning outcomes and focus of responsibility. Of the 74% lower-class and 83% middle-class parents who had aspirations for their children to attend college, 67% of lower- and 44% of middle-status parents expected their children actually to complete college.

Despite their awareness of changes in society toward less differentiation in sex roles, a majority of the parents reported that they held different expectations for boys and girls. Age of a child also has a determining influence on how parents should respond. There was a balance between social and recreational skills and academic ability in the activities and qualities valued in children.

Most of the parents, 98%, perceived the main socialization task of the home as fostering socioemotional development. The school was perceived as having responsibility for fostering intellectual development and academic achievement.

Greathouse, Gomez, and Wurster (1988) found that ethnicity was not a factor in the child-rearing attitudes and practices of the Black and Hispanic mothers they studied; this supports findings in earlier studies (Levine & Bartz, 1979; Strom, Griswold, & Slaughter, 1981). The attitudes and practices of both ethnic groups were desirable and consistent with those that child development specialists view as conducive to positive development in children. It was also concluded that both groups protect, control, apply rules in an authoritarian manner, reward, and utilize guilt to obtain child compliance, just as other researchers have found (Durrett et al., 1975; Griswold, 1975).

Greathouse et al. (1988) investigated parents' locus of control, child-rearing attitudes and practices, and degree of involvement in Head Start of 42 nonworking Black and Hispanic mothers in a southwestern inner city. Most were low-income subjects. The PAAT, used in an earlier study in the same locale (Griswold, 1975), was administered in English or Spanish to assess child-rearing attitudes and practices. Parents and interviewers were matched ethnically. PAAT scores were 136.23 for Hispanic mothers and 137.19 for Black mothers. (Griswold had reported PAAT scores of 137.3 for Hispanics and 134.1 for Blacks.)

Both groups accepted creative functioning in their children and encouraged its development. They were not readily frustrated by their children's behavior. They valued children's play and the influence of play on child development, and saw themselves as facilitators in the teaching-learning process. Black mothers had significantly more education than their Hispanic counterparts, but there was no significant difference in their parenting attitudes and practices.

There was also no significant relationship between locus of control and child-rearing attitudes and practices for the sample. Hispanic mothers exhibited an external locus of control, contrary to the findings of other researchers (Durrett et al., 1975; Levine & Bartz, 1979). The findings are consistent with Buriel's (1981) study of parents' locus of control and child-rearing practices as reported from children's perspectives, suggesting that maternal support was positively related to their internal control and expectancy of their children's success.

My own research findings on Chicano child-rearing practices and the relationship of such practices to child behavior suggest that some lower-SES Chicanas' mothering behaviors are similar to the authoritative style generally characteristic of middle-class white mothers. Yet other lower-SES Chicanas tend to use authoritarian reinforcement patterns that are punitive and controlling, and that discourage verbal give and take. Still other Mexican American mothers tend to be permissive with their young children (Martinez, 1988b).

Evidence of diversity in mothering behaviors was found among a sample of lower-SES, working-class Chicanas during a structured teaching task with their kindergarten-aged children. These results lend support to the findings of Para and Henderson (1982) that Mexican Americans have an extensive range of child guidance practices that include reasoning, positive reinforcement, and punishment. The findings are also consistent with those of Kagan and Ender (1975) that some Mexican American mothers of lower SES tend to use authoritarian reinforcement patterns, which include punishment, in interactions with their children. On the other hand, the permissive child-rearing practices observed in only 4% of the mothers failed to support the findings of previous studies that permissiveness characterizes the child rearing of Mexican American parents (Durrett et al., 1975; Levine & Bartz, 1979).

Those mothers with authoritative patterns of child-rearing practices used (a) inquiry, (b) directives, (c) praise, and (d) physical affection more frequently, and in that order, than other behaviors. The order of the most frequent behaviors observed in the authoritarian mothers was as follows: (a) directives, (b) modeling, (c) visual cues, and (d) positive physical control. Permissive mothers used (a) praise, (b) inquiry, (c) physical affection, and (d) visual cues while they taught their children to make replicas of Tinkertoy models.

Observed maternal behaviors were clearly related to child behaviors. Chicanas encouraged initiative in their children by limiting their directives, frequently praising the children, and knowing when to guide their children physically through solution of the task. Children responded more positively to mothers who expressed approval of them, attracted and maintained the children's attention, and physically facilitated children's solution of the task. Mothers who taught their children primarily by modeling failed to maintain their children's attentiveness to the task. Children were also more verbally negative toward mothers who were punitive or disapproving of their behaviors. Statistically significant linear relationships were found between the following pairs of behavior variables:

(1) The more directives a mother issued, the less a child initiated or became absorbed in the task.
(2) The more a mother praised her child, the more the child questioned the mother.
(3) The more a mother praised her child, the more the child initiated or became absorbed in the task.
(4) The more a mother praised her child, the more the child responded to the mother.
(5) The more a mother modeled the task for her child, the more the child failed to respond to the mother.
(6) The more visual cues a mother gave her child, the more the child responded to the mother.
(7) As the mother's positive physical control increased, the child's positive verbal responses increased.
(8) As the mother's positive physical control increased, the child's physical response decreased.
(9) As the mother's positive physical control increased, the child's frequency of initiating or being absorbed in the task increased.
(10) As the mother's positive physical control increased, the child's failure to respond decreased.
(11) As the mother's negative physical control increased, the child's negative verbal responses increased.

A particularly interesting finding of the study was that 49% of the mothers used authoritative child-rearing practices. The authoritative style is associated with competitive and individualistic middle-class Anglo-American values that are considered antagonistic to communal and cooperative values of Mexican Americans (Baumrind, 1978). Moreover, in Laosa's (1978, 1980a, 1980b, 1980c) research using the Maternal Teaching Observation Technique with Chicanas, maternal behaviors varied with the mothers' educational levels. Chicanas who had completed at least eleventh grade used behaviors more characteristic of authoritative parenting; Chicanas with less than an eleventh-grade education used more authoritarian behaviors in their teaching strategies.

Despite the tenth-grade mean educational level of the lower-SES, working-class mothers in this study, nearly one-half of them demonstrated the authoritative child-rearing pattern generally associated with higher SES. This finding may be attributed to the mothers' acculturation and to the interaction between the family system and other systems in the environment. The mothers studied were three or more generations removed from Mexico, spoke English fluently, and lived in predominantly white neighborhoods of a medium-sized city in the Midwest. Another explanation for the authoritative child-rearing pattern used by nearly one-half of the mothers may be exposure to nonformal means of parent education through the media or community resources. These midwestern Chicano families had clearly adapted to their environment.

PART IV

Native American Families

12

The American Indian Experience

SUZAN SHOWN HARJO

We have been referred to as "Indians" for only 500 years. Prior to that we were, and remain, Tsististas, Lakota, Dine, Muscogee, Ojibway, and several hundred other nations. We still maintain 300 separate languages and dialects. The Indian population today is about 2 million. The population at the time Columbus landed in what is now Cuba in 1492 is in dispute, but many estimates put it at 10 million. The death of Indian people from diseases contracted through contact with Europeans is one of the greatest natural catastrophes of all time. Where these diseases were deliberately inflicted—such as the U.S. Army's delivery of small-pox-infested blankets to certain Indian nations—the catastrophes also fall in the category of national disgraces.

Today, Indian people have the highest birthrate in the United States, and also the highest mortality rate. The average age of death for Indian people is 45, and the median age is only 18. In terms of age, we are the demographic reverse of the United States as a whole.

The experience of most minorities in the United States has been a struggle to gain a place in the melting pot—social acceptance, economic power, and equal rights. The experience of Indian people is just the opposite. Our struggle is to avoid being subjugated and to preserve our land, our water, our traditions, and our unique legal rights. Indian nations are inherently sovereign and have negotiated approximately

AUTHOR'S NOTE: This chapter is adapted from the statement "Native American Experience," made before the House Select Committee on Children, Youth and Families, September 26, 1985.

600 treaties with the U.S. government. In this, we are different from racial and ethnic minorities. We ceded billions of acres of land and untold natural resources in return for a protected land base; water, hunting, gathering, and fishing rights; and educational and health services. Although many provisions of the treaties have been broken unilaterally by the United States, the treaties are still the "Supreme Law of the Land," as they are characterized in the U.S. Constitution. Nothing is more doomed to failure than an effort to toss Indian people into the general melting pot or to deal with Indian people on a strictly racial basis. Our legal status requires that we be dealt with on a government-to-government basis.

We cannot do justice to the suggested subject of Indian experiences with the U.S. government in these few pages. We do welcome, however, the opportunity to present a broad overview, and hope that this will further your interest in examining historical and contemporary Indian issues.

During the colonial period, the British Crown entered into numerous treaties with Indian nations, but did not formulate any coordinated policy. The lines established by the Crown in 1768, beyond which no European settlements were to occur, were routinely violated. Relations between colonists and Indians were often cordial, with Indians providing food, meat, and skills necessary for the immigrants to adjust to their new habitat.

Following the Revolutionary War, the Ordinance for the Regulation of Indian Affairs and the 1787 Northwest Ordinance were passed, promising no taking of Indian lands without Indian consent and requiring laws for the preservation of peace and friendship with the Indians. The first Indian law passed by the First Congress of the United States, the first of the Indian Nonintercourse Acts in 1790, stated that any Indian land transaction without congressional approval would be void, and President Washington interpreted this to the Seneca Nation as assurance that "in future, you cannot be defrauded of your lands."

Indian nations east of the Mississippi, however, were under constant pressure to give up their lands. The infant U.S. government did not enforce its favorable Indian laws against the powerful colonies turned states. During this period, most of the Indian lands in the East were stolen. Following the Indian Removal Act of 1830, most of the Indian population in the southeastern United States was forced to move to Oklahoma. The West at that time was not considered habitable by white people.

The mid-nineteenth century brought a great influx of European settlers to the West, lured by land and gold. And the coming of the railroad brought both accelerated migration and the destruction of the buffalo herds. The U.S. government, reflecting the pressure for Indian land and gold, began an aggressive policy of military action against Indians followed by negotiation of treaties. Between 1853 and 1856, 52 treaties were signed.

Assimilation, always an element of U.S. policy with regard to Indians, dominated U.S. Indian policy in the late nineteenth century and through part of the twentieth century. Assimilation for Indian people meant cultural genocide—a concerted effort to destroy Indian languages, traditions, customary laws, dress, religions, and occupations. Assimilation also meant the abrogation of treaties and the demand that we give up land, water, forests, minerals, and other natural resources.

Three major ways in which the goals of assimilation were to have been accomplished were (a) through federal franchising on Indian nations given to anxious Christian denominations; (b) through a culturally unraveling, imposed educational system designed to separate child from family and instill non-Indian values; and (c) through federal efforts to break up tribal landholdings, turn Indians into individual landowners, and impose taxes on their lands.

The U.S. education efforts directed at Indians were, until recently, based on the premise that Indian people are inferior to white people. The first congressional appropriation for Indian education funds was in 1819, when $10,000 was set aside in a "Civilization Fund." Indian people were to cast aside their traditions and be educated into the culture and religion of the dominant population. In 1871, President Grant delegated to churches the responsibility of nominating Indian agents and directing the education efforts on reservations. In fact, churches were assigned to specific reservations, and others were not allowed entry. The aim of government-sponsored, church-directed education was to strip Indian people of their religious views, practices, and languages. Indian religious ceremonies, including the Sun Dance and Ghost Dance, were prohibited. In schools, children were forbidden to speak their native tongues. By the end of the nineteenth century, there were many off-reservation boarding schools and day schools on reservations.

The establishment of boarding schools for children was a deliberate attempt to disrupt traditional child-rearing practices. Children were forcibly removed from their homes for up to 12 years, and parents and other relatives were not allowed to visit the children during the school year. Children were taught that their traditions were savage and immoral. There are many accounts of parents in this century camping outside the gates of boarding schools to get a glimpse of their children.

Most Indian grandparents and many parents today are the products of boarding and other government schools. Those whose childhoods were spent in boarding schools have little in the way of role models for rearing children. There have been major efforts in the past couple of decades to recover from these past experiences and to reestablish traditional Indian family values. Those values often include an extended family, with sharing of child care among relatives. Extended family identification is central to citizens of Indian nations. The Indian Child Welfare Act of 1978 broke the chain of wholesale expatriation of Indian children when it recognized the traditional kinship system and the nonparental rights of extended family members.

Indian education today, fortunately, is coming under increasing tribal control, primarily as a result of important education reform acts of the 1970s. The result is a culturally relevant curriculum that includes emphasis on tribal history, Indian languages, and increased self-esteem. Indian education is the most decentralized of Indian programs, and the one on which the government has the least hold. While Indian tribes and parents are finally gaining control over Indian schools and have made the few remaining boarding schools into institutions that are administered by Indian boards and serve children with special needs, the federal government under the Reagan administration attempted to lessen the commitment to Indian education. The Bureau of Indian Affairs (BIA) is engaged in an aggressive campaign to get Indian children to attend public schools by redrawing school boundaries, instituting new student counts that will result in less money for BIA schools, and foot-dragging in maintaining school facilities, among other devices. Fortunately, a number of members of Congress are vigilant where Indian education is concerned, and some of these practices have been held in check.

While curricula for Indian-controlled schools are vastly improved, the same is not true for the history texts used by most students in grade schools, high schools, and colleges around this country. Most history courses relegate Indian matters to a few pages or at best a chapter. At Thanksgiving, most schools have an "Indian unit." During Indian unit time, or when there is a day or week set aside as "Indian awareness" time, our office receives many calls from students wanting information on Indian issues, posters, pictures, and so on. We are glad to provide what we can, but wish that an understanding of Indian history and contemporary issues was put in a more natural context.

A recent study of 13 newly issued college history textbooks by Fred Hoxie of the Newberry Library in Chicago revealed that most of the new books still persist in treating Indian history with ignorance, misrepresentation, and apathy. Most of the textbooks reviewed by Hoxie did not include new scholarly work on the native population at the time of Columbus. It makes a big difference in your view of history whether 1 million or 12 million tribal people were here at the time of European immigration to North America. We have many problems with textbooks that refer to the Battle of the Little Big Horn as a "massacre," while the deaths of 300 unarmed and sleeping Indian men, women, and children at Wounded Knee is referred to as an "incident."

The Indian land base has gone from 138 million acres in 1887 to approximately 50 million acres today. There are many reasons for land loss, including flooding for Corps of Engineers projects, creation of national monuments, taking of land for tax defaults and welfare payments, invalidation of wills, and BIA-forced sales on the open market. The 1887 Allotment Act or Dawes Act alone resulted in the loss of more than half the Indian land. Of the 48 million acres left after the Allotment Act took its toll, 20 million acres were desert or semiarid and not suitable for cultivation. The federal government promised to irrigate these lands and "to make the deserts bloom." For most of these arid reservations, this promise remains unfulfilled.

The Allotment Act allocated land on reservations that had been guaranteed by treaties. Every family head was to receive 160 acres and a single person 80 acres. The idea was that Indians should become farmers and thereby become more civilized. This notion of farming was not well received by many tribes and was particularly onerous to many Indians in the Great Plains. The land was to be held in trust status for 25 years. Indians deemed "competent" by the federal government could end the trust status, own the land in fee simple, and become U.S. citizens. Any land outside the allotted acreage was declared to be "excess" and sold to non-Indian settlers. Sometimes in western movies you see white settlers lining up and, at the shot of a gun, running to claim land. Often, the land distributed this way was Indian land declared excess by an act of Congress.

Much of the remaining land has been lost through the inheritance system managed by the federal government. Under this system, a nightmare of fractionated land has developed. Land is passed on to every member of a family to be held jointly, with escalating numbers of landowners through the generations. This has made management and land title issues most difficult, as consent of the landowners has to be gained before any transactions can take place. In many cases, heirs have moved away and their whereabouts are not known. At the Sisseton-Wahpeton Reservation in South Dakota, the first reservation to undergo allotment, people literally own square inches of land. As a result, the land is of little economic value to the Indians, so it is leased out by the Bureau of Indians Affairs to non-Indians. Most non-Indian farmers and ranchers have held very cheap long-term leases on these Indian lands.

Several years ago, Congress passed the Indian Land Consolidation Act to provide authority to tribes and individuals to consolidate and better use land holdings. However, it will take many years before any real improvement can be realized, and the method of separating the fractionated interests from the Indian heirs in one of the act's provisions has been determined to be unconstitutional in one federal circuit court.

During the allotment period, U.S. citizenship was conferred on Indian people, whether they wanted it or not, if their land was held in fee status. In 1919, a law was passed making Indians who had served in World War I U.S. citizens, and in 1924 the Indian Citizenship Act was passed. The federal definition of *Indian* is one who is a citizen of an Indian nation, and courts have held that the Indian definition is political, rather than racial.

The Indian Reorganization Act (IRA), passed in 1936, finally put a formal end to the allotment policy, and the Indian land base has remained relatively constant since that time. The IRA also contained provisions for the establishment of a revolving credit fund to foster economic development and mechanisms for chartering and organizing Indian governments. This interest in tribal self-government was short-lived. During the period from World War II to 1961, a series of disruptive assimilation efforts occurred to force Indians into the melting pot. This era is referred to as the "termination period." During the 1950s, federal Indian policy involved the termination of the tribal-federal relationship with certain Indian governments, the liquidation of their estates, the transfer of federal responsibility and jurisdiction to states, and the physical relocation of Indian people from reservations to urban areas. Termination legislation affected more than 100 tribes, bands, and rancherias; some 12,000 individual Indians were disenfranchised, and 2.5 million acres of Indian land were removed from trust status. Today, many of these tribes are attempting, via federal legislation, to be restored to their former status. In recognition of the disastrous effects of this policy, Congress already has restored several Indian tribes in Wisconsin, Oregon, Oklahoma, and Utah.

Since the 1960s, U.S. policy has placed more emphasis on tribal self-determination. A number of important laws directed at this goal have been enacted, but none in its implementation has met the expectations for reform. Among these laws are the Indian Self-Determination and Education Assistance Act of 1975, the Indian Child Welfare Act of 1978, and the American Indian Religious Freedom Act of 1978.

The Indian Self-Determination and Education Assistance Act directed the secretary of interior, upon the request of any Indian tribe, to contract with the tribe to "place, conduct and administer programs." This was a radical departure from the system of undisguised paternalistic government-run programs on reservations. This is, however, far from a completed process. While there are now schools and health and law enforcement programs administered by tribes, the BIA and the Indian Health Service still have veto power over contracts the tribes wish to negotiate. Often, there are massive bureaucratic and financial obstacles to tribal government efforts to contract to administer their own services. And important training, technical assistance, and funding aspects have yet to be implemented as mandated.

The Indian Child Welfare Act of 1978 was designed to strengthen Indian families by stopping the practice of removing Indian children from their homes and placing them with non-Indian families, off the reservation. From 1969 to 1974, 25-35% of Indian children were separated from their families and placed in foster care, with adoptive families, or in institutions. Some 85% of Indian children in foster care were in non-Indian homes. During this same period, one in four Indian children in Minnesota under age 4 was adopted. In South Dakota, Indian children were 16 times more likely than non-Indian children in that state to be in foster homes. In Washington, Indian children were placed in foster homes and adoptive homes at rates 10 times and 19 times higher, respectively, than non-Indian children in that state. By 1980, Indian children were placed out of homes at a rate five times higher than other children. Placement for children, whether in Indian or non-Indian homes, still is very high. In 1980, Indian children were 22 times as likely to be placed out of the home in South Dakota and 20 times as likely in Minnesota as other children in those states. The Indian Child Welfare Act recognized tribal jurisdictional authority regarding custody proceedings, and the practice of non-Indian adoption over the objection of the extended families has been halted in great part.

Another indication of congressional and administration concern for preservation of Indian culture was exhibited in the passage in 1978 of the American Indian Religious Freedom Act (AIRFA). That act states, "It shall be the policy of the United States to protect and preserve for American Indians their inherent right of freedom to believe, express and exercise the traditional religions of the American Indian, Eskimo, Aleut and Native Hawaiians, including but not limited to access to sites, use and possession of sacred objects, and the freedom to worship through ceremonies and traditional rites."

The hoped-for protection of and access to sacred sites and areas has not been made possible by the American Indian Religious Freedom Act. Governments and courts in the United States seem to have no trouble accepting the fact that there are holy places in Jerusalem, Bethlehem, and Mecca, but they do not give the same credence to areas of spiritual significance to American Indians. Most tribal religions have a center at a particular place, be it a river, mountain, plateau, valley, or other natural feature. The problem of lack of access is exacerbated by the increased development on federal lands in the West, where many Indian religious sites are located. Access to sacred areas is needed for spiritual renewal and communication, and many feel that development of certain areas threatens their religions with extinction.

The First Amendment and AIRFA have not been of much use in protecting Indian people's ability to exercise their religions freely. The courts have taken the curious position that to prohibit an action (i.e., building a ski resort on a mountain sacred to Indians) would constitute the establishment of religion. In an inventive and tragic opinion, a court ruled that the Tellico Dam could flood sacred Cherokee areas, which included many burial sites, because the land was not "central" to their religion. This criterion of centrality is not easily proven, especially since many tribal religious beliefs prohibit the public discussion of those beliefs. The flooding of Indian graves by the Tellico Dam is but an isolated example of the violation of Indian beliefs and sensitivities regarding our ancestors. Nearly all of the human remains unearthed in this country are Indian. Many thousands of Indian human remains are in museums and universities all over the country. The Smithsonian, by its own account, has 12,000 Indian bodies in its collection. The National Congress of American Indians and others are currently discussing this matter with the Smithsonian Institution, and it may need congressional attention for these remains to be returned to tribes for reburial.

The issues described above—the taking of land, forced relocation, an institutionally racist educational system, removal of Indian children from their homes, U.S. government paternalism, obstacles to self-governance, stripping of tribal recognition, and denial of religious freedom—continue to place great stress on Indian families. Symptoms of these policies are, not surprisingly, high unemployment and alcohol and drug abuse. Indian unemployment stands at about 65%; in some tribes, it is as high as 90%. Alcoholism has greatly increased since World War II among Indian people, and it would be difficult to find an Indian family not directly affected by it. The 1980 census shows the alcoholism rate for Indians to be 451% higher than that for the rest of the U.S. population. Even though alcohol and drug abuse is the number one social problem among Indian people, and alcohol-related diseases and accidents are the biggest killers of Indians, the Bureau of Indians Affairs and the Indian Health Service have never made the prevention and treatment of this abuse a priority.

13

Kinship and Political Change in Native American Tribes

DUANE CHAMPAGNE

To understand American Indian families, we need to be aware of the distinctiveness of the various nations. A historical overview of four tribes during periods of rapid political change is presented here. Between 1827 and 1867, four indigenous American Indian societies (Choctaw, Chickasaw, Cherokee, and Creek) from the southeastern quarter of the present United States formed constitutional governments modeled after the U.S. government or local state governments. Under intense pressure from the federal government, as traditional land was taken away from them, American Indian societies handled the changes that were occurring in different ways. The type of kinship system in each tribe had a direct bearing on the speed and acceptance of these transitions.

All four societies were quite small by both contemporary and historical standards. The Cherokee population over the nineteenth century varied from 25,000 to about 43,000, while the Choctaw and Creek populations tended to decline, from about 30,000 to about 10,000 to 12,000. The Chickasaw population ranged between 3,000 and 5,000. Thus the size of the cases limits the generalizability of the results of this study.

AUTHOR'S NOTE: I gratefully acknowledge research assistance from the American Indian Studies Center at the University of California, Los Angeles, and financial support from National Science Foundation, Grant No. R118503914.

Variables

The four societies were similar in many respects that are theoretically linked to social change; therefore, these variables were considered controlled in the study. The major variables are degree of differentiation and solidarity, as measured by the extensiveness of the kinship system. According to the theory of differentiation, more differentiated political systems will have fewer obstacles to change. Thus a society that starts out with a more differentiated political system than the others will encounter fewer institutional obstacles to political change. For example, in a society where political relations are defined in terms of the kinship system, major change in the political system requires an accompanying reorganization of the kinship system. Given that more institutional relations have to be changed, greater resistance to change can be anticipated in less differentiated societies.

Under intense internal and/or external conditions, even non-differentiated systems can change. It is my argument that all four of the nations studied encountered similar levels of intense external political, economic, and cultural forces for change. Therefore, the more differentiated societies should be more capable of accepting and institutionalizing further political changes (Badie & Birnbaum, 1983; Durkheim, 1986; Luhmann, 1982; Parsons, 1966, 1971).

Historical Background

After the War of 1812, the British formally withdrew aid and diplomatic ties to Indian nations east of the Mississippi River. The Spanish, who controlled West Florida, sold it to the United States in 1819. The Spanish did not believe they could defend Florida against the Americans.

The period after 1817 found the Americans in a position to consolidate political control over the eastern half of the present United States. This was a critical time for the Indian nations, who were now forced to contend with a single and considerably more powerful American government. American government policy aimed to persuade the Indians to take up agriculture and Christianity, attend schools, and, most important, cede territory for U.S. settlers. In the Southeast, the rise in the price of cotton sent settlers into the interior in search of land to establish cotton plantations that would export cotton to the textile mills of England. Since 1794, the American government had attempted to induce Indian nations to cede land, and every several years American officials would ask tribal leaders for more land cessions. After 1817, American officials began increasingly to ask the Indian nations to exchange all of their land east of the Mississippi River for roughly the same amount of land located west of the Mississippi river. This was called the "removal policy"; it had been suggested by Thomas Jefferson while he was president.

Until 1828, the Federalists controlled the American government, and they favored a strong central state against states' rights. In the Constitution, the management of Indian relations was delegated to the federal government and not to the several states. Thus the Federalists demanded that all treaties and cessions of Indian land be the business of the federal government and not of the states, which were clamoring for extinguishment of Indian land title. After the election of Andrew Jackson, the federal government favored a much stronger emphasis on removal of Indian tribes west of the Mississippi River. In the late 1820s and early 1830s, Georgia, Alabama, and Mississippi extended their laws over the Indian nations in the Southeast in an attempt to harass the southern Indian nations into removing west of the Mississippi River. The federal government supported the states by arguing that the only reasonable alternative for the southern tribes was for them to be removed.

In 1830-1832 most of the Choctaw were removed to present eastern Oklahoma. The Chickasaw were removed in the late 1830s, and most Creeks were removed in 1836-1837. Most of the Cherokee were forced to remove in 1838-1839. Most members of the four Indian nations did not wish to leave their traditional homelands, and were strongly inclined not to cede land and to retain their political nationality from state and U.S. encroachments. In all four nations, the American threat to territory and of removal was a major impetus for developing strategies for political survival on their traditional homelands (M. D. Green, 1982, p. 22; McLoughlin, 1986, pp. 326-349; *Missionary Herald,* 1829, pp. 153, 382; Young, 1961, p. 9).

Cherokee

The Cherokee had the most differentiated political institutions and the strongest institutions of social solidarity among the four nations. By the beginning of the nineteenth century, Cherokee national political office was not dependent on kinship, and, consequently, the political sphere was also differentiated from the kinship system. The societal community was composed of seven clans that were unified through mythical and ceremonial relations. The clans were represented in all the major regions and villages of the society and helped unify the nation in ceremonial and kinship terms, although not necessarily in political terms. Cherokee clans did not act as corporate political units in regional and national political relations. Cherokee society was composed of villages, in which most of the seven clans were represented. All seven clans participated and had specific roles in ceremonial activities, which thereby enhanced the Cherokee sense of social solidarity. Representatives from the seven clans sat among the inner circle of the town council.

Clans participated in political decisions at the village level. Cherokee villages, however, were corporate units, and each village made its own decisions and sent representatives to the national council, which was composed of delegations from all the villages. The village delegations did not represent clan interests, but represented the decisions of the local village as a group, and thereby were not contingent on clan affiliation.

Owing to pressure to cede land between 1805 and 1810, the Cherokee formed a standing committee to negotiate and manage relations with the American government. The committee was composed of large landholders who had literacy and language skills that would allow them to negotiate with the American government. In the preceding years, several leaders of the Lower Town Cherokee had sold land to the United States without permission from the national council. The threat of further land loss and of removal led the Cherokee to attempt to centralize and regularize their government.

In 1817, the Cherokee national council expanded the powers of the standing committee to include administration of daily government relations with the United States. They also adopted majority rule in the national council. The traditional method of political decision making by unanimous consent from delegations from the 50 villages was considered too unwieldy to accommodate the persistent American pressures. Both the formation of a standing committee and majority rule were direct responses to external political threats to Cherokee national autonomy.

In 1819, the Cherokee reorganized their nation into eight districts for purposes of government and judicial administration. The national council became electoral, and the number of the national council was greatly reduced. All adult males were given the right to vote, although slaves were not able to vote or to participate politically.

Between 1819 and 1927, the Cherokee made laws and incremental improvements to strengthen their government's ability to resist incessant American demands for land cessions and removal. The constitution of

1827 created a bicameral legislature, with the standing committee forming the upper house and the national council the lower house. The primary purpose of the constitutional government was to preserve Cherokee land and national political autonomy.

Between 1810 and the early 1830s, a majority of Cherokee, both conservative subsistence farmers and large landholders, formed a relatively unified coalition against American land and removal threats.

Choctaw

The Choctaw showed little or only nominal national political solidarity. At the turn of the nineteenth century, they were organized by local kinship settlements, each of which had a local leader or captain. There were 90 captains, 30 in each of the three political districts. The Choctaw were divided into two moieties, but the village settlements were composed primarily of local matrilineal, matrilocal kinship groupings.

In Choctaw society a delegation of local settlement leaders, usually a local headman and a warrior leader, represented the local clan settlement in the national and regional councils. Consequently, kinship groupings had direct access to political decision making, and the political system was not differentiated from the kinship system. Decisions at the local level were made by consensus in the settlement council, and consensus among the captains or local clan leaders was required for binding decisions in the national council. Furthermore, Choctaw mythology clearly separated religious roles and political or civil leadership, so that the organization and structure of Choctaw political relations were not explicitly determined by cultural orientations.

The local settlements and the three traditional Choctaw regions retained considerable local and regional autonomy. The three districts shared a common culture and kinship system, but politically they acted independently, and on several occasions during the eighteenth century they were engaged in civil war. During the early nineteenth century, the three political districts remained hostile and noncooperative (Bossu, 1962, pp. 164-165; Linceum, 1870; Romans, 1961, p. 51; Rowland & Sanders, 1927, pp. 90, 108, 116, 145, 150, 155; Swanton, 1931, pp. 50-57).

As with the Cherokee, Choctaw planters assumed more political power as American demands for land cessions and removal intensified. In the early 1820s, incremental political and economic changes were made within the traditional form of government.

In 1830, the chiefs resigned their positions in favor of the northwest district chief, who was declared principal chief and was empowered to negotiate an upcoming removal treaty with the United States. The political centralization and the signing of a removal treaty by the new principal chief precipitated an uprising led by two of the chiefs who had been removed from office. The old district chiefs reasserted the traditional decentralized political order. Considerable negative sentiment was generated toward the views and goals of the previous government. Some of the districts actively opposed further changes in religion, political organization, and education.

The Choctaw signed a removal treaty in 1830, and in the next few years most moved west, to present eastern Oklahoma. There they made incremental changes in their political institution. They wrote a constitution in 1834 that contained a bill of rights and defined voting privileges. They revised the constitution in 1838, 1843, 1850, and 1855. The national council consisted of 30 elected delegates. The Choctaw did not seem to have any difficulty in decreasing the size of the national council from the traditional 90 captains.

The Chickasaw seceded in 1855, and a group of Choctaw planters seized the occasion in 1857 to centralize the government with a new constitution. The new constitution abolished the old district chieftainships and created a single governor over the entire nation. The next year, the conservative small farmers countered with a constitution of their own that preserved intact the autonomy of the traditional three political districts. The conservatives did not want a centralized government or state and wished to preserve the independence of the three districts. In 1860, the smallholders and planters agreed to form a compromise constitution. The compromise preserved the three traditional political districts but reserved administrative power for the governor (Baird, 1979; Debo, 1972, pp. 43-45; *Missionary Herald,* 1831; M. H. Wright, 1929; Young, 1961, p. 26).

Chickasaw

The Chickasaw had a low level of political differentiation. The societal community was based on kinship. Each of the local kinship settlements was led by a chief or captain. The local kinship groups were organized into four principal districts, which had been at one time major villages. The Chickasaw national council was formed of all the captains, the four district chiefs, a hereditary principal chief, a war chief and assistant, and perhaps a head priest. Local kinship groups sent their leaders directly to the national council.

The position of principal chief, whose authority tended to be nominal, was hereditary within a specific clan. Decisions were made by consensus within the local kinship settlements and within the national council. The organization of the political system based on local kinship groupings did not have direct or explicit cultural legitimation. Decisions make in council were informed by Chickasaw worldviews and culture. By the late 1790s, the council no longer met in the traditional sacred village square (Baird, 1974, pp. 7-8; Jennings, 1947; Malone, 1922, pp. 38, 188-193, 208-213; Steacy, 1971).

In 1838, while desperate for somewhere to emigrate after having been pressured by the U.S. government into agreeing to removal, the Chickasaw agreed to join the Choctaw nation, but had to accept Choctaw political institutions. During the early 1840s, the Chickasaw formed a fourth district in the yet decentralized Choctaw government. The Chickasaw traders and planters accepted the decentralized constitutional government of the Choctaw, and tried to use it as a means to eliminate the old Chickasaw kin-based tribal government. The planters were supported by U.S. agents, who refused to recognize the old Chickasaw government. After a series of conflicts in the mid-1840s, the Chickasaw planters reconciled themselves with the conservative majority, but the conservatives had to compromise and accept a constitutional government, because the U.S. government would not recognize their old kin-based government. Furthermore, the conservatives wished to separate from Choctaw society and reestablish their national independence.

In 1846, a Chickasaw constitution was written, and this government formed a nationalistic countermovement to the Choctaw district government. In 1848 the constitution was reorganized, and the Chickasaw campaigned for national independence, which they regained in 1855 with the help of the American government (Baird, 1974, pp. 7-8; Littlefield, 1980, pp. 45-47, 143-144, 149-155; Meserve, 1934, 1938; M. H. Wright, 1929).

Creeks

The Creek confederacy was composed of about 50 locally autonomous villages or tribal towns. Each tribal town had a particularistic religious identity and relation with the Great Spirit. Furthermore, the towns and clans were organized by a symbolic division into red towns and white towns, red clans and white clans. Red towns controlled the government during times of war, and white towns controlled the government during peace. The towns were also divided geographically into upper and lower towns. The upper and lower towns each had a principal red town and a principal white town. The Creek political system was decentralized and segmentary, and organized primarily in cultural and symbolic terms.

The Creeks were the least differentiated of the four nations discussed here in terms of culture and polity. The cultural sphere organized and interpenetrated the political and kinship system. Cultural symbolism defined the organization of the political sphere and the division of labor between the tribal towns. The cultural order, political order, and societal community were nondifferentiated, as the cultural order interpenetrated and organized political and kinship relations.

Participation in extratown political councils, however, did not depend on kinship ties. Delegates to regional and national councils represented their tribal towns as a corporate group and did not represent a clan or moiety grouping. Tribal town leaders represented their villages as independent and autonomous religious and political groupings. Thus national political organization was differentiated from direct kinship relations.

The Creeks did not respond to the intense pressures of the removal period after 1817 with any significant reorganization of their government. In fact, most Creeks actively opposed political and economic change, and in 1813-1814, a majority of villages joined in the fundamentalist Red Stick movement that tried to destroy American-supported economic and political innovations.

By the middle 1830s, the Creeks were pressured into emigrating to present Oklahoma. In the West before the American Civil War, the Creeks did not make any significant alterations in their government. The two principal red towns continued to dominate the government as they had since the late 1790s. Planters controlled the lower town's principal red town, Coweta, and also dominated most of the lower town district. The upper towns were dominated by the more conservative leadership of the principal red town of Tuckabatchee.

In 1867, the Creek large landholders wrote a constitution, which included election by ballot. The conservatives, most of whom were not literate in English, assumed and demanded that elections be held in the traditional style, with individuals lining up behind each candidate. Many conservatives did not understand the new system of voting, and although they claimed the majority, they lost the election. Conservatives claimed the election had been won by fraud. Thereafter, many conservatives rejected the new government and wanted to return to a simplified system, but the U.S. government upheld the constitutional government. Consequently, the conservatives formed a countergovernment and waited for successive elections in order to regain power.

Throughout the rest of the nineteenth century, however, the large landholders dominated the Creek constitutional government. Elections were hotly contested, and on several occasions the conservative Creeks were in open rebellion against the constitutional government. American policy supported the Creek constitutional government and U.S. marshals and troops were supplied to maintain order. On the few occasions that conservative leaders were elected to high executive office, they remained powerless and ineffective (Debo, 1979, pp. 4-24; Ohland, 1930).

Conclusions

The Cherokee formed a state earliest and have the most strongly institutionalized or stable state organization of all the nations discussed here (McLoughlin, 1986). Cherokee society was the most differentiated, based primarily on the differentiation of polity from kinship and culture. The culturally integrated Cherokee societal community, or seven-member clan system, provided stronger societal integration than the more segmentary kinship systems of the Creeks, Choctaw, and Chickasaw.

In contrast to the Cherokee, the Chickasaw and Choctaw National Councils were organized by local kinship groups. The Creek political order and kinship system was interpenetrated and defined by the cultural order. The Creek were the least differentiated owing to the predominantly cultural organization of the Creek towns and kinship system. They were the last to form a state and exhibited the weakest normative institutionalization of their state government.

The ability of American Indian families to adjust to change is related largely to their kinship patterns. Given the intense political pressures of the removal period and the emerging class formations in each society, political centralization, as in the Cherokee case, seems a likely response, but the form of the response is not determined by geopolitical and class relations alone. The societies with less differentiation and solidarity responded to removal pressures by attempting to strengthen their existing institutions.

14

Social Services
With Native Americans

Current Status of
the Indian Child Welfare Act

CHARLOTTE TSOI GOODLUCK

Cultural diversity is a major strength of the indigenous peoples of the
United States, as is their ability to survive and learn from other tribal groups
with different values, languages, and life-styles. American Indians today
represent cultural pluralism in action. In general, the value system is based
on a humanistic ethos, and there is great respect for the individual within
the tribal context. These traditional values and ethics have been translated
into a social welfare policy for today's complex world.

The purpose of this chapter is to discuss the Indian Child Welfare Act
(ICWA) of 1978 (Public Law 95-608), its rationale and implementation,
and the roles of the social worker, as well as to make available for the
reader various resources on the Act.

Historical Overview

Indian history includes various stages of early federal-state-tribal contact, reservation development, development of tribal court systems and
laws, cross-cultural conflict, and the development of the relationship

between each tribe and the U.S. government. The history is problematic and fraught with tension, containing incidents of racial and ethnic conflict, and illustrates extreme value differences on every level. These differences in values include views of the individual and of the family, extended family, tribal systems, and, most important, different styles of parenting. Always in the background has been the issue of whether American Indians should be encouraged or coerced to assimilate, or whether they have the right to retain a separate identity as a sovereign people. Throughout American history, influential politicians and policy developers have debated whether Indian cultures and races should continue as viable entities (Weeks, 1990). These various federal-Indian policies have swung on the continuum between tribal autonomy and assimilation into the American mainstream.

The Indian Child Welfare Act of 1978 is an affirmation of the value of Indian cultures, an affirmation of their right to self-perpetuation and to enculturate tribal children into tribal belief and value systems. The ICWA is a capstone federal piece of legislation that marks a time in history when federal-state-tribal relationships became entwined and actions by various parties became accountable and inclusive of tribal goals for their children.

The ICWA was passed by Congress on November 8, 1978, and signed into law by President Carter after numerous Senate hearings were held on the status of American Indian children, extended families, and tribal issues both on and off the reservations. These congressional hearings have been summarized in numerous articles (see, e.g., Byler, 1977; Dorsey, 1984; H. Green, 1983) and various legal cases (see Grossman, 1985). The most significant finding of the hearings was that "an alarmingly high percentage of Indian families were broken up by the removal, often unwarranted, of their children from them" (Byler, 1977, p. 1). A rate of 25-35% of all American Indian children being placed in substitute care, including foster care, adoption, and other forms of institutionalization (Byler, 1977), is often mentioned. This is a major point in pre-ICWA literature, and it is mentioned in the first section of the Act in the philosophy statement, prior to any of the policy or procedure discussions.

The Act declares that each state dealing with American Indian children in court actions such as child abuse and neglect cases, foster care placements, and preadoption or adoption petitions will incorporate the following policies in their state court proceedings:

(1) Promote tribal Indian family stability and security.
(2) Comply with minimum federal standards for the removal and placement of Indian children.

The Act has three basic sections, as described below.

Child custody proceedings. The first part describes procedures for states and tribes when a child is referred for service. This includes definitions of who is considered an Indian child, tribal court jurisdiction, transfer of jurisdiction, tribal intervention in state court proceedings, notices to tribes and states of each party's role and responsibilities, involuntary and voluntary child proceedings, placement standards and preferences, return of a child to tribal jurisdiction, and adoption policies with regard to parental rights, enforcement, and posttrial rights.

Indian child and family program development. The second part of the ICWA describes information for those tribes who want to develop grants to establish family and children's programs such as parent training, foster care program development, recruitment and training of foster parents, child abuse and neglect prevention programs, and the development of adoption programs within the tribal context.

Record keeping and information. The third part of the Act is concerned with record keeping and information availability, timetables, and, specifically, disclosure of information for enrollment of an Indian child and determination of members' rights or benefits.

The ICWA's First Decade

The initial 10 years of ICWA enactment have brought many positive developments. Areas of significant improvement include an increase in tribal family and children's programs, an increase in tribal service delivery systems on the reservation for abused and neglected children, and an increase in ICWA training and leadership opportunities for direct staff and administrators, at both the state and tribal levels. Numerous state-tribal agreements have been signed and have produced new intra-agency cooperation indicating efforts at problem solving, negotiation, and conflict resolution. In addition, significant ICWA case law has been developed that confirms the original Act's goals and objectives, specifically, to promote the security and well-being of children within the tribal context and to prevent the unnecessary breakup of extended families.

Several national centers have researched and surveyed the impact of the Act (for example, Three Feathers Associates, Oklahoma, and American Indian Law Center, New Mexico). Their findings indicate that the act has made a difference, but many problems continue, for example, with state implementation and continued funding inadequacies at both tribal and state levels. A national study conducted by Three Feathers Associates of Norman, Oklahoma, included a review of individual children's cases in states with large tribal populations. The findings show that American Indian children are still being placed at a high rate, but that these placements are at the direction of the tribal systems (court and social services), under the supervision of tribal workers, within American Indian foster homes, which encourage tribal value systems as a resource for the children.

Since the Act's passage, many cases have come before the various levels of the court system. The American Indian Law Center in Albuquerque, New Mexico, retains many of these legal cases, as does the Native American Rights Fund library in Boulder, Colorado. (The author has also collected numerous cases from newspapers and journals. Given that it is beyond the scope of this chapter to discuss these cases, interested readers should contact the above organizations for more information. See the appendix to this chapter for addresses.)

Preparation of the Social Worker

It is one thing to pass laws about Indian child welfare; it is another to implement those laws. Implementation of the Indian Child Welfare Act is complicated considerably because it often takes place in the context of competing state and tribal jurisdictions, laws, loyalties, and values. Appropriate implementation of the Act therefore requires sophistication in a broad range of issues. Social workers can make an important contribution to this process if they are well informed and prepared.

A social worker must possess professional knowledge, skills, and values in order to be an effective Indian child welfare worker. Those working with different American Indian populations and tribes should have a knowledge base in the following areas:

- American history and tribal history
- tribal value systems
- tribal court systems and tribal children's codes
- tribal extended family structure (kinship and clan systems)
- tribal parenting styles

- natural helping systems and networks
- tribal religions and land bases
- differences among urban, rural, and reservation life-styles of American Indians
- federal, state, and tribal laws and policies
- contemporary child welfare issues (Gibbs, Huang, et al., 1989, pp. 114-147; Goodluck, 1990)
- theoretical frameworks, including general systems theory, family therapy, and the ecological systems approach
- knowledge and competency regarding race, gender, and class issues (Davis & Proctor, 1989)

In addition, the social worker needs particular skills, such as the following:

- communication skills
- ability to assess the positive attributes of individuals, children, and extended families within a holistic (environmental-tribal-social) context (e.g., genogram and ecomap)
- traditional healing practices (e.g., Talking Circle, sweats, and tribal ceremonial rituals)
- contemporary practice strategies (individual, family, group, and tribal network therapy)
- ability to work in cross-cultural situations (Hammerschlag, 1988)
- empowerment skills (Davis & Proctor, 1989)

The social worker also needs to incorporate the following values:

- humanistic ethos
- self-determination
- confidentiality
- respect for the worth and dignity of the individual
- respect for and understanding of different cultures and life-styles

Roles of the Social Worker

Five major social work roles are discussed in the social work education literature (Compton & Galaway, 1989, p. 505). Each of these roles is discussed below in reference to the Indian Child Welfare Act and child welfare practices in general.

Advocate Role

The advocate role is one in which the worker must take a certain position for a particular client system and assert that position in many situations. This can occur when a particular client system is referred to an agency for services or anywhere along the procedural processing of the case within the tribal or state jurisdictional system. The worker must have excellent oral and written skills and extensive knowledge of the Indian Child Welfare Act and its implications for the client system. Advocate roles are important in working across cultural-social-legal systems and with various differing units, which can change often and without notice. Often ICWA cases take many months to complete, and the worker must have patience, strength, hope, and persistence to deal with the situation over the course of time. The worker can apply assertiveness skills and practice by role-playing difficult case situations before they occur. Designing a state policy to facilitate Indian cases at the local level will require an advocate role.

Enabler Role

As an enabler, the worker facilitates change within the client system (individual, family, group, and tribal network) by utilizing direct practice skills. The practitioner must be familiar with the various theories and methods regarding counseling in each of the client systems and have specific practice skills in working with children and families who have experienced separation and loss from their families and tribes. Knowledge of culturally sensitive methods of family therapy with complex extended families within a tribal and rural setting (see, e.g., Schacht, Tafoya, & Mirabla, 1989) is often required. Ethnicity-sensitive practice skills are critical (Lum, 1986, pp. 59-80; Red Horse, 1980) and may include competency and understanding in areas such as power, race, gender, and class (Pinderhughes, 1989).

Mediator Role

The mediator role involves "efforts to resolve disputes that exist between the client system and other persons or organizations" (Compton & Galaway, 1989, p. 509). The worker must be certain of the goals, direction, and objectives of the ICWA because, with the multiple systems interacting, the case in question can become very complex and difficult. The abilities to find common ground, to negotiate, and to compromise are essential in the mediator role. For helpful training in this regard, one may want to take a course in conflict resolution (frequently available at community colleges, law departments, or private consulting firms).

Teacher Role

The teacher role is essential, as in each encounter with the Indian Child Welfare Act, workers must not only be open to learning new ideas about tribal customs, tribal programs, and tribal issues related to the Act, but may often find themselves in the position of needing to educate others involved in the case about issues they have not considered. The teacher role may become important when the worker discusses the case with the specific families involved, other workers, supervisors, judges, and other helping professionals. The Act represents a specialized form of knowledge, and the social worker must continue to educate others about its specifics and how it affects families, tribes, and particular children in particular situations. To be an effective teacher, the practitioner must be familiar with the implementation of the Act, the history of the Act, and current issues and research related to the Act (a list of resources is included in the appendix to this chapter).

Broker Role

In the broker role, workers must link the client system with the appropriate resources. They must be knowledgeable about local, state, tribal, federal, and national resources to make valid and useful referrals among the systems both on and off the reservation, between urban and rural resources, and between state and tribal systems. Some Indian child welfare desks within some states' offices and specific federal Bureau of Indian Affairs office personnel are assigned to work the Act (Steven Lacey, Phoenix Area Office, personal communication). The broker role also involves information and referral processes. This requires vast knowledge about systems and specific personnel in these areas, particularly those working with children and families.

It is highly recommended that the social worker be able to perform any of the roles discussed above when engaging in direct or indirect work with ICWA cases. The worker must be well prepared to deal with the complex interplay among the child, the American Indian extended family, tribal interests, state interests, and private interests. Follow-up and evaluation of each of these social work roles is significant to ensure implementation of the Act as a social service provider. Preparation and education of a worker is a developmental process and requires ongoing knowledge acquisition and practice integration. This chapter is an attempt to provide education, resources, and knowledge about the Indian Child Welfare Act and the roles a social worker can perform in this complex multi-level environment.

Appendix:
Resources on the Indian Child Welfare Act

Books and Articles

American Indian Law Center. (n.d.). *Indian Child Welfare Impact and Improvements under P.L. 95-608 and P.L. 96-272.* Albuquerque, NM: Author.

Association on American Indian Affairs. (1979). Child Welfare Act signed into law. In Association on American Indian Affairs, *Indian family defense.* New York: Author.

Bending, R. et al. (Ed). (1991). *Teaming for Indian families.* Seattle: University of Washington, School of Social Work.

Bureau of Indian Affairs. (n.d.). *Adoption and the American Indian child* (Manual for social workers). Washington, DC: BIA Social Services.

Cross, T. (1986). Drawing on cultural tradition in Indian child welfare practice. *Social Casework, 67,* 238-289.

Fanshel, D. (1972). *Far from the reservation.* Metuchen, NJ: Scarecrow.

Goodluck, C., & Short, D. (1980, October). Working with American Indian parents: A cultural approach. *Social Casework, 61,* 472-475.

Goodluck, C., & Short, D. (1989, February-March). *Indian child welfare digest model practice approach* (ICW: A status report—Case management and planning). Norman, OK: Three Feathers Associates.

Keegan, B. (n.d.). *Child welfare resource development in the Indian community.* Denver: University of Denver, Child Welfare Training Center, Region VIII.

Shore, M. (1978). Destruction of Indian families: Beyond the best interests of Indian children. *White Cloud Journal, 1*(2), 13-16.

Organizations

In addition to the organizations listed below, interested readers can contact BIA area offices for specific regional questions and individual states for Indian child welfare desks and listings for tribal programs and child welfare administrators. Also, the *Federal Register* publishes names, addresses, and phone contacts for tribal ICWA programs

American Indian Law Center
Box 4456, Station C
Albuquerque, NM 87109
(505) 277-5462

Association on American Indian Affairs
432 Park Avenue South
New York, NY 10016
(212) 689-8720

The Indian Family Circle Project
New Mexico Department of Social Services
P. O. Drawer 5160
Santa Fe, NM 87502
(505) 827-8400

National Indian Social Worker's Association
1740 West 41st Street
Tulsa, OK 74107
(918) 446-8432

Native American Adoption Resource Exchange
200 Charles Street
Dorseyville, PA 15238
(412) 782-4457

Native American Rights Fund
National Indian Law Library
1506 Broadway
Boulder, CO 80302
(303) 447-8760

Northwest Indian Child Welfare Association
c/o RRI
Box 751
Portland, OR 97207
(503) 725-3038

Southwest Indian Court Judges Association
Arizona State University
College of Law
Tempe, AZ 85287-7906
(602) 965-6181

Three Feathers Associates
Box 5508
Norman, OK 73070
(405) 360-2919

Urban Indian Child Resource Center
390 Euclid Avenue
Oakland, CA 94610
(510) 356-2121

PART V

Muslim Families

15

The Muslim Family in North America

Continuity and Change

AZIM A. NANJI

Religion and tradition are not static; they change. The erosion they suffer in a wider global context represents a loss of resources. It is far more valuable and fruitful to examine religious and traditional values as a resource—a set of beliefs and values, a way of thinking about and comprehending the human condition—that can be used by those in the eye of the hurricane to create a response, a sense of equilibrium, to preserve some of the content of the resource and to inform their changing lives with it.

In this context, I want to view a threefold process that has affected Muslim families living in North America. The first involves an encounter with a secular and highly industrialized society and a corresponding perception of the erosion of values associated with a Muslim way of life. Second is the development of an awareness of crisis, affecting in particular the second generation, who are sufficiently distanced from the home-country experiences of their parents and whose cultural and national roots are now nurtured within this new environment. Finally, what is emerging is a quest for coherence, a purposeful development of programs and actions to cultivate a sense of Muslim identity. Among a minority of early Muslim immigrants, who may have sought in their quest

AUTHOR'S NOTE: This chapter was originally presented as a Master Lecture at the 1985 annual meeting of the National Council on Family Relations in Dallas, Texas.

229

for a new life to exclude concerns about identity, an essential separation of questions about heritage and the goals they conceived of having in their new land of settlement may have already taken place. But as children were born, grew up, and understood better the framework of a pluralistic religious society and were made aware of their relationship with the Muslim world at large, they chose again to examine the past to rediscover and recover what had been eclipsed in the initial stages of transition. This was also related to the now widespread process within the Islamic world in general that brought a new consciousness about the value of establishing equilibrium among faith, tradition, and the challenges of modern life.

The Muslim concept of the family is based on the notion of kinship. Many ethnic and geographic backgrounds are reflected in the mosaic that forms the Muslim community. Muslim families have faced obstacles in North America. These families are caught up in stereotypes that are related to the political activities and national problems of Muslims in other parts of the world.

During the preparation of this chapter, two relatively minor news items, one from Texas and the other from Oklahoma, came to my attention. In the first, a student was sentenced to five years in prison after he admitted to bombing a Muslim mosque in Houston following the TWA hijacking to Lebanon. The second concerned a proposal to build a religious and cultural center for the Muslims of Central Oklahoma in the city of Edmond. More than 1,000 persons signed a petition opposed to such a center, citing their fear of allowing a terrorist network to be established that would threaten the American way of life! The leaders of the Muslim community, headed by a noted Oklahoma heart specialist, Dr. Nazih Zuhdi, stunned by the opposition, decided not to go through with the deal. An editorial in the *Oklahoma Observer* had these pertinent remarks to make after the event:

> Reaction to the proposed mosque might have been predicted in some rural backwater in Oklahoma, but Edmond is one of the highest per capita income communities in Oklahoma. The mosque was to be located near Central State University. Edmond boasts one of the highest literacy rates in Oklahoma. . . . The community's religious and political hierarchy stepped gently because of Dr. Zuhdi's national reputation as a heart surgeon. Who knows when one of them may need his quick fingers and famous skill? They referred to him as a "good man"—it's his religion that stinks! The thought of having those oily-skinned folks driving in from all over to pollute the pristine

atmosphere of the WASPs was just too much. The holy war was brief—Edmond is safe. But for what? (Troy, 1985)[1]

In the context of this study, these events are significant for two reasons—first, they represent elements of the quite widespread stereotyping about Islam and Muslims that has come to dominate the news and entertainment media and popular consciousness in recent times. Second, reactions such as those in Oklahoma highlight a major dilemma for the growing Muslim community in North America as it seeks to develop networks that will foster and enrich personal and family lives on the basis of Muslim heritage.

Muslims in North America have their roots in many different parts of the world, from Albania to Zanzibar. The Muslims of the world number more than 800 million; less than one-fifth of these are of Arab or Iranian origin, the focus of American media attention about Islam. Historically, the heartland of Islam has been the Middle East, North Africa, and the Indo-Pakistan subcontinent, but the country with the largest number of Muslims in the world—namely, Indonesia—is in Southeast Asia, and there are Muslims in China, the former Soviet Union, and many African countries.

Most of these ethnic and geographic backgrounds are reflected in the North American mosaic. They, like millions of ordinary Muslims, and fellow human beings all over the world, are striving to build a future that will reflect their own heritage of faith and culture. To confound the expectations of the good life of those Muslims in America with specifically political activities and national problems of some of their coreligionists in other parts of the world is to revive many of the mental blocks and stereotyping that have in the past prevented an appreciation of other ethnic and religious groups in the pluralistic society of North America.

Although it is difficult, at this point, to provide accurate figures, it has been suggested that anywhere from 2 to 3 million people in North America identify themselves as Muslims. We know that the early European explorers of the New World were accompanied by those of Moorish background, whose heritage had been shaped by Islam. Certainly, thousands of Muslims of African origin were brought to the Americas in the eighteenth and nineteenth centuries against their will as slaves (Muhammad, 1984). Studies have shown that among emigrants from the Ottoman Empire from 1865 to 1920, at least 80,000 Muslims of Syrian and Lebanese origin came to America (Karpat, 1985). The bulk of the migration from Asia, Africa, and Eastern Europe is more recent and accelerated by the changes in immigration acts that allowed large-scale migration from the Third World. Plausible figures are hard to come by, so it is difficult to verify the estimates that we have for the Muslim population in the New World.

This chapter focuses primarily on those Muslim immigrant groups who have chosen to make their home in North America in this century. To establish a context for their religious background, I would like to begin by delineating the main components of the heritage that diverse Muslim immigrants share and the relationship between this heritage and family life as understood in the past and as challenged in the present. This necessitates some general remarks on Islam and the definition of family life and values in it.

The principle that best defines Islam is that of unity. In the Quran, which Muslims regard as the revealed word of God, unity defines the nature of the divine; it is the defining element in the relationship between material life and spiritual life and between human beings as they interact in society and with the natural environment. With no fundamental division between the spiritual and the material, the quality of human and social interaction that takes place in the total environment reverberates in spiritual life. Thus interactions that revolve around family life, while providing it with an internal momentum and rhythm of its own, are connected with and enriched by living and working with the wider framework of the community and the fellowship that comes from the bonds of faith and common spirituality. To give expression to this principle of unity, there evolved among Muslims a system of law, generally referred to as the Shariah—a code of conduct based on the Quran and the Sunnah, the model behavior of the Prophet Muhammad, that gave concrete expression in all walks of life, including the family, to Islamic values. The Shariah, in a sense, provided an overreaching frame of reference and values within which a comprehensive pattern of daily life unfolded in the community.

This process can perhaps be better understood through the metaphor of an ideal Muslim environment as a series of linked spaces, represented by concentric circles, within which Muslim life unfolds. At the focal point in the center of this total environment one finds the mosque with its characteristic architectural forms, symbolizing the daily interaction between human and divine. The rhythm of the daily prayers, the orientation of the prayer niche towards the Ka'ba in Mecca—the place of worship, according to Muslims, first built by Adam, then rededicated to God's worship by Abraham and again in the seventh century by

Muhammad—provides a continuum in the chain of human history and links Islam to the Judeo-Christian tradition.

The zone that surrounds the mosque in the inner circle is devoted to knowledge. Here one finds the schools and the universities of traditional Muslim society, where learning was acquired and disseminated. Sufficiently distanced and yet interlinked is the next zone—of economic and social relationships. Nestled as it were against this zone, and extending beyond it, is the realm of private and family life—the circle of habitation and housing that, in its architectural form and use of space, emphasizes privacy and family intimacy, guarding it from the zones of public activity and yet assuring, through a code of dress and behavior for men and women, the possibility of balancing privacy with participation in the public spheres of commerce as well as prayer.

Family life in Islam assumes the necessity and regulation of marriage. Disparaging popular images of Muslim women hidden under folds of clothing and shuttered away in exotic harems have created a stereotype of Muslim women as either concubines or oppressed baby-making machines. In reality, the regulations of the Quran sought to define rights as well as obligations for men and women in marriage, assuming a degree of choice: rights of divorce and inheritance, opportunities for participation in the public sphere, and safeguards for a distinctive feminine identity in matters of dress and behavior. As among other religious traditions, notably "fundamentalist" understanding of Christianity and Judaism, some in Islam have interpreted these principles in a very conservative manner to assure a separate and subsidiary role for women in public life, but in the overall context of Muslim history and society, the status and role of women accorded with the larger view of the integrity and vitality of the family as the cornerstone of all social relationships.

The above metaphor defines an all-embracing system influencing and linking all aspects of daily life within the traditional Islamic setting. Each zone complements the others, and within each exist networks that tie them to one another. Family life, as a vital part of this order, thus came to be defined in great detail, with rules governing marriage, divorce, inheritance, and other aspects.

The Quran, within the context of the social circumstances of the times, permitted a man to have a maximum of four wives at one time, thus regulating a system that had allowed for unlimited cohabitation. At the same time, it encouraged the view that equity might be truly possible only within a monogamous household. The Quran recognized the possibility of breakdown in marriage and allowed for divorce after reasonable attempts had been made to reconcile the parties. Marriage was to be accompanied by the signing of a legally binding contract, with the husband specifying the amount of settlement to be made to the wife in the event of divorce. Divorced persons, widows, and widowers were also encouraged to remarry.

Another area of family life touched upon in the Quran is that of inheritance. The Quran prohibited Arab custom whereby a son could inherit his stepmother as part of his father's legacy and then convert the wife's property and gifts into his own. It defined a share of the inheritance for both male and female children, granting, in the context of social roles of the time, the male child twice as much as the female. The widow is granted one-eighth, if there are also children involved; if not, she receives one-fourth.

Some Muslim modernists have argued that such regulations based on a tribal framework offer alternatives that can be adapted when society undergoes detribalization and that the inheritance shares should change accordingly. However, to a large extent, subsequent legal developments ensured that the initial framework of shares continued as the Muslim community grew and changed (Rahman, 1980, pp. 49-51). A particular concern was also expressed for orphans and needy children and the disadvantaged within the family and society, for whom particular care was to be exercised and special funds set aside for their use.

In ideal terms, the physical form of the living environment in Islam— including the places of worship, work, housing, and family networks— can be said to symbolize the vision of unity. This vision, as expressed at ground level, finds expression in the total community context. Such a community is called the Ummah.

The Muslim concept of the family, based on the notion of kinship, provided the individual with identity and status as well as a personal support system within the Ummah at large. The extension of the kinship relationship through marriage created a wider network of contacts. The emphasis on the notions of privacy, intimacy, and seclusion in the sphere of life affecting women, however, gave rise to distinct categories of relationship with those within the kinship sphere and those without. For instance, for Muslims from India, Pakistan, and Bangladesh, this came to be expressed in terms of two dialectically opposed categories, our (*apna*) and those outside (*ghayr*), which in turn denoted the personal and family spheres as against the impersonal, public sphere (Qureshi & Qureshi, 1983, p. 134). Muslim society, in general, thus developed a patrilocal household that was extended through endogamy and was characterized by strong ties of descent. On the whole, this heritage of social grouping and family values characterized the value system of immigrant Muslims. It provided for a strong sense of personal identity within the private, family network, with its element of mutual support and kinship solidarity, reinforced by a strong Islamic emphasis on the centrality of the bonds of the family.

Before turning to a discussion of the specific challenges faced by this heritage in America, I would like to offer some cautionary remarks on methodology in the humanities and social sciences as they deal with family and religious values. In an essay, Mary Douglas (1982), the noted anthropologist, remarks that "events have taken Religious Studies by surprise" (p. 1). As examples, she cites the fact that scholars were unable to foretell the so-called resurgence of Islam, the recent revival of traditional religious forms, and the renewal of right-wing political values based on fundamentalist interpretations of scripture here and elsewhere in the world. Religious studies scholars were taken unawares, she contends, because of the rigid structure of their assumptions and the fact that their eyes were glued to those conditions of modern life identified by Max Weber (Little, 1984) as antipathetic to religion. Surely if, in the social sciences and the humanities, we are to begin to make better sense of the relationship between religious values and social issues and the role of these values in enriching family life, then we need to discard some of these methodological assumptions that have caused us to focus unduly on secularization as a normative and even desirable process viewed from above, affecting those with religion living in enclaves below, as they are buffeted by the hurricane of cultural change.

The first major area of change for Muslim families involved the loss of what was perceived as a complete Islamic environment. Coherence in traditional family life in Islam came from having the security of a well-defined framework of values and institutions to support it. Since the Shariah could not be fully applied in America, and certainly no network of family or kinship ties existed to reinforce it, tradition might guide how families lived, but these traditions were not anchored within the law and in a social setting. In fact, the legal status of individuals within the American system was of a completely different order. It had at its center the individual and not necessarily the corporate family unit. The linkages and networks of Muslim religious and social life did not exist. Mosques and other places for communal gatherings could be created, but they could not serve as networks within a system of interrelated spatial zones and human relationships.

The pattern of housing represented another major impact on family life. Traditional Muslim environments, set within specific quarters in the city, exhibited all the patterns of the networks that anchored human life and activity in Islam. The new family home in America had none of these features. Apartment living or, in time, ownership of a house could not provide the same flow of life. Children did not necessarily grow up in an extended family and kinship network, most dwellers in apartment buildings or neighborhoods might be strangers, and, certainly in the early days, there were no mosques, let alone centers for communal life or neighborhoods.

Perhaps the most significant impact was on the lives of Muslim women. As in their home countries in modern times, many had to choose, of necessity and as an extension of their new roles, to work outside the home. Traditional forms of dress, ways of relating to others, both men and women, outside the family, and the degree of displacement of the dominant role of the husband in the household were all issues that came to the fore. It is conceivable that, in spite of the changes in circumstances, some of the traditional attitudes and values did not pass away. It is often forgotten that in traditionally oriented groups, the greatest stress in times of transition is faced by women.

The overall expectation of the traditional role of the Muslim woman is not very different from that of many other ethnic and religious groups: as a mother, she is the anchor of the family; as a wife, her role is to complement and enhance the image of her husband; and as a home-maker, she is the one on whom the bulk of responsibility falls for the organization and maintenance of the household. These traditional role expectations still contribute a norm in most Muslim families, but clearly some fundamental changes have taken place in the lives of Muslim women in America. The most important is the transition of women from the sphere of work in the private space within the house to the realm of public space in the American workplace. This has meant that the essentially separate worlds of Muslim men and women in the public spheres have now become fused. One corollary of this is that Muslim women in America also tend to participate more actively in the life of prayer and worship in the mosque, whereas in the past they may have prayed almost exclusively at home. Women's social life, however, still revolves around networks linked to the mosque and the local community.

The stresses that mark intergenerational conflict are as much in evidence among Muslims as among other tradition-oriented American groups. Some of these are seen as superficial pandering to aspects of

American youth behavior, such as dating, drinking, and so forth, particularly as far as girls are concerned. Coupled with this is the fear of intermarriage. Again, Muslim girls, who, according to traditional Islamic law, are forbidden to marry outside the faith, represent a vulnerable area of stress in Muslim families. In general, as the new generation grows up, the intergenerational gap in perception of North American versus the past home-country system of values tends to grow wider.

Another area that creates potential fear of loss of values is the system of education. Most traditional Muslim families have ambivalent attitudes toward American educational institutions—on the one hand, they provide the means to enter into the mainstream of American economic life, while on the other, they threaten certain traditional values and modes of thinking. A survey conducted among Muslim students going to school in Edmonton, Canada (Fahlman, 1983, pp. 203-208), illustrates the range of culture conflict faced by Muslim youth:

(1) They suffered a feeling of discrimination (exacerbated, no doubt, in the last few years) because of their ethnic and religious backgrounds.
(2) The Muslim students who chose not to assimilate into the social life of high school students were considered loners or strange.
(3) They expressed a strong concern about peer use of drugs and alcohol, both of which are forbidden to Muslims, and the impact this had on their choice of a school.
(4) The perception of most teachers that the role of the school is to assimilate minority religious ethnic students into the mainstream values of society created pressure to conform to these expectations.

As Muslim youth absorb the values professed in the American educational system, values such as self-reliance, self-sufficiency, and independent decision making, they also become aware of the tension and conflict that can arise within the family as a result of differences in value orientations. This is particularly evident in the role that girls are asked to live up to and the emphasis put on restricting girls from dating and unsupervised contact with boys.

Some see the problem and the ambiguity inherent in the situation. Layla, a 17-year-old Muslim girl, defines it as the "Friday problem"— "Most of my friends go to parties on Friday evening, whereas Friday being the day of congregational prayer in Islam, I must make an effort to go with the family to the Mosque and then for religious education classes."[2] On the other hand, she also recognizes the particular strengths that are derived from these family and religious values: "I couldn't go out on dates, I couldn't go out for dances—I concentrated on school work, the family and the mosque. In a way, my school friends envy me for my grades and the close family ties I have." Anxiety about value conflict and difference is, in some cases, thus balanced by a degree of self-confidence and awareness.

The attitudes and assumptions of teachers and fellow students are, in all likelihood, shared by those who encounter Muslims in their work as human service and family professionals. Just as schools need to develop teacher education programs that address the needs of religious and ethnic minorities, so family and human service professionals also need to develop an understanding of problems specific to groups such as Muslims in a variety of situations. This was brought home to me in a particularly cogent way when I was asked recently to talk about Islam to a National Conference of Administrators of Religious Programs in Corrections Systems in North America. The conference paid particular attention to making chaplains aware of the religious needs of minority groups such as Jews, Muslims, Hindus, and Native Americans.

Their problems were of a practical nature—how to provide space and opportunity for the specific needs of Muslim inmates for prayer and religious instruction; how to develop menus that did not offend Muslim sensibilities; and how to create conditions that allowed Muslims to fulfill their obligations to the work ethic and ensured an opportunity for moral development. In part, the problems are being addressed by making Muslim teachers and counselors available.

In other contexts, the continual search for solutions to these dilemmas has led Muslims to define their life in America within the larger framework of Islam while also seeking to create conditions that can address their problems in local American contexts. Where do we see the signs of the process that I have termed recovery and re-creation of a Muslim identity, and what ramifications do these have for family life? Three examples follow.

The first represents a decision to re-create a total environment for an American Muslim community. Such a task is being carried out by a group of Muslims in the semidesert mountainous region of northern New Mexico near the town of Abiquiu. The site is called Dar-al-Islam, the abode of Islam. The origin of the idea for the project, as recounted by its founders, has quite dramatic overtones:[3]

One rainy night in Makkah, two men set out from different corners of the city toward the Holy Precincts. The two men, Sahl Kabbani from Saudi Arabia and Nuriddeen Durkee of the United States, met by chance at the Kaaba. Sahl, seeing that Nuriddeen was probably from the West, introduced himself. Nuriddeen explained that he was an American Muslim studying Arabic and [Islamic Law] at Makkah University. Sahl, in turn, said that he had studied in America to obtain his degrees in engineering, and added that it had always been his dream to contribute in some way to bring Islam to America in appreciation of the education he received there. The two talked for some time, then decided to develop a Muslim community project to promote Islam in America and made an agreement there, in the shadow of the Kaaba, to work together on it. From that moment on, the project took off. A friend of Nuriddeen's was living in Cairo, introduced them to Hasan Fathi, a famous architect from Egypt. Fathi soon began working on the preliminary plans for the first stage of the project, which was to include a mosque, a school, housing, and other structures. They decided on New Mexico for the location of their project, and soon after, Nuriddeen's wife, Nura, met Princess Moody Bin Khaled, the daughter of the late King Khaled of Saudi Arabia, who contributed the funds necessary for finding the actual site. When the present site was found, it was through the Princess's intercession with her father that the funds for the actual purchase of the land, over 1,000 acres, were obtained. (Spiker, 1985)

The plans for the mosque, which were soon completed, called for the building to be constructed of material indigenous to New Mexico, adobe and brick. The technique of building with adobe had been introduced into America hundreds of years earlier by the Spanish, who, in turn, had probably acquired it during the period of Muslim rule in Spain that lasted for more than 800 years. Quite a lot of the original technique had fallen by the wayside, however, and no one in New Mexico was capable of constructing the exquisite vaulting domes that were such an integral part of traditional designs. So a working seminar for masons, attended by adobe specialists from all over America, was organized. Hasan Fathi, a famous Muslim architect from Egypt, attended and brought with him two Egyptian masons to teach the ancient techniques.

The following year, construction started on the mosque. Already, several of those who had attended the seminar had become Muslims and were working full-time on the project. Within a year of very hectic work, the mosque was completed, and a grand opening was held that was attended by architects and builders from all over the United States. In the words of the director of the center:

We are trying to establish something here that grows out of the earth of America. . . . This will take a long time, with a tremendous effort of hard labor, [building] brick by brick and bit by bit. It is now something that we hope, in the process of the labor involved and the concentration involved, it will produce a synthesis of Islamic feeling, ideals and knowledge with the life of the people of America.

You can see this in the many cultures represented in the children and the teachers here. It's a melting pot, and the time it is taking to build this simple but substantial building is allowing us all to get to know each other and to live together and to know each other's different ideas and experiences of Islam. (Spiker, 1985)

The choice of creating an entire self-contained community represents what the creators of Dar-al-Islam regard as the necessity of ordering Muslim life according to the totality of tradition. Family life will find its place automatically within this organized community and will reflect all the norms that have been defined as Islamic.

The second example is that of an educational institution, the American Islamic College in Chicago, which set out to achieve three objectives:

(1) to establish a college of Islamic study in America that would offer a B.A.
(2) to teach Arabic language, history, and culture
(3) to create a college of education for Muslims and non-Muslims to produce certified teachers for the American school system to teach bilingual and bicultural programs for the Arab and Islamic communities

The project has been supported and funded by the Organization of the Islamic Conference, an international organization of Muslim countries, for whom this is the first project of its kind undertaken outside of the Muslim world.

The college has the atmosphere of a traditional Islamic institution. Men and women occupy separate spaces in the library, cafeteria, and auditorium. In the dormitory, the women live on the first floor, the men on the second, and married couples on the third. The majority of the students reside on campus and must report their whereabouts when they leave. Classes are held five days a week, Saturday being a day of supervised study, with Sunday off. Monday through Saturday, school hours are 8:00 a.m. to 5:00 p.m.

The five daily prayers are performed at the required times. Men and women take turns cooking and cleaning according to a prearranged schedule. Faculty, staff, and students eat communally. The faculty and students are Muslims from a variety of national and ethnic backgrounds, but all are American citizens or permanent residents, as the college cannot yet accept foreign students of nonresident status. The college was incorporated in 1981, and there has been continuing discussion about whether the current format and focus constitute the most suitable vehicle in the North American context.

The third example is a youth-oriented project called al-Ummah: An Experience in Islamic Living (F. Ross-Sheriff, personal communication). The underlying philosophy of the project, as articulated by its director, Dr. Fariyal Ross-Sheriff, is to provide an opportunity for Muslim boys and girls to link resources from the Islamic heritage with an understanding of what it means to grow up in America. The purpose is not to pit one set of values against another, but to create a bridge so that the youth can develop a genuine sense of what it can mean to be a Muslim in America. The emphasis is on cultivating a self-image that blends elements of Islam in a way that will inform the pattern of life in America without excluding this pattern in the life of Muslim youth.

Though the three projects described above reflect an inspiration common to all North American Muslims—that is, the creation of conditions of daily life and sense of identity anchored in their Islamic heritage—they reflect varying strategies of adaptation and incorporation of past experience and traditions. Among the contrasting attitudes expressed, some envisage separate, isolated development, or an encapsulation of community life supported through traditional educational models, while others affirm that a broader and more purposeful integration needs to be worked out for a future Muslim community whose national and cultural aspirations as Muslims will have their context in North America.

Among Muslims in America, as indeed in the world, given their diversity, these strategies can by no means be homogeneous. At the heart of all their responses, one can discern a hope shared by more and more Americans, that of establishing a balance among all the elements of the world they live in: the necessity of human values in an increasingly programmable information-oriented society, the threat to individual and global peace in the secularization of the means of moral decision making, the aspiration for material development, and the desire to build bridges of understanding between Muslims and others. Erik Erikson's (1950) insights have shown us that families across generations strive to create conditions for what he called the "maintenance of the world" (see Benman-Gibson, 1984, p. 59). A recent noted study of American life, *Habits of the Heart* (Bellah, Madsen, Sullivan, Swidler, & Tipton,

1985), points to the necessity of moral tradition and "communities of memory" as vital to the eventual transformation of the social ecology of America. Perhaps in our postmodern world, North American Muslim families' efforts to integrate the values of their faith and tradition in their family lives may represent one element in this revitalization.

Notes

1 *Oklahoma Observer* (1985, September 10). Reprinted with permission.

2. I am grateful to Professor Fariyal Ross-Sheriff of Howard University for sharing her data with me. They are part of a larger study she is currently undertaking on Muslim adolescents.

3. This account is based on a visit to the site and an article in *Saudi Report* (Spiker, 1985).

PART VI

Asian American Families

16

Socialization of
Chinese American Children

YOUNG-SHI OU
HARRIETTE PIPES McADOO

Much attention has been paid to the children of immigrants as they have become acculturated to American society. Many questions related to the socialization of their children have been raised by Asian American parents who have come from other countries, particularly parents from distinctively different language groups. Chinese parents are facing issues related to the impact of language upon their children. They are faced with several important decisions as they prepare to socialize their children, who must learn English in order to be able to move into professional jobs in the broader society.

At the same time, cultural issues must be addressed. How can feelings of self-worth and pride in the culture of the family be maintained while the children are becoming Americanized? What are the psychological effects of being raised with different levels of Chinese in the family? Is it better simply to speak only English in the home, in order to ensure that the child will be brought up as an American citizen without the burden of a different culture? And most important, is it possible for children who come from parents of different racial stock truly to be accepted on a culture-free basis in this society? Or is it necessary to make provisions for maintaining the group's own culture, on a bicultural basis, in order for the children to be able to maintain positive mental health?

Chinese American parents have to make an important decision as soon as their children are born—should they be spoken to in a mixture of English and a Chinese dialect or should they be spoken to only in English? The family can protect the children in the preschool years, but as children become older they find that they must adjust to the larger society. The issue is whether learning Chinese can provide these children with a greater understanding of their own heritage. Is there a way to teach these children that can promote positive self-concepts? What role can the Chinese schools play in addressing these issues?

All of these issues were considered when this study was conducted. Parents were interviewed and then their children were interviewed separately in order to get a picture of the consequences of raising children under two different approaches: speaking only English in the home and exposing the children to Chinese dialects as well as English. The purpose of this study was to determine the degree to which speaking or not speaking Chinese affects how children see themselves and their ethnic group.

Historical Background

The majority of Chinese Americans migrated to America in two main streams of decidedly different character. The first stream started in 1820. Most of the early Chinese immigrants came to the United States to work on the nation's railroads or in the mines. They were regarded and exploited as an abundant source of cheap labor. These early immigrants generally spoke Cantonese dialects, were of lower-class origin, and, in general, were illiterate in their native language.

The second stream of Chinese immigrants, which began in 1847, came largely from the upper and middle classes. Unlike their predecessors, who had limited occupational aspirations, they came to seek higher education or to join their relatives who already possessed advanced degrees in the fields of physical science, art, and medicine. Most of them spoke fluent Mandarin and could read and write in their native language. As a result, they were able to finish school and often received advanced degrees.

Regardless of their socioeconomic status, most of the Chinese immigrants were discriminated against by their employers, classmates, and the American public in general. This discrimination took a variety of forms, from differential wage and salary scales to lack of equal protection under the law, to the development of local, state, and federal legislation controlling the movements of Chinese immigrants and limiting their integration into the larger society. An example of federal legislation was the Chinese Exclusion Act of 1882, which not only limited Chinese immigration but also led to a decline of about 31,000 in the country's Chinese American population.

As a result of the lack of local protection, many Chinese were forced to band together within small towns for their own safety. During the frequent economic recessions and depressions of the nineteenth century, they were also forced to provide economic and social support for their members. Within these enclaves in larger communities, the Chinese immigrants began to develop small industries to help maintain their independence and reduce the possibility of exploitation by employers. These enclaves developed into large ethnic communities in New York, San Francisco, and other large cities that came to be known as Chinatowns.

Chinatowns may be described as ethnic communities in which the Chinese inhabitants have developed and maintained their cultural, economic, social, and psychological independence from the larger society. It was through such communities that the Chinese were able to survive, to establish and maintain their own identity, and to develop positive relationships with the outside world.

Since World War II, there has been a gradual decline in anti-Chinese feelings in the United States. In 1942, Congress repealed the Chinese Exclusion Act. Other discriminatory federal legislation was eliminated in 1965 by the new and more liberal immigration and nationality act. This shift in federal legislation has also had an effect in local Chinese American communities. Since the American attitude toward the Chinese has begun to change, the boundaries around Chinatowns have become absorbed in the larger urban communities.

While there has been a gradual decline in anti-Chinese sentiment nationally, there are still instances of prejudice and discrimination in many urban areas. There also appears to be some conflict and strain within the Chinese community in terms of the issues of maintenance of ethnic identity versus cultural integration into the mainstream of American society. This conflict has been complicated by American society's inadequate attention to the many human service needs of the Chinese community. A report by the JWK International Corporation (1976) indicates that health services in Asian American communities are inadequate. Rose Chao (see Sung, 1977) has noted that the social institutions that served the Chinese American community are now outmoded and obsolete.

There is a great need for mental health and other social services within Chinese American communities. With the gradual shift of many Chinese to a mainstream cultural orientation, there have been conflicts and strains evidenced in both the community and Chinese American families. There appears to be a need for empirical research that looks at family interaction patterns and the conflicts in parent-child relationships in families where the children have chosen to integrate into the mainstream of society.

Child-Rearing Practices

Chinese parents always try to control their children's behavior. In particular, as Sollenberger (1968) has noted, most Chinese parents strictly control their children's aggressive behavior. He found that 74% of Chinese parents demanded their children display no aggressive behavior under any circumstances. The nonaggressive characteristics of the Chinese American may be related to these child-rearing practices. Lack of aggressiveness causing purported reticence in voicing complaints may be an important element in understanding the reason Chinese Americans constitute a neglected ethnic minority group.

The Chinese are also very concerned about the education of their children. In Sollenberger's study, all the mothers indicated that doing well in school was fairly important or very important. In addition, 99% of the mothers expected their children to go to college or graduate school. Ou and McAdoo (1980) have confirmed these results. The high professional level expected of Chinese American children may be seen as evidence of the emphasis placed on academic achievement.

Chinese parents, however, have more dilemmas concerning the education of their children in the United States. It is very difficult for the parents to decide how many languages their children should learn. Parents who can speak more than two Chinese languages (or dialects) have difficulty deciding which language, other than English, should be taught to their children. Some Chinese parents blame the slower academic achievement of their children on the schools' teaching other languages in addition to English. Chao (see Sung, 1977) notes that parents are also divided in their options about bilingual education. Some feel that bilingual education retards the learning of English, and therefore they attempt to assimilate and not teach their children any Chinese language at all, hoping that if English is the only language their children learn, the children will progress more rapidly in school. It is possible, however, that Chinese children who are not taught any Chinese language have less opportunity to respect and appreciate their cultural heritage. Less exposure to Chinese culture, conversely, may be the cause of lower self-concepts, particularly when the child goes to school and meets the dominant societal preference for white over nonwhite. On the other hand, some Chinese parents indicate that Chinese children can learn both English and Chinese well if an appropriate approach is used.

Learning two different languages can increase a child's cognitive functioning as well as decrease the child's identity crises. Also, Huang (1976) has shown that Chinese American parents who demand their children learn a Chinese language often do so despite a certain amount of resistance by their children. (The resistance is probably motivated by the children's fear of being different.) Chinese American children who are taught a Chinese language may feel that they are being forced to learn something that is useless to them.

Thus far, a very limited number of behavioral science studies using scientific methods have been oriented toward a comprehension of the psychological perspectives of the Chinese American, although a few of the studies have used Chinese as subjects. In one type of study, the main purpose of collecting data on Chinese children was to test a general theory further. In another research effort, cross-cultural data from Chinese Americans were used mainly for comparisons to other ethnic groups, rather than to analyze their meaning for the Chinese. Sung (1977) has noted that it can be difficult to employ conventional scientific research methods in a study of the Chinese community because it is a closemouthed society. Sung's publication *Chinese Immigrant Children* (1977) is based on the results of looking, listening, feeling, and being among the people.

Psychological Perspectives on the Children of Immigrants

Self-Concept

A great deal of current research has investigated children's self-concept. Self-concept has been measured by obtaining data from the verbal or overt behavior of a child's expression of his or her own worth. Coopersmith (1967) gave the Self-Esteem Inventory Test to children in fifth and sixth grades. He found significant differences in the behaviors of children differing in self-concept. The low self-concept children tended to be unrealistic, unhappy, depressed, timid, discouraged, and withdrawn. They were passive and preoccupied with emotional difficulties in social groups. On the other hand, the high self-concept children were active and expressive in both their studies and their social activities. It would appear that a positive self-concept is required for a child to lead a creative, significant life.

The preference for the dominant society's language in public schools may have a significant effect on the self-concept and anxiety in bilingual minority children. Minority children may temporarily develop feelings of inferiority for having to learn a new language, unlike their American peers. Fisher (1974) has found that in a bilingual-bicultural program, the self-concepts of minority children are enhanced, whereas minority children in comparable public school settings show some signs of low self-concept and are less receptive to environmental stimuli. The self-concepts of minority children seem to be enhanced when society encourages them to be proud of and to value their minority culture.

Ethnic Attitudes

Three studies have indicated that young Chinese children, regardless of the racial organization of the society in which they live, have unclear ethnic attitudes. One study was conducted in the United States, where there is a dominant/subordinate social structure; another study was conducted in Hawaii, where the races are parallel; and the third study was conducted in Hong Kong. In all of these studies, the Chinese children showed less preference for their own race than did their Caucasian counterparts.

Fox and Jordan (1973) studied racial preference and identification of Black, Chinese American, and white children between the ages of 5 and 7 who were attending New York City schools. Color photographs of Chinese, Black, and white children were shown to subjects, who were asked to show their identification with and ethnic preference by pointing to one of the people in the photographs. Chinese children showed significantly less preference for and identification with their own race than did Black or white children.

Springer (1950) reported similar findings with preschool Chinese children in Hawaii, where the races had parallel status, rather than dominant and subordinate status. Chinese, Japanese, Korean, part Asian, and Caucasian children, aged 3-6 years, were shown photographs representing equal numbers of boys and girls from each nationality and were asked to identify the persons most closely resembling themselves. More than 50% of the Chinese children pointed to pictures of Japanese instead of Chinese children.

Morland (1969) examined race awareness and preference among Hong Kong Chinese children aged 4, 5, and 6. Children pointed to pictures of Chinese and Caucasians and answered which race they belonged to, who they were most like, who they would like to play with, and who they would rather be. Hong Kong Chinese children were aware of their racial uniqueness but were less sure of their racial self-identification and preference. Upper-class children tended to have clearer, more own-race preferences than lower-class children.

Racial attitudes are in the formative stages between the ages of 4 and 7. At that time, ethnoracial cues are being classified in the child's mind. At a later stage, ethnoracial attitudes are crystallized in the form of preferences (Semaj, 1979). Goodman (1964), Porter (1971), and Katz (1976) have all posited an age/stage progression in the ability to perceive, process, and interpret ethnoracial identity by the end of the primary school years.

It has long been felt that negative ethnic attitudes are associated with low self-concept. Recent studies have found that there is no linear relationship between self-concept and racial/ethnic attitudes. John McAdoo (1979) found that Black preschool children of middle-income families had positive self-concepts and positive race identity or preference. However, he found no relationship between self-concept and racial attitudes. Harriette McAdoo (1985) conducted a longitudinal study of self-concept and race attitudes when young Black children were enrolled in preschool day-care programs and again when they were enrolled in the fifth grade. Positive self-concepts were found in all children, regardless of residence in northern or southern states or in rural or urban communities. Self-concepts became more positive over time. All preschool groups indicated majority group preference. At the end of five years, however, the children had markedly changed their race attitudes and preferred and identified more with their own group. Again, no data supported a linear relationship between self-concept and racial attitudes. In the present study, we sought to examine the relationship between ethnic attitudes and self-concept in the psychological construct of children of Chinese immigrants and also the developmental changes that may occur in the two variables.

Bilingualism

Preschool Chinese American children are generally more proficient in Chinese than in English (Kuo, 1974a, 1974b). More than 90% of children of Chinese immigrants are bilingual. Parents speak Chinese to their children and children often reply in Chinese. At preschool age, Chinese American children develop proficiency in English in nursery school through interaction with peers and siblings, but they do not lose their native language proficiency.

The general conclusion may be made that young minority children may have a language handicap when they first enter public school, but their deficiencies in the dominant society's language diminish as they progress through school. Children of immigrant families often learn their native language at home and the dominant society's language at school. In the first and second grades, immigrants' children may have a "language handicap" (W. Jones, 1960; Pinter, 1932; Rigg, 1928) in the dominant society's verbal intelligence tests. However, this handicap may diminish as the children advance through elementary school and have more exposure to the English-speaking community.

Bilingual children of families of low socioeconomic status often live in insulated ethnic communities. Therefore, they may sustain a language handicap (Darcy, 1952) for a longer length of time due to their minimal exposure to the dominant society's language and the emphasis on that language in achievement tests. Minimal exposure to the dominant society's language may be compensated by a stress on the value of developing competence in the language, as Yee and Laforge (1974) found in their study of mental abilities of Chinese children who were attending a school in San Francisco's Chinatown.

In our study, bilingual Chinese children's self-concept and ethnic preference were evaluated. If an impact of bilingualism develops in children of Chinese immigrants, differences in performance may be observed in those children who speak both English and Chinese and those who speak mainly English in the first two years and in the last two years of grade school.

Methodology

Sample Selection

All of the children were American, born of Chinese ancestry. Participants were recruited from a list of Chinese American families within 45 miles of the District of Columbia. The list was developed from membership lists of various Chinese cultural, religious, commercial, and social groups, and public schools in northern Virginia, the District of Columbia, and Maryland.

Subjects were selected on the basis of equal sex and grade distribution. The sample consisted of 96 children (48 male, 48 female) who were first and second graders and 96 children (48 male, 48 female) who were fifth and sixth graders. The mean age was 7.49 years for the younger group and 11.3 years for the older group.

The subjects' parents were of Chinese ancestry and had immigrated to the United States after they were 18 years old. The average length of stay in the United States for both parents was about 15 years.

Of these families, 84% were simple nuclear families consisting of two parents and their biological or adopted children, and 84% of the families had three to five members in the household. Only 16% of the families had more than five members (see Table 16.1).

A Chinese dialect, usually Mandarin, Taiwanese, or Cantonese, was spoken in most of the homes. In order to examine differences in children who knew both English and Chinese and those who knew mainly English, children were separated into above median and below median in native language proficiency on the basis of their scores on the Chinese translation of the Peabody Picture Vocabulary Test (PPVT). Separate medians were determined for each grade and for each sex. The median scores for the younger students, in the first and second grades, were 47 for male children and 59 for female children. For the fifth and sixth graders, medians for both male and female children were 64. Of the children whose families always or mostly spoke Chinese at home, 54% were above median in Chinese vocabulary. Therefore, children who scored above median on the Chinese PPVT were grouped in the English-and-Chinese language group; children who scored below median were put in the mainly English language group.

Parents' socioeconomic status. Parents were very high on the economic ladder as well as highly educated. Fully 88% of the fathers and 45% of the mothers had had graduate or professional education; 35% of the mothers had three or four years of college.

When the parents were asked to give their perceptions of their own and their parents' socioeconomic status, 83% felt that they were middle-class and 15% felt that they were upper-class. They also felt that 71-75% of their own parents were middle-class, while 18% were upper-class in their native land.

An objective measure of socioeconomic status was determined by the standardized Hollingshead and Redlich Socioeconomic Status Scale. On the basis of the father's educational and occupational status, it was

Table 16.1 Frequencies, Means, and Standard Deviations of Sample Characteristics by Grade of Children

Frequency Description of Sample

	Grade 1-2		Grade 5-6		Total	
Variable	f	%	f	%	f	%
Sex						
male	48	50	48	50	96	50
female	48	50	48	50	96	50
total	96	100	96	100	192	100
Hollingshead-Redlich SES						
middle	49	55	54	62	103	59
working	40	45	33	38	73	42
total	89	100	87	100	176	101

Description of Sample by Means and Standard Deviation

	Grade 1-2			Grade 5-6			Total		
Deviation	N	M	SD	N	M	SD	N	M	SD
Child's age (months)	96	89.86	7.32	96	136.56	7.56			
Percentage of English spoken between parent and child	96	38.94	31.59	91	51.64	30.99	187	45.12	31.86
Percentage of Chinese spoken between parent and child	96	57.73	31.79	92	47.11	31.19	188	52.53	31.87
Length of stay in United States (years)									
father	96	13.97	5.29	94	17.64	4.69	190	15.80	5.32
mother	96	12.15	3.65	94	15.38	3.56	190	13.76	3.94

found that 23% of the families were, in fact, upper-class and 77% of the families were middle-class.

Data Collection of Dependent Variables

The dependent variables were as follows: Child variables consisted of (a) self-concept, (b) racial/ethnic attitudes, and (c) Chinese language ability; parental variables were (a) parental attitudes toward Chinese culture and (b) parental attitudes toward the child, his or her ability, and ethnic attitude.

Instruments

Child Measures

Self-concept. Three instruments were used to collect the self-concept data: the Piers-Harris Children's Self-Concept Scale, the Engle Self-Concept Test, and Porter's Self-Portrait Drawing. The Piers-Harris scale is a verbal measure of self-concept, whereas the Engle test and Self-Portrait Drawing are performance measures.

The Piers-Harris Children's Self-Concept Scale is a self-report instrument designed for children over a wide range of ages. Each child answered yes or no to each of 80 items. Items were read to the first and second graders.

In the Engle Self-Concept Test, the child is shown an illustration of two stick figures standing at both ends of a stepladder with five steps. One figure is identified as having positive characteristics (happy) and the other as being negative (sad). The child's self-evaluation statement is rated by his or her placement of a mark on one of the rungs of the ladder illustration. Seven different selections were made (appearance, strength, likability, ability, happiness, bravery, and following rules) for each child. This procedure was developed by Harriette McAdoo (1974) from Engle's factors for Black children.

Porter's Self-Portrait Drawing coding procedure was used to determine self-concept. Each child drew a picture of him- or herself with crayons on white paper, and the drawing was then evaluated. Porter's (1971) scoring scheme was used on the assumption that "the most detailed, colorful, and lively pictures indicated a more favorable self-image" (p. 145). Reliability was achieved by having two coders agree on the presence or absence of each category in the picture.

Ethnic attitudes. Ethnic race awareness, self-identity, and preferences were obtained with a modification of the original Clark's dolls test. Fox and Jordan (1973) had used Clark's questions with color photographs instead of dolls of Chinese and white boys and girls. Photographs of Chinese and white children, similar to the original Fox and Jordan slides, were used in this study. Harriette McAdoo (1974), working with Asian, Black, and African children, had modified the basic race attitude question. In all, this study adapted seven questions from Fox and Jordan and three questions from McAdoo. Race awareness was determined by children's identification of white and Chinese children. Children indicated their racial self-identification by pointing to pictures of children who were like them or most like them. Eight questions were asked to determine Chinese children's ethnic preference in terms of compatibility, appearance, attractiveness, friendliness, and intelligence.

Chinese language ability. The Chinese translation of Form B of·the Peabody Picture Vocabulary Test was used to measure the children's Chinese language ability. Form B was translated into Chinese by the principal investigator of this study and several Chinese scholars, psychologists, linguists, professors, and schoolteachers.

Parent Measures

A parent's protocol translated into both English and Chinese was developed in two parts. The first part consisted of 22 self-rated items that indicated the parent's attitudes toward Chinese culture. Fifteen questions evaluated their attitudes toward raising their children and Chinese philosophy and values in light of their minority status in the United States. Responses to nine questions indicated the extent to which the parents maintained a Chinese subculture by preserving their native language, contact with Chinese organizations and friends, and customs in their life-style. The protocol was pretested on 40 adults and modified before it was administered to the subjects' parents.

The second part of the parent's protocol gathered descriptive data (age of arrival in the United States, native language, education, occupation, religion, family income, and size and type of family). Questions concerning parental expectations of the child's occupation, education, and study of Chinese language were also asked. A subjective rating of the percentage of English and Chinese dialects spoken between parent and child was used to assess the native language usage of the child.

For both instruments, content validity of the items was determined by parents, teachers, and other researchers. Translations and back-translations were made to ensure accuracy.

Data Collection Procedure

Male and female Chinese interviewers were recruited from the metropolitan Washington, D.C., and Baltimore areas. All interviewers spoke English and at least one of the Chinese dialects. All had college degrees, and four out of eight persons had master's degrees. Interviewers were trained by the principal investigators.

Interviews were conducted in the participants' homes. Due to the lengthiness of the battery of tests for the child, most of the children were viewed on two separate occasions within a span of one week. During the first interview with the child, parents were asked to jointly complete the two-part questionnaire. The parents' questionnaire was collected after the second interview with the child. Upon the completion of the interview, a small cash gift was given to participating families.

Results

Parents

Parents' Attitudes Toward Chinese Culture

The parents had positive attitudes toward Chinese culture. A factor analysis of parents' responses to 22 questions on their attitudes toward Chinese culture suggested that their attitudes could be reduced to four factors. In order of importance, these were (a) maintenance of the Chinese language community, (b) pride in Chinese culture, (c) belief in Chinese culture, and (d) preservation of Chinese customs. Parents felt most strongly about exposing their children to Chinese culture so that the children would not lose it. Second, they strongly believed that speaking both Chinese and English would facilitate children's intellectual development. Third, they felt that insults to Chinese honor should not be taken lightly. Fourth, parents felt that, if possible, Chinese should be spoken with other Chinese. Fifth, Chinese parents felt that Chinese schools were very important for their children. The five most important elements of parents' attitudes toward Chinese culture indicated the immigrant parents' strong wish to expose their children to their own culture in order that the children would appreciate and understand it so that they could pass it on to the next generation.

The parents' cultural attitudes were viewed more positively among children in the bilingual group than among children in the group that spoke mainly English. There was no significant difference in attitudes of parents of boys and girls.

The more positive the parents' attitudes were toward Chinese culture, the lower the older boys' self-concept. Parents' attitudes toward Chinese culture were positively related to ethnic preference among younger girls who were in the mainly English group.

Parents' Length of Stay in the United States and Child Measures

Among younger boys and older girls, the longer the mother or father had stayed in the United States, the less Chinese and the more English was spoken between parent and child.

Self-concept. Parents' length of stay in the United States seemed to have an intricate relationship with Chinese boys' self-concept. Negative correlations were found separately between the mother's and father's length of stay and young boys' self-concept. The opposite was true for older boys. The longer the father had stayed in the United States, the higher was the older boys' self-concept. Boys who spoke both English and Chinese had lower self-concepts the longer their parents had lived in the United States. In contrast, mainly English-speaking boys had higher self-concepts the longer the father had lived in the United States.

Among girls, relationships between parents' length of stay in the United States and self-concept were found only in the older group. Negative correlations were found between the mother's length of stay in the United States and self-concept among older girls and English-speaking older girls.

Ethnic preference. Ethnic preference was positively related to parents' length of stay in the United States among English-speaking older boys.

Parents' attitudes toward Chinese culture. As with the use of Chinese in the home, there were also negative correlations between mother's length of stay in the United States and parents' attitudes toward Chinese culture among younger boys and older girls.

Parents' Language Usage With Child and Child Measures

Correlations were examined between the percentage of English and the percentage of main Chinese dialect that was spoken between parent and child. More than one Chinese dialect was spoken in some of the households.

Self-concept. Language usage between parent and child was positively related with boys' self-concept, but not with girls'. Boys who spoke English with their parents had lower racial awareness and self-concepts, and positive correlations were found between the percentage of main Chinese dialect that was spoken and positive self-portrait self-concepts.

Ethnic preference. Ethnic preference was related to language usage in the home only among older boys who spoke both English and Chinese. Older boys' ethnic preference was positively related to the percentage of Chinese that was spoken between parent and child.

Children

The majority of the children had been attending Chinese language schools when they were interviewed. The percentage of Chinese spoken in the home was obtained by subtracting the percentage of English spoken in the home from 100%. Parents spoke more English with boys than with girls, and more Chinese with girls than with boys. Children who scored above median in the Chinese translation of the PPVT spoke more Chinese with their parents than did children in the below median group.

Self-Concept

The self-concepts were high on all of the scales. On the Piers-Harris test, there were no significant sex, grade, or interaction differences on this scale. All of the subjects felt good about themselves.

The Engle self-concept procedure, while it had not been standardized on a national sample, had been found in minority samples to be significantly related to the self-concept scores obtained on the Thomas and Brown scales, which had been nationally normed. High self-concepts in Chinese children were also found for the Engle test. The age differences were significant, but there were no sex or sex-by-grade differences. The younger children felt significantly better about themselves than did the older children; however, both groups had good, positive self-concepts.

The Porter self-portrait scoring procedure was used to determine the characteristics that the children put in their pictures that indicated strong self-esteem. Consistent with the Engle results, the self-concepts of younger children were significantly higher than those of the older children. In both age groups the girls had higher scores than the boys, while there were no sex-by-grade interaction differences.

Language group differences. No significant differences were found between the English-and-Chinese group and the mainly English group in any self-concept measures. Language group differences were found among boys, but not among girls. Among boys, the English-and-Chinese group scored higher than the mainly English group. In the mainly English group, girls scored higher than boys.

Ethnic Attitudes

The overall score on ethnic attitudes, based on responses to only the physical characteristics of children in the pictures, indicated that these children had positive attitudes toward the Chinese racial group.

Race awareness. By the age of 7, the children were almost all clearly aware of racial differences based on physical characteristics.

Self-identification. All of the children were able to identify themselves appropriately with the race of the person in the picture. When asked to point to the child who was like themselves, all made correct identifications.

Ethnic preference. The average ethnic preference was positive for the children, and no grade or sex differences were found in the total ethnic preference scores.

When individual ethnic preference items were examined, some grade and sex differences were found in evaluative measures. On the question, "Which child would you like to play with?" proportionately more of the older children selected the Chinese playmate, indicating a move from no preference in the earlier grades to one of marked Chinese preference in the later grades. Preference for their own skin color was stronger in older children than in younger children.

Only one ethnic preference sex difference was found among children in the early grades. Younger girls preferred Chinese playmates, whereas younger boys preferred white playmates.

Language group differences. No significant differences were found on ethnic preference measures between the language groups. When controlling for grade, no relations were found between children's Chinese vocabulary and any ethnic attitude measures. Regardless of Chinese language ability, Chinese children were aware of race differences in physical characteristics and correctly identified with their own group. The children's Chinese vocabulary had no relationship with ethnic preference, not even with choice of playmate.

Children's rationale for ethnic attitude choices. After all of the choices had been made, each child was asked a series of open-ended questions that attempted to explore the rationale and motivations for the choices they had made. All indicated that they had used some form of physical characteristics for identification. Hair differences, language, and general physical differences were the main items noted by the children. Also mentioned were use of skin color and general cultural differences.

The children were then asked to explain why some children were selected in response to negative attributes and others were selected for positive descriptions. The majority felt that the Chinese child was nicer. The most important reason for selecting the Chinese child positively, at all ages, was the identification with the child as being someone who was like themselves. Only a fourth of the children felt the white child was nicer. Boys said they felt that way because they were American and did not speak Chinese. In contrast, girls chose the white child as being nice because they said that white children looked nicer and were fun to be with.

The children clearly felt that Chinese children (79%) were smarter than white children (21%). There were few sex or grade differences on this attitude. The majority said that they felt the white children were stupid because of their physical appearance, because they were just not smart, and because their behavior was bad. These Chinese American children appeared to have internalized negative attitudes toward a group due to their physical appearance.

Discussion

Self-Concept and Ethnic Attitudes

According to standardized scales for American children, the Chinese American children in this sample have high self-concepts as measured by the Piers-Harris Children's Self-Concept Scale. The mean scores for Engle self-concept, Porter's self-portrait, and ethnic attitude measures show that these Chinese American children have positive attitudes toward themselves and toward their ethnicity.

Positive self-concepts and ethnic attitudes may reflect the middle-class upbringing of the children in this sample by highly educated parents. The dominant society's increasingly positive attitudes toward minority groups may also contribute to the children's positive attitudes toward themselves.

Grade Differences

Self-concept measures. Two performance self-concept measures showed that the older children in this sample had lower self-concepts than did the younger children. This result is consistent with the findings of Piers and Harris (1964), which revealed that third graders in their sample had higher self-concepts than sixth graders among male and female children. It may be that younger children tend to adopt their parents' usually inflated view of them, whereas older children may tend to adjust their feelings of self-worth according to their teachers' and peers' more realistic evaluations. Some questions remain in this inter-pretation of grade differences in self-concept due to the fact that mean scores on the Engle and Porter self-portrait self-concept measures support the Piers and Harris findings, but not the Piers-Harris test itself.

For ethnically different children, lower self-concept among older children may be related to the process of adjusting to a dominant culture. As minority children grow older and interact more with the dominant society, they may become aware of the secondary status of their race and culture, which may decrease their feelings of self-worth.

Ethnic attitude. For the most part, no differences were found between first and second graders and fifth and sixth graders in race awareness, identification, and ethnic preference. Children in this sample seemed to know, prefer, and identify with their ethnicity at an early age.

Grade differences were found in two individual items of ethnic preference. Older children stated that they preferred to play with mem-bers of their own ethnicity and preferred their own skin color, whereas younger children did not seem to have a preference. The preference of skin color may be influenced by the biased beauty standard that the lighter the color, the more beautiful one is. Young Chinese American children may absorb this beauty standard. Older Chinese American children, however, may realize and resolve the conflict between this beauty standard and their feelings of self-worth by developing prefer-ence for their own color. Preference was shown by first and second graders and fifth and sixth graders to their own ethnic group on six other items, and their views are consistent with the parents' positive views toward their own race. This is consistent with Harriette McAdoo's (1985) data on Black children; in that study, young children showed no preferences, but strong ethnic group preferences were clearly noted in older children.

Sex Differences

Sex differences were found only on Porter's self-portrait self-concept test, with girls scoring higher than boys. It is suggested that girls may tend to have higher scores on the self-portrait drawing test because they are more aware of appearance than boys are (Porter, 1971). The lack of sex differences on the Engle or Piers-Harris self-concept measures in ethnic preference or anxiety level suggests that boys and girls are equally well adjusted in the United States. Although Casteneda, McCandless, and Palermo (1956) and other researchers have found that girls are more anxious than boys, this finding is not supported by the Chinese American children in this study.

Psychologically, these Chinese immigrants' children were not affected by their distinct minority status. They not only had high self-concept and ethnic preferences, they also had high self-concept regardless of their ethnic preference.

The high ethnic preferences among these Chinese American children support Harriette McAdoo's (1974) assertion that the self-hatred hypothesis may no longer be valid. The Chinese American children in this sample had more positive race attitudes than did Chinese children of similar ages in an earlier study conducted by Fox and Jordan (1973). The negative attributions that children in the Fox and Jordan study gave to their own group may have been due to the dominant society's attitudes toward minorities at that time or differences in the children's socioeconomic status among samples. Minority children of low socioeconomic status, especially those living in low-income ethnic communities, such as those in the Fox and Jordan study, may not feel as good about their ethnic peers because of their harsher living conditions. In contrast, the group in this sample lived a comfortable middle-class life. Research is needed to explicate the separate and interactive roles of socioeconomic status and the dominant society's attitudes toward minority groups on Chinese American children's ethnic preferences and identification.

Inconsistent with the results of Harriette McAdoo's (1985) five-year longitudinal study, which indicated that minority children had more positive race attitudes over time, no significant grade differences in children's ethnic preferences were found in this study. If further studies indicate that the increase in the child's positive ethnic preference over time is caused more by the dominant society's increase of positive attitudes toward the minority group than by the child's age, then there should not be grade differences as found in the present study. We believe that young Chinese American children tend to adopt their parents' usually inflated view of them, but that they gradually adjust their feelings of self-worth according to their teachers' and peers' more realistic evaluations of them as they grow older.

When bilingual Chinese American children first enter grade school, they enter a new peer group. Rarely do established members of a group adjust to newcomers in their activities (Phillips, Shenker, & Levitz, 1951). Chinese American children, therefore, must adjust to the new values, items, and activities of their new peer group. They are at a disadvantage in becoming popular because of their strength and physical appearance. The more intelligent children may be more sensitive to peers' values and peers' ratings of them, and, therefore, may have lower self-concept than do children who do not feel the factors that make one popular. Less sensitive children may still enjoy their parents' inflated view of them.

Boys and girls react differently to peer group evaluation. Boys are more other-group oriented than girls. They are expected to be well adjusted and socially active in the American society. In the lower grades, their inability to break away from their own group may have a negative impact on Chinese American boys' self-concept. Girls, in contrast, are often reared to be more own-group oriented. They are encouraged not to participate in too many activities outside the home. Therefore, they are not as concerned with their peers' evaluation of them as boys are, and continue to enjoy their parents' inflated view of them.

Chinese American children in the fifth and sixth grades are no longer newcomers in their peer group. They have adapted to their peers' values, customs, and activities. No longer are strength and physical appearance the most important factors in gaining popularity among peers. Other factors, such as their talents, intelligence, self-confidence, friendliness, arithmetic ability, and general academic achievement, can win the respect of the children's peers.

Chinese Language Skills

It is not easy to measure language skills in different dialects spoken by Chinese American children, because some dialect words have no comparable written words. No standardized Chinese language test has been available. The existing Chinese language skill measure is usually appropriate to only one dialect and cannot be used for other dialects.

Chinese Vocabulary and Self-Concept or Ethnic Preference

Asians living in the United States cannot hide their minority status because of their physical appearance, no matter how excellent their English. It will be more beneficial for the security and harmony of the entire society if Asians are encouraged to understand and respect their own cultures than if they are expected to strive to be like Caucasians. Learning the language of one's country of origin, or of one's parents' homeland, can provide many opportunities to understand one's cultural background.

It can be hypothesized that the more proficient Chinese American children are in Chinese, the more positive their ethnic preference and self-concept. One may argue, on the other hand, that the more proficient Chinese American children are in Chinese, the more negative their ethnic preference and self-concept, because the Chinese language may make their minority status more obvious and therefore may make it harder for the children to be accepted by peers in the dominant society.

The general results of this study indicate that there was no relationship between Chinese language skills and self-concept. Only among the older boys was there a positive relationship between Chinese language skills and ethnic preference. This study shows that the Chinese language is not a key element in children's ethnic preference and self-concept. However, the fact that Chinese immigrants' children have high ethnic preference and self-concept, regardless of their Chinese language ability, indicates that the second language does not produce negative effects for the children's ethnic preference and self-concept, and that it might have a positive effect for the older boys' ethnic preference.

Parents' Influence on the Child

The parents' attitudes toward their heritage in a dominant society have always been considered to play a significant role in the child's cognitive development and mental health, especially in competition with nonsupportive socializing agents such as school. Parents can directly or indirectly influence the cognitive functioning and mental health of their children by emphasizing culture in their attitudes and behavior. By taking their children to social events that may ordinarily be considered mainly for adults, Chinese parents can expose their children to adult activities and, indirectly, Chinese culture (Huang, 1976). By placing primary importance on exposing their children to Chinese culture, Chinese parents will probably provide opportunities for their children to reach this end. By choosing to live near good schools, parents show how concerned they are with their children's cognitive functioning and academic achievement. The Chinese traditional values of expecting children to have strong family ties, to be scholars, and to learn Chinese culture are likely to be absorbed by children because parents and children spend so much time together.

The parents' influence on children may be inferred by the children's attitudes toward their own ethnic group or culture. The intercorrelations between parents' attitudes toward Chinese culture and the child's ethnic preferences, Chinese vocabulary, and self-concept may imply some systemic relationship between parent and child. However, one must interpret the relations very carefully, because no directional causal statement can be made from the correlations. However, by the degree to which they are attached to their own people and culture, and the dedication with which they preserve traditional values, practices, and languages in the home, Chinese parents seem to influence their children's self-concept, anxiety, ethnic preference, and Chinese language skills.

Self-Concept

The subjects' parents' attitudes toward Chinese culture and language usage with children were significantly correlated with boys' self-concept. Boys in both the first and second grades and in the fifth and sixth grades had higher self-concept when more Chinese was spoken between parent and child, and lower self-concept when more English was spoken between parent and child. However, for older boys, the more positive the parents' attitudes toward Chinese culture, the lower their self-concept.

Older boys' self-concept may be affected by the dual expectations of their parents for them to achieve and to develop fluency in the Chinese language. Self-concept may be affected when the boys find it difficult to meet both expectations, especially when a degree of bilinguality is necessary for success in the dominant society. Boys in the fifth and sixth grades may be more fluent in English than in Chinese. In order to have the older boys master Chinese as well, parents continue to speak Chinese with their older boys even though the boys may not be proficient in Chinese. This explanation can be supported by the fact that, only among the older boys, there was no positive relationship between

Chinese vocabulary skills and Chinese spoken between parents and children.

Ethnic Preference

In a society in which there is a dominant-subordinate ethnic social structure, minority parents are the main agents in children's retention of positive attitudes toward their own native culture and ethnic groups. No other socializing agent would be more concerned with the children's own-group preference than they. Since most of the Chinese American children in this study had highly positive attitudes toward their own race, it may be inferred that the parents had a significant impact on the children's ethnic preference.

Parents seem to influence the ethnic preferences of girls, especially those in the first and second grades. Parents with strong positive attitudes toward Chinese culture may rear both boys and girls with own-group ethnic preference. According to Chinese tradition, parents may rear girls with a domestic orientation and boys with a more outgoing orientation. Young girls have fewer outside factors affecting their evaluation of their parents' positive attitude toward Chinese culture; therefore, among young girls, the more positive the parents' attitude toward Chinese culture, the stronger their ethnic preference toward their own group. However, among the older children or young boys, who have more experiences beyond the home, ethnic preference may still be affected by their parents' positive attitude toward Chinese culture, but not in systematic relationship. They may also be affected by other unknown parental factors. In general, parents' attitudes toward Chinese culture did not have systematic correlations with boys' or older girls' ethnic preference.

In this study, three parent variables—parents' attitudes toward Chinese culture, language usage with child, and length of stay in the United States—were correlated with the child measures. Symmetrical relationships were found between parent variables and preservation of Chinese language. There was a consistent inverse relationship between the percentage of English and the percentage of Chinese that was spoken between parent and child. Parents spoke more Chinese with their children in the first and second grades than the fifth and sixth grades, and vice versa for English. The longer the parents had lived in the United States, the more English was spoken between parents and male children in the first and second grades and female children in the fifth and sixth grades; conversely, the shorter their length of stay, the more Chinese was spoken between parent and child for younger boys and older girls. The most important component in Chinese parents' attitudes toward Chinese culture in this sample was the maintenance of the Chinese language community. The more positive the parents were toward the Chinese culture, the more Chinese they spoke with the child and the better the child's Chinese vocabulary. Conversely, the less positive the parents' attitudes were toward Chinese culture, the more English was spoken between parent and child, and the lower the child's Chinese vocabulary.

Attitudes toward Chinese culture were more positive in parents whose children were in the Chinese-and-English group than in parents whose children were in the mainly English group. In both language groups, first- and second-grade children seemed to need to balance their abilities in English and Chinese. Young children may feel the dual pressure of doing well in school and of keeping their native language. To alleviate the pressure, Chinese American children may need to develop proficiency in both English and Chinese. In the fifth and sixth grades, bilingual status no longer had a significant psychological impact on children in the Chinese-and-English group. However, older children in the mainly English group spoke more fluently in English than in Chinese by the fifth and sixth grades. If more English is used between parents and older children, not only can the children express their thinking in the most convenient way, but there may be less pressure for the child to develop proficiency in Chinese.

Summary and Conclusions

Little is currently known about the psychological perspectives of Chinese American children. The reason for this is twofold. Social scientists and educators have only recently actively recognized the value and importance of preserving ethnic cultures, not only for members of ethnic groups but also for the larger society. On the other side, members of the Chinese community have only recently begun to be more open about their concerns, voicing them to teachers and policymakers as well as to sociologists and psychologists.

Children of Chinese immigrant families are an overlooked minority group that may need attention. The children have to face the dual problems of adjusting to their minority status in the United States and developing a comfortable degree of binguality in the face of parental and societal forces.

A positive picture, regardless of grade, sex, or language group, emerged for the Chinese American children in this sample. The results probably reflect the children's upbringing in intact, middle- or upper-class families. The children had high self-concepts and Chinese language skills. Older children had lower self-concepts than did younger children. The results are consistent with the findings of Piers and Harris (1964), who found among American children that third graders had higher self-concepts than sixth graders. As noted above, one explanation for this may be that younger children tend to adopt their parents' usually inflated view of them, whereas older children tend to adjust their feelings of self-worth according to their teachers' and peers' more realistic evaluations.

By the age of 7, Chinese American children in this sample were clearly aware of racial differences based on physical characteristics. Furthermore, the children were able to identify themselves with the race of the person in a picture. For the most part, they had developed a strong preference for Chinese children. The parents' very positive attitudes toward Chinese culture seem to have contributed to the children's positive ethnic attitude.

Clearly, parents play an important role in passing the Chinese language to their children. The more strongly the subjects' parents were attached to their own people and culture, the more Chinese and the less English was spoken in the home; the less positive the parents' attitudes toward Chinese culture, the more English and the less Chinese was spoken between parent and child. The amount of Chinese spoken in the home was positively correlated with the breadth of the child's Chinese vocabulary. The fact that fifth- and sixth-grade children had higher Chinese vocabulary skills than first- and second-grade children, despite their increased exposure to English in school, indicates that the Chinese language was preserved among immigrant families.

Too strong an emphasis on the Chinese language, however, apparently had a negative influence on the self-concepts of boys in the fifth and sixth grades. Similarly, the more positive the parents' attitudes were toward Chinese culture, the lower the older boys' self-concepts. Older boys' self-concepts may be affected by the dual expectations of their parents for them to achieve and to develop fluency in the Chinese language. Self-concept is affected because the boys find it difficult to meet both expectations.

The Chinese American children's bilingual status did not affect their self-concept or ethnic preference. Children in both the Chinese-and-English group and the mainly English group showed positive feelings of self-worth and own-group preference. The only difference between the two groups was the amount of Chinese vocabulary known by the children. Children had high self-concepts regardless of their ethnic attitudes, although most of the Chinese children also had positive feelings toward their own ethnic group.

In general, the children of Chinese immigrants in this study seemed to be well adjusted in American elementary schools. Their parents' middle-class socioeconomic status and positive attitudes toward Chinese culture may have contributed to their sense of well-being. Parents' attitudes toward Chinese culture seemed to have significant impacts upon the children's Chinese language skills and ethnic preference. However, as evidenced by the inverse relationships between parents' attitudes toward Chinese culture and self-concept among the boys in the fifth and sixth grades, parents must take great care in creating an environment for children to accept Chinese culture. At the same time, parents should give their children opportunities to practice English— without placing untoward value on English, to the detriment of Chinese culture.

17

Intergenerational Relationships Among Chinese Immigrant Families From Taiwan

CHIEN LIN
WILLIAM T. LIU

The cultural value of filial piety, *hsiao,* which has governed intergenerational relationships among Chinese families for centuries, persists in Taiwan, partly as a result of strong government and institutional reinforcement and support. Both adult children and their parents share the norms, attitudes, and expectations of this cultural value in the Chinese society. However, when Chinese immigrate to the United States, several factors interfere with the maintenance of filial relations: (a) an absence of structural and institutional support, (b) generational differences in the pace of assimilation, and (c) cultural differences between Chinese and American society, including the American emphasis on independence versus the Chinese value of interdependence, the American stress on universalism versus the Chinese preference for particularism, and the American conception of the husband-wife relationship as the dominant dyad versus the Chinese definition of the parent-child relationship as taking precedence over all others.

The intergenerational relationships among Chinese immigrant families are therefore subjected to the stress of the erosion of their own values. Both generations experience these problems, but they seem unable to articulate their precise nature, and have therefore not developed appropriate solutions. The present study is an attempt to understand how the

271

cultural value of *hsiao* is adapted in the vastly different context of the American society.

Background

Hsiao is a complex system that involves a series of obligations of child to parent: most centrally to provide aid, comfort, affection, and contact with the parent (economic and emotional support), and secondly to bring reflected glory to the parent by doing well in educational and occupational activities (success in the outside world). *Hsiao* is deeply ingrained in the Chinese culture and has served as the moral foundation of interpersonal relationships in China for centuries. In terms of economic and emotional support, Confucius demanded from a filial son not merely the formal fulfillment of obligation but also selfless devotion and an attitude of loving warmth and reverence. The 24 filial stories show that the highest priority in the value system in traditional China explicitly demanded that the support of parents by adult children take precedence over all other obligations, including one's love for one's own children. The second dimension of *hsiao* explicitly demands that the child bring glory to the family. One should cultivate one's character to perpetuate one's name for future generations in order to give glory to one's parents (L.-Y. Lee, 1976, chap. 16). Glory for the family can be achieved through educational and occupational achievement.

Hsiao has been woven into virtually every facet of Chinese life. Kinship relations have become a paradigm for nonfamilial social relations. Certain socially significant relationships, such as those between master and apprentice or teacher and student, operate on a simulated father-son basis (Yang, 1959). This paradigm is extended to the relationship between ruler and people. Government officials are referred to as parent-officials (*fu mu kuan*) and the people as children-people (*tse min*). The devotion and reverence expected of people by the ruler is the same as that expected of a son by his father. To encourage the *hsiao* of a son to his parents is also to encourage the loyalty of the people to the ruler. Hence the value of filial piety has been supported by rulers and institutionalized in the legal and political structure of traditional China. From the time of the Han (202 B.C.-A.D. 220) to the Ching Dynasty (1664-1911), filial impiety was one of the 10 unpardonable crimes in Chinese law (Chiu, 1961). This concept is the organizing principle for various institutions. The promotion of an official, for example, is determined, in part, on the basis of filial piety. It is believed that a person who is obedient to his parents can be relied upon.

Following the overthrow of the Kuomintang in 1949, the Communist Chinese government in Peking "liberated" people from the ancient feudal system. Anything related to the old society, including Confucian doctrine, was to be destroyed. The Kuomintang government in Taipei, on the other hand, made a major effort to maintain and glorify the traditional culture. This accentuated the differences between the two governments and supports Taiwan's claim that the Kuomintang is the only legitimate representative of China by virtue of its having preserved the traditional culture. At all levels of the educational system, school officials designate one month of each year as *hsiao-shuen* (filial piety and obedience) month. Speakers are invited each week to give a speech on *hsiao* at a meeting that all students are required to attend. During the month, *hsiao* is used as the subject matter for all school activities (e.g., as the subject of compositions). In 1977, the government further extended this to the total population and designated April as "teaching filial piety month." Supporting one's parents is also laid out in the Civic Law of the Republic of China. It is the children's responsibility to support their parents, regardless of their parents' ability to support themselves.

In a study of the achievement motivation of Chinese teenagers in Taiwan, Yu (1975) found that, by and large, *hsiao* is still a dominant value held by the current generation of Chinese students. Yu reported Taiwan government efforts to maintain and glorify the spirit of *hsiao* through essay contests. Similar efforts were made by such diverse organizations as film companies, the Lion's Club, and the Catholic church. In a study of the value system of Taiwan, Grichting (1970) reported that the preferred location for newlyweds was with the husband's parents; the main reason given for this was mutual support and the "parents' needs."

The origin of filial piety can also be explained in structural terms. As Simmons (1945) and Rosow (1965) have pointed out, the relative position of the elderly in a society is determined by seven conditions: the locus of property ownership, the character of strategic knowledge, the religious links, the nature of kinship and extended family ties, the type of community life, the nature of economic productivity, and the degree of mutual dependence. In traditional China, as demonstrated by Ikels (1980), all seven of these factors were present. The Chinese elderly owned or controlled the productive resources on which the younger people were dependent; their experience was the major source of knowledge; they were seen as a link to the gods, and when they died, they were believed to join the ancestors to be worshiped; they were highly influential because most Chinese villages were relatively small and stable communities; their contribution in the low-productivity economy, even though small, was highly valued; and their network connections were essential for survival. Therefore, practical economic considerations, supernatural sanctions, and community pressure all combined to reinforce filial piety and operated primarily to ensure a measure of security in old age.

In modern society, many unique structural features supporting filial piety are disappearing. Professional training displaces private property as a source of income. Modern society is innovative, and the elderly are hence rendered obsolete. The population is highly mobile, making family stability difficult to maintain. Urbanization and residential mobility weaken local community ties. Productivity is high and individuals, including the elderly, are no longer dependent on families for economic activity. All of these features, and others, tend to threaten the maintenance of filial piety.

In addition to the differences between traditional and modern society, Chinese immigrants to the West face a society with a fundamentally different value system, as discussed below.

Independence versus interdependence. The American value orientation favors economic and social independence. Even though mutual help between generations still exists, especially in the working class, most parents do not expect their children to support them, and they are very cautious about giving help to their adult children. Too much help might cast doubt on the children's abilities to take care of themselves (Sussman, 1953). Chinese, on the other hand, encourage interdependence among family members. A child, no matter how old, should remain emotionally and financially attached to the parents. Grichting's (1970) study of the value system of Taiwan revealed strong indications of a lack of independence training in child rearing. Obedience and cooperation are the values most emphasized. Frequent receiving and giving of help between generations is seen by Chinese as an indication of family solidarity. Most children are expected to turn their earnings over to their parents to be used for general family needs.

To many Americans, death is preferable to "becoming a burden" (Clark & Anderson, 1967). In Chinese thinking, one can find value only in relationships of interdependence. Thus, whereas American parents struggle to be independent to maintain their self-esteem, the Chinese maintain their self-esteem by having someone to depend on.

Father-son versus husband-wife. According to Hsu (1971), each culture has a dominant dyad—that is, a dyad that is accorded central importance and that expresses the fundamental values and commitments of that culture. For Hsu, the dominant dyad is a kind of cultural keystone symbolizing the essence of value and coloring all of the social relationships in the society. In the American kinship system, the husband-wife dyad takes precedence over other dyads in the nuclear family. Chinese society, on the other hand, is dominated by the father-son dyad. According to Hsu's hypothesis on kinship and culture, the dominant dyad in a given society has a tremendous effect not only on other kinship dyads but also on nonkin relationships. All the other nondominant dyads tend to be modified, reduced, or eliminated in favor of the dominant one. In traditional Chinese society, for example, the parents have more to say in the choice of their son's future wife than does the son himself. The needs of the married partners are considered secondary to those of the parents. In American society, the father-son dyad is considered temporary and is superseded by the cohesion between husband and wife.

Whereas in China the father-son dyad is considered of utmost value and the primary model of virtue, in the United States this relationship is of no great consequence—it would be considered aberrant if filial devotion were allowed to interfere with the bond of husband and wife.

Professional commitment versus family loyalty. American society is characterized by the dominant value of universalism. According to this value, persons are judged by an objective standard and that standard is applied independent of any criteria other than those specifically at issue. Chinese society, on the other hand, is a system that Parsons (1966) describes as "shot through with particularistic themes." Kinship takes precedence over other relationships and values in China, and nepotism is a common and accepted practice (Lang, 1946).

Despite its industrialization and modernization in recent years, Taiwan, compared with the United States, remains a relatively small and highly familial society. Occupational success, for example, depends to a large extent upon family network (Mark, 1979). The child moves into an occupational position often provided by family contacts; family solidarity is thus reinforced by participation in the occupational sphere. In the United States, structural differentiation separates family and work. Familial contacts are less significant and unavailable to the immigrant who has only a small network of occupational connections. Moreover, modern occupations are frequently associated with social and geographic mobility; that is, Chinese persons, to be successful in the United States, need to be Americanized. This requires that they eliminate or modify substantially many of their traditional behavior patterns. Professional success thus undermines family solidarity.

Chinese immigrants experience additional strain through their unique migration pattern. Traditionally, migration in China and overseas was a sequential process (Liu, 1966). The able-bodied young men migrated first and made preparations in the host society to provide a cushion for the kin who migrated later. This sequential pattern of migration has been generally adhered to by the Chinese immigrants from Taiwan (L. K. Hong, 1976). Typically, the first immigrants are children who graduate from colleges in Taiwan and are admitted to the United States on student visas. From 1950 to 1969, 22,319 students left Taiwan to pursue studies in other countries (Chang, 1973). According to the data published by the Institute of International Education, more than 20,000 Chinese students have come annually to the United States since 1970. The 1965 Immigration Act expanded the quota for Chinese to 20,000 a year and gave priority to those with needed skills and training. Most of these students with professional degrees eventually readjusted their status to that of permanent residents.

Of the students who came from 1950 to 1969, only 6.5% returned to Taiwan (Chang, 1973). As the students complete their education, secure jobs, marry, and have children, their younger siblings then also apply for visas as students. Meanwhile, the mother may come to visit or, in most cases, to assume the role of caretaker of her newborn grandchildren. She then travels back and forth between the United States and Taiwan. The father might maintain his job in Taiwan and visit his children in the United States for short periods. After the first immigrants have obtained permanent resident status in the United States, either they or their parents, or both, initiate the process of parental immigration. The parents normally immigrate after retirement.

This pattern of sequential migration has been a source of stress in the migrating family. The adult children usually precede their parents in the United States by several years. Living in a different culture at a young age as students and professionals amenable to new ideas, they are influenced by Western culture and develop a value system that differs from that of their parents. The Western reality for the young Chinese person in the United States is that professional socialization involves the adoption of new ideas. The subsequent immigration of elderly parents who are thoroughly imbued with traditional values thus results in severe cultural differences between parents and children.

The main interest of this research is to learn about generational differences in the conception of *hsiao*. Sequential migration, differential rates of assimilation because of age, and the greater involvement of the young in the American society through schooling and work all point to a growing gap between parents and children. Because of the centrality of *hsiao* to Chinese culture, it provides an appropriate focus for the study of intergenerational differences in adaptation to American society.

Data and Method

Data were gathered in both Chicago SMSA and Monterey Park, California. Two types of respondents were included in the sample: (a) Chinese American adults who had emigrated from Taiwan and had at least one parent residing in the area and (b) their parents. Almost all previous research on the nature and types of interaction patterns between two generations has relied on the reports of only one generation (B. N. Adams, 1968; Sussman, 1965; Troll, 1971). Such an approach tends to produce biased results, especially in recent immigrant studies, because of a wide generational gap in attitudes and behaviors within the ethnic group (M. Gordon, 1964; Kiefer, 1974). This research investigated intergenerational relations from both the parents' and their adult children's perspectives. The sample, therefore, included both generations. To isolate the impact of migration on both generations' perceptions of filial norms, child respondents who were 18 years of age or older at the time of migration were chosen. American-born Chinese were excluded to ensure respondent familiarity with filial norms.

A comprehensive list of Chicago Chinese from Taiwan was developed from various sources. Self-administered questionnaires designed in Chinese were mailed to both generations of eligible respondents. In Monterey Park, where a substantial number of Chinese from Taiwan reside in a relatively small geographic area, and where a comprehensive name list was unavailable, a snowball sampling method was used and questionnaires were delivered to each respondent instead of mailing. Altogether, data were collected for 180 parent generations and 129 child generations, or 125 complete households.

The *hsiao* value was measured mainly through six vignettes. These vignettes were initially developed on the basis of the researcher's knowledge of the dilemmas related to filial obligations that Chinese families face. They were later refined through pretest interviews and consultation with Chinese social scientists and mental health research-ers. The vignettes pose hypothetical conflict situations that depict characteristic dilemmas pitting the requirements of filial obligation against other sets of interpersonal demands, such as those between a husband and wife. Respondents were asked to decide what the person should do in each particular circumstance. There were two possible responses to each of the dilemmas: the traditional Chinese solution and a more American solution. By offering the same vignettes to parents and children, it was anticipated that a generation gap would be revealed, as each might interpret the blueprints of conduct in different ways. In addition, respondents were asked what they believed they would do if the situation were to occur in Taiwan versus the United States. The objective was to discern the impact of migration on the structural difference between the two societies. Liu (1966) used the vignette method in a family study in Hong Kong and reported that it might be the best way to elicit information related to cultural values.

The vignettes included situations of conflict revolving around six common problems: promotion, living arrangement, marriage, use of a car, discipline, and education. The aim and content of each vignette are described in detail below.

The Promotion Vignette

The Promotion Vignette dealt with the dilemma between one's obli-gation to one's parents and one's desire for professional achievement. It is a dilemma of central importance because it involves the two major duties of *hsiao*: to display loving care for one's parents and to bring them honor through achievement. There are possible conflicts between these duties. The vignette is translated from the Chinese version as follows:

> Su Ching and Su Ching's parents have lived in Chicago for more than five years. Su Ching's parents have made friends through Chinese church activi-ties and other social events. They regularly see their friends and are satisfied with their environment. Su Ching's company recently wanted to promote Su Ching to the chief of staff of a branch. The branch is located in a small city with very few Chinese. Su Ching's parents express their desire to stay in Chicago. Su Ching is aware of the significance of the promotion in career advancement. However, Su Ching is also aware of the difficulties of either having parents move to a new city or having them stay in Chicago by themselves.

The Living Arrangement Vignette

The Living Arrangement Vignette touches upon the issue of coresidence with one's elderly parents—should the aged parents live with their children at the cost of intrusion into the lives of the younger generation? At issue in this vignette is which dyad, parent-child or husband-wife, will be considered dominant. Elements of this vignette, such as the utility of the living arrangement, are deliberately vague. Thus, although the mother may be better off going to the nursing home for health care reasons, all that is made clear is that the daughter-in-law strongly opposes living with the mother. Hence respondents' priority of commitment can be obtained.

> Mrs. Chen is 68 years old. She has lived in the United States for five years. She has a son and a daughter. The daughter is married to a Caucasian. Because she has trouble with her daughter-in-law, Mrs. Chen lives by herself but keeps in close contact with her children. Recently, Mrs. Chen's health has been failing and she can no longer take care of herself. The son would like to follow Mrs. Chen's wishes to have her stay with his family. However, the daughter-in-law strongly opposes it and suggests sending Mrs. Chen to a nursing home. The reason she gives is that since both she and her husband have to work, a nursing home would be better able to take care of Mrs. Chen.

The Marriage Vignette

The Marriage Vignette deals with the increasing trend toward interracial marriage in the younger generation. It is intended to detect the legitimacy of parental authority in a highly personal area.

> Li Ming is very close to a Caucasian and plans to marry the person. However, when Li Ming's parents found out that Li Ming wants to marry a Caucasian, they strongly disapproved and felt it is shameful to the family.

The Car Vignette

The Car Vignette deals with the issue of whether the parents take priority over their children's resources. It presents a choice between parents' needs and the child's convenience. Unlike the Promotion Vignette, this vignette provides an opportunity for sacrifice that does not threaten the glory of the family. The vignette aims at revealing general dispositions rather than preferences in concrete cases. Therefore, the nature of the parents' need is not specified.

> Wang Hong has to transfer three times on public transportation to get from where he lives to his office. Because of the time and inconvenience of taking public transportation, Wang Hong has tried very hard to save money to buy a car before winter. However, Wang Hong's parents have a need for money and ask Wang Hong to give them the money Wang Hong has saved.

The Discipline Vignette

This vignette deals with the possible conflicts between parents and the daughter-in-law in disciplining the grandchild. It is designed to reveal the locus of family authority and hence to measure some aspects of filial piety. In the traditional Chinese family, the elder generation is clearly the dominant authority. In the United States, however, the parent has the authority to discipline the children, and grandparents normally follow the wishes of the child's parents. This vignette is thus indicative of the degree of Americanization of a family value: the scope of authority retained by the elderly parent.

> Mr. and Mrs. Wang have a 3-year-old son, Hang Chang, who is now being taken care of by Mr. Wang's parents. The arrangement is satisfactory to both Mr. and Mrs. Wang and his parents. On the one hand, Mr. and Mrs. Wang are both working and do not have to worry about the issue of a babysitter; on the other hand, Mr. Wang's parents are both retired and like having a grandson to keep them busy and provide company. Mrs. Wang now feels that Hang Chang is becoming spoiled and naughty. When Mrs. Wang wants to punish Hang Chang for bad behavior, Mr. Wang's parents intervene and stress that the child is only 3 years old and should not be disciplined.

The Education Vignette

The last vignette relates to the dilemma between one's obligation to the parents and one's obligation to the child. Should one sacrifice one's child's education for the support of the parents? In its purest form, this ideal is based on the replaceability of children and the irreplaceability of parents. In earlier days, such a decision might have determined the allocation of food. In modern times, the distribution of other resources is at issue. Because Chinese place heavy emphasis on the child's education, it poses a particularly sharp dilemma.

Mr. Lin lives in Chicago. He has been sending money to his retired parents in Taiwan on a monthly basis. Owing to his dissatisfaction with the quality of the Chicago public schools, Mr. Lin is thinking about transferring his son to a private school. However, the private school costs a lot more. Mr. Lin cannot afford to pay the private school tuition and at the same time send money to his parents in Taiwan.

Findings and Interpretations

A simple description of responses in terms of percentage distributions by generation and parents' gender is presented first. Since each vignette measured a specific aspect of *hsiao,* each is discussed separately. The structural influence on responses to the vignette is also analyzed.

The Promotion Vignette

The majority of respondents indicated that the child should seek the promotion even at the expense of the comfort of the parents. Striving for professional success is well within the domain of filial piety. Most of the adult children in this study came to the United States initially for educational and professional achievement. This choice is consistent with the American emphasis on individual achievement. It is not surprising that when the two sets of filial obligations are in conflict, most children choose the solution that is in their self-interest, particularly when self-interest is consistent with the interests of parents as well as the ideal of *hsiao.*

Parents also place a high value on their child's professional achievement. Such achievement can bring glory not only to the parents themselves but also to the whole family and even to the entire clan. This is revealed by the fact that significantly more parents than children believed the child should accept the promotion.

This intergenerational difference disappeared in the Taiwan context. The difficulties faced by the parents in the vignettes are not applicable in Taiwan, for there they are not isolated in an alien culture. Also, because Taiwan is a relatively small country (about the size of Massachusetts and Connecticut combined), the problems typically posed by long distances and separation are not significant. If the parents are able to take care of themselves, the dilemma is less acute, and the child may freely devote energy to professional success.

The Living Arrangement Vignette

The results of the Living Arrangement Vignette had a different pattern. There was lack of consensus among parents and children, with a more or less even split between the two solutions in the U.S. context. The child respondents were more "Chinese," and adhered more to the traditional norm on living arrangements. More children thought that the son should take the mother home despite the objections of his wife, compared with both mother and father respondents.

The difference between the child and the mother was not statistically significant. However, the difference between the child and the father was highly significant. In addition, there was a significant gender difference between the parent respondents. More mothers than fathers thought that the son should take Mrs. Chan home rather than send her to the nursing home.

The intergenerational and gender differences disappeared when the context shifted to Taiwan. Here, the majority of respondents thought that the son should invite the mother to move in with him even at the cost of hurting his family life and marriage. Since aged parents are better able to function independently in Taiwan, it is less crucial that they live with their children. The fact that significant others are more visible in Taiwan might also explain the greater support for parents and adult children living together.

The Marriage Vignette

The Marriage Vignette is similar to the Living Arrangement Vignette because both depict the dilemma between fulfilling one's obligation to the parents and one's commitment to one's own marriage and family. The majority of respondents in this case thought that the child should marry the Caucasian friend. Both generations gave more weight to the child's personal happiness than to the obligation to fulfill the parents' wishes. The difference in results between this and the Living Arrangement Vignette might be explained by the potential consequences of each unfilial behavior. Being sent to the nursing home by one's children against one's wishes is a sharp rejection from the beloved and a serious disgrace in the Chinese community. This makes the unfilial solution a difficult choice. Although the interracial marriage might create inconvenience and embarrassment, this is much more tolerable. The Caucasian might turn out to be a good in-law, and the parent-child relationship might not be in jeopardy. Inasmuch as the majority population in the

United States is non-Chinese, many parents recognize the unavoidable trend toward interracial marriage among the younger generation.

The consensus pattern remained stable but shifted to a more Chinese solution in the Taiwan context. Apparently, the interracial marriage would be less acceptable in Taiwan. Again, greater visibility of significant others would play a role, as would the greater availability of appropriate mates. More than 60% of the respondents thought that the child should disregard the parents' wishes and marry the Caucasian friend. A quarter of the respondents who approved of the marriage changed their minds when the context shifted to Taiwan; this was found especially among fathers, who seldom opposed it in the U.S. context.

The Car Vignette

The dilemma was less pronounced in the Car Vignette. The majority of respondents chose the Chinese solution. Most respondents thought that the child should give the money to the parents rather than purchase a car for himself. Shanas (1962) used a similar vignette in her study of the health of the elderly in the general U.S. population. Contrary to the finding in the present study, about three-fourths of her respondents (both elderly and those who were responsible for them) thought the child should buy a car rather than use the money to help the parents. It seems that, for Chinese, a car is a convenience that can easily be sacrificed. However, the child was significantly more Chinese than the father. Parents, on the other hand, were somewhat more concerned about their children's comfort. There was no gender difference among the parent respondents.

In the Taiwan context, the preference for the Chinese solution was clearer, probably because the public transportation system in Taiwan is more complete and car ownership is less of a necessity. Also, greater visibility to significant others in Taiwan makes it difficult to choose an unfilial solution.

The Discipline Vignette

The Discipline Vignette involved an issue related to the third generation. Among the child and the mother generations, a shared norm on how to discipline the grandchildren was apparently lacking. There was an almost 50/50 split over whether disciplining of the third generation should follow the parents' rules or should be consistent with the child generation's own principles. The fathers, on the other hand, exhibited a very different pattern. A significantly higher percentage of the fathers thought discipline should be left in the grandparents' hands. Even when the context was shifted to Taiwan, the responses of the respondents exhibited a similar pattern.

The difference between the father and the child generations can be explained by the role of the patriarch in the Chinese family system. The patriarch usually remains the head of the household until he is too old to function well. In the case of our respondents, this power relationship in the family has been changing. The emphasis on independence, occupational autonomy, and the separation of one's conjugal family from one's consanguine family of the younger generation have threatened the traditional authority of the father. While the father generation wants to retain power over the younger generation, the child generation seeks autonomy.

The response pattern of the mother generation is understandable in view of the role difference and the mother-child relationship versus father-child relationship. Also, as reported in anthropological studies of child rearing in Taiwan, grandparents often spoil children, whereas parents are strict with them because they, the parents, will suffer the consequences if the children turn out to be selfish and unfilial (Wolf, 1972, pp. 72-73).

The Education Vignette

As with the Discipline Vignette, the Education Vignette involved the third generation. Unlike the Discipline Vignette, the generation responses were different. A majority of the fathers and children thought that extra available money should be given to parents instead of being used for sending children to an expensive private school. The opinions of the mothers, however, were almost evenly divided. Response patterns in the Taiwan context did not differ much from those in the U.S. context.

Educational attainment has long been an important cultural value in Chinese society, and parents exert great effort to send their children to school. When this task is fulfilled, however, there is also an attempt to strike a balance in resource allocation between parents' needs and children's additional education expenditures. Our data suggest such a norm among the child generation respondents. The fact that Chinese children maintain superior performance in both types of schools in the United States (private and public) is well established (see, for example, "Asian-Americans," 1982). It is perhaps assumed that a child who has graduated, whether from a public or private school, can be successful. Therefore, it is not surprising that the majority of the child generation respondents thought that scarce resources should be devoted to parents' needs.

It should be noted that, among the six vignettes, this vignette had the highest nonresponse rate, which may indicate unresolved conflict. In addition, about 10% of our respondents qualified their answers: If the parents rely on the money for basic living expenses, it should be given to them. Otherwise, the money should be spent on the grandchild's education.

Except for the Promotion Vignette, there was a shifting for all vignettes to a higher percentage of American answers when the social context changed from Taiwan to the United States. At the individual level, the shifting occurred mainly among those who gave the Chinese answer for Taiwan (to the American answer for United States), although small percentages shifted in the opposite direction.

The shifting pattern of the Promotion Vignette deserves closer examination. For the mother and child generations, when the social context changed from Taiwan to the United States, there was a decline in the overall percentage of respondents giving the American answer—that is, the child accepts promotion in another city and leaves the parents alone. In other words, there was greater willingness on the part of the child generation to sacrifice their own occupational achievement to fulfill filial obligation in the new country. The mother generation expected their children to be in close proximity in the alien and new environment, although not necessarily to live in the same household. The difference between the father generation's responses and the mother generation's can be explained by paternal independence and ego needs. Response patterns of the mother and child generations imply that there is a greater degree of perceived incompatibility between occupational achievement and personal services to parents in the U.S. context.

Among the six vignettes, the ones that were more subject to structural influences were Living Arrangement, Marriage, Car, and Promotion. Responses to the Discipline and Education vignettes, which, coincidentally, both involved the third generation, were not as affected.

Summary and Conclusions

Several patterns emerge from the data. First, the child generation respondents were more Chinese in their responses than were the parent generation respondents. In four of the six vignettes—the Promotion, Living Arrangement, Car, and Education—a consistently higher percentage of child generation than parent generation respondents chose the Chinese solution. In other words, the child generation, in general, tended to want to give more to the parents than the parents thought they should, as revealed by the actual percentages.

This response pattern may be attributed to either one or both of two factors. First, the members of the two generations are being considerate of each other. The parents perhaps realize the difficulties the children encounter in struggling for success in a foreign country and want to be helpful rather than burdensome. On the part of the child generation, there may be an overcompensation: After they have made it in the United States, they may feel they have neglected their parents' needs and desires.

A second conclusion that can be drawn is that even though filial piety is still alive in the Chinese community in America, it has undergone a transformation. There has been a shift of emphasis among filial obligations. The vignettes suggest that the child generation is generous in providing resources for the well-being of the parents but is reluctant to be subservient to the wishes of the parents in the areas of personal freedom and the development of self. This reluctance is manifested in the marriage and discipline vignettes, in which more child generation respondents wanted to exercise control over choosing their own marriage partners and disciplining their children.

Third, whereas the father generation was more traditional, there was greater adaptability by the mother generation. The discrepancies between the responses of father and child, in general, were larger than those between mother and child. The different parental roles and the relationship between mother and child enabled mothers to adjust more readily to their children's new lives. Fathers were more sensitive to the context. Their responses shifted the most according to whether the setting was Taiwan or the United States. They tended to be more traditional than mothers and children in the Taiwan context, and more flexible in the U.S. setting. This shift may have resulted from an attempt to maintain their traditional status.

Each generation has its own strategies, reflecting its own specific conditions for adapting to the situations captured in the vignettes. The child generation tries to fulfill its filial obligations, however selectively, while affirming personal autonomy. Mothers adjust their lives to the life-styles of their children. Fathers adapt to the situation in ways that suggest a strong need to maintain their independence and ego.

18

Korean Immigrants' Marital Patterns and Marital Adjustments

PYONG GAP MIN

Social scientists interested in marital patterns of ethnic/immigrant minority groups have focused exclusively on intermarriages (see especially Crester and Leon, 1982; Mindel and Habenstein, 1981), and different forms of in-marriages have been ignored. Several researchers have indicated that cultural differences and other related factors are the causes of instability for intermarriages (see, e.g., Cerroni-Long, 1989; Hong, 1982; Kim, 1972, 1977; Schultz, 1981). However, to the best of my knowledge, only Schultz (1981) has identified cultural differences as a key to understanding problems associated with *international in-marriage*.

The lack of scholarly interest in international in-marriage in the past seems to have been due partly to the fact that this type of marriage was not common among earlier immigrant groups. The vast majority of immigrants to the United States before 1965 were from European countries. Cultural similarities among these white immigrant groups, coupled with the inconvenience of international travel, led most young people to find marital partners within this country, either among in-group members or among out-group members. However, since 1965 a large number of new immigrants have come from non-European countries, especially from Asian countries. The cultural distinctiveness of each of these new immigrant groups, the difficulty in finding in-group

AUTHOR'S NOTE: This chapter is in part based upon work supported by the National Science Foundation under Grant No. SES-8608735.

partners in this country, and the convenience of air transportation seem to contribute to a high rate of international in-marriage among these immigrant groups (Revilla, 1989). Of course, the international in-marriage prevalent among recent Asian immigrant groups had its precedent in the "picture bride" marriage for many of the Japanese and Korean bachelor immigrants at the turn of the century (Chai, 1978; Choy, 1979; Kitano, 1976, p. 40). However, the "picture bride" marriage associated with earlier Asian immigrants did not receive much attention from researchers.

This chapter will shed light on marital patterns and marital adjustment of recent Korean immigrants, with special emphasis on international in-marriage. I have two specific objectives here. First, I will examine Korean immigrants' marital patterns based on data collected in Los Angeles, the largest Korean center in this country. Second, I will discuss the relationship between marital patterns and marital adjustment, focusing on the adjustment problems involved in internationally in-married Korean couples. This study is exploratory in that the findings may be used in formulating hypotheses concerning the relationship between Korean immigrants' marital patterns and marital adjustment rather than to test hypotheses.

Data Sources

A total of 560 employed adult Korean immigrants in Los Angeles and Orange counties were interviewed in the fall of 1986 to investigate the economic and other positive functions of Korean businesses on the Korean community (Min, 1989). The first part of this chapter, concerning Korean immigrants' marital patterns, is based on this data set. The "Kim sample technique" (Shin and Yu, 1984) was used in the Los Angeles study. People bearing the surname Kim constitute roughly 22% of the Korean population; no other nationality is known to have such a surname in any significant number.[1] A list of 1,020 Kims was compiled through random selection from 11 Los Angeles and Orange County public telephone directories. Of these originally selected households, 152 were not eligible for the interview because they were interracially married, American-born, unemployed, or nonimmigrant student households. Of the 868 eligible Korean households, 499 (57.5%) were interviewed. An additional sample (Kims) of 250 households from those not included in the original sample was drawn, and only those Koreans not self-employed were approached for interview. A total of 39 Koreans were successfully interviewed from this additional sample. In addition, 21 Koreans in the secondary labor market were interviewed through purposive sampling, since a very small proportion of Korean workers were employed in this category.

The second half of this chapter discusses the relationship between marital pattern and marital adjustment. It is based on the following three data sources as well as on findings from previous studies using white American samples. First, I talked with many Korean newlywed couples on an informal basis over a long period of time, and these conversations provided me with basic ideas on Korean immigrants' marital adjustment. Second, I interviewed, in 1986 and 1989, several Korean social workers who were working for Korean family and marriage counseling centers in Los Angeles and New York City. All these social workers had helped Korean immigrant battered wives and other Korean women with serious marital problems by giving legal counseling and advice for more than three years before the time of the interviews. The secondhand information provided by these social workers based on their counseling of clients substantiated basic ideas I had derived from my personal observations. Finally, Korean ethnic newspapers publish many articles on Korean immigrants' marital adjustment, and these also provided valuable information. I have subscribed to two ethnic newspapers, the *Korean Central Daily New York* and the *Korea Times New York,* since 1980. The two dailies have published several articles on Korean immigrants' marital adjustment, both based on interviews with couples and contributed by social workers.

Marital Patterns of Korean Immigrants

There are two major data sources for measurement of immigrant/minority groups' intermarriage rates. Marriage license records constitute one such data source. A few states, such as Hawaii and Nebraska, require that marriage license applications include information about the races of both spouses as well as their names. In a few other states, such as California, marriage license applicants are required to provide information about their and their parents' birthplaces, which gives clues to the nationalities of the applicants. Many researchers have measured the intermarriage rates of particular minority/immigrant groups, using state or county marriage license records (Kimura and Kitano, 1974; Kitano and Chai, 1982; Kitano and Yeung, 1982; Leon, 1975; Murguia and Frisbie, 1977; Porterfield, 1982; Risdon, 1954).

The other data source is the Public Use Microfilm Data Sample prepared by the U.S. Census Bureau every 10 years as part of decennial census reports. Census data provide information on a number of variables for intermarried people. Census data enable us to analyze racial/ethnic categories and socioeconomic characteristics of intermarried people as well as the prevalence of intermarriage for a particular minority group, and thus they have been widely used (Alba and Golden, 1986; Gurak and Fitzpatrick, 1978; Lee and Yamanaka, 1989; Lieberson and Waters, 1985; Wong, 1989).

Each data source has limitations in its usefulness for accurately measuring intermarriage rates of particular minority groups and analyzing the relationship between the intermarriage rate and other variables. Census data, compared with marriage registration records, have the advantage of providing sociologically important variables for intermarried people. However, intermarriage studies based on census data do not exclude immigrants married abroad from data analysis. Thus they underestimate the intermarriage rate by including immigrants married in their native countries. Marriage registration records do not include immigrants married abroad, but they exclude those—both immigrants and native-born people—who go abroad and have weddings. Studies based on marriage license records are therefore likely to overestimate the intermarriage rate by excluding from data analysis those in-marriages that occur abroad. This poses a serious problem for estimating intermarriage rates of Korean and other Asian ethnic groups because, as previously indicated, many Asian immigrants bring their partners from their native countries.

Moreover, neither census reports nor marriage registration records provide information on different forms of in-marriage, that is, what proportion of people bring partners from their native countries as opposed to finding coethnic partners in the United States. We therefore need to use survey data to understand in-marriage patterns. To examine marital patterns of young Korean immigrants, three items were included in a questionnaire that focused on welfare functions of Korean immigrant business for the Los Angeles Korean community. Each respondent was first of all asked whether he or she, any of his or her children, or any other relatives living in Los Angeles got married during the last five years. Those who came to Los Angeles from Korea or another part of the United States after marriage were not included. The respondents who answered yes were also asked to identify the sex of the married person and to classify the marital partner into one of the following categories:

(a) Korean in Los Angeles, (b) Korean in another U.S. city, (c) Korean in Korea, (d) white, (e) Mexican or Black, and (f) other Asian (specify the nationality). The first three categories pertain to in-marriage and the others relate to intermarriage. Given that American-born Kims were screened out after the initial telephone contact, as noted above, the data reflect the marital patterns of Korean immigrants rather than Korean Americans in general.

The Korean community in the United States is largely the by-product of the 1965 Immigration Act, which came into full effect in 1968. Census data show that the Korean population in the United States increased from 69,000 in 1970 to 350,000 in 1980, and then to 800,000 in 1990. More than 80% of Korean Americans are believed to be immigrants. The vast majority of the young Koreans in this country who have married during recent years or who have reached marital age immigrated here as children accompanied by their parents. These Korean-born and American-raised children are very often referred to as "1.5-generation Koreans" (Hurh, 1990). The data reflect the marital patterns of these 1.5-generation Koreans.

Since only Koreans with the Kim surname were included in the sample, it is possible that two or more of our respondents are related to one another. Moreover, each respondent was asked to indicate not only his or her own and his or her children's marriages, but also the marriages of any other relatives. Accordingly, it is possible that one marriage was reported by two or more respondents. This can confound the findings concerning the marital pattern of 1.5-generation Koreans. However, I do not consider this to be a serious problem, for two reasons. First, Kims constitute such a large proportion of the Korean population (22%) that the vast majority of Kims are not related to one another. The eleven telephone directories in Los Angeles and Orange counties included nearly 6,000 Kims, and only approximately 540 of them (8%) were interviewed. Second, some marriages may have been reported by two or more respondents, but this overlapping is unlikely to be limited to a particular category of marriage.

As Table 18.1 illustrates, 560 respondents reported that 478 Koreans—the respondents themselves, their children, and other relatives who were Los Angeles residents at the time of marriage—got married during the last five years. Only 8.2% (39 individuals) married out-group members. This figure is lower than the Los Angeles Korean immigrants' out-marriage rate (16.6%) reported by Kitano and Chai (1982) in their study based on Los Angeles marriage license records.[2] Since only

Koreans (Kims) were included in this sample, a significant proportion of out-married Korean families may have been excluded. Thus this study underestimates the Los Angeles Koreans' out-marriage rate.

However, Kitano and Chai's (1982) study based on marriage license records overestimated the Koreans' intermarriage rate. As Table 18.1 shows, approximately 34% of those Koreans married during the last five years found Korean partners in Korea, and almost all of these Koreans got married in Korea. These in-marriages were not included in Los Angeles County marriage license records. Accordingly, Kitano and Chai's study, which failed to take into account Korean international in-marriages, overestimated the Korean immigrants' intermarriage rate.[3] The actual intermarriage rate in the Los Angeles Korean community might have been somewhere between 8% (my estimate) and 16.5%, something like 12%. The intermarriage rate is inversely related to community size. Most other Korean communities are much smaller than the Los Angeles Korean community. The intermarriage rate in these smaller Korean communities might be higher than 12%, the presumed intermarriage rate of the Los Angeles Korean community.

Although the data underestimate the intermarriage rate, they may provide fairly accurate information about different forms of in-marriage. Almost half of those Los Angeles Koreans married during the last five years found Korean partners in the same city. Another 10% married Koreans in other U.S. cities, and 34% brought their marital partners from Korea. Considering the fact that Los Angeles is the home of 200,000 Koreans, with residential concentration in Koreatown, the international in-marriage rate is surprisingly high. The majority of Korean young people living in smaller Korean communities seem to bring their spouses from Korea. Because of the popularity of American residents as prospective spouses in Korea, many Korean Americans can find partners in Korea who are higher than themselves in educational background and social status. This factor apparently encourages many Koreans to visit Korea to look for marital partners. The convenience of air travel to and from Korea and a cheap airfare also seem to contribute to Koreans' high international in-marriage rate. The round-trip airfare from Los Angeles to Seoul can be as low as $750, and an air trip from most other cities to Seoul costs less than $900.

An interesting set of findings reflected in Table 18.1 is that there are significant differences between males and females in marital patterns. A smaller proportion of female immigrants than male immigrants found Korean partners in Los Angeles. This is due to a sex imbalance in favor

Table 18.1 Marital Patterns of Korean Immigrants in Los Angeles

Sex of the Married Person	Category of the Partner												
	Korean in LA		Korean in Other U.S. cities		Korean in Korea		Out-Group Member					Total	
							White	Asian	Other	Total			
	N	%	N	%	N	%	N	N	N	N	%	N	%
Male	127	53.6	17	7.2	87	36.7	2	4	0	6	2.5	237	100
Female	104	43.2	30	12.4	74	30.7	20	13	0	33	13.7	241	100
Total	231	48.3	47	9.8	161	33.7	22	17	0	39	8.2	478	100

of females. The 1980 census indicated that Korean females outnumbered males by 58 to 42 and that sex imbalance is much greater for those at marital ages (20 to 29 years old) with females comprising 68% (U.S. Bureau of the Census, 1983d, p. 50). This suggests that Korean female immigrants have more difficulty finding Korean spouses in this country than do Korean male immigrants. Furthermore, the difficulty of Korean women finding Korean spouses in this country becomes greater because of the tendency of many Korean male immigrants to consider Korean women in Korea, who generally accept the traditional conjugal norms, to be more desirable spouses than American-raised Korean women. Korean immigrant women need to meet their needs by switching to out-group members and/or by bringing partners from Korea. Table 18.1 indicates that a greater proportion of female Koreans than male Koreans were intermarried. However, a smaller proportion of females than males brought their spouses from Korea. Korean immigrant women are reluctant to bring their partners from Korea because of cultural differences in conjugal norms between the United States and Korea. As will be discussed below, a marriage between a Korean immigrant woman and a male from Korea involves more adjustment problems than does one involving a Korean immigrant man and a female from Korea. Because of this difficulty in finding spouses, many Korean immigrant women in their late 20s and early 30s remain single.

Different Forms of In-Marriage and Marital Adjustment

Korean community social workers report that a marriage between a Korean immigrant and a partner from Korea requires greater marital adjustment than does a marriage between two Korean immigrants. They also agree that a marriage between a Korean American woman and a man from Korea involves more adjustment problems than does the opposite combination. Korean ethnic newspapers and magazines are replete with stories about marital problems associated with marriages between Korean American women and men from Korea. The 1980 census reports show that the proportion of Korean divorcees in the United States is five times as high as that found in the Korean general population (Korean National Bureau of Statistics, 1983a, p. 50; U.S. Bureau of the Census, 1984, p. 12). Of course, the divorce rate of Korean immigrants is lower than that of the American native population (the crude divorce rate of Korean immigrant women is 36.8, compared with 72.6 for native-born American women). It is, however, exceptionally high, considering a short period of residence in this country and a low divorce rate in Korea. The high divorce rate of Korean women married to American military personnel inflates the divorce rate of Korean immigrants in general. The marital instability of internationally in-married young Korean couples also seems to contribute to the high divorce rate of Korean immigrants in general.

A marriage between a 1.5-generation Korean and a partner from Korea seems to involve more adjustment problems than one between two 1.5-generation Koreans, for the following reasons. First, the former marriage is likely to involve a higher level of personality/value incongruence than the latter. Marital adjustment research based on white American samples demonstrates that value congruence is positively related to marital quality or successful marital adjustment (Barry, 1970; Hicks & Platt, 1970; Levinger & Breedlove, 1966; Nordland, 1978). Because of the way the decision on marriage is made, an international in-marriage between two Koreans generally involves a higher level of personality incongruence than does a marriage between two Korean immigrants. Those young Koreans who search for Korean partners in the United States go through dating and courtship before they make the decision to marry. If they find themselves incompatible in personality, they will stop dating and try to find other partners. However, international in-marriages take place without these regular processes. A Korean American who wants to find a marital partner in Korea usually makes a one-month visit to Korea to meet several partners recommended by relatives and friends. Thus each partner decides about the marriage within a short period of time, without knowing very much about the personality and background of the other partner. Many partners from Korea decide to marry Korean Americans mainly to come to this country. Once in the United States through marriage, some partners from Korea try to terminate their marital relations so that they can marry old partners. There are many divorce cases in which Korean American partners request that immigration officials send their partners back to Korea. More Korean American women than men seem to be the victims of these "disguised marriages." Many Korean Americans decide to marry spouses from Korea because of the latter's higher level of education and/or family background.

Second, a Korean American and a spouse from Korea seem to experience adjustment difficulties arising from incompatibility between partners in education and social status. Because of the popularity of

Korean Americans as prospective spouses in Korea, many Korean Americans, especially Korean American men, find partners in Korea who are higher than themselves in education and social status. In order to come to the United States, many college-educated women in Korea decide to marry Korean Americans who have completed only high school education. This tendency for Korean American men to marry women with more education than them goes against the general trend in Korea, where the husband is usually more highly educated than the wife. Education and social status hypergamy is known to be a factor in marital conflicts for white Americans (Burgess & Wallin, 1965; Carter & Glick, 1976; Hogan, 1978). The dissimilarity between Korean and Korean American partners in education and/or social status may cause more serious trouble for successful marital adjustment if the Korean American partner has misrepresented his or her educational level and occupation in this country. The gap between the Korean partner's high expectation of American life and reality, plus his or her fall in social status, can lead to great disappointment and frustration, which, in turn, will disrupt marital relations.

Third, a marriage between a Korean immigrant and a partner from Korea is often characterized by adjustment difficulties, especially in the early years, because one partner has to adjust to both immigration and marriage at the same time. Adjustment to a new society is known to be disruptive to family stability (Grant, 1983a). It can have serious negative effects on newly married couples who have not established strong conjugal ties. Newly married brides and grooms from Korea usually do not have support groups (relatives and friends) in this country, and thus they have a sense of alienation, surrounded by the family members of their spouses.

Three additional factors underlie the greater likelihood of marital difficulties in marriages involving Korean American women and men from Korea. First, the husband from Korea is likely to experience greater problems adjusting to a new society than would a wife from Korea. It probably is more difficult for a husband, especially a Korean-raised husband, to learn how to adjust to a new society from his wife than vice versa. Korean cultural norms have taught the husband from Korea that he should exercise authority over his wife. But the fact that he has to learn most things necessary for survival in this country from his wife does not give him the level of authority he likes to exercise. This discrepancy leads him to have a high level of anxiety and frustration, which is very often reflected in violent reactions to his wife. In a marriage of the opposite combination, however, a Korean-raised wife may be able to learn American customs and language from her husband without much psychological difficulty.

Second, a Korean American woman and a husband from Korea may have adjustment difficulties because of cultural differences between partners regarding conjugal relations. A husband from Korea will like to maintain traditional conjugal norms based on male supremacy and strict role differentiation. In contrast, his partner, who finished high school or college in the United States, will insist on a more egalitarian relationship. Several studies have demonstrated that a marriage between a "traditional" husband and a "modern" wife involves a high level of conflict (Araji, 1977; Bowen & Orthner, 1983; Osmond & Martin, 1975; Scanzoni, 1975; J. D. Wright, 1978). A marriage between an American-raised Korean woman and a man from Korea is in most cases a marriage between a "traditional" husband and a "modern" wife.

Third, unions between Korean American women and men from Korea have adjustment difficulties because of the high level of labor force participation by Korean American wives, which may be stressful to their husbands. Most husbands from Korea expect their wives to be full-time homemakers.[4] In reality, most Korean American wives married to men from Korea need to work outside of the home because their husbands are more disadvantaged than they in the American job market, at least in the early years of marriage. It is known that American white males whose wives work outside of the home are subject to greater stress than are those whose wives do not work (Axelson, 1963; Burke & Weir, 1976; Orden & Bradburn, 1969). A wife's participation in the labor market is likely to be more stressful to a husband from Korea than to a Korean American husband.

Summary and Conclusion

In this chapter I have examined marital patterns of 1.5-generation Koreans and have discussed adjustment problems involved in Korean international marriages. To summarize the discussion: Nearly half of those Koreans in Los Angeles who got married during the last five years found Korean partners in the same city. Another 34% brought marital partners from Korea, and only 12% are believed to have married out-group members. Both the international in-marriage and out-marriage rates are likely to be higher in smaller Korean communities, where people must select Korean partners from a smaller pool. Partly because of an unbalanced sex ratio in favor of females, a smaller proportion of Korean females than males found Korean partners in Los Angeles. Moreover, a smaller proportion of Korean females than males brought their marital partners from Korea, which reflects the greater adjustment difficulties involved in marriages between Korean immigrant women and men from Korea than are found in the opposite combination. Owing to a shortage of Korean male partners in the United States and incompatibility with Korean male partners from Korea, a greater proportion of Korean female immigrants than male immigrants choose out-group members as marital partners.

My discussions with community social workers and the evidence found in ethnic newspaper articles suggest that a marriage between a Korean immigrant and a partner from Korea involves greater adjustment difficulties than does a marriage between two Korean immigrants. The greater personality/value incongruence between the partners, the incompatibility between partners in education and/or social status, and the strains and stresses associated with immigration adjustment on the part of the partner from Korea seem to contribute to a lower level of marital adjustment among internationally in-married Korean couples. A marriage between a Korean immigrant woman and a man from Korea is known to involve even greater adjustment difficulties than does a marriage of the opposite combination. Korean American cultural differences in conjugal norms, greater difficulties in immigrant adjustment on the part of husbands from Korea, and a higher level of labor force participation by American-raised wives are believed to have serious negative effects on marital adjustment for couples involving Korean American women and men from Korea.

Many non-European nationals have immigrated to the United States since 1965. The international in-marriage seems to be common among these new immigrant groups. Accordingly, we need to establish viable theoretical and conceptual frameworks that will guide researchers in studying the marital adjustment required by this form of marriage. Value incongruence, marital adjustment problems associated with immigration adjustment, and cultural differences in conjugal relations between partners may be key factors underlying marital problems not only for Korean but also for Filipino, Chinese, and Asian Indian internationally in-married couples.

This is an exploratory study, and more rigorous empirical research on this topic is needed in the future. It would be useful to select three groups of newlywed immigrant couples, representing the three types of in-marriage discussed in this chapter, and administer a structured questionnaire through personal interviews. I hope that tentative conclusions derived from this exploratory study will serve as major hypotheses in a future survey study. A study of this type is valuable for its theoretical significance and policy implications.

Notes

1. Since there is no evidence that Kims are not socially representative of the Korean general population, an unbiased sample of Koreans can be obtained simply by sampling Kims listed in public telephone directories. For a more detailed discussion of the Kim sample technique, see Shin and Yu (1984).

2. According to Kitano and Chai (1982), 30% of the marriages involving at least one Korean partner reported in Los Angeles County for three years (1975, 1977, and 1979) were intermarriages. When we change the unit of analysis from the marriage to the individual Korean, 21% of the Koreans married during the three years were married to out-group members [30 /(30 + 70 × 1 2) = 21]. When we focus only on immigrants, 16.5% of those Koreans included in their study married out-group members.

3. The problem of overestimating the intermarriage rate is not unique to this study. The same problem seems to arise in all studies dealing with recent immigrant groups and using county or state marriage license records as a data source. Nevertheless, to the best of my knowledge, no one has indicated this problem.

4. Although industrialization and urbanization have led to great changes in the traditional family system in South Korea, they have not significantly modified the traditional family ideology on conjugal role differentiation. The wife is still expected to stay home as a full-time homemaker, and the husband's role is limited to earning a living. The 1980 census, for example, shows that only 19% of Korean nonfarm married women were in the labor force (Korean National Bureau of Statistics, 1983b, p. 57).

19

Migration and Family Adjustment

Continuity and Change
Among Vietnamese in the United States

STEVEN J. GOLD

Since 1975, close to 580,000 Vietnamese have fled their homeland and resettled in the United States (Office of Refugee Resettlement [ORR], 1987, pp. 92-93). As a result of this involuntary migration, refugee families are subdivided, taxed by economic hardship, and confronted by American customs that contradict many of their most basic values. Despite these great difficulties, Vietnamese refugees reconstitute family units, rebuild their lives, and provide support for relatives overseas. Accordingly, the Vietnamese family remains a flexible, if embattled, source of social support for many refugees in the United States.

Two Cohorts of Vietnamese Refugees

Vietnamese entered the United States in two major flows. The first group, which numbered about 130,000 and included many members of the Vietnamese military and employees of the U.S. government, left immediately following the communist takeover in spring 1975 (ORR, 1987, p. A-1). A second, more recently arrived group of more than 400,000 refugees (often called the "boat people") exited in the years since the Vietnam-China conflict of 1978 (Nguyen & Henkin, 1984; ORR, 1987, p. A-1).

In many ways, those in the earlier group experienced a smoother resettlement than did those in the later one. They were more highly educated and skilled than the refugees who came later, many knew English upon arrival, they spent little time in Southeast Asian refugee camps, and they often arrived in intact family units (see Table 19.1). Moreover, these early-arriving Vietnamese benefited from three years of cash assistance upon arrival and were often sponsored by American citizens who facilitated job placement and otherwise smoothed resettlement (Montero, 1979; ORR, 1987). This group's flight and resettlement, however, was far from easy—61% had less than 24 hours to prepare for their exit, and 83% had less than a week (Liu, 1979, p. 15). Nearly all left relatives behind, sometimes in communist reeducation camps.

Those in the second group of Vietnamese refugees were less educated and more often rural in origin. Many were members of Vietnam's ethnic Chinese minority group (Desbarats, 1986; Purcell, 1965; Rumbaut, 1986).[1] Their exit, involving open sea voyages in small, overcrowded boats, was subject to attacks by Thai pirates and military forces (Tietelbaum, 1985). Those who survived the high seas had to spend months in rustic refugee camps throughout Southeast Asia before their arrival in the United States.

Because of the risky and difficult conditions of escape, relatively few elderly or female refugees were included among Vietnamese recent arrivals. Consequently, broken families were common among those refugees arriving in the United States since 1978. Finally, recent arrivals' economic difficulties were generally worse than those of the 1975 group because they were eligible for only 18 months of cash assistance and seldom had access to American citizen sponsors who could provide job referrals (Montero, 1979). Hence, despite their shared nationality and motive for exit, the two cohorts of Vietnamese refugees faced different problems related to their own experiences, characteristics, and needs. In general, the recently arrived have made less rapid strides in adjusting to the new society than the 1975 group (ORR, 1987; Rumbaut, 1986).

Methods

Because of the relatively short time Vietnamese have been in the United States, data on their resettlement experience are incomplete. This chapter relies on published sources as well as on my own data, collected in participant observation activities and in in-depth interviews

Table 19.1 Characteristics of Vietnamese Refugees in the United States: 1975 Arrivals and Recent Arrivals

	1975 Arrivals	*Recent Arrivals*
Average years of education	9.5	7.05
Percentage who could not speak English upon arrival	30.6	50
Age		
percentage under 36	49	58
percentage over 56	10	5
percentage with white-collar occupation in Vietnam	78.7	49.2
1980 household income		
percentage less than $9,000	27.6	61
percentage more than $21,000	31	4.6

SOURCE: Data from Nguyen and Henkin (1984, pp. 104-110) and ORR (1983, p. 25).

with Vietnamese refugees in the San Francisco Bay Area between June 1982 and June 1985.

Participant observation took place while I worked one or two days a week at two Vietnamese resettlement agencies in San Francisco from June 1982 to October 1983 and as I visited the homes of a network of Vietnamese refugees weekly for 15 months as a volunteer English teacher. In-depth interviews were completed with 64 Vietnamese refugees and 25 nonrefugee service providers. Interviews ranged from a half hour to several hours weekly over the course of a year. Interviewees were located through participant observation activities, snowball sample referrals, advertisements in refugee publications, the telephone directory, and various compilations of refugee organizations (Indochinese Refugee Action Center, 1982; Indochinese Technical Assistance Project, 1981).

These techniques for contacting respondents were not intended to be random, so my data do not illustrate a cross section of the Vietnamese refugee population. However, I made specific attempts to observe and interview refugees representing a wide variety of social categories, including political activists, religious leaders, resettlement workers, business owners, and recent arrivals. Interviews were conducted in

English. Quotes used in this report were taken directly from taped interviews or field notes. To protect the identities of respondents, all names are pseudonyms.

Vietnamese Family Patterns

The Vietnamese family is traditionally male focused, extended, and shaped by Confucian, Taoist, and Buddhist philosophies (Buttinger, 1958; Haines, Rutherford, & Thomas, 1981; Hickey, 1964; Min, 1988; Slote, 1972; Tung, 1972). Vietnamese families are large (ORR, 1987; Simon, 1983); a great many refugees I interviewed came from families with between 9 and 12 children. Unfortunately, the cost of housing that would permit the unification of these families in urban California is beyond the reach of most Vietnamese refugees, whose average household income was $11,955 in 1979 (U.S. Bureau of the Census, 1983c, Table 97). For example, a refugee describes how the availability of housing has affected his own family:

> Before I left Vietnam, three generations lived together in the same group. My mom, my family including wife and seven children, my elder brother, his wife and three children, my little brother and two sisters—we live in a big house. So when we came here we are thinking of being united in one place. But there is no way. However, we try to live as close as possible.

Although Vietnamese extended families may not be able to reside together in the United States, the family continues to be an issue of central concern in their resettlement experience, and meaningful ties are maintained over distances both short and long (Haines et al., 1981). Through families, Vietnamese refugees provide one another with a variety of resources—from the initial sponsorship needed to enter the United States (ORR, 1984) to the necessities of daily life, to job referrals and the investment capital required to open a small business (Finnan & Cooperstein, 1983; Gold, 1985; Haines et al., 1981; Indochinese Community Center, 1983; Velasco, Ima, Stanton, & Yip, 1983). Through a family-based exchange of information, support, and resources, some of the social, economic, and psychological trauma of the immigration experience is eased. Concurrently, the stability provided by this exchange allows refugee parents to fulfill some of their traditional responsibilities and hence offers their families continuity that might otherwise be unobtainable. A Vietnamese refugee describes how the Vietnamese family is ideally suited for solving problems of resettlement in the United States:

> To Vietnamese culture, family is everything. There are aspects which help us readjust to this society. It is easy for us because of tradition of helping in the family.
>
> We solve problems because [the] family institution is a bank. If I need money—and my brother and my two sisters are working—I tell them I need to buy a house. I need priority in this case. They say okay, and they give money to me. And after only two years, I bought a house.
>
> Some Americans ask me, "How come you came here with empty hands and now you have a house?" I told them, it is easier for us because my brother and sister help with the down payment. Now I help them. They live with me and have no rent.
>
> The family is a hospital. If mom is sick, I, my children, and my brother and sisters care for her. We don't need a nurse. She stays home, so we don't need to send her to nursing home.

The viability of extended families is revealed by their ability to care for relatives in distant places. I interviewed many Vietnamese refugees who, despite their very small incomes, exchanged sums of hundreds or even thousands of dollars with friends and relatives in the United States and overseas. Refugees regularly sent canned goods, clothes, medicine, and dollars (for instance, hidden in the battery compartment of a pocket calculator) to their families in Vietnam, knowing that these items stood a good chance of being confiscated or stolen.

Vietnamese refugees also engage in international financial transfer activities to give money to relatives. In such arrangements, a refugee in the United States gives a sum of money to another refugee. Then the recipient informs his relatives in Vietnam to give money to the first refugee's family in Vietnam. The Vietnamese tradition of treating an entire family as a single fiscal entity allows these transactions to take place over distances of thousands of miles.

Family Businesses

Vietnamese families pool labor, capital, and know-how to run a variety of economic enterprises. For many refugees, small business provides not only a means of economic support, but an opportunity to solve adjustment problems as well, since family entrepreneurship allows them to maintain a degree of autonomy unavailable under other conditions of employment (Bonacich, 1973). I interviewed the owners of restaurants, grocery and dry goods stores, barber and beauty shops, retail shops, and a variety of service enterprises, all of which depended upon family-based resources to obtain competitive advantages in the business world. Many features of family-oriented entrepreneurship that are associated with other Asian groups, including reliance on low-cost family labor and use of rotating credit associations (commonly called Hui) to amass capital, are evident among Vietnamese refugees (Finnan & Cooperstein, 1983; Gold, 1985; Light, 1972; Tran, 1986).

Family needs and resources in themselves may play a major role in the opening and operation of businesses. For example, a study of refugee food-related enterprises found the following:

> Data show that the Indochinese define success differently than Americans in food-related enterprises. Profit . . . is not the sole or even the main criterion for success. [Instead] the enterprises provide employment and social contact for family and kin . . . provide the basic nutritional needs of one's family. Working together provides the family with a setting in which positive adjustment can be made. (Indochinese Community Center, 1983, p. 9)

For many refugees, small business functions as an extension of the family itself. Within Vietnamese culture, the linking of small business activities to family patterns is bolstered by the fact that financial matters are traditionally the responsibility of female family members. "In Vietnam, the woman was always the money manager of the family, and was referred to as Noi Tuong, or 'Chief of Domestic Affairs'" (Finnan & Cooperstein, 1983, p. 31).

> The urban Vietnamese financial aid society is notable not only for its speculative characteristics but also for the fact that it is managed by women.
>
> There are some women who manage two, three and up to five *HO* (savings and mutual lending societies) simultaneously and know how to manipulate the funds of all without a hitch. (Nguyen, 1949, pp. i, 9)

Drawing upon this tradition, Vietnamese families use a division of labor in which the husband takes a job while the wife opens a small business such as a grocery or restaurant. This arrangement offers the family a high degree of economic security and minimizes risk. The husband's income supports the family while the wife's business becomes established. He also helps by working at the business during evenings and weekends. If the husband is laid off, income derived from the enterprise can support the family. In addition to providing a stable source of income, this arrangement also allows the family to act in accordance with Vietnamese norms about family life, hence easing some of the difficulty of resettlement and allowing the family to maintain a good reputation within the refugee community. A Vietnamese resettlement worker elaborates:

> Southeast Asians have our family to back us up. We are not like Americans— when the children are 18 years old, the American parents kick them out. For us, it is common for the children to stay at home until they are married. So we can rely on family to help lower labor costs during early years of business operation.
>
> In our family, the wife runs the small business. I help out on weekends and with the accounting. We get no pay, so it is easier to cover expenses and avoid bankruptcy.

Small business activities are valued by refugee families because they can be passed on to children. By creating small businesses that can be given to children, parents hope to spare the younger generation the trauma of instability that they, as refugees, suffered. For example, one Vietnamese couple opened a grocery store that bore their teenage daughter's name. They planned to give it to her as a wedding gift.

Despite the many benefits Vietnamese refugees enjoy through their participation in family businesses, some disadvantages were noted as well. Several refugees described losing large sums of money that they had invested in a relative's failed enterprise. Similarly, a number said that they were obliged to work in family businesses for subminimum wages even though they were offered better-paying jobs in the larger economy. For example, an ethnic Chinese woman reported that her family moved from Iowa to San Francisco to escape an uncle who compelled them to work in his laundry.

Adaptability

Although Vietnamese remain committed to traditional customs, many realize that their economic well-being would be hindered if they were to retain these practices in the United States. Consequently, many families appear to be adopting Western family patterns rapidly, such as use of day care, small family size, and women's employment outside the home (Gold, 1987; Gordon, 1987; ORR, 1987).

Problems Faced by Vietnamese Families

Vietnamese refugees frequently confront major obstacles in adapting to the United States. These include broken family status, economic difficulties, role reversals, generational conflict, and scarcity of coethnic marriage partners. One of the most basic problems that Vietnamese families confront is being split up in the process of selective immigration (Gordon, 1987). Broken families are very common among Vietnamese refugees, especially the recent arrivals, who are disproportionately young and male (Gordon, 1982). Being apart from extended family causes refugees both emotional and economic hardship (Caplan, Whitmore, & Bui, 1985; Owan, 1985).

One way refugees compensate for their broken families is by including distant relatives and unrelated persons in their extended family units. Several factors can be seen as important to the creation of pseudofamilies (Owan, 1985). First is the high degree of emphasis placed upon the extended family by Vietnamese culture (Slote, 1972; Tung, 1972). Valuing family solidarity, brothers, sisters, nephews, uncles, cousins, distant relatives, and unrelated persons will unite in the United States. A second source of connection that brings unrelated individuals together to form extended families can be found in relationships forged in the refugee camps of Southeast Asia. Bonds created in the camps are treated with a great deal of seriousness and are frequently maintained in the United States. Third is the physical closeness that characterizes recently arrived refugee enclaves. Because of financial difficulties, Vietnamese refugees are forced to share dwellings and may be placed with others by resettlement agencies. Refugees meet coethnics in immigrant enclaves, in coffee shops, at resettlement agencies, and while on the job or in classes. These meetings often evolve into familylike relationships.

Finally, forms of chain migration (A. Cohen, 1969; Glazer & Moynihan, 1963) appear to be important in creating extended families. Chain migration involves a process by which established refugees encourage and sponsor the migration of friends or relatives from the country of origin, refugee camps, or locations elsewhere in the United States, and provide accommodations for them.[2] One Vietnamese family of this type in Oakland, California, consisted of a couple in their mid-20s, their two small children, the husband's two brothers and sister, the sister's fiance, and an unrelated individual. The members of the family had left Vietnam at different times and the group had taken its current form only in California.

The inclusion of unrelated individuals in extended families facilitates the sharing of information, money, and emotional support. This process appears to be an efficient means of providing the necessities of life to refugees who have few resources and limited connections.

Economic Difficulties

Despite popular stereotypes about the economic success of new immigrants and model minorities, recently arrived Vietnamese refugees share many of the social characteristics associated with other disadvantaged urban minority groups.[3] Their population is marked by welfare dependency, unemployment, underemployment, health problems, and overcrowded housing (ORR, 1987).[4]

Few recently arrived Vietnamese hold professional or managerial occupations in the United States. If employed, they tend to work as laborers or operators, or in service occupations such as electronics assembly worker, driver, factory worker, clerk, janitor, or food handler. Such jobs are often poorly paid, part-time, seasonal, and without benefits (U.S. Bureau of the Census, 1983c, Table 196B). The members of a household of young Vietnamese—each of whom had spent three or four years in the United States in a succession of futureless, minimum-wage jobs—expressed frustration at their inability to get decent jobs in America: "If you had a diploma or a good job in Vietnam, you can just throw it away. It won't do you any good here. You can only get a job for $4.50 here, so forget about your old one."

These economic difficulties cause many problems for refugee families. One is overcrowded housing conditions. Vietnamese refugees have the largest number of occupants per housing unit of any ethnic group in San Francisco (Finnan & Cooperstein, 1983, p. 123).[5] Another economic problem experienced by Vietnamese refugees is welfare dependency. The dependency rate for Vietnamese refugees in the United States for less than three years is 64% (ORR, 1987, pp. 34-35). Data suggest that family-related issues are associated with welfare dependency. For example, a recent survey found that more than 33% of Southeast Asian refugees between the ages of 25 and 44 who were not employed cited "family needs" as their reason for not seeking employment (ORR, 1987, p. 112).

My fieldwork revealed that refugees' concern over the cost of medical care for their large families was a major factor in their staying on welfare. Ty Nguyen, a resettlement worker, describes this issue:

> You must realize that refugees here—they really want to work, to be self-sufficient. No one really wants to rely on another person. But why, then, do

you see most of them still stay on welfare? It's not completely their fault. The policy is not an incentive for them to become self-sufficient.

If they work at the entry level job, they get $3.25, $3.50 an hour. They can make $450, $500 a month. Then why do they stay on welfare for only $240 a month?

This is why. Everyone knows that here, the medical bill is the worst—so everyone has in their mind how to pay it. Especially for the refugee who has many children. If they work, then they lose government medical benefits, and low-wage jobs don't provide. And that's why, myself, I think that's why we still have a lot of refugees on welfare.

Role Reversals

Economic necessity often requires the women or children of refugee families to enter the labor force. This results in various degrees of reversal of the "provider" and "recipient" roles that existed among family members in Vietnam (Sluzki, 1979). The most common shift of roles occurs between husband and wife, with the wife taking on the breadwinner role as well as some of the status and power that accompanies it. This may be because women's jobs, such as house cleaner, hotel maid (a major source of employment for female refugees in San Francisco), and food service worker, are much more readily available than the male-oriented unskilled occupations that the men seek. In other cases, the mother becomes breadwinner as she supports the family by working in a menial job while the father attempts to find professional employment. Finally, women may have to assume the breadwinner role because of the absence of a spouse in the United States. Role reversals also occur in families where both the husband and wife work, since the wife was not employed outside the home before the family came to the United States.

The process by which mother rather than father becomes the primary source of a refugee family's income indicates the adaptability of Vietnamese families. At the same time, however, the inversion of traditional family roles often provokes hostility and resentment (Liu, 1979). Several social workers with refugee clients commented that self-destructive, violent, psychosomatic, or antisocial reactions—such as wife or child abuse, depression, or alcoholism—occur as a result of family role reversals (Cohon, 1981).

The relative increase in women's power as a result of their earning capabilities is an issue of great concern for refugee families. This is due, in part, to the fact that these role changes occur just when families are attempting to reestablish some sense of stability so long absent because of their flight from the country of origin. A male Vietnamese social worker, Doan Nguyen, feels that despite the disruptive effects of role changes, in the long run they are beneficial:

> I think the role change—the phenomenon that the man is losing his status and the woman gaining—I see that, in a way, it negatively affects the traditional unit of the family. But it is also positive in terms of sharing, in terms of educating the children, in terms of financial matters.
>
> [Gold: If the woman gets a job, and later the husband finds employment, will she go back to being a housewife?]
>
> It is my impression that she might not go back to being a mere housewife. Because, besides the political reasons, the Vietnamese decision to settle in the United States is also very much economic. And if both parents go to work, they will try to keep it that way.
>
> And also, the husband and wife each may have responsibility to send money back to their families in Vietnam.

A Vietnamese woman who has taken over a typically male position in career and family because of her husband's death expresses both pride and anxiety about her newly acquired power and responsibility:

> I brought my children here. I raised them and I went to graduate school, all on my own. When I started this resettlement agency, my son asked me, "Mom, can you really do this?" That really hurt me. I could bring the children here—I raised them by myself. But then, I see even my son cannot trust me to be in executive position. So how can other people?
>
> Because the situation put me in the role of the man—automatically I'm doing it, but I'm not aware. Because I picture myself—we are in a boat in the middle of the ocean and the boat is on fire. So we have to jump in the ocean. That means we swim or die, we have no choice. That's what it is like for the single mother refugee.

Generational Conflicts

Generational conflicts are common to the families of nearly all immigrant groups because the children are growing up in a different social milieu from the one in which their parents were raised (Eisenstadt, 1954, 1956). These conflicts may be especially severe for Vietnamese families in this country for two reasons. First, they are moving from a society that is very age graded and respectful of elders to one that stresses individual equality and glorifies youth (Bellah, Madsen, Sullivan, Swidler, & Tipton, 1985). Second, because of the rapid rates of assimila-

tion experienced by Vietnamese youth, cultural gaps between the upwardly mobile young and their traditional parents and grandparents may be
extreme ("Elderly Southeast Asian refugees," 1987, pp. 1-3).

For example, while Vietnamese traditions promote family cooperation,
the dynamics of the Vietnamese family may hinder the development and
expression of the kind of individualism that American-oriented adolescents
see as appropriate (Brower, 1981). A Vietnamese Buddhist monk describes
how refugee families confront the issue of self-determination:

> Okay, there is some breakdown in the family. Kids are growing and become
> American and the grandfather and grandmother stick to the old culture. So
> we have to become involved in this problem.
>
> It's tough. And I think that if you work with the refugees, you will notice
> that the kids, they are completely American after 7 years in America. They
> want to date, they want to go out with their boyfriend, girlfriend.
>
> This idea never existed in Vietnam. So the older generation cannot stand
> this stuff. And the kids feel terribly upset when mother says, "Hey—you have
> to stay home."

In Vietnam, it is customary for parents to make the children's life
decisions for them. A successful refugee exemplifies this position:

> I am a father. I was a professor, I am an educator. I need to be there and the children
> need to study. I have to give guidance on what to do and how to do things.
>
> Let me cite example. My son age was 13 in 1975 (when we arrived in the
> U.S.). He completed eighth grade in Vietnam and the church that resettled us
> placed him in high school. After two years, in June 1977, he completed tenth
> grade. I had him take the California high school proficiency exam. He passed
> it. And so I had him skip eleventh and twelfth grade, go directly to Kenyatta
> College. After two years, I got him transferred to Berkeley. In March '82 he
> graduated in chemistry at Berkeley.

Many American-oriented Vietnamese youth object to this tradition.
Arguments over life decisions yield family conflict. A Vietnamese social
worker, who has been in the United States several years longer than the
man quoted above, describes how she has come to see the validity of letting
children choose their own careers and goals in the American fashion:

> I tell the refugees that come to my resettlement center of my own experience. I
> applied for my son to go to Berkeley. I got him a full scholarship. I decide for him
> to major in economics. But he didn't want economics, he wanted electronics. Now

he is in the electronics field, his work is easier. He works for Apple Computer. They sent him to Stanford. He has done well, so his own way is the best.

Same with my daughter. I wanted her to be a doctor, but she didn't get into medical school. She dropped out and worked in a doctor's office. She found out that she was good in accounting. She went back to college and got A+ easily. She studied management. They hired her to introduce computers in University Hospital.

She said, "See mom, if you let me select my major . . . " That's another example I show my clients. If I didn't force my daughter into medical, she might have gone into management easier. I share with the refugee my lesson: let the children do what they love.

While young Vietnamese experience one side of the problem of generational conflict, the elderly confront another. Although elderly individuals are uncommon within the Vietnamese American population (less than 2% of Southeast Asians entering the United States in 1986 were age 65 or older; ORR, 1987, p. 10), they are considered to be very important family members. In interviews, refugee families described many problems they experienced with aged family members. Elderly Vietnamese have difficulties learning English, finding employment, and making their way in the United States. Families who have successfully adapted to American life express concern over the relative isolation of their elderly.[6] A Vietnamese refugee who was a law professor before arriving in California describes his ambivalence toward the rapid rate with which his children are accepting American ways of life:

My mom is 82. She doesn't speak English at all. And the children learn the American way. They come home, and in some cases, they want to imitate American behavior. The children use the wrong terms of address with Grandmother. She says, "Now you are American and you are impolite to me!"

In the community, criteria have changed. They tolerate children who do not study as hard. But the children still act with discipline at home. Next generation will be different. We are happy we are still in control. We are really afraid that the next generation will fall into a crisis of identity.

Generational conflicts such as these affect not only individual families, but the entire refugee community as well. Disputes between a traditionalistic but powerful older generation and a more assimilation-oriented younger generation are manifested at many levels within the Vietnamese community of the San Francisco Bay Area. A young refugee describes these concerns:

So I'm here just starting all over again. They [the older generation] say, "Oh Vietnamese culture" and that is the way it is supposed to be. You never put down a parent, because of their pride, because they are afraid that people will know the bad thing about someone. It won't work here.

A Surplus of Male Refugees

A final problem confronted by Vietnamese families is a relative scarcity of Vietnamese females in the United States (L. W. Gordon, 1982, 1987; ORR, 1986).[7] The lack of Vietnamese women of marriageable age, together with economic difficulties, prevents many Vietnamese males from establishing their own families in the United States. Male Vietnamese refugees who find difficulty in establishing courting relationships with coethnics sometimes express hostility toward the female members of their community, who, by virtue of their small numbers, enjoy many options in mate choice. Two Vietnamese refugees commented:

> In Vietnam, it was easy to meet a girlfriend because so many men were killed in the war. But in America, Vietnamese ladies only like you if you have a good job, nice clothes, a good car, and plenty of money. They look for money, not love.

> There was a girl I knew in the refugee camp. We were good friends. I came to the United States, Oakland. She moved to Los Angeles. At first I used to write to her. I saw her, but she is not friendly anymore. She only likes a man who has a lot of money.

Lacking the opportunity to get married or find stable employment, many recently arrived male Vietnamese refugees live lives that reveal striking parallels to those led by the Chinese laborers who endured a marginal existence without families in America's Chinatowns 100 years ago (Light, 1972; Lyman, 1974).

Conclusions

Vietnamese refugees have had to flee their homeland under dire circumstances and face great challenges in their adjustment to the United States. However, the Vietnamese family unit provides these refugees with many assets in facilitating resettlement. Two family-based resources are cooperation and flexibility. Vietnamese families reveal these characteristics as they share resources and information to support family members in the United States and overseas.

At the same time, however, Vietnamese families face many serious problems as they work to adjust to the United States. These include broken families, economic difficulties, role reversals, generational conflicts, and a lack of female refugees. With the exception of generational conflicts, these problems weigh more heavily upon the recently arrived refugees than they do on the 1975 cohort, because the former are the more disadvantaged of the two groups.

While the mass of Vietnamese continue to confront serious difficulties in their attempts to adjust to the United States, the successes of the 1975 cohort and the accomplishments of refugee youth who have been making remarkable strides in higher education offer evidence that problems of resettlement are being solved by members of this population (Efron, 1990).[8]

Notes

1. Data collected by Rumbaut (1986) and Desbarats (1986) indicate that ethnic Chinese refugees from Vietnam experience "disadvantage . . . with respect to both acculturation and economic self-sufficiency variables" (Desbarats, 1986, p. 405).

2. Secondary migration among Vietnamese refugees in the United States has been significant. For example, in fiscal 1982, 23,977 refugees entered California from other states. This number constitutes about 4% of all refugees in the United States at that time. Similarly, in the same year, 4,733 refugees left the state of Texas. This number is greater by more than 1,000 than the 3,509 refugees who remained in the Lone Star State that year (ORR, 1984, p. A-16).

3. This problem is more severe for the recently arrived cohort than for the 1975 arrivals, who have made significant progress in adjusting to the American economy (ORR, 1987, p. 124).

4. In 1979, 41.4% of Vietnamese refugee families in California were below the poverty line (versus 7.6% for the native-born) (U.S. Bureau of the Census, 1983c, Table 196A).

5. The average numbers of occupants per housing unit are as follows: Vietnamese, 4.3; White, 1.8; Black, 2.5; Hispanic, 2.8.

6. Difficulties with aged family members are most common among 1975 arrivals, since elderly persons are far more common among this cohort than among recent arrivals (see Table 19.1).

7. "The Vietnamese refugee population is particularly remarkable for its excess of males over females, which is pronounced among persons in their teens and twenties. . . . In 1984, among the arriving 18-year-old Vietnamese, males outnumbered females by three to one" (L. W. Gordon, 1987, p. 4).

8. For example, the number one student in the Air Force Academy's class of 1987 was a Vietnamese refugee.

PART VII

Practice With Ethnic Families

20

Ethnic Sensitivity for Practitioners

A Practice Model

WYNETTA DEVORE
HARLAN LONDON

A Historical Perspective

The English were the first to arrive in America as colonists. They came as pilgrims fleeing oppression and searching for a new home. America was a haven, a place where they could carve out their own history. By the middle of the eighteenth century they were well established. They did not leave behind the language and customs of England; rather, these became dominant forces in government, commerce, and religion. Although there were modifications, the English way ruled the New World setting and became the model for those who would follow.

Blacks arrived from Africa in 1619, close to the time of arrival of the English. Their initial status was that of indentured or bonded servants. This limited freedom for Blacks slowly eroded as legislation denied them freedom. Slavery, a lifetime of servitude, became well established. Without power, Blacks were dependent upon white masters for rations of food, clothing, the daily organization of their lives, and their living conditions (Sowell, 1981, pp. 10-11). Despite this servitude, they would become an integral part of American life.

Other groups were to follow the English and the Blacks. They did not arrive at the same time, nor did they settle in the same places. Their arrival may be examined in relation to economic and political forces in their own nations and in America. The Irish, early arrivals, settled in the Northeast, as did the Italians and the Jews. Germans moved a little more to the west, into Pennsylvania, which they shared with the Scotch-Irish, who drifted into the Carolinas. The Scandinavians settled in the Midwest, and the Orientals were on the West Coast. Later arrivals, Mexican Americans and Cuban refugees, settled in the Southwest and Florida. Blacks remained, for the most part, in the South, where they had begun as servants (Sowell, 1981).

American Indians, who already held claim to the land, were found in various locations. Legend asserts that they were friends to the earliest immigrants in the northeast. They also encountered the immigrants who were moving west.

Immigrants from around the world have accepted the invitation to the tired, the poor, the masses yearning to breathe free. This appeal at the base of the welcoming Statue of Liberty includes the masses yearning for freedom, the wretched refuse of overcrowded lands, as well as the homeless. The torch has served as a constant beacon to the troubled of other countries to seek a new life, often a second chance.

Those who respond in the present are unlike the earlier European settlers mentioned here. They come from places unknown to the earliest settlers, unknown to many of us today. Their arrival and impact upon our life has been reported in the popular press (Daly, 1982; Fauriol, 1984; Friedrich, Church, Doerner, et al., 1985; McGrath, Fuller, Smith, et al., 1982; Morgan, 1983; Sheils, 1983; West, 1982). The newest waves of immigrants are from Ethiopia, Ghana, Afghanistan, Laos, and South Korea. Many others continue to arrive from Israel, Cuba, and Mexico.

While it is not the task of this chapter to provide an ethnic history of America, it is important that those persons who are charged with the delivery of social services to older and newer ethnic families be responsive to the origins, languages, religions, and many other ethnic variables that make up these families' life-styles, including patterns of interpersonal relationships. These may include parent-child, marital, and sibling as well as intergenerational relationships.

A Social Work Response to Ethnicity

The call for ethnic sensitivity is not new. We have known for some time of the need to be responsive to national and racial characteristics.

Many years ago, Mary Richmond (1917, p. 382) suggested that there were two possible errors in dealing with foreign families. The first was to think of them as members of a nationality having fixed characteristics; the second was to ignore national and racial characteristics and try to apply the same standards of measure to all persons. Those choosing the latter course would be "liable to surprises," for they would soon discover that national characteristics cannot be ignored altogether.

Despite this caution, the field of social work did ignore racial and national characteristics for a time. Egalitarian motives led to the conclusion that if a practitioner had an understanding of basic human needs and the dynamics of human behavior, then he or she could provide equal service to all. Others believed that explicit attention to the relationships among ethnicity, social class, and behavior was in some manner incongruent with social work's commitment to equality and the call for the recognition of the uniqueness of each individual (Devore & Schlesinger, 1987).

It was not until 1973 that the Council on Social Work Education (CSWE) incorporated ethnicity into its criteria for accreditation. Undergraduate and graduate programs were to attend to this area as well as to other neglected areas of diversity. Again in 1984 the expectation was present in the council's manual of accreditation (CSWE, 1984). The mandate has met with mixed results. There are those who are diligent in their commitment to examining course syllabi at regular intervals to assure compliance. Others have established special courses dealing particularly with ethnic minority groups—Blacks, Puerto Ricans, Chicanos, American Indians. Even with the mandate and tacit cooperation, there are still those who question the validity of the effort.

As she describes her experience in ethnicity training for family therapists, McGoldrick (1982) reports two major resistances to ethnicity training. The first is the attitude that ethnicity is a subject that we all understand, and so, with so many other critical areas of study, little time, if any, need be devoted to ethnicity. The second resistance is a reluctance to define ethnic differences. Stereotyping—labeling—is feared. This resistance has been felt from minority groups who fear that, in discussions of ethnic differences from a general perspective, their less powerful group would be lost.

Most certainly we must be aware of the dangers in labeling; we must realize that stereotypes are indeed exaggerations, useful to those who would seek to maintain prejudices that allow for the legitimation of racist attitudes and behaviors. The ethnicity-sensitive practitioner is aware of the difference between honored ethnic traditions and labeling for destructive reasons.

Self-Awareness and Ethnicity

The process of building ethnic sensitivity requires self-awareness—the ability and willingness to examine one's own ethnicity, attitudes, and actions. Siporin (1975) describes self-awareness as "an accurate perception of one's own behavior on others" (p. 78). It requires a third eye and a third ear to view oneself in action and to examine "the innermost recesses of oneself." In those innermost recesses is the ethnic self. It is through "thinking and feeling" the impact of one's own ethnicity that one comes to realize how much is involved in ethnic identity. A total perception of "appropriate" family life emerges, including fact and fantasy about family economics, roles, and the like (Devore & Schlesinger, 1987). McGoldrick (1982) adds that persons who are secure in their own ethnic identities can act with greater freedom, flexibility, and openness to persons of different ethnic backgrounds.

This examination and continuing awareness helps the practitioner to realize that ethnicity is here to stay. It will continue as a vital force in the lives of many Americans. It cannot be viewed as "a marginal phenomenon nor as a vestigial cultural legacy in the evolution toward social homogeneity" (Korbin & Goldscheider, 1978). The expectations of sociologists Robert Park (1950), Warner and Srole (1945), and Handlin (1951) were that ethnicity would end, that it would be quickly absorbed, replaced by an American culture. Milton Gordon (1964) suggests that "the sense of ethnicity has proved to be hardy" (p. 24). It has survived in various forms, with various names, and it has not perished. It is conspicuous in ethnic communities, suggesting that ethnic institutions and social networks, although changing, remain a major source of group identification (Korbin & Goldscheider, 1978).

Ethnicity Revitalized

For a time, ethnicity languished. The call by young Black Americans, "Say it loud, I'm Black and I'm proud," as well as "Black is beautiful," encouraged other groups to search for and reclaim their heritage (Greely, 1981; Novak, 1971). As they claimed their past, there was no effort toward separateness; rather, they retained their ethnic identity and heritage while holding full membership in American society.

More recent arrivals, closer to their ethnic origins, look for full membership as well. But they are often in the throes of cultural transitions. The process often challenges the validity of their languages, religions, education, and life-styles—evidence of a treasured ethnic background. The resultant stresses may be extreme for those who lack sufficient support systems. Family life, enjoyed in the past in the context of community, is experienced in isolation. There is enmeshment, the drawing in for protection in a seemingly hostile environment, or disengagement as certain family members challenge the old ways as they take on values and life-styles that are more acceptable in mainstream society (Landau, 1982, pp. 555-556).

Social workers need guidelines as they work with families who have already begun the acculturation process and with those who have arrived more recently. It is not expected that all practitioners can or should become familiar with all ethnic groups in our country. A more effective approach would be for them to become acquainted with the diverse ethnic groups within the communities where they practice.

We suggest that the following assumptions and principles are useful in working with the many ethnic groups found in a community. They serve to sensitize practitioners who use a variety of approaches in their practice. The goal is to develop an awareness of ethnicity as a continuing force in the life of individuals and families.

The Ethnic Reality

There are many perspectives on ethnic family life in the United States. Sociologists have examined how ethnic group membership, minority status, culture, and social class affect individual, family, and group life. It is continually recognized that social class position has a significant effect on daily life. Milton Gordon (1964) characterizes the point at which social class and ethnic group membership meet as "ethclass." This concept explains the role that social class membership plays in defining the basic condition of life influenced by ethnicity at the same time that it accounts for differences between groups at the same social class level.

Devore and Schlesinger (1987) elaborate on this concept, suggesting that at the point of ethclass there is a convergence of identifiable dispositions in behaviors that may be termed the ethnic reality, "ethclass in action." Family dispositions on such matters as child rearing, sibling responsibility, marital relations, and appropriate care for the aged are often affected by ethnicity. The ability to act on the dispositions may well be influenced by social class position.

Ethnic minority families often find themselves in the lower stratification as a result of their history of racism and discrimination in employment, housing, education, and the delivery of social services. This is their ethnic reality. Families of white ethnic groups in the majority society are more often able to set and achieve material goals. Yet, they are aware of others still plagued by the isolation of the lower strata.

Assumptions and Principles
for Ethnicity-Sensitive Practice

Practitioners who are sensitive to ethnicity begin with a basic knowledge of human behavior, including knowledge of human development, role theory, personality theory, individual and family life cycles, and systems theory. In addition, they need to have knowledge of the structures of social service agencies, their goals, and their functions. This is followed by the self-awareness discussed earlier. A third important area of knowledge concerns the impact of the ethnic reality on the daily lives of families, along with a recognition of the significance of ethnicity in identity formulation. Finally, practitioners need to be able to adapt and modify the skills and techniques of practice in ways that will respond to the ethnic reality. These four components have been termed the "layers of understanding."

The assumptions and principles for ethnicity-sensitive practice presented here build upon such accepted social work values as preferred concepts of people, preferred outcomes for people, and preferred instruments for dealing with people (Levy, 1973). They take into account the ethnic reality and its relationship to the individual and family life cycles, the layers of understanding, and the view that social work is a problem-solving endeavor.

We present first the basic assumptions for ethnicity-sensitive practice:

(1) Individual and collective history have bearing on problem generation and solution.
(2) The present is most important.
(3) Ethnicity has significant influence on individual identity formation.
(4) Ethnicity is a source of cohesion, identity, and strength, as well as a source of strain, discordance, and strife.

Workers who are sensitive to their clients' ethnicity must be aware that the history of immigration to this country has not ended. New waves of immigrants provide new challenges. There are new Asian families and Vietnamese and Cambodian refugees who, like the early settlers, fled oppression and war at home.

There are problems of language, education, and economics, as well as problems in individual and family life-cycle development. Racism hampers movement in employment and disrupts attempts on the part of ethnic minority members to become an integral part of some communities. This is collective history, it is the present. Yet, there are individual strengths and family coping skills that have been useful in the past. The strengths and coping skills found within the family's present ethnic reality may offer solutions in its movement toward becoming an integral part of the community.

Tension, stress, and discomfort often occur in the present. The nature of daily living is such that individuals and families find themselves in turmoil. Practice response needs to be related to the present pain, but the past must not be ignored. Both past and present racism, anti-Semitism, and sexism influence life in the present. The obligation is to attend to current issues with the understanding that distribution and intensity of problems are often related to the ethnic reality (Devore & Schlesinger, 1987).

Routine and habitual dispositions of life become so thoroughly a part of the individual that they require no examination. These unarticulated dispositions become part of the core of the self. They are the rhythms of the ethnic community conveyed through the sounds that children hear as they grow. The sounds are ordinary and routine, yet they convey the joy or sadness of life in the family and community. The sights, sounds, and smells of the environment can be integral parts of the individual's ethnic reality (Devore & Schlesinger, 1987).

Understanding and knowledge of the past as it relates to history, customs, traditions, and beliefs are required for ethnicity-sensitive practice. The problem of the present must receive primary attention. Practitioners must, however, recognize that history, custom, and belief will affect the perception of the problem and the possible solutions (Devore & Schlesinger, 1987).

While ethnicity provides individuals with a sense of cohesion and identity drawn from the strength of the group, it also may be the source of strain, discordance, and strife. Sotomajor (1977) has written of the contributions made by language as it identifies a group. As the years pass, the language of the immigrant may be lost or unappreciated by first, second, and third generations. McGoldrick (1982) suggests that it is important to learn what languages are spoken in the family. More recent arrivals must struggle with language immediately.

The Hmong community of Syracuse, New York, provides new immigrants from Cambodia, their homeland, with tutors as soon as they arrive so that they can learn the English language quickly. While their native language provides a sense of security in the community, there is a potential for distress as barriers are placed before those who do not speak English. Obstacles may be found in the many institutions that serve the community at large—schools, potential employers, or social welfare agencies. Language, a force for identity and strength, may at the same time present strain and strife. Tutors help to provide the tools for greater security.

In addition to the assumptions set forth above, there is a set of guiding principles for ethnicity-sensitive practice:

(1) Attention must be paid to individual and systemic needs as they emerge out of client need and professional assessment.
(2) Practice skills and techniques must be adapted to respond to the needs or dispositions of various ethnic and class groups.
(3) The route to the social worker will affect problem definition and intervention strategies.

In the recent past, we have seen a shift in the focus of many social workers. While the historical mandate for focus on social change has not been forgotten, considerable energy has been invested in clinical concerns. There is a continuing need for social workers to address public issues at the same time that they hear private troubles. Such integration is urgent if practice is to respond to the needs and sensitivities of various groups and individuals.

Public schools are not always sensitive to relatively unfamiliar religious practices that may require that children attend services rather than school. Hospitals may be unfamiliar with dietary habits or religious dietary laws that demand that patients refuse prescribed diets despite their therapeutic advantage. Child-care workers, unaware of the strengths of the extended family, may question the wisdom of leaving young children with aging family members. In all of these cases, there is a need to attend to the troubles generated by long-held ethnic traditions while seeking ways to encourage appropriate institutional policy change.

The emerging literature on ethnicity and practice tells us that we must reconsider the ways in which we use the techniques and skills familiar to us. At times we are confronted by behaviors that defy our training and education. Blacks may be uncommunicative, the Irish fail to talk, the Norwegians withhold information. Each causes us to sense failure, and our techniques seem useless. However, the Black fails to communicate with a white representative of mistrusted institutions, the Irish individual is embarrassed about admitting failure, and the Norwegian withholds information out of respect and politeness, in order not to say less-than-positive things about the family (McGoldrick, 1982). Once practitioners understand such behaviors, they may move forward, adapting to the needs of the ethnic groups they serve.

Too often, problem definition has been taken away from the client and assumed by others, who conclude that their definition has greater legitimacy than the client's. As problems are defined, many clients are sent to social workers. They travel a route that is coercive, sent by the county, child protective agencies, a drug rehabilitation service, the schools, and medical services. The careful observer will note that there are disproportionate numbers of ethnic minority persons among those who are coerced. Their low income status and racial characteristics render them powerless in times of distress. Others define their problems and send them to the social worker.

Those whose routes are voluntary are more likely to define their own problems. They may respond to the urging of a family member or a member of the clergy. Unlike those who are coerced, they are more likely to be found in the middle and upper social strata, including a cross section of ethnic groups.

The assumptions and principles provided above guide ethnicity-sensitive practice, which is good social work practice based on values that have served the profession well.

A Word of Caution

Jay Lappin (1983, p. 127) warns us of the "house ethnic," the ethnic practitioner who is automatically assigned to clients who are of similar ethnic heritage. Neither the client nor the practitioner is consulted. It is the agency's assumption that it is not respectful to assign clients to practitioners of ethnic groups other than their own. However, such policy denies both client and practitioner the opportunity to make a choice. A more appropriate response would be a commitment to ethnic sensitivity in practice that would transcend ethnocentricity.

A second warning comes from Montalvo and Gutierrez (1984), who caution that families may "use their cultural heritage as a mask, a justification for curtailing needed problem-solving" (p. 46). Traditional gender assignments cover up exploitation and spousal abuse. Past parent-child conflict around the role of father as head of the household may mask real problems in the present related to unemployment. To make ethnicity more central than interactions with the surrounding environment is to initiate emotional and technical excess (Montalvo & Gutierrez, 1984). While it is important to be sensitive to ethnicity, it is equally important to realize that this is but one facet in the lives of individuals and families.

Appendix: Resources

When the vast amount of research on ethnicity is examined, only a few studies emerge that have a clearly positive perspective on the use of the model discussed in this chapter. The following bibliography, with some annotation, represents selected works on ethnicity that tend to support a positive rather than a negative perspective.

Allen, J. A., & Burwell, N. Y. (1980). Ageism and racism: Two issues in social work education and practice. *Journal of Education for Social Work, 16,* 71-77.

Bernal, G., & Fores-Ortiz, Y. (1982). Latino families in therapy: Engagement and devaluation. *Journal of Marital and Family Therapy, 8,* 357-365.
    The authors present guidelines that lead to successful engagement of Latino families in family therapy. These include use of the clients' own language, particularly the polite form; appropriate use of power and authority in giving advice; and attention to the position of the father in the family. Workers are cautioned to distinguish migration and/or cultural conflicts from family conflicts. In addition, workers must understand the various aspects of Latino culture that may come from Mexico, Puerto Rico, or Cuba.

Borus, J. F. (1979). Psychotherapy in the goldfish bowl. *Archives of General Psychiatry, 36,* 187-190.
    This article explores the therapeutic advantages and liabilities accrued to the indigenous therapist (whether professional or paraprofessional),

utilizing the five-year experience of 10 indigenous therapists in a community of Italian immigrants with strong family and cultural ties.

Davis, L. E. (Ed.). (1984). *Ethnicity in social group work practice.* New York: Haworth.
  This volume heightens awareness and understanding of the needs and resources of minority ethnic groups and presents the contribution that social work with groups can make to the strengthening of both ethnic and universal identity so necessary in contemporary society. Chapters explore social group work practice with American Indians, Asians, Asian Pacific Americans, Hispanic Americans, and Black Americans.

Dresp, C. S. W. (1985). Nervios as a culture-bound syndrome among Puerto Rican women. *Smith College Studies in Social Work, 55,* 115-136.

Eilberg, A. (1984). Views of human development in Jewish rituals: A comparison with Eriksonian theory. *Smith College Studies in Social Work, 55,* 1-23.

Gomez, E., Zurcher, L. A., Farris, B. E., & Becker, R. (1985). A study of psychosocial casework with Chicanos. *Social Work, 30,* 477-482.
  The results of the authors' study of short-term psychosocially oriented casework with Chicanos provide a model for practice. Data suggest that it is important for workers to consider clients' cultural beliefs and the natural helping systems used by clients. The most significant finding was the development and reinforcement of positive feelings about clients' self-concept as Mexican Americans.

Griffith, M. S. (1977). The influences of race on the psychotherapeutic relationship. *Psychiatry, 40,* 27-40.
  The influences on the therapeutic relationship of racial differences between client and therapist are receiving renewed attention in the psychological literature. This review examines the psychotherapeutic relationship under varying racial matches of white and Black clients and therapists. It seeks to sharpen the sensibilities of therapists to some of the racial factors contributing to premature termination of treatment.

Hall, E. H. (1982). Working with the strengths of Black families. *Child Welfare, 61,* 536-544.
  The author discusses deterrents to effective practice with Black families and identifies family strengths that can be incorporated into a resilient practice approach. An important prerequisite of intervention is an understanding and awareness of ecosystem problems and an ability to work toward eliminating or modifying barriers that can impede the helping relationship.

Hill, R. (1977). Family therapy workshop: When family and therapist are of different races. *Journal of Contemporary Psychotherapy, 9,* 45-46.

Jenkins, S. (Ed.). (1981). *The ethnic dilemma in social services.* New York: Macmillan.

This volume presents a study of ethnic issues in the design and delivery of social services.

Jones-Morrison, B. (1982). Socio-cultural dimension: Nursing homes and the minority aged. *Journal of Gerontological Social Work, 5,* 127-145.

Findings from recent studies of minorities in long-term care settings are used to illustrate the ways in which racial or ethnic factors influence the design and use of institutional long-term care. Minorities historically have not used nursing homes to any great extent because of shorter life expectancy than found in the general population, the availability of relatives to provide care, cultural aversion, geographic location, and economic factors.

Kumabe, K. T., Nishida, C., & Hepworth, D. H. (1985). *Bridging ethnocultural diversity in social work and health.* Honolulu: University of Hawaii, School of Social Work.

This monograph is presented for the use of students, faculty, and practitioners to assist them in the critical analysis of ethnocultural factors in day-to-day practice, enhancing the delivery of health care to ethnic groups. Work with Samoan-Hawaiian and Filipino families and an intercultural marriage (Japanese/Caucasian) are highlighted.

Lieberson, S. (1985). Unhyphenated whites in the United States. In R. D. Alba (Ed.), *Ethnicity and race in the USA* (pp. 159-180). London: Routledge & Kegan Paul.

This chapter is intended for use by students and practitioners who wish to broaden their knowledge of ethnicity and racial diversity in the United States.

Lum, D. (1992). *Social work practice and people of color: A process-stage approach* (2nd ed.). Pacific Grove, CA: Brooks/Cole.

McAdoo, H. P. (Ed.). (1988). *Black families* (2nd ed.). Newbury Park, CA: Sage.

This interdisciplinary research volume includes a crisp demythologization of negative images about the Black family. The writers challenge many concepts presented in the social science literature. The book is a move toward continued examination of Black families on a conceptual level and the testing of some of the theories that have been brought forth about these families.

McAdoo, H. P., & McAdoo, J. L. (Eds.). (1985). *Black children.* Beverly Hills, CA: Sage.

This volume is designed to explore in depth the unique experiences and situations that are common to Black children and their parents. The book begins with the assumption that all children, during their childhood, regardless of race, ethnicity, social class, or gender, must complete similar developmental tasks if they are to become competent adults. It then documents how these developmental tasks are uniquely experienced in the environment of children's growth and development. It further explores the diversity of childhood experiences confronted by children who are members of Black families.

McGoldrick, M., Pearce, J. K., & Giordano, J. (Eds.). (1982). *Ethnicity and family therapy.* New York: Guilford.

This anthology presents intervention strategies for practice with a vast array of ethnic families. Following a conceptual overview on family therapy and an ecological model of ethnic families, paradigms of ethnic families are presented. Clinical questions such as cultural differences, attitudes toward problem solving, and family role behavior are considered.

Majors, R., & Nikelly, A. (1983). Serving the Black minority: A new direction for psychotherapy. *Journal of Non-White Concerns in Personnel & Guidance, 11,* 142-152.

The authors contend that the forces that generate racism must be addressed before psychotherapy can respond to the needs of the Black client. Therapy must encompass external, social, and economic factors to serve the Black minority. As therapists recognize the importance for Blacks of pride, childhood trauma, effects of racism, and having a place in the world of work, they will be capable of responding more fully and effectively to the Black client. It is argued that white therapists can learn to win the trust of Black clients, to make use of the resources in the immediate Black environment, and to deal directly and honestly with the issues of racism.

Martin, J. M., & Martin, E. P. (1985). *The helping tradition in the Black family and community.* Silver Spring, MD: National Association of Social Workers.

The authors present a systematic way of viewing the Black family and the Black community. In addition to explaining the forces responsible for the rise, development, and decline of the Black helping tradition, they provide a model for social work practice from a Black perspective. Among the key concepts presented are mental aid, social class cooperation, male-female equality, racial and religious consciousness, racism, bourgeoisie and sheet ideology, and patriarchy.

Myer, D. F. (1976). The relevance of ethnic awareness to effective education: Implications for drug educators. *Journal of Drug Education, 6,* 127-136.

The author asserts that effective education goals can be sabotaged by unrecognized ethnicism in the teacher, the school, or the materials used. Teachers/facilitators of effective strategies should develop a sensitivity to all types of ethnicism, become aware of the cognitive and affective realities of other ethnic groups, and work toward programs that are free of ethnic discrimination, whether overt or covert.

Niedert, L. J., & Farley, R. (1985). Assimilation in the United States: An analysis of ethnic and generation differences in status achievement. *American Sociological Review, 50,* 840-850.

This article is a review of differences in socioeconomic status among various ethnic groups over the generations. The author explores the issues of assimilation, success in educational credentials, and per capita income by comparing several ethnic groups' achievement as judged by these measures.

Parnajpe, A. C. (Ed.). (1985). Ethnic identities and prejudice: Perspectives from the Third World [Symposium]. *Journal of Asian and African Studies, 20,* 133-244.

This is an interesting collection of essays that shows the distinctiveness of cultural diversity among societies around the globe. Despite many differences in the form and content of these essays, many common themes emerge, suggesting that a sense of peoplehood is rooted in many cultures.

Red Horse, J., Lewis, R., Feit, M., & Decker, J. (1978). Family behavior of urban American Indians. *Social Casework, 59,* 67-72.

American Indian urban family networks are described, along with examples of problems that occur when service professionals are ignorant of Indian culture and family dynamics. Levine's social conservation model provides the theoretical orientation. The values, group standards, and accountability of Indian communities are enforced by their family networks, which are structurally open and include several households.

Sachdev, P. (1984). *Adoption: Current issues and trends.* Ontario, Canada: Butterworth.

Through 20 essays, this book examines a wide range of pertinent issues central to the concerns of human service professionals in the adoption field, providing a reconnaissance view of the issues of the 1980s and future developments. The volume serves as a guide for practitioners in their everyday practice concerns and for administrators in their efforts to develop policies and programs.

Shen-Ryan, A. (1985). Cultural factors in casework with Chinese-Americans. *Social Casework, 66,* 333-340.

Workers need to understand how the influence of the teachings of Confucius, Lao-tse, and Buddha affect Chinese families' ways of thinking. New Chinese immigrants may have lost the family resources that supported them in the past, but continue to find it difficult to look for help outside the family. Workers may find it essential to focus on external factors until trust is established. Use of educational techniques, gentle interpretation of resistance, transference, and reassurance are suggested techniques. Workers are seen as responsible for recognition of the culture of the Chinese as an important component of practice.

Solomon, B. B., & Fores-Ortiz, Y. (1976). *Black empowerment: Social work in oppressed communities*. New York: Columbia University Press.

This book is intended for use by students and practitioners wishing to prepare for effective social work practice with Black clients.

Stanford, E. P. (Ed.). (1973). *Minority aging: Institute on Minority Aging proceedings*. San Diego, CA: San Diego State University, School of Social Work.

This volume focuses on gaps in research models that exclude minority aged, curriculum development expansion, existing theories and needed theories of minority elderly in self-determination and consumer participation, environment and health, and impact of social policy.

Vaux, A. (1985). Variations in social support associated with gender, ethnicity and age. *Journal of Social Issues, 41,* 89-110.

This article reviews studies allowing comparison of support across gender, ethnicity, and age, and suggests that social support varies across subgroups of the population. Women (older rather than adolescents, and younger rather than older adults) seem to be at an advantage with respect to some kinds of support. Support from friends seems more variable than that from family members. Associations between support and well-being also vary across subgroups, and advantages in support do not always translate into advantages in well-being.

Yoshioka, R. B. (1975, Fall). Intervention techniques and Asian American identity: The problem of alienation and self-esteem. *International Mental Health Research Newsletter, 17,* 2-4.

The author reports on the group encounter method to help 17 Americans with different Asian ethnic backgrounds to reduce feelings of alienation from American society and to enhance self-esteem. It is recommended both that the educational community become more therapeutic and that the therapeutic community become more aware of cultural behavior.

21

Family Ethnicity

A Challenge for the Future

HARRIETTE PIPES McADOO

The United States is now at a point in history where it can no longer be blind to the ethnic groups, particularly those of color, that are steadily growing in its midst. Now, more than one American in four can claim nonwhite or Hispanic ancestry (Rix, 1990). If present trends continue until the end of the twentieth century—increases due to immigration and birthrates—the Asian American presence will have increased by 22%, the Hispanic American presence by 21%, African Americans by 12%, and Americans of European descent by only 2% (Henry, 1990). These dramatic changes will cause difficulties if no attempt is made to prepare all of us for this new reality in America. We will need to learn more about each other and to reach out and appreciate the diversity that we all bring to our shared future.

What Is Needed

Policies are needed on both national and local levels to ensure that members of ethnic groups are treated fairly at home, on the job, and in public accommodations.

Ethnic families are most seriously in need of services. They must be given the tools and insights to be able to work with prevailing assumptions, exclusions, and slights that may be their lot from those of the dominant groups. The dominant group has parallel needs that should be addressed. However, there is small hope that such service needs will be realized. One of the requisites of being in a powerful and dominant group is that one is not even aware of being in that position. It comes with the territory. Until one has an itch, one does not scratch. Until one feels the pain of exclusion, one will not seek to overcome exclusionary tactics in others.

Members of the dominant group can do much to promote the freedom of ethnic families, and there is much that only they can do. They understand the perceptions of the dominant group, and only they are able to make cultural translations. There is room for liberal persuasion in all groups.

The major tasks will fall to members of ethnic families. They will need to fight their own pain and then move on to fight for the right to opportunities for members of their families and other families of color.

Professional Tasks That Must Be Undertaken to Serve Ethnic Families

Professionals who work with diverse ethnic groups must have a clear understanding of their own ethnic identification. All of us are biased; it is part of the human condition. We tend to share the preconceptions inherent in our own group experiences. We are often unaware of these preconceptions, for they become part of our consciousness before we are even aware of them. They are passed on to us with our mothers' milk. Inherent also are the preconceptions we carry that are part of the society's view of the world, or our interpretation of how persons in powerful positions perceive others. Our interpretations of the bias of the powerful group within our own culture may be even further distorted through the perceptions of a person who is part of neither group. As Kumabe, Nishida, and Hepworth (1985) have stated, professionals, as well as clients, are repositories of their own ethnic, occupational, religious, and racial subcultures. They are the repositories of the mainstream culture as well. African Americans may perceive Asian Americans from the context of their own culture, but within that perception is also the image of how African Americans feel white Americans perceive them. All of these may be out of concert with the way Asian Americans feel or really are. These perceptions may never be checked for accuracy. They are not open for verification. But they become part of the whole view of a given group, and biases and misperceptions continue on and on.

We are not culture free or value free as individuals. Yet, as members of the helping professions, we mistakenly think that we can handle ourselves in ways that nullify our own biases. When asked to intervene within the ethnic system of a family, we will often find that a great deal of "mental garbage" enters into the picture. Professionals' visions of who we are and our view of who the clients are may clash.

Before we can develop services that are appropriate for clients from ethnic groups, helping professionals must develop our awareness of our own ethnic heritages and cultural fabrics. This work on self-awareness is a continuous and ongoing process. The development of our own cultural awareness and understanding is not an easy task. It is never completed, for interpretations will continue to arise that will have cultural or ethnic connotations that may interfere with the process of providing services to clients.

References

Ablon, J. (1964). Relocated American Indians in the San Francisco Bay Area: Social interaction and Indian identity. *Human Organization, 23,* 296-304.

Ackerman, L. A. (1971). Marital instability and juvenile delinquency among the Nez Perces. *American Anthropologist, 73,* 595-603.

Adams, B. N. (1968). *Kinship in an urban setting.* Chicago: Markham.

Adams, R. (1937). *Interracial marriage in Hawaii.* New York: Macmillan.

Alba, R., & Golden, R. M. (1986). Patterns of ethnic marriage in the United States. *Social Forces, 65,* 202-223.

Allen, W. R. (1978a). Black family research in the United States: A review, assessment, and extension. *Journal of Comparative Family Studies, 9,* 167-189.

Allen, W. R. (1978b). The search for applicable theories of Black family life. *Journal of Marriage and the Family, 40,* 117-129.

Allen, W. R. (1981). Moms, dads, and boys: Race and sex differences in the socialization of male children. In L. Gary (Ed.), *Black men.* Beverly Hills, CA: Sage.

Alvarez, R. (1973). The psycho-historical and socio-economic development of the Chicano community in the United States. *Social Science Quarterly, 53,* 920-942.

Alvirez, D. (1981). Socioeconomic patterns and diversity among Hispanics. *Research Bulletin, 4,* 11-14.

Alvirez, D., & Bean, F. (1976). The Mexican American family. In C. H. Mindel & R. W. Habenstein (Eds.), *Ethnic families in America: Patterns and variations.* New York: Elsevier.

Alvirez, D., Bean, F., & Williams, D. (1981). The Mexican-American family. In C. H. Mindel & R. W. Habenstein (Eds.), *Ethnic families in America: Patterns and variations* (2nd ed., pp. 269-292). New York: Elsevier.

Anderson, E. (1989). Sex codes and family life among poor inner-city youth. *Annals of the American Academy of Political and Social Science, 501,* 59-78.

336   Family Ethnicity

Andrade, S. (1982). Social science stereotypes of the Mexican American woman: Policy implications for research. *Hispanic Journal of Behavioral Science, 4,* 223-243.

Andrews, F. M., Morgan, J. N., Sonquist, J. A., & Klem, L. (1973). *Multiple classification analysis.* Ann Arbor: University of Michigan, Institute for Social Research.

Applebome, P. (1988, January 3). Amnesty requests by aliens decline. *New York Times,* pp. 11, 12Y.

Araji, S. K. (1977). Husbands' and wives' attitude-behavior congruence on family roles. *Journal of Marriage and the Family, 39,* 302-320.

Arce, C. (1982, March). Maintaining a group culture. *ISR Newsletter.*

Aschenbrenner, J. (1973). Extended families among Black Americans. *Journal of Comparative Family Studies, 4,* 257-268.

Aschenbrenner, J. (1975). *Lifelines: Black families in Chicago.* New York: Holt, Rinehart & Winston.

Asian-Americans: A "model minority." (1982, December 6). *Newsweek,* pp. 39-42, 51.

Association on American Indian Affairs. (1974). The destruction of Indian families. In Association on American Indian Affairs, *Indian family defense.* New York: Author.

Attenave, C. L. (1977). The wasted strengths of Indian families. In S. Unger (Ed.), *The destruction of American Indian families.* New York: Association on American Indian Affairs.

Axelson, L. (1963). Marital adjustment and marital role definitions of husbands and working and non-working wives. *Journal of Marriage and the Family, 25,* 189-195.

Aylesworth, I. S., Ossorio, P. G., & Osaki, I. T. (1980). Stress and mental health among Vietnamese in the United States. In R. Endo, S. Sue, & N. Wagner (Eds.), *Asian-Americans: Social and psychological perspectives* (Vol. 2). Palo Alto, CA: Science & Behavior.

Baca Zinn, M. (1975). Political familism: Toward sex role equality in Chicano families. *Aztlan: Chicano Journal of the Social Sciences and the Arts, 6,* 13-26.

Baca Zinn, M. (1980). Employment and education of Mexican-American women: The interplay of modernity and ethnicity in eight families. *Harvard Educational Review, 50,* 47-62.

Baca Zinn, M. (Ed.). (1982, April). Social science research on Chicanos: A symposium [Special issue]. *Social Science Journal, 19,* 1-8.

Bach, R. L., Bach, J. B., & Triplett, T. (1981-1982). The flotilla "entrants": The latest and most controversial. *Cuban Studies/Estudios Cubanos, 11-12.*

Badie, B., & Birnbaum, P. (1983). *The sociology of the state.* Chicago: University of Chicago Press.

Baird, D. W. (1974). *The Chickasaw people.* Phoenix, AZ: Indian Tribal Series.

Baird, D. W. (1979). Peter Pitchlynn and the reconstruction of the Choctaw Republic. In H. G. Jordan & T. M. Halen (Eds.), *Indian leaders: Oklahoma's first statesmen* (pp. 12-28). Oklahoma City: Oklahoma Historical Society.

Barnett, L. D. (1963). Interracial marriage in California. *Marriage and Family Living, 25,* 424-427.

Barnett, L. D. (1975). Interracial marriage in California. In D. Wilkinson (Ed.), *Black male/white female: Perspectives on interracial marriage and courtship.* Morristown, NJ: General Learning.

Barry, W. A. (1970). Marriage research and conflict: An integrative view. *Psychological Bulletin, 73,* 41-54.

Bartz, K., & Levine, E. (1978). Childrearing by Black parents: A description and comparison of Anglo and Chicano parents. *Journal of Marriage and the Family, 40,* 709-719.

Baruch, G. K., & Barnett, R. C. (1986). Consequences of fathers' participation in family work: Parents, role strain and well-being. *Journal of Personality and Social Psychology, 51,* 983-992.

Baumrind, D. (1971). Current patterns of parental authority. *Developmental Psychological Monographs, 11,* Part 2, 1-103.

Baumrind, D. (1975). *Early socialization and the discipline controversy.* Morristown, NJ: General Learning.

Baumrind, D. (1978). Parental disciplinary patterns and social competence in children. *Youth & Society, 9,* 239-276.

Bean, F. D., & Bradshaw, B. (1970). Intermarriage between persons of Spanish and non-Spanish surname: Changes from the mid-nineteenth to the mid-twentieth century. *Social Science Quarterly, 51,* 389-395.

Bean, F. D., Curtis, R., & Marcum, J. (1977). Families and marital status among Mexican Americans. *Journal of Marriage and the Family, 39,* 759-767.

Bean, F. D., & Tienda, M. (1988). *The Hispanic population of the United States in the 1980's.* New York: Russell Sage.

Becerra, R. M. (1988). The Mexican American family. In C. H. Mindel, R. W. Habenstein, & R. Wright (Eds.), *Ethnic families in America: Patterns and variations* (3rd ed. pp. 141-159). New York: Elsevier.

Beigel, H. G. (1975). Problems and motives in interracial relationships. In D. Wilkinson (Ed.), *Black male/white female: Perspectives on interracial marriage and courtship* (pp. 67-87). Morristown, NJ: General Learning.

Beiser, M. (1974). A hazard to mental health: Indian boarding schools. *American Journal of Psychiatry, 131,* 305-306.

Bellah, R. N., Madsen, R., Sullivan, W. M., Swidler, A., & Tipton, S. M. (1985). *Habits of the heart: Individualism and commitment in American life.* Berkeley: University of California Press.

Benman-Gibson, M. (1984, November-December). Erik Erikson and the "ethics of survival." *Harvard Magazine,* pp. 59-64.

Berk, B., & Hirata, L. C. (1972). Mental illness among the Chinese: Myth or reality. *Journal of Social Issues, 29,* 149-166.

Bernal, G. (1982). Cuban families. In M. McGoldrick, J. K. Pearce, & J. Giordano (Eds.), *Ethnicity and family therapy* (pp. 186-207). New York: Guilford.

Bernard, J. (1966). *Marriage and family among Negroes.* Englewood Cliffs, NJ: Prentice-Hall.

Berry, B. (1958). *Race and ethnic relations: The interaction of ethnic and racial groups.* Boston: Houghton Mifflin.

Billingsley, A. (1968). *Black families in white America.* Englewood Cliffs, NJ: Prentice-Hall.

Billingsley, A. (1970). Black families and white social science. *Journal of Social Issues, 26,* 127-142.

Billingsley, A., & Greene, M. C. (1974). Family life among the free Black population in the 18th century. *Journal of Social and Behavioral Sciences, 20,* 1-17.

Bird, G. B. (1972). *The Cheyenne Indians: Their history and ways of life* (Vol. 2). Lincoln: University of Nebraska Press.

Blackwell, J. E. (1975). The Black family in American society. In J. E. Blackwell (Ed.), *The Black community: Diversity and unity.* New York: Dodd, Mead.

338   Family Ethnicity

Blackwell, J. E. (Ed.). (1985). *The Black community: Diversity and unity* (2nd ed.). New York: Harper & Row.

Blanchard, E. L. (1980). Organizing American Indian women. In *Conference on the Educational and Occupational Needs of American Indian Women.* Washington, DC: U.S. Department of Education, National Institute of Education.

Blanchard, J. D., & Warren, R. L. (1975). Role stress of dormitory aides at an off-reservation boarding school. *Human Organization, 34,* 41-49.

Blassingame, J. W. (1972). *The slave community.* New York: Oxford University Press.

Blea, I. I. (1992). *La Chicana and the intersection of race, class and gender.* New York: Praeger.

Blood, R. O., & Wolfe, D. (1960). *Husbands and wives.* New York: Free Press.

Blumenthal, W. H. (1976). *American Indians dispossessed.* New York: Arno.

Boggs, S. T. (1953). Cultural change and the personality of Ojibwa children. *American Anthropologist, 60,* 47-58.

Bonacich, E. (1973). A theory of middleman minorities. *American Sociological Review, 38,* 583-594.

Bossu, J. B. (1962). *Travels in the interior of North America, 1751-1762.* Norman: University of Oklahoma Press.

Boswell, T. D., & Curtis, J. R. (1984). *The Cuban American experience: Culture, images, perspectives.* Totowa, NJ: Rowman & Allanheld.

Bowen, G. L., & Orthner, D. K. (1983). Sex role congruency and marital quality. *Journal of Marriage and the Family, 45,* 223-230.

Bowman, P. J. (1983). Significant involvement and functional relevance: Challenges to survey research. *Social Work Research, 19,* 21-26.

Bowman, P. J. (1984). A discouragement-centered approach to studying unemployment among Black youth: Hopelessness, attributions and psychological distress. *International Journal of Mental Health, 13,* 68-91.

Bowman, P. J. (1988). Post-industrial displacement and family role strains: Challenges to the Black family. In P. Voydanof & L. C. Majka (Eds.), *Families and economic distress* (pp. 75-97). Newbury Park, CA: Sage.

Bowman, P. J. (1989). Research perspectives on Black men: Role strain and adaptation across the adult life cycle. In R. L. Jones (Ed.), *Black adult development and aging* (pp. 117-150). Berkeley, CA: Cobbs & Henry.

Bowman, P. J. (1990a). The adolescent to adult transition: Discouragement among jobless Black youth. In V. C. McLoyd & C. Flanagan (Eds.), *New directions in child development: Responses to economic crisis* (pp. 87-105). San Francisco: Jossey-Bass.

Bowman, P. J. (1990b). *Black men as family providers: Role strain, coping resources and life happiness. The African American experience.* Detroit, MI: Wayne State University Press.

Bowman, P. J. (1990c). Coping with provider role strain: Cultural resources among Black husband-fathers. *Journal of Black Psychology, 16,* 1-22.

Bowman, P. J. (in press). Toward a cognitive adaptation theory of role strain: Relevance of research on Black fathers. In R. L. Jones (Ed.), *Advances in Black psychology* (Vol. 2). Berkeley, CA: Cobbs & Henry.

Bowman, P. J., & Howard, C. S. (1985). Race-related socialization, motivation and academic achievement: A study of Black youth in three-generation families. *Journal of the American Academy of Child Psychiatry, 24,* 134-141.

Bowman, P. J., Jackson, J. S., Hatchett, S., & Gurin, G. (1982, Autumn). Joblessness and discouragement among Black Americans. *Economic Outlook U.S.A.*, pp. 85-88.

Bowman, P. J., & Sanders, R. (1989). Black unmarried fathers across the life cycle. In J. L. McAdoo (Ed.), *Empirical research in Black psychology* (pp. 9-15). Rockville, MD: National Institute of Mental Health.

Boyd, M. (1971). Oriental immigration. *International Migration Review, 5,* 48-61.

Boyd, M. (1974). The changing nature of Central and Southeast Asian immigration to the United States: 1961-1972. *International Migration Review, 8,* 489-519.

Boyd-Franklin, N. (1988). *Black families in therapy: A multisystems approach.* New York: Guilford.

Boyer, R. M. (1964). The matrifocal family among the Mescaleroi: Additional data. *American Anthropologist, 66,* 593-602.

Brightman, L. (1971). Mental genocide: Some notes on federal schools for Indians. In *Inequality of education* (pp. 15-19). Cambridge, MA: Harvard University, Center for Law and Education.

Bronfenbrenner, U. (1982, November). *The changing family in a changing world: America first?* Paper presented at UNESCO international symposium, Children and Families in a Changing World, Munich.

Brower, I. C. (1981). Counseling Vietnamese. In *Bridging cultures: Southeast Asian refugees in America* (pp. 224-240). Los Angeles: Asian American Community Mental Health Training Center.

Brown, D. (1970). *Bury my heart at Wounded Knee: An Indian history of the American West.* New York: Holt, Rinehart & Winston.

Brown, J. (1970). Economic organization and the position of women among the Iroquois. *Ethnohistory, 17,* 151-167.

Bullock, P. (Ed.). (1978). *Minorities in the labor market: American Indians, Asian Americans, Blacks, and Chicanos.* Los Angeles: University of California, Industrial Relations Institute.

Burgess, E. W., & Wallin, P. (1965). Factors in broken engagement. In R. S. Cavan (Ed.), *Marriage and the family in the modern world* (pp. 172-184). New York: Crowell.

Buriel, R. (1981). The relation of Anglo and Mexican-American children's locus of control beliefs to parents' and teachers' socialization practices. *Child Development, 52,* 104-113.

Burke, R. J., & Weir, T. (1976). Relationship of wife's employment status to husband, wife, and pair satisfaction and marital performance. *Journal of Marriage and the Family, 38,* 279-287.

Burma, J. (1963). Interethnic marriage in Los Angeles, 1948-1959. *Social Forces, 42,* 156-165.

Burton, R., & Whiting, J. (1961). The absent father and cross sex identity. *Merrill-Palmer Quarterly, 7,* 85-95.

Buttinger, J. (1958). *The smaller dragon.* New York: Praeger.

Byler, W. (1977). The destruction of American Indian families. In S. Unger (Ed.), *The destruction of American Indian families* (pp. 1-11). New York: Association on American Indian Affairs.

Byler, W., Deloria, S., & Gurwitt, A. (1974). American Indians and welfare: The problem of child adoption. *Current*, pp. 30-37.

Cabeza de Baca, F. (1972). The pioneer women. In L. Valdez & S. Steiner (Eds.), *Aztlan: An anthology of Mexican American literature* (pp. 260-265). New York: Random House.

Cabezas, A. (1977). Evidence for the low mobility of Asian Americans in the labor market. In P. Bullock (Ed.), *Minorities in the labor market*. Los Angeles: University of California, Institute of Industrial Relations.

Cade, T. (Ed.). (1970). *The Black woman: An anthology*. New York: New American Library.

Canino, I. A., & Canino, G. (1980). Impact of stress on the Puerto Rican family: Treatment considerations. *American Journal of Orthopsychiatry, 50,* 535-541.

Canino, I. A., Earley, B. F., & Rogler, I. H. (1980). *The Puerto Rican child in New York City: Stress and mental health.* Bronx, NY: Hispanic Research Center.

Caplan, N., Whitmore, J. K., & Bui, Q. L. (1985). *Southeast Asian refugee self-sufficiency study* (Report prepared for the Office of Refugee Resettlement). Ann Arbor: University of Michigan, Institute for Social Research.

Cardes, C. (1983, November). Spanish research comes alive in Miami. *APA Monitor.*

Carrillo-Beron, C. (1974). *Traditional family ideology in relation to locus of control: A comparison of Chicano and Anglo women.* San Francisco: R. & E. Research Associates.

Carter, H., & Glick, P. C. (1976). *Marriage and divorce: A social and economic study.* Cambridge, MA: Harvard University Press.

Castenada, A., McCandless, B., & Palermo, D. (1956). The children's form of the manifest anxiety scale. *Child Development, 27,* 317-322.

Casuso, J., & Camacho, E. (1985). *Hispanics in Chicago.* Chicago: Chicago Reporter and the Center for Community Research Assistance, Community Renewal Society.

Cazenave, N. A. (1979). Middle-income Black fathers: An analysis of the provider role. *Family Coordinator, 28,* 583-593.

Cazenave, N. A. (1980). Alternate intimacy, marriage, and family life styles among low-income Black Americans. *Alternative Lifestyles, 3,* 425-444.

Cazenave, N. A. (1981). Black men in America: The quest for "manhood." In H. P. McAdoo (Ed.), *Black families* (pp. 176-185). Beverly Hills, CA: Sage.

Centers, R. B., Raven, H., & Rodrigues, A. (1971). Conjugal power structure: A reexamination. *American Sociological Review, 36,* 264-278.

Cerroni-Long, M. (1984). Marrying out: Socio-cultural and psychological implications of intermarriage. *Journal of Comparative Family Studies, 16,* 25-46.

Chai, A. (1978). A picture bride from Korea: The life history of a Korean American woman in Hawaii. *Bridge Magazine, 6*(4), 37-41.

Chang, S. Y. (1973). China or Taiwan: The political crisis of the Chinese intellectual. *Amerasia Journal, 2,* 47-81.

Cheng, C. K., & Yamamura, D. S. (1957). Interracial marriage and divorce in Hawaii. *Social Forces, 36,* 377-384.

Cheung, L., Cho, E. R., Lum, D., Tank, T. Y., & Yau, H. B. (1980). The Chinese elderly and family structures: Implications for health care. *Public Health Reports, 95,* 491-495.

Chilman, C. (1968). Fertility and poverty in the United States. *Journal of Marriage and the Family, 30,* 207-227.

Chilman, C. (1983). *Adolescent sexuality in a changing American society: Social and psychological perspectives for human services professions.* New York: John Wiley.

Chilman, C. (1988). Public policies and families with economic problems. In C. Chilman, F. Cox, & E. Nunnally (Eds.), *Families in trouble* (Vol. 1). Newbury Park, CA: Sage.

Chiswick, B. R. (1982). The economic progress of immigrants: Some apparently universal patterns. In B. R. Chiswick (Ed.), *The gateway* (pp. 119-158). Washington, DC: American Enterprise Institute for Public Policy Research.

Chiu, T.-T. (1961). *Law and society in traditional China.* Paris: Mouton.

Choy, B. Y. (1979). *Koreans in America.* Chicago: Nelson-Hall.

Clark, M., & Anderson, B. (1967). *Culture and aging.* Springfield, IL: Charles C Thomas.

Cohen, A. (1969). *Custom and politics in urban Africa.* Berkeley: University of California Press.

Cohen, L. (1977). The female factor in resettlement. *Society, 14*(6), 27-30.

Cohn, R. M. (1978). The effects of employment status change on self-attitudes. *Social Psychology, 41,* 81-93.

Cohon, J. D., Jr. (1981). Psychological adaptation and dysfunction among refugees. *International Migration Review, 15,* 255-275.

Cole, J. (1990, May 30). Melange: Commencement 1990. *Chronicle of Higher Education,* p. B2.

Cole, J. (1992). Commonalities and differences. In M. V. Andersen & P. Collins (Eds.), *Race, class and gender.* Belmont, CA: Wadsworth.

Collado, E. (1980, January). Hispanic intermarriage in New York City. *Research Bulletin, 3,* 5-6.

Compton, B., & Galaway, B. (1989). *Social work processes* (4th ed.). Belmont, CA: Wadsworth.

Conner, J. (1974). Acculturation and family continuities in three generations of Japanese Americans. *Journal of Marriage and Family, 36,* 159-165.

Conner, J. (1977). *Tradition and change in three generations of Japanese Americans.* Chicago: Nelson-Hall.

Cooney, R. S., Rogler, L. H., Hurrer, R., & Ortiz, V. (1982). Decision making in Puerto Rican families. *Journal of Marriage and the Family, 44,* 621-631.

Cooney, R. S., Rogler, L. H., & Schroeder, E. (1980). Puerto Rican fertility: An examination of social characteristics, assimilation, and minority status variables. *Research Bulletin, 3* 3-4.

Coopersmith, S. (1967). *The antecedents of self-esteem.* San Francisco: W. H. Freeman.

Cordova, D. (1980). Educational alternatives for Asian-Pacific women. In *Conference on the Educational and Occupational Needs of Asian-Pacific-American Women,* pp. 135-156. Washington, DC: U.S. Department of Education, National Institute of Education.

Correa, G. (1980). Puerto Rican women in education and potential impact on occupational patterns. In *Conference on the Educational and Occupational Needs of Hispanic Women.* Washington, DC: U.S. Department of Education, National Institute of Education.

Cortes, C. (1980). *The Cuban experience in the United States.* New York: Arno.

Council on Social Work Education, Commission on Accreditation. (1984). *Section 11, Evaluation Standard 13, cultural diversity.* New York: Author.

Crester, G. A., & Leon, J. (1982). Intermarriage in the U.S.: An overview of theory and research. *Marriage and Family Review, 5,* 3-15.

Cromwell, R., Corrales, R., & Torsiella, P. (1973). Normative patterns of marital decision-making power and influence in Mexico and the U.S.A.: A partial test of resource and ideology theory. *Journal of Comparative Family Studies, 4,* 177-196.

Cromwell, V. L., & Cromwell, R. E. (1978). Perceived dominance in decision making and conflict resolution among Anglo, Black, and Chicano couples. *Journal of Marriage and the Family, 40,* 749-759.

Cross, W. E. (1985). Black identity: Rediscovering the distinction between personal identity and reference group orientation. In M. B. Spencer, G. K. Brookins, & W. R.

Allen (Eds.), *Beginnings: The social and affective development of Black children.* Hillsdale, NJ: Lawrence Erlbaum.

Cross, W. E. (1987). A two-factor theory of Black identity: Implications for the study of identity development in minority children. In J. Phinney & M. J. Rotheram (Eds.), *Children's ethnic socialization, pluralism, and development* (pp. 117-133). Newbury Park, CA: Sage.

Cross, W. E. (1990). *Shades of Black: Diversity in African-American identity.* Philadelphia: Temple University Press.

Cuellar, I., Harris, L., & Jasso, R. (1980). An acculturation scale for Mexican American normal and clinical populations. *Hispanic Journal of the Behavioral Sciences, 2,* 199-217.

Curran, J. W., Jaffe, H. W., Hardy, A. M., Morgan, W. M., Selik, R. M., & Dondero, T. J. (1988). Epidemiology of HIV infection and AIDS in the United States. *Science, 239,* 610-616.

Daly, M. (1982, December 20). Making it. *New York,* pp. 32-38.

Darcy, N. (1952). The performance of bilingual Puerto Rican children on verbal and on non-language tests of intelligence. *Journal of Educational Research, 45,* 499-506.

David, H. P. (1970). Involuntary international migration: Adaptation of refugees. In E. B. Brody (Ed.), *Behavior in new environments: Adaptation of migration populations.* Beverly Hills, CA: Sage.

Davis, L. E., & Proctor, E. K. (1989). *Race, gender, and class: Guidelines for practice with individuals, families, and groups.* Englewood Cliffs, NJ: Prentice-Hall.

Davis, M. (1961). Adoptive placement of American Indian children with non-Indian families: Part II. One agency's approach to the Indian adoption project. *Child Welfare, 40,* 12-15.

Debo, A. (1972). *The rise and fall of the Choctaw republic.* Norman: University of Oklahoma Press.

Debo, A. (1979). *The road to disappearance: A history of the Creek.* Norman: University of Oklahoma Press.

DeGeyndt, W. (1973). Health behavior and health needs in urban Indians in Minneapolis. *Health Service Reports, 33,* 360-366.

Delgado, M. (1980, September). Providing child care for Hispanic families. *Young Children, 35,* 26-32.

Delgado, M. (1987). Puerto Ricans. In *Encyclopedia of social work* (Vol. 2, pp. 427-432). Silver Spring, MD: National Association of Social Workers.

Delgado, M., & Delgado, D. (1982). Natural support systems: Source of strength in Hispanic communities. *Social Work, 27,* 83-90.

Delgado, S. (1971). Chicana: The forgotten woman. *Regeneración, 2,* 2-4.

Deloria, V. (1970). *Custer died for your sins: An Indian manifesto.* New York: Avon.

Deloria, V. (1978). Kinship with the world. *Journal of Current Social Issues, 15,* 19-21.

Demerson, B. A. (1991). Family life on Wadmalaw Island. In M. S. Twining & K. Baird (Eds.), *Sea Island roots: African presence in the Carolinas and Georgia* (pp. 57-87). Trenton, NJ: Africa World Press.

de Rodriguez, L. V. (1973). Social work practice in Puerto Rico. *Social Work, 18,* 32-40.

Desbarats, J. (1986). Ethnic differences in adaptation: Sino-Vietnamese refugees in the United States. *International Migration Review, 20,* 405-427.

de Silva, E. (1981). *Survival and adjustment skills to the new culture: Working with Hispanic women who have settled in the United States.* Paper presented at the National Conference on Social Welfare, San Francisco.

Devore, W., & Schlesinger, E. G. (1987). *Ethnic sensitive social work practice* (2nd ed.). Columbus, OH: Merrill.

DeVos, G. (1973). *Personality patterns and problems of adjustment in American-Japanese intercultural marriages.* Taiwan: The Orient Cultural Service.

Diaz, G. M. (Ed.). (1980). *Evaluation and identification of policy issues in the Cuban community.* Miami: National Cuban Planning Council.

Diaz-Guerrero, R. (1955). Neurosis and the Mexican family structure. *American Journal of Psychiatry, 112,* 411-417.

Dlugokinski, E., & Kramer, L. (1974). A system of neglect: Indian boarding schools. *American Journal of Psychiatry, 131,* 670-673.

Dobbins, M. P., & Mulligan, J. (1980). Black matriarchy: Transforming a myth of racism into a class model. *Journal of Comparative Family Studies, 11,* 195-217.

Doben, D. (1959). Religious practice and marital patterns in Puerto Rico. *American Catholic Sociological Review, 20,* 203-219.

Dorsey, C. (1984). *The Indian Child Welfare Act and law affecting Indian juveniles.* Boulder, CO: Native American Rights Fund.

Douglas, M. (1982, Winter). Effects of modernization on religious changes. *Daedalus, 3-4.*

Du Bois, W. E. B. (1903). *Souls of Black folk.* Chicago: McClurg.

Du Bois, W. E. B. (1969). *The Negro American family.* New York: New American Library. (Original work published 1908)

Dulles, F. (1959). *The United States since 1865.* Ann Arbor: University of Michigan Press.

Durkheim, E. (1986). *Durkheim on politics of the state.* Stanford, CA: Stanford University Press.

Durrett, M. E., O'Bryant, S., & Pennebaker, J. W. (1975). Child-rearing reports of white, Black, and Mexican-American families. *Developmental Psychology, 11,* 871.

Earl, L., & Lohman, M. (1978). Absent fathers and Black male children. *Social Work, 23,* 413-415.

Education Commission of the States & State Higher Education Executive Officers. (1987, July). *Focus on minorities: Trends in higher education participation and success.* Denver, CO: Author.

Edwards, O. I. (1970). Patterns of residential segregation within a metropolitan ghetto. *Demography, 7*(2), 185-192.

Efron, S. (1990, April 29). Few Viet exiles find U.S. riches. *Los Angeles Times,* pp. A1, A34-A35.

Eisenstadt, S. N. (1954). *The absorption of immigrants.* London: Routledge & Kegan Paul.

Eisenstadt, S. N. (1956). *From generation to generation: Age groups and social structure.* New York: Free Press.

Elder, G. (1974). *Children of the Great Depression: Social change in life experience.* Chicago: University of Chicago Press.

Elderly Southeast Asian refugees: Still strangers in a strange land. (1987, May 15). *Refugee Reports, 8*(5), 1-7.

Endo, R. (1980). Social science and historical materials on the Asian American experience. In R. Endo, S. Sue, & N. Wagner (Eds.), *Asian-Americans: Social and psychological perspectives* (Vol. 2). Palo Alto, CA: Science & Behavior.

Endo, R., Sue, S., & Wagner, N. (Eds.). (1980). *Asian-Americans: Social and psychological perspectives* (Vol. 2). Palo Alto, CA: Science & Behavior.

Erikson, E. (1950). *Childhood and society.* New York: W. W. Norton.

Estevez, G. A. (1983). Resettling the Cuban refugees in New Jersey. *Migration Today,* *11*(4-5), 35-42.

Estrada, L. (1987). Hispanics. In *Encyclopedia of social work* (Vol. 1, pp. 730-739). Silver Spring, MD: National Association of Social Workers.

Evans, B. J., & Whitfield, J. R. (1988). *Black males in the United States: An annotated bibliography from 1967 to 1987.* Washington, DC: American Psychological Association.

Fahlman, L. (1983). Culture conflict in the classroom. In E. Waugh (Ed.), *The Muslim community in North America* (pp. 202-211). Edmonton: University of Alberta Press.

Falicov, C. (1982). Mexican families. In M. McGoldrick, J. K. Pearce, & J. Giordano (Eds.), *Ethnicity and family therapy* (pp. 134-163). New York: Guilford.

Falicov, C., & Karrer, B. (1980). Cultural variations in the family life cycle: The Mexican American family. In E. Carter & R. McGoldrick (Eds.), *The family life cycle* (pp. 383-425). New York: Gardner.

Family Planning Perspectives. (1983). Vol. 15(4), 197.

Farley, R., & Allen, W. R. (1987). *The color line and the quality of American life.* New York: Russell Sage.

Farris, C. (1976). Indian children: The struggle for survival. *Social Work, 21,* 386-389.

Fauriol, G. (1984, May-June). U.S. immigration policy and the national interest. *Humanist.*

Feagin, J. (1968). The kinship ties of Negro urbanites. *Social Science Quarterly, 69,* 600-655.

Fernandez-Marina, R., Maldonado Sierra, E., & Trent, R. (1958). Three basic themes in Mexican and Puerto Rican family values. *Journal of Social Psychology, 48,* 167-181.

Fillmore, L. W., & Cheong, J. (1980). The early socialization of Asian-American female children. In *Conference on the Educational and Occupational Needs of Asian-Pacific-American Women.* Washington, DC: U.S. Department of Education, National Institute of Education.

Finnan, C. R., & Cooperstein, R. (1983). *Southeast Asian refugee resettlement at the local level* (Office of Refugee Resettlement Report). Menlo Park, CA: SRI International.

Fisher, R. A. (1974). A study of non-intellectual attributes of children in a first grade bilingual-bicultural program. *Journal of Educational Research, 67,* 323-328.

Fitzpatrick, J. (1971). *Puerto Rican Americans: The meaning of migration to the mainland.* Englewood Cliffs, NJ: Prentice-Hall.

Fitzpatrick, J. (1981). The Puerto Rican family. In C. H. Mindel & R. W. Habenstein (Eds.), *Ethnic families in America: Patterns and variations* (2nd ed., pp. 189-214). New York: Elsevier.

Fitzpatrick, J. P., & Gurak, D. T. (1979). *Hispanic intermarriage in New York City.* Bronx, NY: Hispanic Research Center.

Fong, P., & Cabezas, A. (1980). Economic and employment status of Asian-Pacific women. In *Conference on the Educational and Occupational Needs of Asian-Pacific-American women* (pp. 255-321). Washington, DC: U.S. Department of Education, National Institute of Education.

Fortes, M. (1949). *The web of kinship.* London: Oxford University Press.

Fox, D., & Jordan, V. (1973). Racial preference and identification of Black, American Chinese, and white children. *Genetic Psychology Monographs, 88,* 229-286.

Fradd, S. (1983). Cubans to Cuban Americans: Assimilation in the United States. *Migration Today, 11*(4-5), 34-41.

Frazier, E. F. (1939). *The Negro family in the United States.* Chicago: University of Chicago Press.

Frazier, E. F. (1968). *The free Negro family.* New York: Arno.

Friedrich, O., Church, G., Doerner, W., Brew, D., & Urquhart, S. (1985, July 8). Immigrants. *Time*, pp. 24-33.

Frisbie, W. (1986). Variations in patterns of marital instability among Hispanics. *Journal of Marriage and Family Therapy, 48,* 99-106.

Fujii, S. (1980a). Elderly Asian-Americans and use of public services. In R. Endo, S. Sue, & N. Wagner (Eds.), *Asian-Americans: Social and psychological perspectives* (Vol. 2). Palo Alto, CA: Science & Behavior.

Fujii, S. (1980b). Elderly Pacific Island and Asian-American women: A framework for understanding. In *Conference on the Educational and Occupational Needs of Asian-Pacific-American Women* (pp. 343-357). Washington, DC: U.S. Department of Education, National Institute of Education.

García, F. (1980). The cult of virginity. In *Conference on the Educational and Occupational Needs of Hispanic Women.* Washington, DC: U.S. Department of Education, National Institute of Education.

Garcia-Preto, N. (1982). Puerto Rican families. In M. McGoldrick, J. K. Pearce, & J. Giordano (Eds.), *Ethnicity and family therapy* (pp. 164-186). New York: Guilford.

Gary, L. E. (Ed.). (1981). *Black men.* Beverly Hills, CA: Sage.

Gibbs, J., Huang, L. N., & Associates. (1989). *Children of color: Psychological interventions with minority youth.* San Francisco: Jossey-Bass.

Gibson, G. (1985). *Prevention and the Mexican American elderly.* Paper presented at the annual meeting of the Gerontological Society on Aging, San Antonio, TX.

Gil, R. M. (1968). *The assimilation and problems of adjustment to the American culture of one hundred Cuban refugee adolescents.* Unpublished master's thesis, Fordham University, Bronx, NY.

Gil, R. M. (1983). Issues in the delivery of mental health services to Cuban entrants. *Migration Today, 11*(4-5), 43-48.

Gilfillan, J. (1901). The Ojibwe in Minnesota. In *Collections of the Minnesota Historical Society* (Vol. 9, pp. 1-116). St. Paul: Minnesota Historical Society.

Gillespie, D. L. (1971). Who has the power? The marital struggle. *Journal of Marriage and the Family, 33,* 445-457.

Gillian, D. (1990, June 7). On slang, prosecution's guilty. *Washington Post,* p. D3.

Glazer, N., & Moynihan, D. P. (1963). *Beyond the melting pot.* Cambridge: MIT Press.

Glazer, N., & Moynihan, D. P. (1975). *Beyond the melting pot* (3rd ed.). Cambridge: MIT Press.

Glick, P. C. (1981). A demographic picture of Black families. In H. P. McAdoo (Ed.), *Black families* (pp. 106-126). Beverly Hills, CA: Sage.

Glick, P. C. (1988). Demographic pictures of Black families. In H. P. McAdoo (Ed.), *Black families* (2nd ed., pp. 111-132). Newbury Park, CA: Sage.

Gold, S. J. (1985). *Refugee communities: Soviet Jews and Vietnamese in the San Francisco Bay Area.* Unpublished doctoral dissertation, University of California, Berkeley.

Gold, S. J. (1987). Dealing with frustration: A study of interactions between resettlement staff and refugees. In S. Morgan & E. Colson (Eds.), *People in upheaval* (pp. 108-128). New York: Center for Migration Studies.

Golden, J. (1975). Patterns of Negro-White intermarriage. In D. Wilkinson (Ed.), *Black male/white female: Perspectives on interracial marriage and courtship* (pp. 9-16). Morristown, NJ: General Learning.

Gonzales, S. (1980). La Chicana: An overview. In *Conference on the Educational and Occupational Needs of Hispanic Women*. Washington, DC: U.S. Department of Education, National Institute of Education.

Goode, W. J. (1960). A theory of role strain. *American Sociological Review, 11*, 483-496.

Goodluck, C. T. (1990). Mental health issues of Native American transracial adoptions. In P. Grabe (Ed.), *Adoption resources for mental health professionals* (pp. 215-230). New Brunswick, NJ: Transaction.

Goodman, M. (1964). *Race awareness in young children*. New York: Crowell-Collier.

Goodman, M. E., & Beman, A. (1971). Child's-eye-views of life in an urban barrio. In N. Wagner & M. Haug (Eds.), *Chicanos: Social and psychological perspectives*. St. Louis: C. V. Mosby.

Gordon, I. (1983). *The American family in social-historical perspective* (3rd ed.). New York: St. Martin's.

Gordon, L. W. (1982, April). *New data on the fertility of Southeast Asian refugees in the U.S.* Paper presented at the annual meeting of the Population Association of America, San Diego.

Gordon, L. W. (1987, May). *The missing children: Mortality and fertility in a Southeast Asian refugee population*. Paper presented at the annual meeting of the Population Association of America, Chicago.

Gordon, M. (1964). *Assimilation in American life*. New York: Oxford University Press.

Grant, G. (1983a). Immigrant family stability: Some preliminary thought. *Journal of Children in Contemporary Society, 15*, 27-37.

Grant, G. (1983b). Impact of immigration on the family and children. In M. Frank (Ed.), *Newcomers to the United States* (pp. 26-37). New York: Haworth.

Granzberg, G. (1973). The psychological integration of culture: A crosscultural study of Hopi type initiation rites. *Journal of Social Psychology, 90*, 3-7.

Greathouse, B., Gomez, R., & Wurster, S. (1988, January-April). An investigation of Black and Hispanic parents' locus of control, childrearing attitudes and practices and degree of involvement in Head Start. *Negro Educational Review, 39*(1-2), 4-17.

Grebler, L., Moore, J. W., & Guzman, R. (1970). *The Mexican American people: The nation's second largest minority*. New York: Free Press.

Grebler, L., Moore, J. W., & Guzman, R. (1973). The family: Variations in time and space. In L. Duran & H. Bernal (Eds.), *Introduction to Chicano studies: A reader*. New York: Macmillan.

Greely, A. (1981). *The Irish Americans*. New York: Harper & Row.

Green, H. (1983). Risks and attitudes associated with extra-cultural placements of American Indian children: A critical review. *Journal of the American Academy of Child Psychiatry, 22*, 63-67.

Green, M. D. (1982). *The politics of Indian removal: Creek government and society in crisis*. Lincoln: University of Nebraska Press.

Green, R. (1975). The Pocahontas perplex: The image of Indian women in American culture. *Massachusetts Review, 16*, 698-714.

Grey-Little, B. (1982). Marital quality and power processes among Black couples. *Journal of Marriage and the Family, 44*, 633-645.

Grichting, W. (1970). *The value system in Taiwan, 1970*. Taipei, Taiwan.

Griswold, D. L. (1975). *An assessment of the child-rearing information needs and attitudes of Anglo, Black and Mexican-American mothers*. Unpublished doctoral dissertation, Arizona State University.

Grossman, T. (1985). [Indian Child Welfare children's case review, American Indian Law Center, Albuquerque, NM]. Unpublished list of legal citations.

Gurak, D. T. (1981). Family structural diversity of Hispanic ethnic groups. *Research Bulletin, 4*, 6-10.

Gurak, D. T., & Fitzpatrick, J. P. (1978). Intermarriage patterns in the U.S.: Maximizing information from the U.S. Census Public Use Samples. *Review of Public Data Use, 6*, 333-343.

Gurak, D. T., & Rogler, L. (1980). Hispanic diversity in New York City. *Research Bulletin, 3*, 1-5.

Guthrie, G., & Jacobs, P. (1966). *Child rearing and personality in the Philippines.* University Park: Pennsylvania State University Press.

Gutman, H. (1965). *The Black family in slavery and freedom, 1760-1925.* New York: Pantheon.

Gutman, H. (1977). *The Black family in slavery and freedom, 1760-1925.* New York: Random House.

Haines, D., Rutherford, D., & Thomas, P. (1981). Family and community among Vietnamese refugees. *International Migration Review, 15*, 310-319.

Haley, A. (1976). *Roots: The saga of an American family.* Garden City, NY: Doubleday.

Hallowell, A. I. (1963). American Indians, white and Black: The phenomenon of trans-culturation. *Current Anthropology, 4*, 519-531.

Hamamsy, L. S. (1957). The role of women in a changing Navajo society. *American Anthropologist, 39*, 101-111.

Hamilton, M. (1973). The women of La Raza. In D. Moreno (Ed.), *La mujer—en pie de lucha* (pp. 90-105). Mexico City: Espina del Norte.

Hammerschlag, C. (1988). *The dancing healers.* New York: Harper & Row.

Hammond, J., & Enoch, J. R. (1976). Conjugal power relations among Black working-class families. *Journal of Black Studies, 7*, 107-133.

Handlin, O. (1951). *The uprooted: The epic story of the great migrations that made the American people.* New York: Grossett & Dunlap.

Hare, N. (1976). What Black intellectuals misunderstood about the Black family. *Black World, 20*, 4-14.

Harmsworth, H. (1965). Family structure on the Fort Hill Indian reservation. *Family Life Coordinator, 14*, 7-9.

Harris, L. (1980, May 26). Americans uneasy about U.S. policy on accepting Cuban Refugees. *ABC-Harris Survey, 2*(64).

Hawkes, G., & Taylor, M. (1975). Power structure in Mexican and Mexican-American farm labor families. *Journal of Marriage and the Family, 37*, 806-811.

Hays, W. C., & Mindel, C. H. (1973). Extended kinship relations in Black and white families. *Journal of Marriage and the Family, 35*, 51-56.

Heiss, J. (1975). *The case of the Black family: A sociological inquiry.* New York: Columbia University Press.

Henry, W. (1990, April 9). Beyond the melting pot. *Time*, pp. 28-31.

Hernandez, A. R. (1974). *The Cuban minority in the U.S.: Final report on the need identification and program evaluation.* Washington, DC: Cuban National Planning Council.

Herskovits, M. J. (1941). *The myth of the Negro past.* New York: Harper.

Hetherington, D. (1966). Effects of paternal absence on sex-typed behavior in Negro and white males. *Journal of Personality and Social Psychology, 4*, 87-91.

Hetherington, M., Cox, M., & Cox, R. (1978). The aftermath of divorce. In J. Stevens & M. Mathews (Eds.), *Mother-child, father-child relationships*. Washington, DC: National Association for the Education of Young Children.

Hickey, G. C. (1964). *Village in Vietnam*. New Haven, CT: Yale University Press.

Hicks, M. W., & Platt, M. (1970). Marital happiness and stability: A review of the research in the sixties. *Journal of Marriage and the Family, 32,* 553-574.

Hilger, I. M. (1951). *Chippewa child life and its cultural background* (Bulletin 146). Washington, DC: U.S. Bureau of American Ethnology.

Hilger, I. M. (1952). *Arapahoe child life and its cultural background* (Bulletin 148). Washington, DC: U.S. Bureau of American Ethnology.

Hill, R. B. (1972). *The strengths of Black families*. New York: Emerson Hall.

Hill, R. B. (1977). *Informal adoption among Black families*. Washington, DC: National Urban League.

Hirata, L. C. (1980). Social mobility of Asian women in America: A critical review. In *Conference on the Educational and Occupational Needs of Asian-Pacific-American Women*, pp. 323-341. Washington, DC: U.S. Department of Education, National Institute of Education.

Hogan, D. P. (1978). The variable order of events in the life course. *American Sociological Review, 43,* 573-586.

Homma-True, B. (1980). Mental health issues among Asian-American women. In *Conference on the Educational and Occupational Needs of Asian-Pacific-American Women*, pp. 65-87. Washington, DC: U.S. Department of Education, National Institute of Education.

Hong, L. K. (1976). Recent immigrants in the Chinese-American community: Issues of adaptations and impacts. *International Migration Review, 10,* 509-514.

Hong, S. (1982). Another look at marriages between Korean women and American servicemen. *Korean Journal, 22,* 21-30.

Hood, J. C. (1986). The provider role: Its meaning and measurement. *Journal of Marriage and the Family, 48,* 349-359.

Hopps, J. (1982). Oppression based on color. In J. Hopps (Ed.), Social work and people of color [Special issue]. *Social Work, 27,* 3-6.

Hostbjor, S. (1961). Social services to the Indian unmarried mother. *Child Welfare, 40,* 7-9.

Hsu, F. L. K. (1971). *Kinship and culture*. Chicago: Aldine.

Huang, L. (1976). The Chinese American family. In C. H. Mindel & R. W. Habenstein (Eds.), *Ethnic families in America: Patterns and variations*. New York: Elsevier.

Hunt, L., & Coller, R. (1956). Intermarriage and cultural change: A study of Philippine-American marriage. *Social Forces, 35,* 223-230.

Hunter, A. (1984). *Working wives and mothers: An investigation of the work decisions of Black women, 1900 to 1940*. Unpublished master's thesis, Cornell University, Ithaca, NY.

Hurh, W. M. (1990). The 1.5 generation: A paragon of Korean-American pluralism. *Korean Culture, 22,* 21-30.

Hwang, S.-S. (1990). The problems posed by immigrants married abroad on intermarriage research: The case of Asian Americans. *International Migration Review, 24,* 563-576.

Hyman, H. H., & Reed, J. S. (1969). Black matriarchy reconsidered: Evidence from secondary analysis of sample surveys. *Public Opinion Quarterly, 33,* 346-454.

Ikeda, K., Ball, H., & Yamamura, D. (1962). Ethnocultural factors in schizophrenia: The Japanese in Hawaii. *American Journal of Sociology, 68,* 242-248.

Ikels, C. (1980). The coming of age in Chinese society: Traditional patterns and contemporary Hong Kong. In C. L. Fry (Ed.), *Aging in culture and society* (pp. 80-100). Brooklyn, NY: J. F. Bergin.

Indians seek to rebury remains of ancestors. (1982, March 14). *New York Times*, p. A22.

Indochinese Community Center. (1983). *Entrepreneurship among Southeast Asian refugees*. Washington, DC: Office of Refugee Resettlement Report.

Indochinese Refugee Action Center. (1982). *Survey of refugee self-help initiatives*. Washington, DC: Author.

Indochinese Technical Assistance Project. (1981). *Indochinese mutual assistance association and resource directory*. Unpublished manuscript.

Ishizuka, K. (1978). *The elder Japanese*. San Diego: Campanile.

Jackson, J. (1972). Comparative life styles and family and friend relationships among older Black women. *Family Coordinator, 21*, 477-486.

Jackson, J. S. (Ed.). (1991). *Life in Black America*. Newbury Park, CA: Sage.

Jackson, J. S., & Gurin, G. (1987). *National survey of Black Americans, 1989-80* (Vols. 1-2). Ann Arbor: University of Michigan, Institute for Social Research.

Jackson, J. S., Tucker, M. B., & Bowman, P. J. (1990). Conceptual and methodological problems in survey research on Black Americans. In R. L. Jones (Ed.), *Advances in Black psychology* (Vol. 1). Berkeley, CA: Cobbs & Henry.

Jaco, D., & Wilber, G. (1975). Asian Americans in the labor market. *Monthly Labor Review, 98*, 33-38.

Jennings, J. (1947). Nutts trip to the Chickasaw country. *Journal of Mississippi History, 9*, 41-47.

Jewell, S. K. (1988). *Survival of the Black family: The institutional impacts of U.S. social policy*. New York: Praeger.

Jiménez-Vásquez, R. (1980). Some issues confronting Hispanic American women. In *Conference on the Educational and Occupational Needs of Hispanic Women*, pp. 213-249. Washington, DC: U.S. Department of Education, National Institute of Education.

Jimson, L. B. (1977). Parent and child relationships in law, and in Navajo custom. In S. Unger (Ed.), *The destruction of American Indian families*. New York: Association on American Indian Affairs.

Johnson, C. L. (1977). Interdependence, reciprocity and indebtedness: An analysis of Japanese American kinship relations. *Journal of Marriage and the Family, 39*, 351-363.

Johnson, C. S. (1934). *Shadow of the plantation*. Chicago: University of Chicago Press.

Jones, J. (1985). Fertility-related care. In H. P. McAdoo & T. Parkam (Eds.), *Services to young families* (pp. 167-206). Washington, DC: American Public Welfare Association.

Jones, R. (1980). *Black psychology*. New York: Harper & Row.

Jones, W. (1960). A critical study of bilingualism and nonverbal intelligence. *British Journal of Educational Psychology, 30*, 71-76.

JWK International Corporation. (1976). *Identification of problems in access to health services and health careers for Asian Americans* (Vol. 2) (Contract No. HRA-230-75-0193). Washington, DC: U.S. Department of Health, Education and Welfare, Office of Health Resources Opportunity.

Kagan, S., & Ender, P. B. (1975). Maternal response to success and failure of Anglo-American, Mexican-American, and Mexican children. *Child Development, 46*, 452-458.

Kahn, R. L., Wolfe, D. M., Quinn, R. P., Snoek, J. D., & Rosenthal, R. A. (1964). *Organizational stress: Studies in interrole conflict and ambiguity.* New York: John Wiley.

Kain, E. (1982). *The secret lives of spinsters.* Unpublished manuscript.

Kain, E. (1987). Trends in the demography of death. In H. Wass, F. M. Berardo, & R. A. Neimeyer (Eds.), *Dying: Facing the facts* (pp. 79-96). Washington, DC: Hemisphere.

Kalish, R., & Moriwaki, S. (1973). The world of the elderly Asian American. *Journal of Social Issues, 29,* 187-209.

Kalish, R., & Yuen, S. (1971). Americans of East Asian ancestry: Aging and the aged. *Gerontologist, 11,* 36-47.

Kamerman, S., & Kahn, A. (1978). *Family policy: Government and families in fourteen countries.* New York: Columbia University Press.

Kamerman, S., & Kahn, A. (1981). *Child care: Family benefits and working parents.* New York: Columbia University Press.

Kane, P., & Wilkinson, D. (1974). Survival strategies: Black women in *Ollie Miss* and *Cotton Comes to Harlem. Critique: Studies in Modern Fiction, 16,* 101-109.

Kaplan, C., & Van Valey, T. (1980).*Census '80: Continuing the factfinder tradition.* Washington, DC: U.S. Department of Commerce, Bureau of the Census.

Karpat, K. H. (1985). The Ottoman emigration to America. *International Journal of Middle Eastern Studies, 17,* 175-209.

Katz, P. A. (1976). The acquisition of racial attitudes in children. In R. A. Katz (Ed.), *Towards the elimination of racism.* New York: Pergamon.

Kearns, B. J. (1970). Child-rearing practices among selected culturally deprived minorities. *Journal of Genetic Psychology, 116*(2), 149-155.

Kelly, C. (1990). E pluribus unum: The impossible dream? In G. Thomas (Ed.), *U.S. race relations in the 1980s and 1990s: Challenges and alternatives.* New York: Hemisphere.

Kenkel, W. (1985). *The family in perspective* (5th ed.). Houston, TX: Cap & Gown.

Keshena, R. (1980). Relevancy of tribal interests and tribal diversity in determining the educational needs of American Indians. In *Conference on the Educational and Occupational Needs of American Indian Women,* pp. 231-250. Washington, DC: U.S. Department of Education, National Institute of Education.

Kiefer, C. (1974). *Changing cultures, changing lives: An ethnographic study of three generations of Japanese Americans.* San Francisco: Jossey-Bass.

Kikumura, A., & Kitano, H. (1973). Interracial marriage: A picture of the Japanese Americans. *Journal of Social Issues, 29,* 67-81.

Kim, B.-L. C. (1972). Casework with Japanese and Korean wives of Americans. *Social Casework, 53,* 273-279.

Kim, B.-L. C. (1977). Pioneers of intermarriage: Korean women in the United States. In H. Sunwoo & D. S. Kim (Eds.), *Korean women in struggle for humanization* (pp. 59-66). Association of Korean Christian Scholars in America.

Kim, B.-L. C. (1980). Asian wives of U.S. servicemen: Women in triple jeopardy. In *Conference on the Educational and Occupational Needs of Asian-Pacific-American Women,* pp. 359-379. Washington, DC: U.S. Department of Education, National Institute of Education.

Kim, H., & Mejia, C. (1976). *The Filipinos in America: 1983-1974.* New York: Oceana.

Kimura, A., & Kitano, H. H. (1974). Interracial marriage: A picture of Japanese Americans. *Journal of Social Issues, 29,* 67-81.

Kimura, Y. (1957). War brides in Hawaii and their in-laws. *American Journal of Sociology, 63,* 70-76.

Kish, L. (1965). *Survey sampling.* New York: John Wiley.

Kitagawa, E. M., & Hauser, P. M. (1973). *Differential mortality in the United States.* Cambridge, MA: Harvard University Press.

Kitano, H. (1961). Differential child rearing attitudes between the first and second generation Japanese in the United States. *Journal of Social Psychology, 53,* 13-19.

Kitano, H. (1964). Inter- and intra-generational differences in maternal attitudes towards child rearing. *Journal of Social Psychology, 63,* 215-220.

Kitano, H. (1976). *Japanese Americans: The evolution of a subculture* (2nd ed.). Englewood Cliffs, NJ: Prentice-Hall.

Kitano, H., & Chai, L. K. (1982). Korean interracial marriage. *Marriage and Family Review, 5,* 35-48.

Kitano, H., & Kikumura, A. (1980). The Japanese American family. In R. Endo, S. Sue, & N. Wagner (Eds.), *Asian-Americans: Social and psychological perspectives* (Vol. 2). Palo Alto, CA: Science & Behavior.

Kitano, H., & Yeung, W.-T. (1982). Chinese interracial marriage. *Marriage and Family Review, 5,* 35-48.

Korbin, F., & Goldscheider, C. (1978). *The ethnic factor in family structure and mobility.* Cambridge, MA: Ballinger.

Korean National Bureau of Statistics. (1983a). *1980 population and housing census report: Vol. 1. Complete enumeration.* Seoul: Economic Planning Board.

Korean National Bureau of Statistics. (1983b). *1980 population and housing census report: Vol. 2. Percent sample.* Seoul: Economic Planning Board.

Kraus, M. (1959). *The United States to 1865.* Ann Arbor: University of Michigan Press.

Krush, T., & Bjork, J. (1965). Mental health factors in an Indian boarding school. *Mental Hygiene, 49,* 94-103.

Kumabe, K. T., Nishida, C., & Hepworth, D. H. (1985). *Bridging ethnocultural diversity in social work and health.* Honolulu: University of Hawaii, School of Social Work.

Kuo, E. (1974a). Bilingual pattern of a Chinese immigrant group in the United States. *Anthropological Linguistics, 16,* 128-140.

Kuo, E. (1974b). The family and bilingual socialization: A sociolinguistic study of a sample of Chinese children in the United States. *Journal of Social Psychology, 92,* 181-191.

Kurokawa, M. (1968). Lineal orientation in child rearing among Japanese. *Journal of Marriage and the Family, 30,* 129-136.

Kuttner, R., & Lorinez, A. (1976). Alcoholism and addiction in urbanized Sioux Indians. *Mental Hygiene, 51,* 530-542.

Lacy, S. (1975). Navajo foster homes. *Child Welfare, 54,* 127-128.

Lammermeier, P. (1973). Urban Black family of the nineteenth century: A study of Black family structure in the Ohio Valley, 1950-1880. *Journal of Marriage and the Family, 35,* 440-456.

Landau, J. (1982). Therapies in families in cultural transition. In M. McGoldrick, J. K. Pearce, & J. Giordano (Eds.), *Ethnicity and family therapy.* New York: Guilford.

Lang, O. (1946). *Chinese family and society.* New Haven, CT: Yale University Press.

Laosa, L. M. (1978). Maternal teaching strategies in Chicano families of varied educational and socioeconomic levels. *Child Development, 49,* 1129-1135.

Laosa, L. M. (1980a). Maternal teaching strategies and cognitive styles in Chicano families. *Journal of Educational Psychology, 72,* 45-54.

Laosa, L. M. (1980b). Maternal teaching strategies in Chicano and Anglo-American families: The influence of culture and education on maternal behavior. *Child Development, 51,* 759-765.

Laosa, L. M. (1980c). Measures for the study of maternal teaching strategies. *Applied Psychological Measurement, 4,* 355-366.

LaPorte, B. (1977). Visibility of the new immigrants. *Society, 14*(6), 18-22.

Lappin, J. (1983). On being a culturally conscious family therapist. In C. Falicov (Ed.), *Cultural perspectives in family therapy* (pp. 122-136). Rockville, MD: Aspen.

Lavender, A. D. (1986). *Ethnic women and feminist values.* Lanham, MD: University Press of America.

Lee, G. R. (1980). Kinship in the seventies: A decade review of research and theory. *Journal of Marriage and the Family, 42,* 923-934.

Lee, L.-Y. (Trans.). (1976). *The hsiao ching.* Taipei, Taiwan: Confucius.

Lee, S., & Yamanaka, K. (1989). Intermarriage in the Asian American population. *Journal of Comparative Family Studies, 20,* 287-305.

Leigh, G. K. (1982). Kinship interaction over the family life span. *Journal of Marriage and the Family, 44,* 197-207.

Leon, J. J. (1975). Sex-ethnic marriage in Hawaii: A non-metric multidimensional analysis. *Journal of Marriage and the Family, 37,* 775-781.

Levine, E. S., & Bartz, K. W. (1979). Comparative child-rearing attitudes among Chicano, Anglo, and Black parents. *Hispanic Journal of Behavioral Sciences, 1*(2), 165-178.

Levinger, G., & Breedlove, I. (1966). Interpersonal attraction and agreement: A study of marriage partners. *Journal of Personality and Social Psychology, 3,* 367-372.

Levy, C. (1973, Winter). The value base of social work. *Journal of Education for Social Work, 9.*

Lewis, O. (1965). *La vida: A Puerto Rican family in the culture of poverty, San Juan and New York.* New York: Random House.

Lewis, R. (1981). Patterns of strengths of American Indian families. In *The American Indian family: Strengths and stresses* (Proceedings of the Conference on Research Issues). Isleta, NM: American Indian Social Research and Development.

Li, P. S. S. (1975). *Occupational mobility and kinship assistance: A study of Chinese immigrants in Chicago.* Unpublished doctoral dissertation, Northwestern University.

Lieberson, S., & Waters, M. (1985). Ethnic mixtures in the United States. *Sociology and Social Research, 70,* 43-52.

Liebow, E. (1967). *Tally's corner: A study of street corner men.* Boston: Little, Brown.

Light, I. H. (1972). *Ethnic enterprise in America.* Berkeley: University of California Press.

Linceum, G. (1870). *The traditional history of the Chanhta Nation.* Unpublished manuscript.

Little, D. (1984). *Religion, order, and law.* Chicago: University of Chicago Press.

Littlefield, D. (1980). *The Chickasaw freedmen: A people without a country.* Westport, CT: Greenwood.

Litwak, E. (1960a). Geographic mobility and extended family cohesion. *American Sociological Review, 25,* 385-394.

Litwak, E. (1960b). Occupational mobility and extended family. *American Sociological Review, 25,* 9-21.

Litwak, E., & Szelenyi, I. (1969). Primary group structures and their functions: Kin, neighbors, and friends. *American Sociological Review, 34,* 465-481.

Liu, W. T. (1966). Family interactions among local and refugee Chinese families in Hong Kong. *Journal of Marriage and the Family, 28,* 314-323.

Liu, W. T. (1979). *Transition to nowhere: Vietnamese refugees in America.* Nashville, TN: Charter House.

Liu, W. T., & Yu, E. S. (1975). Asian-American youth. In R. J. Havighurst (Ed.), *Youth: The seventy-fourth yearbook of the National Society for the Study of Education* (Part 1, pp. 367-389). Chicago: National Society for the Study of Education.

Longeaux y Vásquez, E. (1972). The women of La Raza. In L. Valdez & S. Steiner (Eds.), *Aztlan: An anthology of Mexican American literature,* (pp.271-278) New York: Random House.

Loo, F. V. (1980). Asian women in professional health schools with emphasis on nursing. In *Conference on the Educational and Occupational Needs of Asian-Pacific-American Women.* Washington, DC: U.S. Department of Education, National Institute of Education.

Lopez, J. (1973). Chicana women's statement. In D. Moreno (Ed.), *La mujer—en pie de lucha* (pp. 48-50). Mexico City: Espina del Norte.

Lott, J. T. (1980). Migration of a mentality: The Filipino community. In R. Endo, S. Sue, & N. Wagner (Eds.), *Asian-Americans: Social and psychological perspectives* (Vol. 2). Palo Alto, CA: Science & Behavior.

Luhmann, N. (1982). *The differentiation of society.* New York: Columbia University Press.

Lum, D. (1986). *Social work practice and people of color.* Monterey, CA: Brooks/Cole.

Lyman, S. (1970). *The Asian in the West.* Reno: University of Nevada, Desert Research Institute, Western Studies Center.

Lyman, S. (1971). Marriage and the family among Chinese immigrants to America, 1850-1960. *Phylon, 29,* 321-330.

Lyman, S. (1974). *Chinese Americans.* New York: Random House.

Mack, D. (1971). Where the Black matriarchy theorists went wrong. *Psychology Today, 4*(24), 86-87.

Mack, D. E. (1978a). The power relationship in Black and White families. In R. Staples (Ed.), *The Black family: Essays and studies* (pp. 144-149). Belmont, CA: Wadsworth.

Mack, D. E. (1978b). Power relationships in Black families. *Journal of Personality and Social Psychology, 30,* 409-413.

Magner, D. (1990, June 13). More than half of Blacks and Hispanics said to live "at the margin." *Chronicle of Higher Education,* p. A2.

Maldonado, D. (1975). The Chicano aged. *Social Work, 20*(3), 213-216.

Malone, J. (1922). *The Chickasaw Nation: A short sketch of a noble people.* Louisville, KY: John P. Morton.

Mann, E. S., & Salvo, J. J. (1985). Characteristics of new Hispanic immigrants to New York City: A comparison of Puerto Rican and non-Puerto Rican Hispanics. *Research Bulletin* (Hispanic Research Center), *8,* 1-8.

Mark, L. L. (1979). *The Taiwanese lineage and industrial enterprise: Two case studies.* Unpublished manuscript.

Marsiglio, W. (1987). Commitment to social fatherhood: Predicting adolescent males' intentions to live with their child and partner. *Journal of Marriage and the Family, 49,* 82-91.

Martin, E. P., & Martin, J. M. (1978). *The Black extended family.* Chicago: University of Chicago Press.

Martineau, W. (1977). Informal social ties among urban Black Americans. *Journal of Black Studies, 8,* 83-104.

Martinez, E. (1988a). Child behavior in Mexican American/Chicano families: Maternal teaching and child-rearing practices. *Family Relations, 37,* 175-280.

Martinez, E. (1988b). Mexican American/Chicano families: Challenging the stereotypes. In H. B. Williams (Ed.), *Empowerment through difference: Multicultural awareness in education* (pp. 248-269). Normal, IL: Glencoe.

Maunez, J. (1973). The Puerto Rican community: Its impact on the emotional development of children and youth. In R. E. Moran (Ed.), *Ecological and cultural factors related to emotional disturbances in Puerto Rican children and youth* (pp. 129-130). Rio Piedras: University of Puerto Rico, College of Education.

McAdoo, H. P. (1974). The socialization of Black children: Priorities for research. In L. Gary (Ed.), *Social research and the Black community.* Washington, DC: Howard University Press.

McAdoo, H. P. (1977). *The impact of extended family variables upon the upward mobility of Black families.* Washington, DC: U.S. Department of Health, Education and Welfare, Office of Child Development.

McAdoo, H. P. (1978a). Factors related to stability in upwardly mobile Black families. *Journal of Marriage and the Family, 40,* 761-776.

McAdoo, H. P. (1978b). Minority families. In J. Stevens & M. Matthews (Eds.), *Mother/child, father/child relationships.* Washington, DC: National Association for Young Children.

McAdoo, H. P. (Ed.). (1981). *Black families.* Beverly Hills, CA: Sage.

McAdoo, H. P. (1983). *Extended family support of single Black mothers* (Report No. NIMH 5 RO1 MN32159). Rockville, MD: Department of Health and Human Services, Public Health Service, Alcohol, Drug Abuse and Mental Health Administration and National Institute of Mental Health.

McAdoo, H. P. (1984, Spring). Poverty equals women and their children. *Point of View,* pp. 8-9.

McAdoo, H. P. (1985). Racial attitude and self-concept of young Black children over time. In H. P. McAdoo & J. L. McAdoo (Eds.), *Black children: Social, educational, and parental environments* (pp. 213-242). Beverly Hills, CA: Sage.

McAdoo, H. P. (Ed.). (1988). *Black families* (2nd ed.). Newbury Park, CA: Sage.

McAdoo, H. P. (1990). A portrait of African American families. In S. E. Rix (Ed.), *The American woman 1990-91: A status report* (pp. 71-93). New York: W. W. Norton.

McAdoo, J. L. (1979). *Parent-child interaction and the development of racial group identity and self-concepts of preschool children.* Unpublished manuscript.

McAdoo, J. L. (1988). The role of Black fathers in the socialization of Black children. In H. P. McAdoo (Ed.), *Black families* (2nd ed., pp. 257-269). Newbury Park, CA: Sage.

McAdoo, J. L. (1990). Understanding African American teen fathers. In P. E. Leone (Ed.), *Understanding troubled and troubling youth* (pp. 229-245). Newbury Park, CA: Sage.

McGoldrick, M. (1982). Ethnicity and family therapy. In M. McGoldrick, J. K. Pearce, & J. Giordano (Eds.), *Ethnicity and family therapy* (pp. 3-30). New York: Guilford.

McGoldrick, M., Pearce, J. K., & Giordano, J. (Eds.). (1982). *Ethnicity and family therapy.* New York: Guilford.

McGrath, P., Fuller, T., Smith, V. E., Whitaker, M., Niessen, B., Weathers, D., & Whitmore, J. (1982, February 1). Refugees or prisoners. *Newsweek,* pp. 24-29.

McLanahan, S. S., Wedemeyer, N. V., & Adelberg, T. (1981). Network structure, social support, and psychological well-being in the single-parent family. *Journal of Marriage and the Family, 43,* 601-612.

McLoughlin, W. G. (1986). *Cherokee renascence in the new republic.* Princeton, NJ: Princeton University Press.

McLuhan, T. C. (1974). *Touch the earth: A self-portrait of Indian existence.* New York: Outerbridge & Dienstfrey.

Medicine, B. (1969). The changing Dakota family and the stresses therein. *Pine Ridge Research Bulletin, 9.*

Medicine, B. (1975). The role of women in native American societies. *Native Historians, 8,* 50-54.

Merton, R. K. (1968). *Social theory and social structure.* New York: Free Press.

Meserve, J. B. (1934). Governor William Leander Byrd. *Chronicles of Oklahoma, 12,* 432-443.

Meserve, J. B. (1938). Governor Benjamin Franklin Overton and Governor Benjamin Crooks Burney. *Chronicles of Oklahoma, 16,* 221-233.

Metcalf, A. (1976). From schoolgirl to mother: The effects of education on Navajo women. *Social Problems, 23,* 535-544.

Middleton, R., & Putney, S. (1960). Dominance in decisions in the family: Race and class differences. In C. V. Willie (Ed.), *The family life of Black people* (pp. 16-22). Columbus, OH: C. E. Merrill.

Miller, I. W., & Norman, W. T. (1979). Learned helplessness in humans: A review and attribution-theory model. *Psychological Bulletin, 86,* 93-119.

Min, P. G. (1988). Korean immigrant families. In C. H. Mindel, R. W. Habenstein, & R. Wright (Eds.), *Ethnic families in America: Patterns and variations* (3rd ed., pp. 199-229). New York: Elsevier.

Min, P. G. (1989). *Some positive functions of ethnic business for an immigrant community: Koreans in Los Angeles.* Final report submitted to the National Science Foundation, Queens College, Department of Sociology.

Mindel, C. H., & Habenstein, R. W. (Eds.). (1981). *Ethnic families in America: Patterns and variations* (2nd ed.). New York: Elsevier.

Mindel, C. H., Habenstein, R. W., & Wright, R. (Eds.). (1988). *Ethnic families in America: Patterns and variations* (3rd ed.). New York: Elsevier.

Miranda, M., & Ruiz, R. (1981). *Chicano aging and mental health.* Rockville, MD: National Institute of Mental Health.

Mirandé, A. (1977). The Chicano family: A reanalysis of conflicting views. *Journal of Marriage and the Family, 39,* 747-756.

Mirandé, A. (1979). Machismo: A reinterpretation of male dominance in the Chicano family. *Family Coordinator, 28,* 473-479.

Mirandé, A. (1980). The Chicano family. *Journal of Marriage and the Family, 42,* 892-896.

Mirandé, A., & Enriquez, E. (1979). *La Chicana: The Mexican American woman.* Chicago: University of Chicago Press.

Missionary Herald. (1829). Vol. 25, 153, 348-349, 382.

Missionary Herald. (1831). Vol. 27, 18-19, 185, 353.

Mittlebach, F., & Moore, J. (1968). Ethnic endogamy: The case of Mexican Americans. *American Journal of Sociology, 74,* 50-62.

Mizio, E. (1974). Impact of external systems on the Puerto Rican child. *Social Casework, 55,* 76-83.

Moen, P., Kain, E. L., & Elder, G. H., Jr. (1983). Economic conditions and family life: Contemporary and historical perspectives. In R. R. Nelson & F. Skidmore (Eds.),

American families and the economy: The high costs of living (pp. 213-253). Washington, DC: National Academy Press.

Montalvo, B. (1974). Home-school conflict and the Puerto Rican child. *Social Casework, 55,* 100-110.

Montalvo, B., & Gutierrez, M. (1984, July-August). The mask of culture. *Family Therapy Networker,* pp. 42-46.

Montero, D. (1979). *Vietnamese Americans: Patterns of resettlement and socioeconomic adaptation in the United States.* Boulder, CO: Westview.

Montero, D. (1980). The elderly Japanese Americans: Aging among the first generation immigrants. *Genetic Psychology Monographs, 101,* 99-118.

Montiel, M. (1970). The social science myth of the Mexican-American family. *El Grito: A Journal of Contemporary Mexican American Thought, 3,* 56-63.

Montiel, M. (1973). The Chicano family: A review of research. *Social Work, 18,* 22-31.

Montiel, M. (Ed.). (1978). *Hispanic families: Critical issues for policy and programs in human services.* Washington, DC: COSSMHO.

Moore, J. W., & Pachon, H. (1985). *Hispanics in the United States.* Englewood Cliffs, NJ: Prentice-Hall.

Moran, R. (Ed.). (1973). *Ecological and cultural factors related to emotional disturbances in Puerto Rican children and youth.* Rio Piedras: University of Puerto Rico, College of Education.

Morgan, T. B. (1983, May). The Latinization of America. *Esquire,* pp. 47-56.

Morland, J. K. (1969). Race awareness among American and Hong Kong Chinese children. *American Journal of Sociology, 75,* 360-374.

Morris, A. (1984). *The origins of the civil rights movement.* New York: Free Press.

Moynihan, D. P. (1965). *The Negro family: The case for national action.* Washington, DC: Government Printing Office.

Muhammad, A. (1984). Muslims in the United States: An overview of organizations, doctrines and problems. In Y. Y. Haddad et al. (Eds.), *The Islamic impact* (pp. 195-217). Syracuse, NY: Syracuse University Press.

Muñoz, R. (1973). Family structure and the development of the child. In R. Moran (Ed.), *Ecological and cultural factors related to emotional disturbances in Puerto Rican children and youth* (pp. 80-81). Rio Piedras: University of Puerto Rico, College of Education.

Muramatsu, M. (1980). Family planning practice among the Japanese. *Eugenics Quarterly, 7,* 23-30.

Murguia, E., & Frisbie, W. P. (1977). Trends in Mexican-American intermarriage: Recent findings in perspective. *Social Science Quarterly, 58,* 374-389.

Murillo-Rohde, I. (1976). Family life among mainland Puerto Ricans in New York City slums. *Perspectives on Psychiatric Care, 14,* 174-179.

Murrillo, N. (1971). The Mexican-American family. In N. Wagner & M. Haug (Eds.), *Chicanos: Social and psychological perspectives.* St. Louis: C. V. Mosby.

Nagel, G. (1975). American Indian life: Unemployment, ill health, and skid rows. *Current, 169,* 34, 43.

National Center for Health Statistics. (1979). *Health United States: 1979* (DHEW Publication No. [PHS] 80-1232). Washington, DC: Government Printing Office.

National Council of La Raza. (1986). *The education of Hispanics: Status and implications.* Washington, DC: Author.

Nava, Y. (1973). The Chicana and employment: Needs analysis and recommendations for legislation. *Regeneración, 2,* 7-8.

Neighbors, H. W., Jackson, J. S., Bowman, P. J., & Gurin, G. (1983). Stress, coping and Black mental health. *Journal of Prevention in Human Services, 2,* 5-29.

Nguyen, L. T., & Henkin, A. B. (1984). Vietnamese refugees in the United States: Adaptation and transitional status. *Journal of Ethnic Studies, 9*(4), 110-116.

Nguyen, V. V. (1949). *Savings and mutual lending societies (HO).* New Haven, CT: Yale University, Southeast Asian Studies.

Nieto, C. (1974). Chicanas and the women's rights movement: A perspective. *Civil Rights Digest, 6,* 36-43.

Nievera, F. C. (1980). Some effects of childrearing practices on the value systems of Asian-American women. In *Conference on the Educational and Occupational Needs of Asian-Pacific-American Women,* pp. 39-64. Washington, DC: U.S. Department of Education, National Institute of Education.

Nieves, J., & Martinez, M. (1980). Puerto Rican women in higher education in the United States. In *Conference on the Educational and Occupational Needs of Hispanic Women,* pp. 87-115. Washington, DC: U.S. Department of Education, National Institute of Education.

Nobles, W. (1974). African root and American fruit: The Black family. *Journal of Social and Behavioral Sciences, 20,* 52-64.

Nobles, W. (1978). Toward an empirical and theoretical framework for defining Black families. *Journal of Marriage and the Family, 40,* 679-688.

Nobles, W. (1988). African-American family life: An instrument of culture. In H. P. McAdoo (Ed.), *Black families* (2nd ed., pp. 44-53). Newbury Park, CA: Sage.

Nordland, A. (1978). Attitudes, communication and marital satisfaction. *International Journal of Sociology of the Family, 8,* 115-117.

Novak, M. (1971). *The rise of the unmeltable ethnics.* New York: Macmillan.

Office of Refugee Resettlement (ORR). (1983). *Report to Congress.* Washington, DC: Author.

Office of Refugee Resettlement (ORR). (1984). *Report to Congress.* Washington, DC: Author.

Office of Refugee Resettlement (ORR). (1986). *Report to Congress.* Washington, DC: Author.

Office of Refugee Resettlement (ORR). (1987). *Report to Congress.* Washington, DC: Author.

Ohland, M. (1930). The government of the Creek Indians. *Chronicles of Oklahoma, 8,* 45.

Olsen, D., Russell, C., & Sprenkel, D. (1982). The circumplex model of marital and family systems: VI. Theoretical update. *Family Process, 22,* 69-83.

Orden, S. R., & Bradburn, N. M. (1969). Working wives and marital happiness. *American Journal of Sociology, 74,* 392-407.

Osako, M. (1976). Intergenerational relations as an aspect of assimilation: The case of Japanese Americans. *Sociological Inquiry, 46.*

Osako, M. (1980). The effects of Asian-American kinship systems on women's educational and occupational attainment. In *Conference on the Educational and Occupational Needs of Asian-Pacific-American Women,* pp. 211-236. Washington, DC: U.S. Department of Education, National Institute of Education.

Osmond, M. W., & Martin, P. Y. (1975). Sex and sexism: A comparison of male and female sex-role attitudes. *Journal of Marriage and the Family, 37,* 744-758.

Ou, Y., & McAdoo, H. P. (1980). *Ethnic preference and self-concept in Chinese children.* Paper presented at the 88th Annual Meeting of the American Psychological Association, Montreal.

Owan, T. C. (1985). Southeast Asian mental health: Transition from treatment services to prevention—a new direction. In T. C. Owan (Ed.), *Southeast Asian mental health: Treatment, prevention services, training and research* (pp. 141-167). Washington, DC: U.S. Department of Health and Human Services.

Pacific/Asian American Mental Health Research Center Research Review. (1983, January). Vol. 2, 1-11.

Padilla, A., & Ruiz, R. (1973). *Latino mental health: A review of literature.* Washington, DC: National Institute of Mental Health.

Palisi, B. J. (1966). Ethnic generation and family structure. *Journal of Marriage and the Family, 28,* 49-50.

Para, E. & Henderson, R. W. (1982). Mexican-American perceptions of parent and teacher roles in child development. In J. A. Fishman & G. D. Keller (Eds.), *Bilingual education for Hispanic students in the U.S.* (pp. 289-299). New York: Teachers College, Columbia University.

Park, R. (1950). *Race and culture: Essays in the sociology of contemporary man.* New York: Free Press.

Parsons, T. (1966). *Societies: Evolutionary and comparative perspectives.* Englewood Cliffs, NJ: Prentice-Hall.

Parsons, T. (1971). *The system of modern societies.* Englewood Cliffs, NJ: Prentice-Hall.

Pearlin, L. I. (1983). Role strains and personal stress. In H. B. Kaplan (Ed.), *Psychological stress: Trends in theory and research* (pp. 30-32). New York: Academic Press.

Pearlin, L. I., Lieberman, M., Menaghan, E., & Mullan, J. (1981). The stress process. *Journal of Health and Social Behavior, 22.*

Pearlin, L. I., & Schooler, C. (1978). The structure of coping. *Journal of Health and Social Behavioral Sciences, 19*(3), 2-21.

Pedraza-Bailey, S. (1980). *Political and economic migrants in America: Cubans and Mexican Americans.* Unpublished doctoral dissertation, University of Chicago.

Penalosa, F. (1967). The changing Mexican-American in Southern California. *Sociology and Social Research, 51,* 405-417.

Penalosa, F. (1968). Mexican family roles. *Journal of Marriage and the Family, 30,* 680-689.

Perez, J. (1979). *A profile of the Puerto Rican community in the United States.* New York: National Puerto Rican Forum.

Peters, M. (1974). The Black family—perpetuating the myths: An analysis of family sociology textbook treatment of Black families. *Family Coordinator, 23,* 349-357.

Peters, M., & McAdoo, H. P. (1983). The present and future of alternative lifestyles in ethnic American culture. In E. Macklin & R. Rubin (Eds.), *Contemporary families and alternative lifestyles.* Beverly Hills, CA: Sage.

Phillips, E., Shenker, S., & Levitz, P. (1951). The assimilation of the new child into the group. *Psychiatry, 14,* 319-325.

Pian, C. (1980). Immigration of Asian women and the status of recent Asian women immigrants. In *Conference on the Educational and Occupational Needs of Asian-Pacific-American Women* (pp. 181-210). Washington, DC: U.S. Department of Education, National Institute of Education.

Piers, E., & Harris, D. (1964). Age and other correlates of self-concept in children. *Journal of Educational Psychology, 55,* 91-95.

Pinderhughes, E. (1989). *Understanding race, ethnicity, and power.* New York: Free Press.

Pinkney, A. (1975). The family. In A. Pinkney, *Black Americans*. Englewood Cliffs, NJ: Prentice-Hall.

Pinter, R. (1932). The influence of language background on intelligence tests. *Journal of Social Psychology, 3*, 235-240.

Porter, J. (1971). *Black child, white child*. Cambridge, MA: Harvard University Press.

Porterfield, E. (1982). Black-American intermarriage in the United States. *Marriage and Family Review, 5*, 17-59.

Portes, A. (1969). Dilemmas of a golden exile: Integration of Cuban refugee families in Milwaukee. *American Sociological Review, 34*, 505-518.

Portes, A. (1979). Labor functions of illegal aliens. *Society, 14*(6), 31-37.

Portes, A., & Bach, R. L. (1985). *Latin journey: Cuban and Mexican immigrants in the United States*. Berkeley: University of California Press.

Portes, A., Clark, J. M., & Bach, R. L. (1977). The new wave: A statistical profile of recent Cuban exiles to the United States. *Cuban Studies/Estudios Cubanos, 7*(1), 1-32.

Poston, D., Alvirez, D., & Tienda, M. (1976). Earnings differentials between Anglo and Mexican American male workers in 1960 and 1970; Changes in the "cost" of being Mexican American. *Social Science Quarterly, 57*, 618-631.

Project on the Status and Education of Women. (1975). *Spanish speaking women and higher education: A review of their current status*. Washington, DC: Association of American Colleges.

Purcell, V. (1965). *The Chinese in Southeast Asia*. London: Oxford University Press.

Queralt, M. (1984). Understanding Cuban immigrants: A cultural perspective. *Social Work, 29*, 115-121.

Qureshi, R. B., & Qureshi, S. M. (1983). Pakistani Canadians: The making of a Muslim community. In E. Waugh (Ed.), *The Muslim community in North America* (pp. 127-148). Edmonton: University of Alberta Press.

Rahman, F. (1980). *Major themes of the Quran*. Minneapolis: Bibliotheca Islamica.

Rainwater, L. (1966, April). Some aspects of lower class sexual behavior. *Journal of Social Issues, 12*, 96-108.

Red Horse, J. (1980). Family structure and value orientation in American Indians. *Social Casework, 61*, 462-467.

Red Horse, J. (1981). American Indian families: Research perspectives. In *The American Indian family: Strengths and stresses* (Proceedings of the Conference on Research Issues). Isleta, NM: American Indian Social Research and Development Association.

Red Horse, J., Lewis, R., Feit, M., & Decker, J. (1978). Family behavior of urban American Indians. *Social Casework, 59*, 67-72.

Reiss, P. J. (1962). The extended kinship system: Correlates of the attitudes on frequency of interaction. *Journal of Marriage and the Family, 24*, 333-339.

Reiss, P. J. (1981). *The family construction of reality*. Cambridge, MA: Harvard University Press.

Reiss, P. J., & Oliveri, M. E. (1983). The family's construction of social reality and its ties to its kin network: An exploration of causal direction. *Journal of Marriage and the Family, 45*, 81-91.

Rendón, A. (1971). *Chicano manifesto: The history and aspirations of the second largest minority in America*. New York: Collier.

Revilla, L. (1989). Dating and marriage preferences among Filipino Americans. *Journal of the Asian American Psychological Association, 13*, 72-79.

Riccatille, R. (1974). The sexual stereotypes of the Chicana in literature. *Encuentra Femenil, 1*, 48-56.

Richmond, M. (1917). *Social diagnosis.* New York: Russell Sage.

Rigg, M. (1928). Some further data on the language handicap. *Journal of Educational Psychology, 19,* 252-257.

Rincón, B. (1974). La Chicana, her role in the past and her search for a new role in the future. *Regeneración, 2,* 36-39.

Risdon, R. (1954). A study of interracial marriages based on data for Los Angeles County. *Sociology and Social Research, 39,* 92-95.

Rix, S. E. (Ed.). (1990). *The American woman, 1990-91: A status report.* New York: W. W. Norton.

Rodriguez, A., & Vila, M. E. (1982). Emerging Cuban women of Florida's Dade County. In R. E. Zambrana (Ed.), *Work, family, and health: Latino women in transition* (pp. 55-67). Bronx, NY: Fordham University, Hispanic Research Center.

Rodriguez, C., Sanchez-Korrol, V., & Alers, J. (1980). *The Puerto Rican struggle: Essays on survival.* New York: Puerto Rican Migration Research Consortium.

Rogg, E. M. (1974). *The assimilation of Cuban exiles: The role of community and class.* New York: Aberdeen.

Rogg, E. M., & Cooney, R. S. (1980). *Adaptation and adjustment of Cubans: West New York, New Jersey.* Bronx, NY: Fordham University, Hispanic Research Center.

Rogg, E. M., & Homberg, J. J. (1983). The assimilation of Cubans in the United States. *Migration Today, 11*(4-5), 8-11.

Rogler, L. H., & Cooney, R. S. (1980). Intergenerational change in ethnic identity in the Puerto Rican family. *Research Bulletin, 3,* 1-3.

Rogler, L. H., Santana-Cooney, R., Costantino, G., Earley, B. F., Gurak, D. T., Malgady, R., & Rodriguez, O. (1983). *A conceptual framework for mental health research on Hispanic populations.* Bronx, NY: Fordham University, Hispanic Research Center.

Romans, B. (1961). *A concise natural history.* New Orleans: Pelican.

Rosenberg, M. (1965). *Society and the adolescent self-image.* Princeton, NJ: Princeton University Press.

Rosow, I. (1965). And then we were old. *Transaction, 2*(2), 20-26.

Rossi, A. S. (1985). Introduction. In A. S. Rossi (Ed.), *Gender and the life course* (pp. xiii-xvii). New York: Aldine.

Rowland, D., & Sanders, A. G. (1927). *Mississippi provincial archives 1729-1740* (Vol. 1). Jackson: Press of the Mississippi Department of Archives and History.

Rubel, A. L. (1966). *Across the tracks: Mexican-Americans in a Texas city.* Austin: University of Texas Press.

Rubin, R. (1974). Adult males and the self attitudes of Black children. *Child Study Journal, 4,* 33-46.

Rumbaut, R. G. (1986, August). *The structure of refuge and Southeast Asian refugees in the U.S.: A portrait of a migration and resettlement, 1975-1985.* Paper presented at the 81st Annual Meeting of the American Sociological Association, New York City.

Ryder, N. B. (1965). The cohort as a concept in the study of social change. *American Sociological Review, 30,* 843-861.

Samora, J., & Lamanna, R. (1967). *Mexican-Americans in a Midwest metropolis: A study of East Chicago* (Advance Report No. 8). Los Angeles: University of California, Graduate School of Business Administration, Division of Research.

Sánchez, E. (1973). Machismo vs. momism in Puerto Rico. In R. Moran (Ed.), *Ecological and cultural factors related to emotional disturbances in Puerto Rican children and youth.* Rio Piedras: University of Puerto Rico, College of Education.

Santiago, G. (1973). The impact of some factors to the Puerto Rican community on children's development. In R. Moran (Ed.), *Ecological and cultural factors related to emotional disturbances in Puerto Rican children and youth.* Rio Piedras: University of Puerto Rico, College of Education.

Sarbin, T. R., & Allen, V. L. (1969). Role theory. In G. Lindzey & E. Aronson (Eds.), *Handbook of social psychology* (pp. 488-568). Reading, MA: Addison-Wesley.

Scanzoni, J. H. (1971). *The Black family in modern society.* Boston: Allyn & Bacon.

Scanzoni, J. H. (1975). Sex roles, economic factors, and marital solidarity in Black and white marriages. *Journal of Marriage and the Family, 37,* 130-144.

Schacht, A., Tafoya, N., & Mirabla, K. (1989). Home-based therapy with American Indian families. *American Indian and Alaska Native Mental Health Research, 3*(2), 27-42.

Scheirbeck, H. (1980). Current educational status of American Indian girls. In *Conference on the Educational and Occupational Needs of American Indian Women.* Washington, DC: U.S. Department of Education, National Institute of Education.

Schnepp, G., & Yui, A. (1955). Cultural and marital adjustment of Japanese war brides. *American Journal of Sociology, 61,* 48, 50.

Schryock, H. S., Siegel, J. S., & Associates. (1975). *The methods and materials of demography.* Washington, DC: U.S. Department of Commerce, Bureau of the Census.

Schultz, S. L. (1981). Adjusting marriage tradition: Greeks to Greek Americans. *Journal of Comparative Family Studies, 12,* 205-218.

Schur, C. L., Bernstein, A. B., & Berk, M. L. (1987). The importance of distinguishing Hispanic subpopulations in the use of medical care. *Medical Care, 25,* 627-641.

Scoffield, R., & Sun, C. A. (1960). Comparative study of the differential effect upon personality of Chinese and American child training practices. *Journal of Social Psychology, 52,* 221-224.

Sears, R. R., Maccoby, E. E., & Levin, H. (1957). *Patterns of child rearing.* Stanford, CA: Stanford University Press.

Semaj, L. (1979, January). *Reconceptualizing the development of racial preference in children: The role of cognition.* Paper presented at the Fourth Conference on Empirical Research in Black Psychology, San Diego.

Sena-Rivera, J. (1979). Extended kinship in the United States: Competing models and the case of la familia Chicana. *Journal of Marriage and the Family, 41,* 121-129.

Sexton, C. S., & Perlman, D. S. (1989). Couples' career orientation, gender role orientation, and perceived equity as determinants of marital power. *Journal of Marriage and the Family, 51,* 933-941.

Sexton, P. (1965). *East Harlem.* New York: Harper & Row.

Shanas, E. (1962). *The health of older people.* Cambridge, MA: Harvard University Press.

Sheils, M. (1983, January 17). A portrait of America. *Newsweek,* pp. 20-23.

Shepro, T. (1980). Impediments to Hispanic women organizing. In *Conference on the Educational and Occupational Needs of Hispanic Women* (pp. 117-137). Washington, DC: U.S. Department of Education, National Institute of Education.

Shimkin, D., Shimkin, E., & Frate, D. (1978). *The extended family in Black societies.* Chicago: Aldine.

Shin, E.-H., & Yu, E.-Y. (1984). Use of surname in ethnic research: The case of Kim in the Korean-American population. *Demography, 21,* 347-359.

Shin, M. (1978). Father absence and children's cognitive development. *Psychological Bulletin, 85,* 295-324.

Simmons, L. W. (1945). *The role of the aged in primitive society.* New Haven, CT: Yale University Press.

Simon, R. J. (1983). Refugee families' adjustment and aspirations: A comparison of Soviet Jewish and Vietnamese immigrants. *Ethnic and Racial Studies, 6,* 492-504.

Siporin, M. (1975). *Introduction to social work practice.* New York: Macmillan.

Slote, W. H. (1972). Psychodynamic structures in Vietnamese personality. In W. P. Lebra (Ed.), *Transcultural research in mental health* (pp. 114-133). Honolulu: University Press of Hawaii.

Sluzki, C. E. (1979). Migration and family conflict. *Family Process, 18,* 381-394.

Smeeding, T. M., & Zill, N. (1990). *Measuring the impact of the Family Support Act on families and children: What's there vs. what's ideal.* Washington, DC: National Academy of Sciences, Research Forum on the Family Support Act.

Sollenberger, R. (1968). Chinese American child-rearing practices and juvenile delinquency. *Journal of Social Psychology, 74,* 13-23.

Sotomajor, M. (1977). Language, culture and ethnicity in developing self-concept. *Social Work, 58,* 195-203.

Sowell, T. (1981). *Ethnic America: A history.* New York: Basic Books.

Spiker, A. Q. (1985). The Islamic community flourishes in southwest U.S. *Saudi Report, 7*(26), 4-5.

Spindler, L. (1962). Menomine women and culture change. In *American Anthropological Association memoir 91.* Menasha, WI: American Anthropological Association.

Springer, D. (1950). Awareness of racial differences of preschool children in Hawaii. *Genetic Psychology Monographs, 41,* 214-270.

Stack, C. (1974). *All our kin: Strategies for survival in a Black community.* New York: Harper & Row.

Staples, R. (Ed.). (1971a). *The Black family: Essays and studies.* Belmont, CA: Wadsworth.

Staples, R. (1971b). The myth of the Black matriarchy. In R. Staples (Ed.), *The Black family: Essays and studies* (pp. 149-159). Belmont, CA: Wadsworth.

Staples, R. (1971c). Towards a sociology of the Black family: A theoretical and methodological assessment. *Journal of Marriage and the Family, 33,* 119-138.

Staples, R. (1976). The Black American family. In C. H. Mindel & R. W. Habenstein (Eds.), *Ethnic families in America: Patterns and variations.* New York: Elsevier.

Staples, R. (1977). The myth of the Black matriarchy. In D. Wilkinson & R. Taylor (Eds.), *The Black male in America* (pp. 174-187). Chicago: Nelson-Hall.

Staples, R. (1980). Racial and cultural variations among American families: A decennial review of the literature on minority families. *Journal of Marriage and the Family, 42,* 157-173.

Staples, R. (1982). *Black masculinity: The Black male role in American society.* San Francisco: Beach Scholar.

Staples, R., & Mirandé, A. (1980). Racial and cultural variations among American families: An analytic review of the literature on minority families. *Journal of Marriage and the Family, 42,* 887-904.

Staton, R. (1972). A comparison of Mexican and Mexican-American families. *Family Coordinator, 21,* 325-329.

Steacy, S. (1971). The Chickasaw Nation on the eve of the Civil War. *Chronicles of Oklahoma, 49,* 52.

Steinberg, S. (1989). *The ethnic myth, race, ethnicity, and class in America* (2nd ed.). Boston: Beacon.

Steward, M., & Steward, D. (1973). The observations of Anglo, Mexican, and Chinese-American mothers teaching their young sons. *Child Development, 44,* 329-337.

Strauss, A. (1954). Strain and harmony in American-Japanese war-bride marriages. *Marriage and Family Living, 16,* 99-106.

Streit, F., & Nicolich, M. J. (1977). Myths versus data on American Indian drug abuse. *Journal of Drug Education, 7,* 117-122.

Strom, R. D., Griswold, D., & Slaughter, H. (1981). Parental background: Does it matter in parent education? *Child Study Journal, 10,* 243-260.

Suárez, C. (1973). Sexual stereotypes—psychological and cultural survival. In National Education Association, *Education for survival.* Washington, DC: National Education Association.

Sudarkasa, N. (1975). An exposition on the value premises underlying Black family studies. *Journal of the National Medical Association, 19,* 235-239.

Sudarkasa, N. (1980). African and Afro-American family structure: A comparison. *Black Scholar, 11,* 37-60.

Sudarkasa, N. (1981). Interpreting the African heritage in Afro-American family organization. In H. P. McAdoo (Ed.), *Black families* (pp. 37-53). Beverly Hills, CA: Sage.

Sudarkasa, N. (1988a). Interpreting the African heritage in Afro-American family organization. In H. P. McAdoo (Ed.), *Black families* (2nd ed., pp. 27-43). Newbury Park, CA: Sage.

Sudarkasa, N. (1988b, Summer). Reassessing the Black family: Dispelling the myths, reaffirming the values. *Sisters,* pp. 22-23, 38, 39.

Sue, S., & Kirk, B. (1973). Differential characteristics of Japanese and Chinese American college students. *Journal of Counseling Psychology, 20,* 142-148.

Sue, S., & McKinney, H. (1975). Asian Americans in the community mental health care system. *American Journal of Orthopsychiatry, 45,* 111-118.

Sue, S., & Sue, D. (1971). Chinese-American personality and mental health. *Amerasia Journal, 1,* 36-49.

Sue, S., & Wagner, J. (Eds.). (1973). *Asian-Americans: Psychological perspectives.* Palo Alto, CA: Science & Behavior.

Sung, D. (1977). *Chinese immigrant children.* New York: City College of New York, Department of Asian Studies.

Sussman, M. B. (1953). The help pattern in the middle class family. *American Sociological Review, 18,* 22-28.

Sussman, M. B. (1959). The isolated nuclear family: Fact or fiction? *Social Problems, 6,* 333-340.

Sussman, M. B. (1965). Relationships of adult children with their parents in the United States. In E. Shanas & G. Streib (Eds.), *Social structure and the family* (pp. 65-92). Englewood Cliffs, NJ: Prentice-Hall.

Sussman, M. B. (1970). The urban kin network in the formulation of family theory. In R. Hill & R. Konig (Eds.), *Families in East and West.* Paris: Mouton.

Sussman, M. B., & Burchinal, L. (1962). Kin family network: Unheralded structure in current conceptualizations of family functioning. *Journal of Marriage and the Family, 24,* 231-240.

Swanton, J. A. (1931). *Source materials for the social and ceremonial life of the Choctaw Indians* (Bulletin 103). Washington, DC: U.S. Bureau of American Ethnology.

Szapocznic, J. (1980). *A programmatic mental health approach to enhancing the meaning of life of the Cuban elderly.* Washington, DC: COSSMHO.

Szapocznic, J., & Kurtines, W. (1980). Acculturation, biculturalism, and adjustment among Cuban Americans. In A. Padilla (Ed.), *Acculturation: Theory, models, and some new findings* (pp. 57-68). Boulder, CO: Westview.

Szapocznic, J., Scopetta, M. A., Arnalde, M., & Kurtines, W. (1978). Cuban value structure: Treatment implications. *Journal of Consulting and Clinical Psychology, 46,* 961-970.

Taeuber, I. (1966). Migration and transformation: Spanish surname populations and Puerto Ricans. *Population Index, 12.*

Taylor, R. J. (1983). *The informal social support networks of the Black elderly: The impact of family, churchmembers and best friends.* Unpublished doctoral dissertation, University of Michigan, Ann Arbor.

Taylor, R. J., Jackson, J. S., & Quick, A. (1982). The frequency of social support among Black Americans: Preliminary findings from the national survey of Black Americans. *Urban Research Review, 8.*

Taylor, R. J., Leashore, B. R., & Tolliver, S. (1988). An assessment of the provider role as perceived by Black males. *Family Relations, 37,* 426-431.

Teicher, J. (1968). Identity problems in children of Negro/white marriages. *Journal of Nervous and Mental Disease, 146.*

Temple-Trujillo, R. (1974). Conceptions of the Chicana family. *Smith College Studies in Social Work, 45,* 1-20.

TenHouten, W. D. (1970). The Black family: Myth and reality. *Psychiatry, 23,* 145-173.

Thomas, V. G. (1990). Determinants of global life happiness and marital satisfaction in dual career Black couples. *Family Relations, 39,* 174-178.

Thompson, J. D., & Van Houten, D. R. (1970). *The behavioral sciences: An interpretation.* Reading, MA: Addison-Wesley.

Thornburg, H., & Grinder, R. (1975). Children of Aztlan: The Mexican-American experience. In R. Havighurst (Ed.), *Youth: The seventy-fourth yearbook of the National Society for the Study of Education* (pp. 340-366). Chicago: National Society for the Study of Education.

Thurston, R. G. (1974). *Urbanization and socio-cultural change in a Mexican American enclave.* San Francisco: R. & E. Research Associates.

Tietelbaum, M. S. (1985). Forced migration: The tragedy of mass expulsion. In N. Glazer (Ed.), *Clamor at the gates: The new American immigration* (pp. 261-283). San Francisco: Institute for Contemporary Studies.

Tinker, J. (1973). Intermarriage and ethnic boundaries: The Japanese American case. *Journal of Social Issues, 30,* 49-66.

Tran, A. K. (1986). *Economic base of the Vietnamese community in the Los Angeles and Orange County area.* Unpublished manuscript, University of California, Los Angeles, Department of Asian-American Studies.

Triandis, H. C., Lambert, W., Berry, J., Lonner, W., Hernon, A., Brislin, R., & Draguns, J. (Eds.). (1980-1981). *Handbook of cross-cultural psychology* (Vols. 1-6). Boston: Allyn & Bacon.

Troll, L. E. (1971). The family of later life: A decade review. *Journal of Marriage and the Family, 33,* 263-290.

Troy, F. (1985, September 10). Heathen days: No mosque for Edmond. *Oklahoma Observer.*

Tung, T.-M. (1972). The family and the management of mental health problems in Vietnam. In W. P. Lebra (Ed.), *Transcultural research in mental health* (pp. 107-113). Honolulu: University Press of Hawaii.

Tyler, I. M., & Thompson, S. (1965). Cultural factors in casework treatment of a Navajo mental patient. *Social Casework, 46,* 215-220.

Uhlenberg, P. (1980). Death and the family. *Journal of Family History, 5,* 313-320.

Unger, S. (Ed.). (1977). *The destruction of American Indian families.* New York: Association on American Indian Affairs.

United Nations. (1980). *United Nations demographic yearbook, 1980.* New York: Author.

U.S. Bureau of the Census. (1973). *Japanese, Chinese and Filipinos in the U.S.* (Subject Report PC[2]-1G). Washington, DC: Government Printing Office.

U.S. Bureau of the Census. (1978). *The social and economic status of the Black population in the United States: An historical view, 1790-1978* (Current Population Reports, Special Studies, Series P-23, No. 80). Washington, DC: Government Printing Office.

U.S. Bureau of the Census. (1980a). *Household and family characteristics: March 1979* (Current Population Reports, Series P-20, No. 352). Washington, DC: Government Printing Office.

U.S. Bureau of the Census. (1980b). *Marital status and living arrangements: March 1979* (Current Population Reports, P-20, No. 349). Washington, DC: Government Printing Office.

U.S. Bureau of the Census. (1980c). *Persons of Spanish Origin in the United States: March 1979* (Current Population Reports, Series P-20, No. 354). Washington, DC: Government Printing Office.

U.S. Bureau of the Census. (1980d). *Population profile of the United States: 1979* (Current Population Reports, Series P-20, No. 350). Washington, DC: Government Printing Office.

U.S. Bureau of the Census. (1981a). *Age, sex, race, and Spanish origin of the population by regions, divisions, and states: 1980* (Supplemental Report PC80-S1-1). Washington, DC: Government Printing Office.

U.S. Bureau of the Census. (1981b). *Race of the population by states: 1980* (Supplemental Report PC80-S1-3). Washington, DC: Government Printing Office.

U.S. Bureau of the Census. (1982). *Ancestry and language in the United States, November, 1979* (Current Population Reports, Series P-23, No. 116). Washington, DC: Government Printing Office.

U.S. Bureau of the Census. (1983a). *Characteristics of the population below the poverty level* (Current Population Reports, Series P-60, No. 138). Washington, DC: Government Printing Office.

U.S. Bureau of the Census. (1983b). *General social and economic characteristics: U.S. summary* (Report PC80[1]-C1). Washington, DC: Government Printing Office.

U.S. Bureau of the Census. (1983c). Detailed population characteristics: Part 6. California. In *1980 census of population: Vol. 1. Characteristics of the population.* Washington, DC: Government Printing Office.

U.S. Bureau of the Census. (1983d). General population characteristics: Part 1. United States summary. In *1980 census of population: Vol. 1. Characteristics of the population.* Washington, DC: Government Printing Office.

U.S. Bureau of the Census. (1984). Detailed population characteristics: Part 1. United States summary. In *1980 census of population: Vol. 1. Characteristics of the population.* Washington, DC: Government Printing Office.

U.S. Bureau of the Census. (1990). *The Hispanic population in the U.S., March 1989* (Current Population Reports, Series P-20, No. 444). Washington, DC: Government Printing Office.

U.S. Department of Health and Human Services. (1982). *Vital statistics of the United States, 1978* (Vol. 2, Part A) (DHHS Publication No. 83-1101). Washington, DC: Government Printing Office.

U.S. Department of Health and Human Services. (1985). *Vital statistics of the United States, 1980* (Vol. 2, Part A) (DHHS Publication No. 85-1101). Washington, DC: Government Printing Office.

U.S. Department of the Interior. (1977). *Facts on American Indians and Alaskan Natives.* Washington, DC: Bureau of Indian Affairs.

U.S. Department of the Interior. (1980). *The Indian people.* Washington, DC: Bureau of Indian Affairs.

U.S. Department of Labor. (1971). *The New York Puerto Rican: Patterns of work experiences, poverty profiles* (Regional Reports No. 4). New York: Author.

U.S. Department of State, Bureau of Public Affairs. (1980). *Refugees: A global issue* (Current Policy No. 201). Washington, DC: Government Printing Office.

U.S. House of Representatives Select Committee on Aging. (1987). *Minority participation rates in Older Americans Act programs.* Washington, DC: Administration on Aging.

U.S. Senate. (1985). *A compilation of the Older Americans Act of 1965 and related provisions of the law as amended through October 9, 1984* (Serial No. 99-A). Washington, DC: Government Printing Office.

Valle, R., & Vega, W. (1982). *Hispanic natural support systems: Mental health promotion perspectives.* Sacramento: State of California, Department of Mental Health.

Vasquez, E. (1970). The Mexican American woman. In R. Morgan (Ed.), *Sisterhood is powerful* (pp. 379-384). New York: Vintage.

Vasquez, M., & Gonzalez, A. (1981). Sex roles among Chicanos. In A. Baron, Jr. (Ed.), *Explorations in Chicano psychology* (pp. 50-70). New York: Praeger.

Vega, W. A. (1990, November). Hispanic families. *Journal of Marriage and the Family, 52,* 1015-1024.

Vega, W. A., Kolody, B., & Valle, J. (1986). The relationship of marital status, confidant support, and depression among Mexican immigrant women. *Journal of Marriage and the Family, 48,* 597-605.

Vega, W. A., Patterson, T., Sallis, J., Nader, P., Atkins, C., & Abramson, I. (1986). Cohesion and adaptability in the Mexican American and Anglo families. *Journal of Marriage and the Family, 48,* 857-867.

Velasco, A., Ima, K., Stanton, B. K., & Yip, B. (1983). *Adjustment strategies of the Vietnamese refugees in San Diego, California: Six ethnographic case histories.* San Diego: Union of Pan Asian Communities.

Ventura, S. J. (1982, May 13). Births of Hispanic parentage, 1979. *Monthly Vital Statistics Report, 31,* 1-11.

Vidal, M. (1971). Woman: New voice of La Raza. In *Chicanas speak out.* New York: Pathfinder.

Viera, S. (1980). The need for an anthropological and cognitive approach to the education of Hispanic women. In *Conference on the Educational and Occupational Needs of Hispanic Women,* pp. 277-289. Washington, DC: U.S. Department of Education, National Institute of Education.

Virgil, J. (1980). *From Indians to Chicanos: A sociocultural history.* St. Louis: C. V. Mosby.

Wallerstein, J. (1985). The over-burdened child: Some long-term consequences of divorce. *Social Work, 30,* 116-123.

Warner, W. L., & Srole, L. (1945). *The social systems of American ethnic groups.* New Haven, CT: Yale University Press.

Weeks, P. (1990). *Farewell, my nation: The American Indian and the United States 1820-1890.* Arlington Heights, IL: Harlan Davidson.

Weiss, M. (1970). Selective acculturation and the dating process: The patterning of Chinese-Caucasian interracial dating. *Journal of Marriage and the Family, 32,* 273-278.

Wenk, M. G. (1969). Adjustment and assimilation: The Cuban experience. *International Migration Review, 3,* 38-49.

West, R. (1980). An American family. *Texas Monthly, 8*(3).

Westermeyer, J. (1977). The ravage of Indian families in crisis. In S. Unger (Ed.), *The destruction of American Indian families.* New York: Association on American Indian Affairs.

Wilkinson, D. (Ed.). (1969). *Black revolt: Strategies of protest.* Berkeley, CA: McCutchan.

Wilkinson, D. (1970). Tactics of protest as media: The case of the Black revolution. *Sociological Focus, 3,* 13-21.

Wilkinson, D. (1974). Racial socialization through children's toys: A socio-historical examination. *Journal of Black Studies, 5,* 96-109.

Wilkinson, D. (Ed.). (1975a). *Black male/white female: Perspectives on interracial marriage and courtship.* Morristown, NJ: General Learning.

Wilkinson, D. (1975b). Black youth. In R. Havighurst (Ed.), *Youth: The seventy-fourth yearbook of the National Society for the Study of Education* (pp. 285-305). Chicago: National Society for the Study of Education.

Wilkinson, D. (1978a). The Black family, past and present: A review essay. *Journal of Marriage and the Family, 40,* 829-835.

Wilkinson, D. (1978b). Toward a positive frame of reference for analysis of Black families: A selected bibliography. *Journal of Marriage and the Family, 40,* 707-708.

Wilkinson, D. (1979). [Review of *The Black extended family*]. *Contemporary Sociology, 8* 296-297.

Wilkinson, D. (1980a). Minority women: Social-cultural issues. In A. M. Brodsky & R. Hare-Mustin (Eds.), *Women and psychotherapy.* New York: Guilford.

Wilkinson, D. (1980b). Play objects as tools of propaganda: Characterizations of the African American male. *Journal of Black Psychology, 7,* 1-16.

Wilkinson, D., & Taylor, R. (Eds.). (1977). *The Black male in America: Perspectives on his status in contemporary society.* Chicago: Nelson-Hall.

Williams, A. (1980). Transition from the reservation to an urban setting and the changing roles of American Indian women. In *Conference on the Educational and Occupational Needs of American Indian Women* (pp. 251-282). Washington, DC: U.S. Department of Education, National Institute of Education.

Williams, N. (1990). *The Mexican-American family: Tradition and change.* New York: General Hall.

Willie, C. V. (1977). The Black family and social class. In D. Wilkinson & R. Taylor (Eds.), *The Black male in America* (pp. 335-348). Chicago: Nelson-Hall.

Willie, C. V., & Greenblatt, S. L. (1978). Four classic studies of power relationships in Black families: A review and look to the future. *Journal of Marriage and the Family, 40,* 691-696.

Wilson, K. L., & Portes, A. (1980). Immigrant enclaves: An analysis of the labor market experience of Cubans in Miami. *American Journal of Sociology, 86*(2).

Wilson, W. J. (1978). *The declining significance of race: Blacks and changing American institutions.* Chicago: University of Chicago Press.

Wilson, W. J. (1987). *The truly disadvantaged: The inner city, the underclass, and public policy.* Chicago: University of Chicago Press.

Wissler, C. (1966). *Indians of the United States.* Garden City, NY: Anchor.

Witt, S. (1974). Native women today, sexism and the Indian woman. *Civil Rights Digest, 6,* 29-35.

Wolf, M. (1972). *Women and the family in rural Taiwan.* Stanford, CA: Stanford University Press.

Wong, M. (1989). A look at intermarriage among the Chinese in the United States. *Sociological Perspectives, 32,* 87-107.

Wright, J. D. (1978). Are working women really satisfied? Evidence from several national surveys. *Journal of Marriage and the Family, 40,* 301-313.

Wright, M. H. (1929). Brief outline of the Choctaw and the Chickasaw nations in the Indian territory 1820-1860. *Chronicles of Oklahoma, 7,* 388-418.

Yanagisako, J. (1975). The process of change in Japanese-American kinship. *Journal of Anthropological Research, 31,* 196-224.

Yang, C. K. (1959). *The Chinese family in the communist revolution.* Cambridge: MIT Press.

Ybarra, L. (1977). *Conjugal role relationships in the Chicano family.* Unpublished doctoral dissertation, University of California.

Ybarra, L. (1982). When wives work. *Journal of Marriage and the Family, 44,* 169-177.

Yee, L., & Laforge, R. (1974). Relationship between mental abilities, social class, and exposure to English in Chinese fourth graders. *Journal of Educational Psychology, 6,* 826-834.

Young, M. (1961). *Redskins, ruffleshirts, and rednecks: Indian allotments in Alabama and Mississippi, 1830-1860.* Norman: University of Oklahoma Press.

Yu, E. (1975). *The significance of hsiao and achievement motivation in Taiwan.* Unpublished doctoral dissertation, University of Notre Dame.

Zambrana, R. (1980). Research issues: Family, health, and employment patterns of Hispanic women. *Research Bulletin, 3,* 10-12.

Zapata, J., & Jaramillo, P. (1981). Research on the Mexican-American family. *Journal of Individual Psychology, 37,* 72-85.

Zavaleta, N. (1981). Variations in Hispanic health status. *Research Bulletin, 4,* 1-6.

Zinn, M. B., & Eitzen, D. (1990). *Diversity in families.* New York: Harper & Row.

Zollar, A. C., & Williams, J. S. (1987). The contribution of marriage to life satisfaction in Black adults. *Journal of Marriage and the Family, 49,* 87-92.

Zuniga, M. E. (1992). Families with Latino roots. In E. W. Lynch & M. J. Hanson (Eds.), *Developing cross-cultural competence: A guide for working with young children and their families* (pp. 151-179). Baltimore: Paul H. Brookes.

Author Index

Ablon, J., 24, 39
Abramson, I., 154
Ackerman, L. A., 39
Adams, B. N., 277
Adams, R., 41
Adelberg, T., 15
Alba, R., 290
Alers, J., 150
Allen, V. L., 135
Allen, W. R., 15, 54, 55, 90, 91, 120, 121, 123, 133
Alvarez, R., 26, 48
Alvirez, D., 19, 33, 46, 48, 151, 153, 191
Anderson, B., 274
Anderson, E., 121
Andrade, S., 141, 152, 158
Andrews, F. M., 94
Applebome, P., 142
Araji, S. K., 297
Arce, C., 147, 153
Arnalde, M., 170
Aschenbrenner, J., 83, 91, 92
Asian-Americans, 284
Association on American Indian Affairs, 25, 224
Atkins, C., 154
Attenave, C. L., 40

Axelson, L., 297
Aylesworth, I. S., 22, 52

Baca Zinn, M., 26, 33, 36, 56, 147, 148, 153, 154, 158
Bach, J. B., 167, 168, 173
Bach, R. L., 165, 167, 168, 169, 173, 176
Badie, B., 209
Baird, D. W., 213, 214
Ball, H., 47, 53
Barnett, L. D., 43, 52
Barnett, R. C., 125
Barry, W. A., 295
Bartz, K., 189, 190
Bartz, K. W., 189, 190, 192, 193
Baruch, G. K., 125
Baumrind, D., 188, 189, 192, 195
Bean, F., 48, 151, 153, 191
Bean, F. D., 44, 153, 164, 166, 167, 169, 170, 174, 175
Beigel, H. G., 43, 52
Beiser, M., 50
Bellah, R. N., 241, 310
Beman, A., 34
Benman-Gibson, M., 241
Berk, B., 53
Berk, M. L., 172

369

Council on Social Work Education, Commission on Accreditation, 319
Cox, M., 155
Cox, R., 155
Crester, G. A., 287
Cromwell, R., 48
Cromwell, R. E., 36, 48, 115, 153
Cromwell, V. L., 36, 48, 115, 153
Cross, W. E., 8, 133
Cuellar, I., 154
Curran, J. W., 78
Curtis, J. R., 165, 167, 168, 170, 171, 172, 173, 174, 176
Curtis, R., 153

Daly, M., 318
Darcy, N., 252
David, H. P., 169, 173
Davis, L. E., 221
Davis, M., 50
Debo, A., 213, 216
Decker, J., 33, 39
DeGeyndt, W., 24
Delgado, D., 159
Delgado, M., 144, 159, 191
Delgado, S., 49, 56
Deloria, S., 50, 51
Deloria, V., 24, 25, 51
de Rodriguez, L. V., 50
Desbarats, J., 301, 314
De Silva, E., 141
Devore, W., xii, 4, 6, 9, 319, 320, 321, 323
DeVos, G., 41, 52
Diaz, G. M., 171, 172
Diaz-Guerrero, R., 35, 47
Dlugokinski, E., 51
Dobbins, M. P., 30
Doben, D., 47
Doerner, W., 318
Dondero, T. J., 78
Dorsey, C., 218
Douglas, M., 235
Draguns, J., 135
Du Bois, W. E. B., 122, 125
Dulles, F., 156
Durkheim, E., 209

Durrett, M. E., 36, 188, 189, 192, 193

Earl, L., 121
Earley, B. F., 19, 56, 169
Education Commission of the States & State Higher Education Executive Officers, 184
Edwards, O. I., 24
Efron, S., 314
Eisenstadt, S. N., 310
Eitzen, D., 4, 13
Elder, G., 73
Elder, G. H., Jr., 77
Elderly Southeast Asian refugees, 311
Ender, P. B., 186, 193
Endo, R., 21, 22, 42
Enoch, J. R., 114, 115, 118
Enriquez, E., 35, 56, 191
Erikson, E., 241
Estevez, G. A., 172
Estrada, L., 146
Evans, B. J., 121

Fahlman, L., 237
Falicov, C., 147, 151, 155, 158, 159
Family Planning Perspectives, 145
Farley, R., 121, 123
Farris, C., 25, 50
Fauriol, G., 318
Feagin, J., 92
Feit, M., 33, 39
Fernandez-Marina, R., 29, 34
Fillmore, L. W., 40
Finnan, C. R., 303, 305, 308
Fisher, R. A., 250
Fitzpatrick, J., 33, 36, 50, 148, 149
Fitzpatrick, J. P., 44, 290
Fong, P., 47
Fortes, M., 82
Fox, D., 250, 256, 263
Fradd, S., 168, 176
Frate, D., 91, 92
Frazier, E. F., 30, 120, 122, 123, 125
Friedrich, O., 318
Frisbie, W., 141, 145
Frisbie, W. P., 44, 289

Hong, L. K., 276
Hong, S., 287
Hood, J. C., 123
Hopps, J., 6
Hostbjor, S., 24
Howard, C. S., 126, 135
Hsu, F. L. K., 275
Huang, L., 249, 266
Huang, L. N., 221
Hunt, L., 52
Hunter, A., 77
Hurh, W. M., 291
Hurrer, R., 154
Hyman, H. H., 112

Ikeda, K., 47, 53
Ikels, C., 273
Ima, K., 303
Indochinese Community Center, 303, 305
Indochinese Refugee Action Center, 302
Indochinese Technical Assistance Project, 302
Ishizuka, K., 39

Jackson, J., 54
Jackson, J. S., 7, 92, 126, 135
Jaco, D., 47
Jacobs, P., 52
Jaffe, H. W., 78
Jaramillo, P., 154
Jasso, R., 154
Jennings, J., 214
Jewell, S. K., 110
Jiménez-Vásquez, R., 19, 36, 37
Jimson, L. B., 39
Johnson, C. L., 21, 37, 39
Johnson, C. S., 85
Jones, J., 146
Jones, R., 126
Jones, W., 252
Jordan, V., 250, 256, 263
JWK International Corporation, 247

Kagan, S., 186, 193
Kahn, A., 64

Kahn, R. L., 125
Kain, E., 77, 78
Kain, E. L., 77
Kalish, R., 21, 39
Kamerman, S., 64
Kane, P., 54
Kaplan, C., 22, 25, 26
Karpat, K. H., 231
Karrer, B., 158, 159
Katz, P. A., 251
Kearns, B. J., 185
Kelly, C., 12
Kenkel, W., 35
Keshena, R., 33, 51
Kiefer, C., 277
Kikumura, A., 40, 41, 52
Kim, B.-L. C., 52, 53, 287
Kim, H., 39, 46, 52
Kimura, A., 289
Kimura, Y., 52
Kirk, B., 21, 30
Kish, L., 126
Kitagawa, E. M., 60
Kitano, H. H., 289
Kitano, H., 40, 41, 52, 288, 289, 291, 292, 299
Klem, L., 94
Kolody, B., 155
Korbin, F., 320
Korean National Bureau of Statistics, 294, 299
Kramer, L., 51
Kraus, M., 151
Krush, T., 50
Kumabe, K. T., xii, 4, 5, 11, 333
Kuo, E., 251
Kurokawa, M., 52
Kurtines, W., 170
Kuttner, R., 39

Lacy, S., 19, 50
Laforge, R., 252
Lamanna, R., 26
Lambert, W., 135
Lammermeier, P., 30
Landau, J., 321
Lang, O., 275

Montiel, M., 16, 19, 48, 49, 50, 57
Moore, J. W., 48, 152, 165, 169, 173, 174, 176
Moore, J., 41, 44, 49
Moran, R., 50, 56
Morgan, J. N., 94
Morgan, T. B., 318
Morgan, W. M., 78
Moriwaki, S., 21, 39
Morland, J. K., 251
Morris, A., 126
Moynihan, D. P., 5, 90, 121, 307
Muhammad, A., 231
Mullan, J., 179
Mulligan, J., 30
Muñoz, R., 50
Muramatsu, M., 21, 39
Murguia, E., 44, 289
Murrillo, N., 48
Murrillo-Ronde, I., 36

Nader, P., 154
Nagel, G., 47
National Center for Health Statistics, 45
National Council of La Raza, 184
Nava, Y., 47
Neighbors, H. W., 135
Nguyen, L. T., 300, 302
Nguyen, V. V., 305
Nicolich, M. J., 39
Nieto, C., 48, 49, 55
Nievera, F. C., 19
Nieves, J., 20, 29, 46
Nishida, C., xii, 4, 5, 11, 333
Nobles, W., 19, 31, 54, 91, 125, 135
Nordland, A., 295
Norman, W. T., 135
Novak, M., 320

O'Bryant, S., 36, 188, 189, 192, 193
Office of Refugee Resettlement, 300, 301, 302, 303, 306, 308, 312, 313, 314
Ohland, M., 216
Oliveri, M. E., 94, 108
Olsen, D., 154
Orden, S. R., 297
Orthner, D. K., 297

Ortiz, V., 154
Osaki, I. T., 22, 52
Osako, M., 39, 40, 46
Osmond, M. W., 297
Ossorio, P. G., 22, 52
Ou, Y., 248
Owan, T. C., 307

Pachon, H., 165, 169, 173, 174, 176
Pacific/Asian American Mental Health Research Center Research Review, 30
Padilla, A., 19, 48
Palermo, D., 263
Palisi, B. J., 15, 38
Para, E., 191, 192, 193
Park, R., 320
Parsons, T., 209, 275
Patterson, T., 154
Pearce, J. K., xii, 8, 159
Pearlin, L. I., 124, 125, 135, 179, 181
Pedraza-Bailey, S., 166
Penalosa, F., 27, 35, 47
Pennebaker, J. W., 36, 188, 189, 192, 193
Perez, J., 36
Perlman, D. S., 112
Peters, M., 19, 159
Phillips, E., 264
Pian, C., 21, 22, 39
Piers, E., 262, 269
Pinderhughes, E., 222
Pinkney, A., 30, 31, 54
Pinter, R., 252
Platt, M., 295
Porter, J., 251, 255, 263
Porterfield, E., 289
Portes, A., 142, 161, 165, 167, 168, 169, 173, 176
Poston, D., 48
Proctor, E. K., 221
Project on the Status and Education of Women, 36
Purcell, V., 301
Putney, S., 114

Queralt, M., 165, 167, 169, 173
Quick, A., 92

Subject Index

About the Authors

Phillip J. Bowman is Associate Professor in the Graduate Programs in Counseling Psychology and Human Development and Social Policy at Northwestern University. He received his Ph.D. in social psychology at the University of Michigan, where he directed an innovative five-year postdoctoral training program in survey research and Black mental health. While at Michigan, he also collaborated with James S. Jackson and others to complete several national surveys of Black adults of three-generation Black families and Black youth. He has also researched chronic role strains of African Americans. His articles have appeared in the *International Journal of Mental Health, Journal of the American Academy of Child Psychiatry,* and the *Journal of Black Psychology.* His recent publications include *Postindustrial Displacement and Family Role Strains, Adolescent to Adult Transition, Coping With Provider Role Strain, Research Perspectives on Black Men,* and *Organizational Psychology: African American Perspectives.* He is married and the father of two sons and a daughter.

Duane Champagne, a Native American from the Chippewa Tribe, is an Associate Professor in the Sociology Department of the University of California, Los Angeles. He received his B.A. and M.A. from North Dakota State University and his Ph.D. from Harvard University. He did postdoctoral studies at Harvard University and at the University of California, Irvine. He is the author of *American Indian Societies: Strategies and Conditions of Political and Cultural Survival,* and *Social Order and Political Change.* He has published in the *American Sociological Review, Urban Education,* and several American Indian studies journals. Since 1986, he has been editor of the *American Indian Culture and Research Journal.* He is married to Liana M. Champagne, a Harvard University Ed.D., and they have three children.

Catherine Street Chilman holds the rank of Professor Emerita, School of Social Welfare, University of Wisconsin—Milwaukee. She received her A.B. degree in sociology from Oberlin College, her M.A. in social work from the University of Chicago, and her Ph.D. in psychology from Syracuse University. She has taught and directed programs at Syracuse University, Hood College, the University of Michigan, and the University of Wisconsin. She also held senior research positions in the U.S. Department of Health, Education and Welfare during the 1960s. She has served as President of the Groves Conference on Marriage and the Family and on its board and program committees. She has received several honors from that organization as well as from the University of Chicago and the National Council on Family Relations. Her books include *Growing Up Poor*; *Your Child: Six to Twelve*; *Adolescent Sexuality in a Changing American Society*; and *Families in Trouble* (author and coeditor of a five-volume series). She has published widely in scholarly and professional journals and has given lectures in many parts of the world, including Chile. She is a widow and has three grown daughters, all with professional careers, plus six grandchildren.

Wynetta Devore is a Professor in the School of Social Work at Syracuse University. She received her M.S.W. and Ed.D. from Rutgers University. She is coauthor of *Ethnic Sensitive Social Work Practice,* now in its third edition, and other publications on counseling ethnic minority families. She was coinvestigator, with Harlan London, in a training grant to provide ethnic sensitivity training for staff in several residential treatment centers in Upstate New York. She is professionally active in the American Public Health Association's Section on Social Work, the National Council on Social Work Education, and the National Association of Black Social Workers. She has two adult children.

Steven J. Gold is Associate Professor of Sociology at Whittier College. He received his Ph.D. from the University of California, Berkeley. His research interests involve the adaptation and community formation activities of immigrants, as well as visual sociology. From 1987 to 1990 he was President of the International Visual Sociology Association and is author of *Refugee Communities: A Comparative Field Study*. He has published articles in the *Journal of Contemporary Ethnography, Ethnic and Racial Studies, Contemporary Jewry, Research in Community Sociology,* and *Qualitative Sociology*. He is married and has two children.

Charlotte Tsoi Goodluck, a member of the Navaho Nation, is an Assistant Professor in the Department of Sociology and Social Work at Northern Arizona University. She received her B.A. from Prescott College, an M.S.W. from Smith College School for Social Work and is CISW. She worked for Jewish Family and Children's Service in Phoenix on a special project with American Indian children and their families, Region VIII Family Resource Center, American Indian Law Center, and has been a social work educator for six years. She has published in the area of American Indian child welfare and women's issues. Her latest publication is "Mental Health Issues of Native American Transracial Adoptions," in *Adoption Resources for Mental Health Professionals* (edited by P. Grabe). She is a board member of Native Americans for Community Action and currently lives in Flagstaff, Arizona.

Suzan Shown Harjo, a citizen of the Cheyenne and Arapaho Tribes, is President and Executive Director of the Morning Star Foundation, Cochair of the Howard Simons Foundation for Indian Journalists, and Vice President of Native Children's Survival. Since 1974, she has developed key federal Indian policy in Washington, D.C., conducting more than 300 successful legislative and appropriations efforts. A leading force behind the 1989 law establishing the National Museum of the American Indian on the Capitol Mall, she is a member of the Museum's Board of Directors and the Smithsonian Institution's Cultural Education Committee, and served as a trustee of the predecessor Museum of the American Indian in New York City from 1983 to 1990. She has been a Common Cause National Governing Board member and Executive Director of the National Congress of American Indians. She also served as Special Assistant in the Office of the Secretary of the Interior during the Carter administration. Her testimony and policy statements are included in hundreds of congressional hearing records, and her political analyses have appeared in the *Miami Herald, Los Angeles Times, Chicago Tribune, USA Today, Los Angeles Herald, Christian Social Action, Environmental Action,* and the *Village Voice,* as well as in tribal newspapers. She is a poet, born in El Reno, Oklahoma, and is the mother of a daughter and son.

Shirley J. Hatchett received her Ph.D. from the University of Michigan in social psychology. She was one of the major collaborators on the National Survey of Black Americans, the only probability sample drawn of Black Americans. She has worked as a Senior Research Scientist at the University of Michigan Institute of Social Research and has been involved in several studies, one of which concerned the level of interactions among newlywed couples in Detroit. She is coauthor of *Black Racial Attitudes: Trends and Complexities.*

James S. Jackson is a Professor of Social Psychology and Public Health and a Research Scientist at the Institute for Social Research at the University of Michigan. He is the Director of the Program for Research on Black Americans and the African-American Mental Health Research Center. He is a co-author of *Hope and Independence: Blacks' Response to Electoral and Party Politics* and an editor of the books *Aging in Black America, Life in Black America,* and *The Black American Elderly.* He has also directed twelve major national sample surveys of the black population and has conducted research and published in the areas of racial and ethnic influences on life course development, attitude change, reciprocity, social support, and coping and health. He is married and has two daughters.

Edward L. Kain is Associate Professor and Chair of Sociology and Anthropology at Southwestern University in Georgetown, Texas. He received his B.A. in sociology and religion from Alma College in Alma, Michigan, and his Ph.D. in sociology from the University of North Carolina at Chapel Hill. While on the faculty at Cornell University, he served on the Board of Directors of the New York State Council on Family Relations and the Employment Services Committee of the National Council on Family Relations. His papers on patterns of singlehood, women's labor force participation, marital status and mental health, social class and child rearing, mortality, and HIV infection and AIDS have been published in *Social Science History, Journal of Abnormal Psychology, Teaching Sociology, American Demographics,* and *Early Child Development and Care.* He is author of *The Myth of Family Decline.* He is the proud uncle of two nephews and a niece.

Chien Lin received her Ph.D. in sociology from the University of Illinois at Chicago and taught sociology at the National Cheng Chi University in Taiwan. She has published several papers on intergenerational relations and filial piety, and on mental health among Chinese Americans, in both English and Chinese professional journals.

William T. Liu received his Ph.D. in sociology from Florida State University and did postdoctoral work at the University of Chicago and at Yale University. He has taught at the University of Notre Dame and the University of Illinois at Chicago, where he also serves as the Director of the Pacific/Asian American Mental Health Research Center. He served on the staff panel of the President's Commission on Mental Health during the Carter administration and was consultant to the Bureau of the Census for both the 1980 and 1990 censuses. His books include *Family and Fertility* (1967), *Chinese Society Under Communism* (1967), *The Emergent Woman* (1970), *Kinship and Fertility* (1980), *Transition to Nowhere: Vietnamese Refugees in American* (1979), *Abortion: New Directions for Policy Studies* (1977), and *Methodological Problems in Minority Research* (1982).

Harlan London is an Associate Professor of Family Studies and Chair of the Department of Child and Family Studies in the College for Human Development at Syracuse University. He received his B.A. from Philander Smith College, his M.A. from Boston University, and his Ph.D. from the Maxwell School of Citizenship at Syracuse University. He has been a postdoctoral fellow at the Institute of Survey Research at the University of Michigan. He has published in the areas of coping strategies in Black families and counseling with ethnic minority families. He recently completed a national study of United Methodist clergy families, and has published on the subject of the changing roles of clergymen. He is a member of the Board of Directors of the National Council on Family Relations, and Chair of the Ethnic Minorities Section. He is married to Arcenia Phillips London, and they have three children and two grandchildren.

Estella A. Martinez is an Assistant Professor of Family Studies at the University of New Mexico in the Division of Innovative Programs in Education, College of Education. She was formerly at the University of Utah. She received her B.A. at Fort Lewis College, her M.S. at Colorado State University, and her Ph.D. in family ecology at Michigan State University. She has published in the areas of child rearing and the family ecology of Mexican American/Chicano families in *Family Relations* and *Journal of Applied Family and Child Studies* and in books such as *Child Rearing in the Home and School* and *Empowerment Through Difference: Multicultural Awareness in Education.* She is a single parent and the mother of two sons and a daughter.

Harriette Pipes McAdoo is a Professor at Michigan State University, Department of Family and Child Ecology, and has been a professor at Howard University in the School of Social Work. She has been a Visiting Lecturer at Smith College, University of Washington, and the University of Minnesota. She received her B.A. and M.A. from Michigan State University, her Ph.D. from the University of Michigan, has done postdoctoral studies at Harvard University, and was a fellow at ISR, University of Michigan. She is Director of the Groves Conference on Marriage and the Family and Director of the National Council on Family Relations. She was formerly a National Adviser to the White House Conference on Families (presidential appointment) and was a member of the Governing Council of the Society for Research in Child Development. She was the first person honored by NCFR with the Marie Peters Award for Outstanding Scholarship, Leadership, and Service in the Area of Ethnic Minority Families. She has published on racial attitudes and self-esteem in young children, Black mobility patterns, coping strategies of single mothers, and professional Kenyan and Zimbabwean women. She is coeditor of *Young Families: Program Review and Policy Recommendation* and *Black Children: Social, Educational, and Parental Environments* and is coauthor of *Women and Children, Alone and in Poverty.* She is married to John Lewis McAdoo and they have four children and two grandchildren.

John Lewis McAdoo is on the faculty of Michigan State University and was formerly at the University of Maryland School of Social Work and Community Planning. He received his B.A. from Eastern Michigan University and his M.S.W. and Ph.D. from the University of Michigan. He did postdoctoral studies at Harvard University, was a Postdoctoral

Fellow in the Johns Hopkins University School of Public Health, and was a summer Fellow at the Institute of Survey Research at the University of Michigan. He has taught at Smith College and Howard University College of Education. He has published on male-female relations, Black adolescent fathers, parent-child interactions, parenting by Black fathers, and fear of crime among the elderly. He was awarded the Margaret Dawson Award for Outstanding Achievement by the Tri-Services National Institute of Dyslexia in 1987. He and his wife, Harriette Pipes McAdoo, coedited *Black Children: Social, Educational, and Parental Environments.* They have four children and two grandchildren.

Pyong Gap Min is an Associate Professor of Sociology at Queens College of the City University of New York. He received a bachelor's degree from Seoul National University, Korea, specializing in history. He earned a master's degree in history and two Ph.D. degrees, one in education and the other in sociology, all from Georgia State University. He teaches classes in the subjects of Asian Americans, minority groups, and marriage and the family. As a Korean/Asian American specialist, he has published a number of articles on Korean and Asian Americans in sociological journals. His book is *Ethnic Business Enterprise: Korean Small Business in Atlanta.* He is currently completing a book, *Ethnic Business and Ethnic Solidarity: Koreans in New York.* He and his wife, Hyun Suk, have three teenaged children.

Azim A. Nanji, a native of Kenya, was educated at Maherere University and received his Ph.D. from McGill University in 1972. His is currently Professor of Islamic Studies and Chair of the Department of Religion and Member of the Center for African Studies at the University of Florida. He has also taught at McGill and Dalhousie universities in Canada and at Oklahoma State University. He was Margaret Gest Professor at Haverford College during 1988-1989. His publications include *The Nizari Ismaili Tradition, The Religious World,* and the forthcoming *The Fruits of Two Wisdoms: Religion and the African Imagination,* besides various chapters and journal and encyclopedia articles. He has also been the recipient of several awards and fellowships from the Rockefeller Foundation, the National Endowment for the Humanities, the Canadian Council, and the Killiam Trust. Married, he lives with his wife, Razia, and daughter, Tasneem, in Gainesville, Florida. His son, Karim, is an undergraduate at Haverford College.

Young-Shi Ou is a staff psychologist at the Regional Institute of Children and Adolescents in Baltimore, Maryland. He was formerly a Research Associate at Columbia Research Systems, Inc., where he co-conducted the research for the chapter appearing in this volume. He is also a licensed psychologist in Maryland. He was an Adjunct Professor at the University of the District of Columbia. He received his Ph.D. in psychology from Howard University. He is married and has three children.

Juan J. Paz, D.S.W., is currently on the faculty of Arizona State University School of Social Work. He completed his doctorate at Howard University and his master's of social work at the University of Houston. A native of the Southwest, he is Cochair of the NASW Latino Caucus and is actively involved in the area of health care service delivery along the United States/Mexico border. He also has extensive research experience in gerontology. He is married to Herminia Cubillos, and both he and his wife have recently been consultants in the areas of long-term care and health care for the National Council of La Raza and the American Association of Retired Persons.

Zulema E. Suárez received her Ph.D. from the University of Chicago School of Social Service Administration. She is an Assistant Professor at the University of Michigan School of Social Work, where she teaches minority- and gender-sensitive interpersonal practice. Her primary research interests are in the areas of Latino health and poverty. A native of Cuba, she is single and has no children.

Niara Sudarkasa (née Gloria A. Marshall) is President of Lincoln University in Pennsylvania. She was formerly Professor of Anthropology and Associate Vice President for Academic Affairs at the University of Michigan. While at Michigan she also served as Director of the Center for Afro-American and African Studies. She began her undergraduate education at Fisk University, and received her A.B. from Oberlin College and her M.A. and Ph.D. from Columbia University. She is the author of *Where Women Work* and numerous other publications on women, trade, and migration among the Yoruba in Nigeria, Ghana, and other West African countries. She has also published widely on the African background of African American family organization. She is married to John L. Clark and her son, Michael Sudarkasa, is an attorney-at-law.

Doris Wilkinson is a Professor of Sociology at the University of Kentucky. She received her B.A. from the University of Kentucky, her M.A. and Ph.D. in medical sociology from Case Western Reserve University, and her M.P.H. from Johns Hopkins University. She has been a Ford Fellow at Harvard University. She is the co-editor of *Race, Gender, and the Life Cycle: The Afro-American Experience* and has published more than 45 articles in such distinguished journals as *Phylon, Journal of Marriage and Family, British Journal of Sociology,* and *Social Problems.* She has been President of the District of Columbia Sociological Society and the Society for the Study of Social Problems and is the current President of the Eastern Sociological Society. She also received the American Sociological Association's DuBois-Johnson-Frazier Award.